Far from the Mountain

To Krishna & Family

Best Wishes

Jai

jai parasram

Far from the Mountain

political notes and commentaries

© Jai Parasram 2013

All rights reserved. Except for use in review, no part of this publication may be reproduced or transmitted in any form or by any means, electronic or mechanical, including photocopy, recording, any information storage or retrieval system, or on the internet, without permission in writing from the author.

http://www.jyoticommunication.blogspot.com/

Disclaimer:

Whilst the author has taken all reasonable care to ensure the accuracy of the information presented in this book he does not make any warranties regarding the accuracy or completeness of the information within.

The views, opinions and comments expressed in this book are those of the author and not necessarily those of Paria Publishing Company Limited and/or its staff and/or its agents and/or its assigns or any other affiliate. Paria Publishing Company Limited accepts no liability and will not be held accountable for same.

Produced by:

 www.pariapublishing.com

Typeset in Times and My Underwood
Printed by Lightning Source, U.S.A./U.K.
ISBN 978-976-8244-04-8

Dedication

To my granddaughter Aurora and others of her generation who will grow up in a foreign state but would always have roots in Trinidad and Tobago, so they may understand some of the issues that shaped our political history from a perspective that is different from what the history books will report.

To dear wife, Seromanie, for her love, support and patience all through my journalism career; my sons, Shiva, Amit, Ajay and Jivesh; and daughters in law Nirmala, Heather and Fazeela – to help them understand my dedication to and passion for my native land.

Contents

Dedication	v
Publisher's Note	xii
Foreword by Dr. Hamid Ghany	xiv
Preface	xvii
Acknowledgements	xix
Introduction by Ajay Parasram The long road to de-colonisation: Understanding our political present	xxi
Section 1: The futile search for common ground	**1**
A divided opposition: the struggle for survival	2
Common sense and the politics of opposition	11
The trouble with disunity	13
How to win an election, or lose one	16
Who's the leader? Time running out for UNC Alliance	18
Let the people decide	21
Don't celebrate COP victory yet	26
Political lessons from Canada	28
Super weekend for TT politics	30
Politics by numbers: gambling with T&T's future	34
Panday is not dead yet; UNC support still strong	37
Time to focus on T&T's future; tomorrow is too late	40
The trouble with polls	42
Basdeo Panday and the politics of opposition	45
Basdeo Panday: look in the mirror	50
Section 2: The aftermath of 2007	**52**
Ajay Parasram: Democracy in Portions?	53
Griffith challenges COP leader	58
COP bickering exposes vulnerability of opposition politics	60
Dookeran says deal with the UNC-A is an option	65
Panday expulsion is a brilliant strategy of distraction	66
Leave the laptop; get on with the people's business	70
Speaker's agenda lost in propaganda over laptop affair	72
Don't save face, save the nation	75
Food prices and survival back home in TT	78

TT minister calls for supermarket boycott; blames grocers for high food prices	81
Looting, assault and robbery a routine affair in TT	82
Revenge of the stepchild	84
What agriculture incentives?	88
Has Rowley's time come?	91
Now is the time to stand up for T&T	93
Failed state or failing?	96
Manning announces enquiry into construction sector, UDeCOTT	99
Why does Trinidad and Tobago need a new form of indentureship?	101
Is Manning making Grenada a colony of Trinidad and Tobago?	105
Why is the opposition giving the government a free ride?	108
Free speech at risk in TT?	110
Improve media standards, but don't curtail freedom	112
One year after Manning's 26-15 victory, do we like it so?	114

Section 3: Challenging the status quo — 118

Time to change, unite and save T&T: Jack Warner	119
Jack ready to hit the road if UNC refuses to change	121
"Send me off in a blaze of glory"	123
Can Couva North be Panday's Waterloo?	126
Panday, Dookeran want independent inquiry into Bakr's affidavit	128
Time to defend our freedom	130
Does Jeremie's "Friend or Foe" exclude PM Manning?	132
Ramesh might challenge Panday for UNC leadership	134
Who will lead UNC?	137
Warner, Dookeran keep unity flame ablaze	140
Warner urges constituents to work for unity to destroy Ravanas of T&T	141
Dookeran praises Warner, launches new search for political unity	143
It's time to end battles and unite to win the war	145
PM Manning says Rowley was not fired over UDeCOTT	147
Manning calls Rowley "a raging bull"; defends UDeCOTT	148
UNC delegate tells Panday step aside and let Kamla lead	150
Dookeran slams gov't; talks of Panday-Manning alliance	152
Manning and Panday meeting because they need each other	154
Opposition political games hurting T&T	156

Section 4: A new dawn for the rising sun — 160

Kamla to take on Bas, Ramesh for UNC leadership	161
Kamla's gamble	163
Don't celebrate Kamla's victory yet	166

The future is ours to control	169
Challenging the UNC status quo	171
All not well in Panday camp	173
The will of the majority must prevail in UNC election	175
Nomination day marks start of home stretch in epic UNC election battle	178
Warner fought for Mark to get senate leader's seat	180
Media, politics and the truth	182
Kamla praises Panday but says he's too wounded to lead	184
You are a loser, Kamla tells Panday	186
Is there life after the election?	188
What is the UNC protecting?	190
Ajay Parasram: Has the UNC lost its way?	194
Kamla beats Bas; says it's people's victory	197
Kamla takes charge of the UNC; praises media	199
Panday's control of the UNC is a betrayal of the people	201
Kamla unseats Panday	204
Don't let Panday stand in the way of progress	205
Section 5: Kamla rises	**208**
Kamla files no confidence motion in government	209
Who shot Calder Hart?	211
Opposition unity is good news but at what price?	213
COP, UNC agree on two-way contest in next election	215
Manning tells PNM get ready for election	217
Manning makes a gamble but is the opposition ready?	218
Manning's options: prorogue or dissolve?	221
Kamla wants Manning to fire housing minister, UDeCOTT board	223
Kamla wants Manning's resignation	225
Parliament dissolved	226
Manning's gamble. Don't celebrate yet	227
Manning was facing palace coup: Kamla	230
The Rowley factor is the PNM albatross	231
Kamla declares victory at hand; leaders sign unity accord	234
The Fyzabad Declaration April 21, 2010	235
Manning's dirty politics won't hurt Kamla	238
Opposition team can easily win majority in May 24 vote	240
Political games in the PNM	242
It's worth it to dream of a united T&T	245
Jack exposes PNM conspiracy to smear him	248
Stand up for T&T	250
One million to choose the way forward for T&T	252

Kamla's victory speech May 24, 2010	257
Manning graceful in defeat	261
"Yes we can"; T&T takes a quantum leap forward	261

Section 6: The challenge of leadership — **264**

The test begins for Kamla's experiment in participatory democracy	265
PM Kamla's inaugural address	268
Manning's resignation	271
Kamla appoints first cabinet	272
Jack the giant killer topples Bas and Patrick and puts Kamla in charge	274
No room for complacency	277
Does the PNM deserve forgiveness?	279
PP wins LGE; no one will divide us again - Kamla	281
PNM must confess its sins in order to move on	282
Opposition infighting is bad news for T&T and PNM	284

Section 7: New issues and major challenges — **287**

Kamla's yellow dress was always green	288
Police must not be allowed to hold a nation to ransom	290
Can Rowley justify his own mutiny?	291
Is the PSA uprising really about money?	293
Are we there yet?	296
Is Rowley a drowning man clutching at straws?	298
PM exposes secret spy network; President, media on list of victims	300
Manning should be censured for making mischief	304
What is Manning contemplating?	306
It's time for Rowley to stop the pappyshow	309
PNM kills hanging bill	311
Let's grow food and build houses	312
Kamla fires Mary King	315
Did Rowley really visit NY mission on Nov. 5?	316
Workers must start asking their unions some questions	317
Don't be fooled by Rowley's crocodile tears	320
Rowley should learn to lead or just get out of the way	321
Afro Trinis commit majority of crimes in T&T: Sandy	323
Don't give a moose a muffin	325
PM Kamla says PNM didn't deal with crime	326
If you think Manning is quitting politics, watch for Santa Claus	330
The SOE worked. Now let's keep criminals on the run	333
Don't put on your campaign jerseys yet	335
What's Panday trying to prove?	337

Section 8: Testing time for PP as T&T turns 50	**340**
Rowley should not be offended by Kamla's act of humility and respect	341
Ira Mathur: We need more humility	343
McLeod's departure from MSJ won't damage coalition	347
Rowley must start leading instead of just being a rabble rouser	350
So what's wrong with a welfare state?	354
Doctors must honour their oath and put patients first	356
Kamla still strong but protests will continue	359
Battle for San Fernando East	361
Choose a side Abdulah; you can't have it both ways	363
Roget's "war" more important than a settlement at Petrotrin	365
Rowley's gamble could inflict critical political injury on him and his party	367
Now is the time for the PNM to get rid of its albatross	369
Lee Sing is new Rowley target	371
Leave Kamla alone	373
It's time that COP gets over its political tabanca	375
COP's gamble could be costly and lead to its own demise	378
Partnership will stand - with or without COP	380
Trust Kamla to keep partnership together	383
Labour's best deal ever is to remain a part of the People's Partnership	386
Labour united in 1976 but failed to win power	389
Is Lee Sing getting ready to lead the PNM?	392
COP needs to be careful it does not shoot itself	394
All's well that ends well, but stormy seas lie ahead	397
Time for Abdulah to make up his mind about the PP	400
PP remains strong because it welcomes dissent	403
Labour advancing political agenda at the expense of workers	406
Abdulah must show leadership and resign as a government senator	408
Music that celebrates humanity cannot be imprisoned within the narrow walls of racism	410
Time for labour to remove the mask	412
Labour still has the best representation in the PP government	415
Progress means some inconvenience	417
The facts show Jack did nothing wrong	420
Why does Rowley want to waste Parliament's time again?	422
A thought for Emancipation Day: Are we free yet?	424
PM Kamla verbatim: National Day of Prayer August 26, 2012	425

Epilogue: We still have a long way to go 428
And now - it is time to close the book. 430

Appendix: Remembering ttt – A Personal View 433

Publisher's Note

We met Jai Parasram in July this year when we were introduced to this veteran journalist by Dr. Hamid Ghany, with whom we had collaborated in 2012 on the production of the official commemorative magazine of the Government of Trinidad and Tobago to mark the 50th anniversary of the Independence of our nation.

Dr. Ghany had a good hunch that Jai's manuscript would be a good fit with Paria Publishing's overall work. The author's concept for this book, "Far from the Mountain", immediately caught our interest. As a publishing house specialised in the history of Trinidad and Tobago, we saw a two-fold uniqueness in this book: on the one hand, it presented contemporary history in a diary form, which allowed for a depth and spontaneity that "hindsight research" wouldn't, and on the other hand, its content had previously been published as a blog, which gave it inter-medial linkages that we always look for.

Jai was of course known to us as an early pioneer of television journalism in Trinidad and Tobago. Jai rose through the ranks of Trinidad's national television service, Trinidad and Tobago Television (ttt) as a reporter, writer, producer, anchor and News Director, and we are happy that he added his memories of TTT as an appendix to this book. Unfortunately, these pages do not have any sound, because like ourselves, many Trinidadians and Tobagonians of a "certain generation" would remember his voice very well from TTT's nightly news programme "Panorama".

As a much-respected journalist Jai Parasram travelled the Caribbean, always focused on "telling the story" — telling THE story, concisely and with wit and the sort of sparse commentary that leave it open to the viewer or reader to draw his or her own conclusions. This skill of the journalist of four decades is also very evident in "Far from the Mountain". Whether you intend to read the short chapters consecutively, or browse and dip into the pages wherever fancy takes you — Jai's journalistic genius will always add value to your reading experience.

What attracted us particularly to this manuscript was the "witness to history" format. Jai's epistles accompany an important period of change in Trinidad and Tobago's political history. On an almost month-by-month basis, he summarises and annotates events surrounding the emergence of Kamla Persad-Bissessar as prime minister of the country. Jai, ever the master storyteller, weaves facts of the past that are easily forgotten in the urgency of the present into an overall narrative that makes them memorable and logical. And the savvy political strategist also shimmers through these pages. Jai takes position and does not spare with ammunition, so reader, be prepared for numerous volleys!

"Although I live in Canada, my feet remain grounded in Trinidad and Tobago," Jai told us. With "Far from the Mountain", Jai Parasram has left a legacy of great academic value and a virtual "how to" book for budding journalists, all seasoned with a pinch of homesickness that gives this book its patriotic flavour.

GERARD A. BESSON
CASCADE, 22 AUGUST 2013

Foreword

I have known Jai Parasram for the better part of two decades. Our paths have crisscrossed over the years and we have maintained a friendship that has been sustained through periods of intense connection and discussion and periods of absence through physical distance.

Jai is a patriot who was one of the pillars at Trinidad and Tobago Television (TTT) having joined the company on 16th February, 1972. He has seen politics and society at close range from both sides of the camera and he has a compelling story to tell.

For most of his career, he has reported and analysed the news, but there is a side to his amazing life that has not recorded the extent to which he has, in fact, helped to make the news.

Jai represents the quintessential Trinidadian who has broken all of the stereotypes that would apply to him in the land of his birth by virtue of the fact that his professional reputation as a renowned producer, editor and broadcaster have earned him acclaim internationally.

As a highly respected journalist at the Canadian Broadcasting Corporation (CBC) in Toronto, which he joined on 13th June, 1988, Jai has earned the accolades befitting someone whose talent is rare. His voice resonated over the black and white (and later colour) airwaves of TTT in his native Trinidad and Tobago in the 1970s and 1980s and that grounding led him to win journalism awards locally, regionally and in Canada for his work.

His numerous awards for journalistic excellence include the following :

1983   The Caribbean Publishers and Broadcasters (CPBA) Award for Best Documentary for his coverage of the 7th Non-Aligned Countries Summit in New Delhi, India.

1984   BWIA News Media Award for Best Current Affairs programme for the TTT National News Review – 1984.

1985   BWIA News Media Award for Best Documentary entitled "From Columbus to Commonwealth" that covered the 1985 Commonwealth Heads of Government Conference (CHOGM) in Nassau, The Bahamas.

1985   BWIA News Media Award for Best Current Affairs programme for the TTT National News Review for 1985.

1987   BWIA News Media Award for Best Current Affairs programme for his submission of "Money is No Problem" which had been submitted as part of his Master of Journalism (MJ) thesis at Carleton University in Canada.

1987   Special Award for contribution to Journalism in Trinidad and Tobago presented by The All Trinidad Sugar and General Workers' Trade Union.

1998   GEMINI Award (the most prestigious award for television journalism in Canada) awarded to the CBC Newsworld news team (of which he was one of the news producers) for their coverage of the crash of a SWISSAIR aircraft in Peggy's Cove, Nova Scotia.

Jai was part of a team that launched the well-known CBC cable news and current affairs television network "Newsworld" (now called Canada News Network) on 31st July, 1989. It was only the second twenty-four hour all-news channel to be established in North America after CNN had started "Headline News" some time before. He was a main driver of the growth of "Newsworld" in Canada as an editor, writer and producer.

Oftentimes, the passage of time and the forgetfulness of post-colonial societies that do not bother to document their histories will wipe away the richness of their own past glories. Jai, like so many others who have hit more than the proverbial glass ceiling in West Indian societies, had to be part of an inevitable diaspora that allowed very good homegrown talent to blossom elsewhere because of the smallness and inequalities of these West Indian societies that scream equality and whisper discrimination of all types.

Jai has made a pause here to let us have an insight into his own contribution to his passage across the digital divide with a collection of hundreds of blogs that he has written over a five-year period that tells the story of the fall of the Manning regime and the arrival of the first female Prime Minister, Mrs. Kamla Persad-Bissessar, into office.

Much has been said and written about this period of the political history of Trinidad and Tobago, but this story is told through the eyes of a person whose journalistic and political instincts can intimately describe the political rise of Kamla Persad-Bissessar. Academics, journalists and activists of all political persuasions will find this book to be meticulously compiled, yet easy to read as they can relate to its subjects and objects.

In reading this book, it is important to do so far from the mountain because that is how it was written. Jai has never lost sight of that mountain that he has always been able to see from the plains of Caroni or through the lenses of the cameras at the CBC.

HAMID A. GHANY, PH.D. (LSE, LONDON)
THE UNIVERSITY OF THE WEST INDIES, ST. AUGUSTINE, TRINIDAD
25 AUGUST 2013

Preface

Several years ago I started writing regular commentaries, mainly about political developments in my native Trinidad and Tobago. They formed an integral part of my personal blog (www.jyoticommunication.blogspot.com), which remains a permanent fixture on the Internet.

The intention was to stay in touch and offer my personal views on how I saw my home country develop. The result is a collection that is neither a history book nor an academic text. It is the work of a journalist who tries to shed light on and seeks to explain some of the issues during a critically important period in Trinidad and Tobago's political development between 2007 and 2012. It presents a view from afar, perhaps even a clearer view, because from a distance it is always easier to get a proper view of the mountain.

This series of news items, columns and commentaries reflect my thoughts and views on how I saw my country struggle, stumble and then make positive steps as it tried to move forward under a government that, for the first time in the country's history, represents people from every stratum in the society, regardless of class, social standing, ethnicity or religious belief.

The period covered in these pages saw the consolidation of power by the People's National Movement (PNM) under Patrick Manning following his ascension to office by presidential decree in 2001; the near-death experience of the United National Congress (UNC); the conflicts within the party that once governed the country; the birth of the Congress of the People (COP); the selfless struggle by a dedicated few to revive the UNC and finally the rise of Kamla Persad-Bissessar to lead the party and the country.

Within four months of becoming political leader of the UNC Kamla and her political colleagues formed a national coalition of interests that won a decisive political victory in a general election that was not due until 2012. The powerful People's Partnership toppled Patrick Manning and his PNM administration and Kamla became the first woman to lead a government of Trinidad and Tobago.

What you are holding in your hands is by no means exhaustive and is really a snapshot of the period, compressing time and space to build a political narrative.

My hope is that you will find material here to generate a national conversation on where we are today and where are heading as we continue our journey past the first 50 years since we pulled down the Union Jack and hoisted our own national flag with a pledge to create a new state forged from the "love of liberty" where each of us would "find an equal place."

I thought of calling this "A political lime" because in a sense that is what it is – an honest, from-the-heart conversation tinged with my own bias as I responded to the daily events and the changing political fortunes. I have to confess that it pained me to write some of what you would find in these pages but I felt a patriotic obligation to write down my thoughts for posterity.

JAI PARASRAM
TORONTO, ONTARIO, CANADA

Acknowledgements

Production of a work of this nature, I have discovered, is a mammoth undertaking and is very different from what I have done for decades - creating news stories and getting them to air.

And that is why I must acknowledge with deepest gratitude the assistance of Ms. Alice Besson for her tedious efforts in getting the manuscript ready for publication, and both Alice and Mr. Gerry Besson of Paria Publishing for believing in me.

Thanks also to my friend, Dr. Hamid Ghany, for introducing me to Alice and Gerry, and for his counsel over the years. Hamid and I have worked on many projects since we first met and I am particularly pleased that he has endorsed this one.

I wish to also acknowledge Mr. Anand Rampersadsingh. I wrote my first commentaries for Anand's online site (hotlikepepperradio.com) for his radio station and he generously allowed me to reproduce them on my personal blog, JYOTI, which I started in February 2008.

Thanks also to my many friends and colleagues in Trinidad and Tobago and Canada who encouraged me to write. I am also grateful to Ms. Ira Mathur, for generously allowing me to include one of her commentaries in this collection. Ira is a brilliant writer and storyteller and I am honoured to include her work in this volume.

I also wish to acknowledge my friends Richard Hosein and Capil Bissoon, for circulating my work online to a wide international audience. My grateful thanks as well to, Ram Jaggessar, who kept telling me why it was necessary not only to write but also to get this work published.

I would be ungrateful if I did not acknowledge my children – Shiva, Amit, Ajay and Jiv and their respective spouses, Lisa, Heather and Fazeela – for the encouragement and ideas for this book. Ajay wrote the introduction to this volume and co-authored some of the material.

I wish to express my deepest appreciation to Ajay and Fazeela for putting aside their own work to edit and proof read the manuscript and offer useful comments. It was a painstaking and meticulous process for which I shall be eternally grateful.

And my dear wife, Seromanie, who is one of my greatest fans and also a most brutal critic of everything I write. She refused to let me give up.

Finally, I don't think it would have been possible for me to complete this work if it had not been for the inspiration from my granddaughter, Aurora. I wanted to do it for her and the children of her generation and whenever I felt overwhelmed and thought of giving up I looked at her photo, which reminded me that I had an obligation to her and generations to come to publish this work.

Jai Parasram
Toronto, Ontario, Canada

Introduction by Ajay Parasram

The long road to de-colonisation: Understanding our political present

There's no such thing as history, only histories. The book you hold in your hands is a particular reading of history in Trinidad and Tobago covering the tumultuous national politics of the last half a decade. The author's objective is to stimulate a national conversation about our future, and by way of introducing this important collection, these first few pages seek to make one single point that I hope you will keep in mind while reading the book: Trinidad and Tobago is not yet free, but rather, still engaged in a long process of de-colonisation.

It may seem insulting to patriots to say that we are not free. After all, Port of Spain occupies a seat at the United Nations in New York, the islands follow a Westminster parliamentary model with a bureaucracy and a novel coalition government that illustrates the state's willingness to experiment with democratic practices. But in acknowledging that we are still in a process of political experimentation, it opens the door to political possibilities that are as yet uncharted.

The way that Trinidad and Tobago is governed does not truly reflect the aspirations of the people of the country any more so than it does in most other postcolonial societies. One of the reasons for this is that the structure of government has its origins in the colonial planning of the British government; our nation-state was written first with the subduing of the indigenous populations, then sown with slave labour and indentured servitude.

Colonial statecraft, Eric Williams has observed, follows a capitalist logic of transforming the land for the purpose of resource exploitation and the subduing of dark-skinned people for the interest of creating wealth for the coloniser. The British achieved this goal by implementing European understandings of property, elite-level governance, and ensuring a suitable level of disunity amongst the colonised population such that they would not rise up against them.

We, like so many other postcolonial states, have made the mistake of thinking that self-rule marks the end of colonialism, but the legacy of colonialism is deeply woven into our institutions and politics. The last half century of independence should be thought of as part of a process of de-colonising and we must be bold in our experimentation with new ways of living freely together.

Though much of the popular literature on nationalism and state development suggests that countries follow a similar path, postcolonial statecraft took the form of serving the interests of resource and labour exploitation to serve Europe. In Trinidad and Tobago, it began with subjugation of indigenous Arawak and Caribs who resisted colonial penetration until the late 17th century. By the 19th century, the idea was to turn the physical territory into a satellite state of the British empire, creating large-scale commercial farms that compromised local ecosystems so that wealth could be sucked from the land and used to benefit local estate owners and investors rather than using it for the betterment of those who toiled the land. And in typical colonial fashion, colonised peoples were told that this was ultimately in their own interests; that Europeans were offering a guiding hand-up into the riches of the modern world that people of the global south couldn't hope to access on their own.

The French-Creoles, and later the British, accomplished this feat through purchasing African slaves and forcing them to work the land to produce profit for white planters who both owned the land and controlled the satellite-colonial government. As Eric Williams has shown, the emancipation of slaves by British decree came about less as a result of moral revelation and more as a result of the proven inefficiency of slave labour. After emancipation, freed slaves became workers. As workers rather than property, these free men and women were able to withhold labour in order to negotiate somewhat better conditions and economic benefits. This was a tumultuous time for the global economy because British planters were now competing against American planters who scoffed at the idea of ending slavery, thus putting economic pressure on the European government to find a cheap source of labour rather than bargaining with the workers of African descent.

Fortunately for the planters, the British Empire was busy starving millions to death in Asia around the same time. Indian and Chinese farmers, facing famines that were engineered by British commercial farming demands sailed across the *kali pani* (black water) to Trinidad, Fiji, Guyana, and elsewhere. According to Mike Davis, between 1876 and 1878, six million Indians and 12 million Chinese died as a result of colonial authorities prioritising crops for imperial interests rather than feeding the local population.

The planters made sure that Africans and Asians could not truly influence politics. Planters controlled the government and wrote laws that made participation in politics conditional on wealth and land-ownership. The new Indian and Chinese indentured labourers were required to repay the cost of their voyage to the British and were indentured for upwards of 20 years at a time in order to do so. Perversely, the British raised the necessary capital to finance this mass migration of indentured labourers by taxing the free African population. Consequently, from the beginning of indentureship there was a conflict of interest between the African population and the Asian population.

Starved and desperate Asians occupied the former slave barracks and toiled for sub-market wages to repay their debt to the colonial administrators. Yet in so doing, they represented a kind of scab-labour, undermining the collective attempts of the African workers to force better working conditions and distribution of resources. These same administrators drafted laws to take the money needed to finance the labour immigration from the African population through taxation and legal maneuvers. Over time a political economy of race developed in Trinidad, rooted to economics that emulated the interest of the coloniser over the interests of the colonised.

As Bridget Brereton has argued, there is no one history of Trinidad and Tobago. National-histories are plentiful and articulate a particular standpoint. Brereton describes a British, French-Creole, Afro-Creole, Indigenous, Tobagan, Afro-centric, Indo-centric, Hindu-centric, and opens the door for Syrian, Chinese, and Lebanese-centric ones as well. In her 2007 essay, "Contesting the Past: Narratives of Trinidad and Tobago history" Brereton writes, "Nationalisms are invented, and their claims to historical continuity are always expressions of ideological and political concerns, and this is equally true of the construction of ethnicities and ethnic narratives."

The collective traumas and indignities of colonisation, broadly defined, seeded and nurtured a pernicious politics of race-based partisanship that continues to affect the elected politics of today. National politics, the main focus of this book, has tended to emphasise a rhetoric of race in order to mobilise voters.

Part of the entrenched principles of colonialism lies in the idea that the public's participation in its own governance ends with the ballot-box or fundraising for the party of their choice. To de-colonise our society, the practice of politics needs to change in order to involve the regular participation of citizens in shaping the outcome of their land well beyond casting a ballot. The anger that fuels race-based politics answers in part to the incentive structure of first-past-the-post politics and it retards the process of de-colonisation. Formerly colonised people have every right to be enraged by the legacies of colonisation, but that anger ought to be directed at the institutions that continue to pit one formally colonised group against another. If we are indeed "forged from the love of liberty, in the fires of hope and prayer," we can surely do better.

This collection of editorial commentaries does not lay claim to being an objective account of history, nor does it seek to represent any "nation" within the state. Rather, the author offers the keen eyes and ears of a seasoned Trinidadian journalist who has, in his own words, seen his country "struggle, stumble, and then move forward." If we consider the evolving politics of Trinidad and Tobago as part of the long process of de-colonising, we may forgive some of the missteps of previous and current governments while demanding serious accountability and the meaningful involvement of ordinary citizens in their own governance.

Trinidad and Tobago is a complex society where solidarities cross "national" boundaries and cover gender, sexuality, labour, development, ecology, and more to show the fragility of imagined national solidarities. Having been given the privilege of introducing this volume, I will share one final point with readers. I have known the author for 29 years and in this time period, not one day has elapsed where Jai Parasram has not devoted a considerable amount of time and energy in pursuit of de-colonising Trinidad and Tobago, though he would not use those words.

In these pages you will not find a solution, but a call to action. As you turn the page, I urge you to embrace de-colonisation such that we might all "stumble, struggle, and then move forward" on the long march to freedom.

Section 1
The futile search for common ground

A divided opposition: the struggle for survival

"We wished one another well and said we would meet again next week… it took us 10 years for us to meet again as a cabinet."

Those are the words of Roodal Moonilal, the MP for Oropouche East and Government Chief Whip, talking about how the Basdeo Panday United National Congress (UNC) administration lost the government. Roodal was the Communication and Information Technology Minister in the government and had just entered electoral politics, having lost to Patrick Manning in the 2000 general election; a year later he soundly defeated a turncoat UNC, Trevor Sudama, in an election that was forced by the betrayal of three members of the governing party — Ramesh Lawrence Maharaj, Trevor Sudama and Ralph Maraj. The three had conspired with then opposition leader Patrick Manning to usurp the government; Panday learned of the scheme and told President Arthur Robinson to dissolve parliament and call fresh elections, which Robinson reluctantly did.

The dissident MPs who had campaigned with the UNC in the 2000 election in which the UNC was elected with a majority of one seat (UNC 19; PNM 16; NAR 1) began their revolt within months of the new government taking office, complaining of what they said was a perception of corruption within the administration. It turned out that they were the ones who helped create the perception. In the 2007 general election campaign that Manning and his People's National Movement (PNM) won, Manning stated publicly that Ramesh was "his best friend," having given him the information that he used to label Panday and the UNC as corrupt.

Ramesh was an angry man. He was the outsider who Panday brought into the party to replace Kelvin Ramnath after Panday rejected Ramnath and people like the UNC's founding chairman, Dr. Rampersad Parasram. Ramnath and Parasram had won control of the UNC executive in the party's internal election, a fact that did not sit well with Panday. Once he dispensed with them, Ramesh moved in to help Panday organise the party, which entered government in 1995 in a coalition with the National Alliance for Reconstruction (NAR) led by ANR Robinson.

In 2000 Ramesh found himself in the same position as Kelvin and company; his Team Unity had won control of the UNC's national executive but Panday refused to accept it. While he installed the executive as required by the UNC constitution, Panday never treated Ramesh with the respect or courtesy that he had earned as a deputy leader. Instead he handed that privilege to Kamla Persad-Bissessar, who ran in the internal election against Ramesh but did not win.

There were other factors at play as well. Ramesh had seen himself as the heir apparent to Panday, but suddenly other people were moving into what he assumed was his rightful place — people like Carlos John, dubbed by Ramesh and his Team Unity group as a Johnny Come Lately who had no business in the cabinet or the party. Carlos was indeed new, but he was not irrelevant. He was there protecting the interest of Lawrence Duprey, the Executive Chairman of the powerful conglomerate, CL Financial.

Carlos had developed a strong friendship with Panday, and especially Panday's wife, Oma. As a business associate of Duprey, Carlos was needed to keep an eye on things within the cabinet — or so Ramesh felt.

Panday had run a pretty good government between 1995 and 2000 and his re-election with a clear majority had left some serious questions that made Panday uncomfortable. His party had 19 of the 36 seats but two of them were the subject of a legal battle with the PNM arguing that the election of Winston Peters (Mayaro) and Bill Chaitan (Pointe-a-Pierre) were null and void because both men held citizenship of the U.S. and Canada respectively on nomination day, and therefore were not qualified to be candidates. If the PNM had won its case, it might have won those seats by default reducing Panday's UNC to 17 seats and giving Manning and the PNM 18. The matter never reached a conclusion.

Ramesh, as Panday's Attorney General, knew that the new government was not standing on firm ground, so he engineered Panday's fall by putting government corruption on the national agenda with the assistance of Ralph and Trevor. He took it one extra politically dangerous step — a courtship with Manning. Ramesh and Manning met privately and cut a deal for Panday to lose his parliamentary majority and then ask the president to fire Panday and appoint Manning as prime minister. They were clever about it; they did not want fresh elections so they voted with the government to pass the budget but once that was out of the way they moved for the kill, presenting Manning as their leader. A newspaper headline reading "Done Deal" became an albatross around Ramesh's neck that remains his greatest political liability.

Panday acted swiftly. He went to Robinson with a request to dissolve parliament. Robinson initially objected, saying that since it was so soon after the last election Panday should consider whether the EBC — the Elections and Boundaries Commission — would be ready and able to hold another election. Panday argued that such an issue was irrelevant and demanded that Robinson dissolve parliament. The president had no choice; he had to abide by the constitution.

The election was on December 10, 2001 and the contest was mainly between the PNM and UNC as it had been a year before. However, the group that Ramesh had headed to contest the internal election became the thorn in Panday's side. Team Unity became a third political party and ran candidates against the UNC with a campaign that was ostensibly based on integrity and morality; in reality Ramesh and his team had just one motive — to topple Panday.

The result was a tie with the PNM and UNC winning 18 seats each in the 36-member legislature. Ramesh had won. His party's 14,207 votes were insignificant at the national level but important enough to rob Panday's UNC of the one critical seat — Tunapuna. Both the UNC and PNM lost ground with the UNC support falling from 307,791 (51.7 percent of the popular vote) to 279,002 (49.9 percent). The PNM maintained its 46.5 percent but public apathy caused it to lose some of its numeric support. The Team Unity campaign cost the UNC more than 28,000 votes; by contrast the PNM lost only 16,000.

What happened next created an unusual political precedent and set the stage for a new direction in the politics of Trinidad and Tobago. Panday as the incumbent head of the government had the right to seek a vote of confidence and govern. His party also had the higher popular vote but in the country's first-past-the-post electoral system that did not matter; it was clear that Panday could not govern. With the parliament tied at 18-18 neither the UNC nor the PNM could convene parliament. There was only one way to break the deadlock — negotiate some form of compromise. Panday seized the initiative and invited Manning to join with him to form a government of national unity, which Manning immediately rejected.

President Robinson called in Panday and Manning and asked them to work out a governing formula since without a Speaker the parliament could not convene and would have to be dissolved without ever sitting. Trinidad and Tobago was certainly not ready for another election, which would likely have returned the same result.

Several meetings and negotiating sessions later an "amicable" accord — the Crowne Plaza Accord — was drafted. Panday somehow felt that he had scored a victory and according to one commentator "all but hugged and kissed" Manning as the two met the media. "Come on kid, let's go home," Panday told Manning. And they went their separate ways.

The two had agreed on the choice of a Speaker of the House of Representatives (and a lot more that was later discarded) and decided they would abide by whatever decision Robinson made in choosing a prime minister.

Some of Panday's advisers were wary of that situation and suggested that he should return to the people. Others, who were more influential, assured Panday that Robinson would follow precedent and reappoint Panday since he was the incumbent and should naturally be given an opportunity to form a government and convene parliament, now that the matter of a Speaker was settled. That was a blundering miscalculation.

Panday and Robinson had never truly sealed a truce since their political divorce in 1987. When Robinson became kingmaker with his two Tobago seats in 1995, Panday had little choice but to cut a deal with him and unseat Manning as prime minister. However, that arrangement never worked. Panday sought to solve the problem by setting a new precedent in appointing an active politician to the post of head of state. Panday had hoped that with this 'stroke of genius' he would get rid of Robinson. It was another blundering miscalculation. Robinson was not the passive president Panday had hoped for and he and Panday had open conflicts during the UNC administration. Panday even campaigned against Robinson's party in the Tobago House of Assembly election in 2001, causing the PNM to win a strong majority.

With such a record of animosity and hostility, it is surprising that Panday trusted Robinson to be fair and objective in his choice of a prime minister or to even follow parliamentary convention. Those who felt comfortable with Robinson assured him that the president would follow convention to protect his legacy. Panday, the seasoned politician and fighter, fell for that.

He and his political colleagues were in a celebratory mood when they concluded that last cabinet meeting on December 20, 2011. The next move was Robinson's and Moonilal and the other members of cabinet left, confident that they would be back after Christmas to continue their work.

On Christmas eve, Robinson delivered the shocking news in an address to the nation broadcast live on radio and television. He had decided to ask Manning to form a government, having decided that someone with strong "moral and spiritual values" must lead the government. It was the nightmare before Christmas for some; a gift from the Lord for others. Christmas 2001 was a turning point in the political history of Trinidad and Tobago.

The Crowne Plaza Accord fell apart. The new prime minister found it impossible to convene parliament because he needed a majority in the House of Representatives to elect a speaker, without whom the parliament would be stillborn. Robinson came to Manning's rescue and allowed the parliament to be prorogued, giving Manning a free hand to govern without accounting to the parliament or facing the scrutiny of the opposition.

With the full resources of the state and some loyal friends with special skills, Manning governed for nine months as a law unto himself, consolidating his power while undermining the opposition. The lingering question about those nine months is whether Manning and the president were acting within the letter and spirit of the constitution. Perhaps they were in breach but the opposition never formally challenged the legality except to refuse to cooperate each time Manning tried to convene parliament.

In the general election of October 7, 2002, Manning's PNM increased its share of the vote by more than 48,000 while the UNC was able to get just over 5,000 more than it did in the previous election. The PNM won 20 of the 36 seats, with the other 16 going to the UNC. In less than two years after winning re-election with a clear majority, Panday was back in a familiar position — leader of the opposition, when he could have been prime minister. He pledged that he would never forgive Ramesh.

Manning was determined never to lose power again. He had foolishly called an early election in 1995 during the fourth year of his first administration and he ended up losing the government to Panday. His fall was partly precipitated by his decision to place the Speaker of the House of Representatives, Oka Seepaul, under House Arrest and the firing of her brother, Foreign Affairs Minister, Ralph Maraj. Both Ralph and Manning's Finance Minister, Brian Kuei Tung walked over to Panday. Manning blamed many people and advanced several excuses for his loss, including the silly story that his colleague, Wendell Mottley, leaked the election date to Panday and the UNC. However, the most chilling issue was the blame he himself accepted — that he did not adequately take care of "his people" in his first administration and he would never make that mistake again.

Trinidad and Tobago politics had been polarised along ethnic lines since 1956 with the arrival of Eric Williams on the political scene. Williams had gathered a strong team but was clever enough to make a clear separation between the Hindu Indians and the Muslims and Christians. Manning went beyond that and kept only one Indian within his inner cabinet — his trusted friend and ally Lenny Saith. There were others but their "Indianness" was subordinate to the PNM's politics.

The power brokers in the UNC knew that the time had come for Panday to take his exit and decided to tell him so. Jack Warner, who had been a silent supporter and financier since the first Panday administration (1995-2000), Ameer Edoo and former PNM senior cabinet minister Errol Mahabir went to see Panday at his home and convey the news. Panday reluctantly agreed to leave but only on condition that there was an orderly leadership transition. At a special meeting of the UNC national executive in October 2002 Panday announced that he would quit as leader after a transition team had worked out the details of the transfer of power. The late Kelvin Ramnath and Kamla Persad-Bissessar were members of the team, which never met and never did anything to change the status quo.

In the meantime, Manning was firmly in charge. Robinson, the man who put Manning in charge, had publicly warned against "a creeping dictatorship" within the Panday administration, but that same label was made to fit Manning much later when people across the country — including prominent members from the ranks of the PNM like Ken Valley and Keith Rowley — rose up to challenge Manning.

In planning for the 2002 election, the backroom players were already looking for a new leader. Kamla had been preparing for that role from the time she entered electoral politics at the national level as a candidate for the UNC in 1995, but the power brokers were looking at someone else.

Winston Dookeran had fallen out with Panday back in 1987 when Panday and some of his loyalists from the former United Labour Front (ULF) walked away from the Robinson National Alliance for Reconstruction (NAR) government. The ULF was one of the political groups that had merged with others to form NAR. However, the lopsided 33-3 victory gave Robinson strength he never expected and there was no room for dissent within the homogenous political movement.

Robinson's agenda didn't jive with Panday's and before long, there was open political warfare over several issues, including race. When Panday left, Winston stayed with Robinson because he was convinced that it was the right thing to do. He acknowledged that he owed his political presence in parliament to Panday's leadership (he was the MP for Chaguanas) but felt that Panday's approach was wrong. In the 1991 general election when Panday had formed a new party — the UNC — Hulsie Bhaggan defeated Winston in Chaguanas. Winston emerged on the national landscape later as Governor of the Central Bank during the Panday administration and when Manning refused to renew his contract it seemed like his time had come to return to politics.

One of the key players in the resurrection of Winston was Kamaluddin "Charch" Mohammed, a founding member of the PNM whom Manning had unceremoniously discarded along with Errol Mahabir (both men had been deputy PNM leaders under Williams and their race and politics didn't suit Manning). Charch arranged a special dinner at the home of a prominent member of the Muslim community in Charlieville when Panday sealed the deal for Winston to return to politics in the safe seat of St. Augustine, which Gerry Yetming reluctantly gave up and moved to St Joseph. There was an understanding that he would be the future leader of the party.

Panday and the UNC had planned to break the news to the media at the St Augustine Constituency Office where Yetming would shake hands with Winston. The media were alerted but Winston was shy about the event and suggested that it be handled privately.

There was something about the event that was just not right. Kamla was not amused about Winston, whom she saw as a threat to her future leadership. And when she showed up for the event the media came with her. She insisted that she never invited them. The UNC communications staff quickly solved the problem and invited the media to hear the worst kept secret and capture the photo-op. Panday was not pleased. He had refused to invite Kamla to the event and the next morning, holding one of the daily papers in his hands he remarked, "The woman spoil meh picture". He was referring to a picture of the key players, including Kamla.

That incident was a watershed moment in the UNC and the political change that would come later. When the UNC *jefes* visited Panday to tell him it was time for him to leave, it was Winston's name that came up as the new leader but that change didn't happen until much later.

On September 2, 2005, Panday announced that he would be willing to hand over the party's leadership if he could remain as UNC chairman. Once both men agreed on that each of them faced the UNC electorate unopposed. While it was no contest for those two posts in the internal election, each of the two ran a slate of candidates for the remaining 16 executive posts.

In the election on October 2, Panday's slate won 12 of the posts, including two of the three deputy leader positions and the vice-chairmanship. Dookeran's slate won the others. That's when the trouble started that ended nearly five years later with a humiliating defeat for Panday at the hands of Kamla, the same person whom Panday had shunned more than once.

Members of the slate backed by Dookeran, which included Jack Warner as a deputy leader, demanded that Panday step down as leader of the opposition, a seat that rightfully belonged to the leader of the opposition party. Panday refused and turned to Ramesh, the man who had betrayed him and sent him from government to opposition.

Many years before, Panday had stated that he would "sleep with the devil" if it suited his political cause. He did it with Robinson to become prime minister and now he was ready to get in bed with Ramesh for a second time. This coincided with another significant political development. Jack fell out with Winston and returned to the Panday camp. His agenda was unchanged; he still wanted Panday to go, but he felt that Dookeran's approach was wrong. His argument was that certain people like former UNC cabinet minister Gerald Yetming had no real concern for the party and its principles and were more interested in hijacking Winston and taking charge of the party. That was Panday's position as well, which he used to justify his opposition to Winston's leadership.

Winston found himself in a political straitjacket, unable to effect the changes he wanted to see in the UNC as he prepared it to win government. Panday refused to cooperate and with a national executive that Panday controlled, Winston became politically impotent within the UNC.

In February 2006 Panday announced that he and Ramesh were once more a team and that Ramesh would be present at a UNC rally later in the month at the party's stomping ground at the Mid Centre Mall in Chaguanas. Winston attended the rally on February 19 and criticised Panday for bringing Ramesh back into the UNC. It was a tactical error. The propaganda ahead of the rally had primed the UNC supporters to be hostile to their leader. When Winston went after Ramesh, it earned him boos from the crowd.

Yetming had previously had a stormy relationship with Ramesh and the latter's return caused him to make his exit from the UNC. The pieces of the jigsaw were falling into place. Winston and his advisers were no longer working with the executive. In effect, the UNC was split between a Panday faction and one headed by its elected leader.

Winston's political fortunes inside the UNC were waning, having lost the support of Jack and Roodal Moonilal who moved to Panday's side. Panday was also losing ground, but on a personal level.

On April 24, 2006 a magistrate convicted him of fraud for failing to disclose a London bank account and jailed him for two years. The next day, President Max Richards fired Panday as leader of the opposition and in a move intended to show Dookeran the door. UNC MPs announced their support for deputy leader, Kamla, who was appointed opposition leader on February 27, 2006. Panday was granted bail a day later and offered his resignation as chairman of the party, which the executive refused. The drama continued to undermine the credibility of the UNC and as the tension increased Winston began organising a party within the UNC, ignoring the national executive, which Panday controlled.

As opposition leader, Kamla flexed her political muscle and appointed her own senators. Panday ostensibly tried to heal the wounds but the effect had been lethal. UNC supporters were growing tired and losing interest while Manning was getting stronger and bolder. Those who mattered in the UNC were not listening to Winston. To make matters worse, Panday was now heading a governing council of the party that comprised deputy leaders Wade Mark, Kamla and Jack as well as Ramesh and Tim Gopeesingh, who was the party's CEO. There was no room for Winston, so he closed the book on the UNC and walked away.

On September 10, 2006, his supporters organised a rally in Freeport at which Winston announced his resignation from the UNC and the formation of the Congress of the People (COP), under his leadership. Panday got what he wanted and returned as interim leader as well as chairman of the UNC.

The stage was now set for a three-way political battle for Trinidad and Tobago that would eventually lead to the political demise of both Panday and Manning and the rise of Kamla as the only person to ever challenge Panday and win.

These opening commentaries ahead of the 2007 general election focus on the need for the opposition to come together as the only means of rescuing Trinidad and Tobago from the reign of a dictator in the making.

The later sections deal with the upheaval inside the UNC, leading to the Movement for Change led by Jack Warner and including Ramesh and Mayaro MP Winston "Gypsy" Peters; the rise of Kamla and the historic UNC internal election of 2010 that saw Panday suffer the most humiliating defeat of his political career; the fall of the Manning PNM at the hands of a powerful coalition of interest that included both Kamla and Dookeran; and some of the major events that directed the national conversation.

This first volume ends with the celebration of Trinidad and Tobago's 50th anniversary of independence in 2012.

Common sense and the politics of opposition

You've no doubt heard the saying that common sense is not so common. Well in case you're wondering, it's true. Take the politics of Trinidad and Tobago today. The common sense reality is that the nation is under siege by criminals — kidnappers, murderers, thieves and thugs. The government is bankrupt of any ideas about how to deal with the crime and its performance generally is so pathetic, people will gladly trade their government for a viable alternative.

But where is that government in waiting?

Basdeo Panday knows. And that's why he is calling for all politicians who oppose the PNM to unite to remove the Manning regime from office. It's good common sense. But Manohar Ramsaran and Sadiq Baksh and other born-again politicians dressed in the robes of "new politics" are quick off the mark to shoot down this plan.

They claim to be close to the grassroots, to be gifted with the common touch, capable of understanding what it is like to move from the ground floor up. Yet they lack the vision to see plain ol' common sense. Panday, on the other hand, understands the predicament of the people today and is ready — or so he says — to build a coalition to achieve the primary goal: boot out the PNM. Panday's recent judicial victory gives him more political muscle and lends credence to the UNC.

Patrick Manning commands the full resources of the state. And he has certain "community leaders" on his side who are more than willing to "lend their expertise" to ensure that Manning returns to power. That itself puts any opposition at a monumental disadvantage. But common sense tells you that there is within the opposition enough talent and commitment to convince a confused and desperate electorate that they can change things.

Do a quick analysis and the picture gets into sharp focus. PNM and its allies are clear on their goal. And they are united. The opposition is also clear but fragmented. Each opposition group has the same primary goal, so the common sense thing to do would be to make the next election a one-on-one battle: one opposition candidate versus a PNM in each of the 41 constituencies. It's the only hope in hell that the opposition has any chance of unseating the PNM.

The obvious question is: why try this approach again? Well the circumstances are quite different. This is neither 1981 nor 1986. It's close to 1995, except much worse. In fact there is so much dejavu you have to pinch yourself to know you're awake and it's real.

Think of it: Manning fighting and persecuting a top (Indian) official, the courts hounding and putting Panday on trial for a charge that gets tossed out, crime on the rise, and Panday and the UNC are fighting a third force, the NAR. Sounds familiar? Well that was 1995. In that election, Panday beat the odds and put Manning out of business. Panday can do it again, but only if there is a one-on-one fight. And it's pie-in-the-sky to think that Dookeran and his COP can do it; they missed their opportunity a long time ago and it won't come back.

People are fed up. They want to move the PNM. They know Manning has failed them in every aspect of national life. They live in self-imposed prisons. In spite of the oil windfalls, the economy is under threat. Although many people are seeing more money in their pockets everybody knows that this is for short-term political expediency. Keeping Manning in office is the last thing any right-thinking person wants.

But the constituency that's clamouring for change — which happens to be the majority — is confused because it has to split its loyalty among the various opposition elements. And what makes this a truly difficult situation is that each opposition party is fishing in the same lake for the same fish. Manning, on the other hand, has his exclusive pond. And he keeps it like a modern-day fish farm, where more and more fish are added artificially.

And therein lies a fundamental problem, but also a reason for optimism. The opposition has a lake; he has a pond. That's not confusing as it might seem.

Remember that in each constituency, four out of every six qualified electors don't vote. They are the fish that the opposition can catch this time; even two out of four will make the difference. And some of the PNM fish are ready to swim away. So why can't everybody understand that the only common-sense thing to do is sit down, work things out, collate ideas and strategies and fight one battle to win the war? Even with a combined one-to-one effort, beating Manning will still be like climbing a greasy pole. But it's the only way. And the opposition can do it.

Here's why. For starters, the opposition has 15 seats in parliament and ran a close second in three others. That means, in a one-on-one fight chances of winning these 18 seats are very good. In a splintered multi-party race, it's a given that Manning will run away with several of these seats. But 18 is just three seats short of a majority. There are five new constituencies and a combined, responsible opposition can win those additional seats from among the five.

So why isn't everybody clutching on to this lifeline?

Simple. Politicians aren't as smart as they want us to believe. They don't have the common sense to see that's the most obvious thing to do. They prefer to be selfish and lose everything than to build a strong coalition and win the prize, because unfortunately, like my mother always told me, "common sense not so common."

(May 28, 2007)

The trouble with disunity

There is a sense of deja-vu with the recently concluded deal for a united alliance of opposition parties, headed by the UNC. And the notable absence of the COP from the group adds to it.

Rewind to 1981. There was an alliance then too with the United Labour Front (ULF), Tapia and the Democratic Action Congress (DAC). And the arrogant new kid on the block wanted nothing to do with the likes of Basdeo Panday, Lloyd Best and A.N.R. Robinson. Karl Hudson Phillips and his Organisation for National Reconstruction (ONR) were going to change the face of national politics and end the PNM's reign. The result of that election was predictable as is the forthcoming one, given the present state of affairs.

There are some significant differences between then and now, which means there is still a quickly closing window of opportunity for opposition politicians to determine once and for all if they want to remove the PNM or remain stuck in the quicksand of political pettiness.

In 1981 the politics was different. George Chambers had just inherited the PNM following the demise of the party's founder, Dr. Eric Williams.

Chambers had little time to put his own stamp on anything and continued with the Williams agenda. A whole generation had known no other party in government and people were not yet ready to change that. Also, when Chambers called the election the nation was still mourning the death of a man who was loved even by those who didn't know him or disagreed with his politics.

Chambers guided the PNM back to Whitehall on a landslide, primarily because of a sympathy vote. What was also significant that year was that the ONR did better than the Alliance but ended without a single seat. Chambers was almost a soothsayer when he declared in Woodford Square, "They are too wicked. Not a damn seat for them."

The Alliance experiment that year didn't work. Each party kept its identity and didn't run under a single symbol. Robinson won his two Tobago seats, Best and Tapia remained irrelevant and Basdeo Panday went back to parliament with his traditional ULF seats. The moral of the story then as it is now: splintering the opposition returns the government to office.

And that brings us back to where we are 26 years later in 2007.

Once again, we have an Alliance. And once again we have a new party "full of sound and fury" arguing that it will change things with its "new" politics. The fundamental difference this time is that the Congress of the People (COP) is led by a man who was disenchanted with the UNC, unlike Hudson Phillips, who was a former PNM Attorney General. Winston Dookeran is fishing in the opposition pond; Hudson Phillips was in the government's.

This brings up a critical part in the 2007 political equation.

Dookeran and the COP have claimed that they have majority support among those who oppose the PNM. In translation, that means the COP believes it can win the opposition constituencies. But there's little evidence of that. The UNC has kept its base, in spite of the witchhunt by the PNM that has not really left anyone burning at the stakes.

Over the years from 1995 to 2002 the UNC vote increased, with a peak in 2000 of more than 307,000, accounting for more than 50 percent of the popular vote. It dipped in the next election, then went up again, ending with a net gain over 1995 by the time it was pushed out of office by President Robinson on Christmas eve 2001.

So the real issue that makes 2007 so critically different from 1981 is that the COP is courting votes from the opposition constituencies while leaving PNM strongholds alone. The bulk of ONR's 90,000 votes in 1981 came from disenchanted PNM supporters. Still the party lost every seat.

The COP, therefore, by using this strategy of facing the polls alone, is engineering a PNM victory by splintering the vote in opposition constituencies to allow the strong possibility of the PNM winning in some areas with a minority vote.

What is also different this time is that none of the frontline leaders in the present Alliance, except Basdeo Panday, has true political clout. And the Alliance is making the same fundamental mistake of 1981 by not declaring who is its leader.

Politics in Trinidad and Tobago is based on allegiances more than policy. So it really comes down to who's the leader. Williams, Robinson, Manning and Panday have had strong, dedicated followings (Chambers didn't, but won on the strength of Williams). People want to identify the leader who will take them to government before they make that choice.

That was a principal fault in the 1981 Alliance. They fixed the problem five years leader when Panday handed the leadership of the NAR to Robinson, but that failed because the opposition became a single party with no room for dissent and discussion among its different components. Today the Alliance is back to collective leadership, which is confusing the electorate.

And if the COP is counting on cutting a new political path, it should do the analysis first and it will see that it has to rethink its position if it is serious about beating the PNM.

Loyalty dies hard. Eric Williams used to say that he could put a crapaud in his strongholds and win. He was right. Ask Hulsie Bhaggan why Chaguanas rejected her or Rupert Griffith what really happened in Arima. They were seen as traitors to their respective parties; people voted for the party, seeing them only as symbols of the organisation.

Dookeran must know that. He's no idiot. Manohar Ramsarran trounced him in 1991 in Chaguanas where he had won a landslide. So that raises the most important question of the day: what is the COP's real agenda? Is it seeing the big picture or is it happy with giving Manning a constitutional majority?

Manning has created the best opportunity for the opposition to boot him out of office, but the opposition is engaged in turf wars and pettiness. And at the end of the day, there will be plenty of finger-pointing. By then the true losers will be the people who would have every reason to say their leaders failed them — again.

(July 2007)

How to win an election, or lose one

I don't know Steve Alvarez and have had no contact with him, but if comments attributed to him in Irene Medina's Newsday story on August 7, 2007 are true, I would say he's either ducking a significant political issue or naïve about the business into which he is getting. Medina's story quotes Alvarez as saying that the UNC Alliance will not choose a leader until after the general election because "we don't want the media to focus on one person."

Alavarez and anybody who shares that view are missing the whole point.

Patrick Manning and his PNM administration have created every opportunity for a strong opposition to unseat his regime. Just look at the mayhem that plagues the society with the government showing scant attention to public safety or the irresponsible squandering of the country's resources.

Ask people everywhere in Trinidad and Tobago and they will tell you it's time for the PNM to go. Even some PNM supporters are fed up and ready to change the guard, if not the party. But almost in the same breath you will hear another familiar line: "who we go put?" And that's what Alvarez is missing.

I refuse to believe he's that naïve. In a previous column I wrote about the mistakes the Alliance (ULF, DAC and TAPIA) made in 1981. Selwyn Ryan and other political commentators have written extensively about the confused electorate that returned the PNM to office in 1981. The people were confused because Basdeo Panday, Lloyd Best and A.N.R. Robinson made the same mistake Alvarez is encouraging the Alliance to make today.

By ducking the question of leadership the UNC Alliance is demonstrating a clear lack of confidence in its electoral chances and its leaders. Or perhaps it is just frightened to deal with the reality. Basdeo Panday is the de facto leader of the UNC Alliance. Alvarez and his colleagues are frightened to challenge that because they lack a constituency.

Panday is the only one among them who has one. It's the same one he has had since he entered politics forty years ago: the dispossessed and disadvantaged masses.

PNM propaganda has put a tremendous amount of negative baggage on the man who presided over the most effective government the nation has ever known. And it is popular these days to engage in Panday-bashing, which is getting to be some kind of new national sport. Yet his commanding political presence makes it difficult for anyone to challenge him.

And that's where the UNC Alliance is missing the boat. You cannot tell people you lack the confidence to decide who among you can lead the party to victory and take over the government. If you can't do that, why should anybody vote for you?

That was the issue in 1981. People voted for the ULF and the DAC, not the Alliance. That year, the other parties at least had some kind of track record and identities. No non-UNC component in the UNC Alliance has demonstrated it can command support to even win one seat on its own anywhere in the country; the UNC remains the only credible element in the group. And that brings us back the dilemma facing the UNC Alliance. They want to push Panday out because they feel — perhaps with good reason — that the baggage he now carries will be devastating. As each "leader" jockeys for position, he sees the faint light at the end of the tunnel leading to Whitehall. So why rock the boat now and put out that light? Each knows he cannot face the electorate as a leader and win. So, instead of dealing with the problem, they hide behind useless rhetoric such as the comment attributed to Alvarez.

A voter has every right to care about the media focus in an election campaign, especially one so crucial as the election at hand. And the media have every right to focus on a leader.

A responsible political party has an obligation to get its act together, determine who is its leader, create a platform for change and then convince the people that it presents the best hope to fix the damage done over the past six years of PNM misrule.

The media report the news. That's their role and responsibility in a democracy. When they focus on a leader of a party, they focus on the person who will likely be the next prime minister. They have every right to focus on the leader, so it's absolute nonsense for any politician to even suggest that the reason for not selecting a leader now is because the UNC Alliance doesn't want the media to focus on one person.

Trinidad and Tobago is in a political crisis. Time is running out and the people are still holding hope that they will find the alternative they so desperately need. There is still time. Perhaps the UNC Alliance should look beyond the narrow view of the current "leaders."

I live in Toronto, so I don't have a vote in this election. But in the present circumstances, that's a good thing because it spares me the dilemma of deciding who gets that vote. Unfortunately, the tens of thousands who want to vote remain confused because of the indecision and grandstanding.

However, if I did have a vote, here's how I would like to "invest" it. Give me a strong, united opposition party. The UNC, its alliance members and the COP all have people with talent and commitment to the national good. Each group has valid and useful programmes to rescue the nation. Bring the ideas together, bring the people together and decide on a leader. If people still have a problem with Basdeo Panday, give Jack Warner or Kamla Persad-Bissessar the task of leading the nation out of its current misery. I would vote for that. And I can guarantee that the majority of the electorate will.

Who's the leader? Time running out for UNC Alliance

Basdeo Panday made it clear Friday night in Rio Claro that he's not going away and he also said that as far as he is concerned there are going to be three parties contesting the upcoming general election.

In other words, there will be no deal with the Congress of the People (COP). In a week of rumours and behind the scene intrigue in the opposition ranks this new episode in the Trinidad and Tobago political soap opera came as no surprise.

COP leader Winston Dookeran had also made the same pronouncement, although in less dramatic fashion, possibly leaving room for some kind of compromise. According to Dookeran, he would not talk unity with Panday as leader of the UNC.

So was he leaving the door open? Perhaps.

So it was no shocking news when the Trinidad Express heard from "sources" that a move was afoot to dump the UNC leader for the opposition leader, who happens to also be a deputy political leader of the United National Congress.

For her part, Kamla Persad-Bissessar was batting in her crease and quickly informed the media that she knew of no such moves in the party's back room. And when the media ambushed Bas to inquire about whether he met a certain party financier in London, inquiring what they talked about, the wily Bas informed the reporter that the hot topic was the *vindaloo* at the Indian restaurant where he dined with Lawrence Duprey.

But the drama became rather interesting Friday night in Rio Claro. Kamla ended her brief address with an impassioned plea for unity in the opposition. She said Patrick Manning's policy of divisiveness and discrimination was destroying the country and only a united opposition could save the nation. The nation was crying for unity, she declared.

Was she the one who could deliver it? Was she saying if Bas can't do it she can? What made it more interesting was that it came within minutes of Jack Warner's stern message to the COP that it was "rude and farse" to even suggest that the UNC should merge with it.

Jack's position was this: how can an upstart party with no track record be so bold as ask the UNC to merge with it when the UNC was a party that had served the country for 19 years, built and sustained its constituency on the basis of democracy, and had the most effective and productive track record in government in the history of the country. So why were these two deputies not singing from the same song sheet?

Well, the chief set matters straight when he came out swinging with his pronouncement that "Red (the COP colour) dead, and PNM gone."

Panday was in charge; he was going nowhere unless he died or his constituents in Couva North told him to leave, and he didn't expect any of that to happen before the next election. He was sending a clear message to pretenders to the throne. But not clear enough to the electorate. He still didn't say what the people had come to hear: who's the leader? And then he slammed the door on any unity deal with Dookeran and the COP. There will be three parties in the next election, he said.

So where does this all lead and what does it mean? If I were Patrick Manning I would pull the date from my back pocket right away because it sounded like a good time to profit from the splintered opposition factor.

But before you start blaming Panday alone for this, check the script of this political soap and the way the drama unfolded. It was Bas who handed Dookeran the leadership of the UNC. It was Bas who offered the olive branch and it was Dookeran who looked the other way. And while

Dookeran was posing as leader of the UNC, he was secretly building a party within the party and making plans to become a new messiah. The famous Freeport declaration was both unethical and dishonest.

Here's why. Up to days before that event, Dookeran was saying he wanted to mend fences in the UNC and make the leadership thing work. How could you say that, and in less than one week put together a mass meeting to be crowned leader of a new party? So don't point that finger at one person. Bas alone didn't write that script; he merely gave it the counterpoint for good drama. And that's bad politics. The real issue in the next few days, weeks and months is not who to blame but how to win an election.

Every serious politician knows that a day is a lifetime in politics. Basdeo Panday is the personification of compromise and deal making. He's been doing it for 40 years. He handed Robinson a party and made him prime minister, fought openly with him, left and formed his UNC, then came back to government as prime minister with Robinson as his ally as Manning sat sulking in the opposition leader's chair.

Panday tossed out Kelvin Ramnath and anointed Ramesh Lawrence Maharaj but when he was ready to dispense with his former Attorney General he brought Kelvin out of retirement to show Ramesh who was boss. So don't write off a deal of some kind. In fact, expect one.

But this raises the much bigger question of leadership. Was Kamla making a play and suggesting that opposition unity was bigger than one person? Was Panday saying the matter was settled? Who's holding an ace? And where's the Jack? Is someone planning to hang a Jack or make the best strategic use of the Jack?

When the UNC created an alliance with other small parties and pressure groups it left the leadership question wide open. One member of the alliance said it was better that way because it would ensure that the media didn't focus on just a leader during the election campaign. Panday's take on the leadership matter was that it was better to decide that in consultation with the parliamentary caucus, after the election. That, he said, would be more democratic.

That, I would argue, is politically foolish. I can't believe Panday is ready to make the same mistake he made in his 1981 Alliance with A.N.R. Robinson's Democratic Action Congress (DAC) and Lloyd Best's Tapia. Three parties, no leader. The result was a confused electorate, a PNM landslide and the end of the Alliance.

In an election as important as the one that's coming, people must be clear about a few things: why am I voting for this party, what makes it different, why should I bother to change what I have? But most important, who is going to be prime minister?

So far we have not heard anything about policy from the UNC Alliance. It's been small stuff and lots of venom-spitting but nothing to convince the nation that it deserves to be in Whitehall. Panday is sounding like the leader he is with fire in his belly. But both he and the UNC Alliance are short-changing the electorate.

I sincerely believe that people want change. Patrick Manning has given people enough reasons to be fed up and frustrated, but so far the opposition — both the COP and the UNC Alliance — have failed to seize the opportunity and offer the people an alternative. In three weeks, the UNC Alliance will hold its coming out rally. Panday has set high expectations. Let's hope that if he gets the 15,000 he is counting on that he will tell them once and for all, here's your leader.

And let us not delude ourselves into believing that a leader is anyone who is called a leader. The people of Trinidad and Tobago know who is a leader and they know who is not. Bas knows that too. A leader, according to former American President John Quincy Adams, "inspires others to dream more, learn more, do more and become more."

No team wins without a leader. There are many wannabe leaders in the UNC Alliance, but few have what it takes. Come on Bas. Time is running out. Level with the people. Who's the leader? Tell them who is the next prime minister.

Let the people decide

So we are back to square one. Basdeo Panday and Jack Warner offered the olive branch to Winston Dookeran, seeking opposition unity, but as expected, the leader of the Congress of the People (COP) said an emphatic no.

In fact, Dookeran says instead of responding to Jack Warner in 21 days, he will be having a 21-gun salute to mark his election victory. If that's the final word (and I sincerely doubt it) it looks like the UNC Alliance must go to the electorate as a united opposition with a third party on the ballot paper.

Last week, Panday made that clear at a meeting in Rio Claro, a few days before he called on Dookeran to meet him one-on-one "anytime, any place" to talk opposition unity. And that brings up the most nagging question about this whole unity matter. Leadership. From what I am hearing and reading, the party is asking its supporters and those seeking an alternative to the PNM to go blindly into the voting booth and make a decision about the future of their nation without knowing which leader they are choosing.

Basdeo Panday is on record as saying it's best to let the parliamentarians who emerge from the election choose the leader, because it's possible that any one among the leadership contenders can lose his or her seat. Well that's true in any election. Every leader takes that risk.

In Canada we have had at least one instance where a party won an election but its leader lost his seat. The party decided — rightly or wrongly — that the best way to resolve the problem was to ask one legislator in a "safe" riding (constituency) to quit and force a byelection in which the defeated leader ran and won, thereby taking his place in the provincial legislature and becoming premier.

We might argue that there's something undemocratic about that on the basis that the electorate decided that while it wanted the party, it didn't care for the leader, and that another leader should have been allowed to take over the party. But consider the other side of argument, which is that the membership of the party chose their leader to take them into an election and by giving the party a clear mandate to govern, they stated unequivocally that they wanted that leader to be their premier.

The leader then had little choice but to seek the back-door entry into the legislature. And that really is the essence of leadership in our party system of democratic governance. Otherwise we should just go back to a system of electing independents.

That original Westminster idea is a formula for gridlock because in the end, the parliament would be comprised of 41 independent members, each serving the interests of his or her constituents first and the national interest second. By that formula you will have leadership musical chairs. And there's the danger that an individual MP might abdicate his or her constituency obligations for those of stronger lobbyists. That's why the party system emerged. With all its flaws, it works because people can choose a party for what it represents and believes in.

However, we are dealing with today's conventional politics and the job at hand. There is a party. And it refuses to elect a leader. How can a party that emerged from among the people deny its supporters the right to have a leader? It's unfair to ask supporters and members to choose a leaderless organisation with the hope that one person from the party will become the leader and prime minister when the party wins the election. Let us assume the party goes ahead with this plan and wins, what will be the result? That's easy to predict: chaos, bickering and an impotence that will affect the governing of a country that today needs leadership more than anything else. Each of the members would have a right to be leader. How will the party make that final decision?

No matter what formula you use, it will still come down to alliances and deal making, which is unfortunately a part of politics everywhere. And if you look at the structure of the party today, it is clear even now who will be the leader in such a scenario. The most dominant UNC Alliance member is the UNC itself. The fact that it is called the UNC Alliance and uses the UNC's rising sun symbol sends a clear signal that this is a group of UNC and the others, not the others and the UNC. The message is that everyone accepts that the UNC still has its support and strength.

Basdeo Panday is the undisputed UNC leader and all the MPs who sit the parliament today are members of his party. Suppose Alvarez, Cadiz et al run in safe seats and win, they, along with Panday, will be eligible to lead as would Jack Warner, Kamla Persad-Bissessar, Kelvin Ramnath, Roodal Moonilal and Ramesh Maharaj. In other words, every MP would have an equal claim and would have to build alliances within the caucus to determine who will be the prime minister. People will form blocs. That's normal human behaviour and standard political practice.

And while the party makes deals and fights among itself creating new factions of allegiances, Trinidad and Tobago will remain leaderless. What will emerge will be a fractured group of MPs and a party in name only.

Someone will be the prime minister and the others who sought leadership would have to either follow or get out of the way. And we would be truly naïve if we believe that the people don't know that.

So why not do it right now?

One Alliance leader worries that the media would focus too much on the leader. Well, I have stated before, that it is the media's right and responsibility to do that because every leader must pass the media's scrutiny if he or she wants to be prime minister.

The media represent the people as a fourth estate of government. In a democracy, they are there to seek out the issues on behalf of the people and report on them as fairly and objectively as they can so that the people can form an informed opinion on which they can act. That's how democracy works.

The reluctance of the UNC Alliance to choose its leader today leaves the voter confused and makes Basdeo Panday the leader if for no other reason than the fact that among the UNC Alliance leadership, he commands the strongest support among the people and because of his domineering political persona.

The present negotiation for seat allocation is really about leadership. Why would any of the leaders agree to weaken his position by giving up 'safe' seats to a potential opponent for the leadership? So in the end, the process would serve the individual, not the people.

On the other hand, if the UNC Alliance were to settle the question of leadership today then it can move on to select the best candidates to represent the people and serve the national interest, not the ones best suited to the parochial interests of would-be leaders.

When Basdeo Panday handed A.N.R. Robinson the leadership of the National Alliance for Reconstruction (NAR), he was acting on the same premise — that his decision that day was the best in the national interest. There was no doubt that his party had the most winnable seats. The Democratic Action Congress (DAC) component that Robinson led was a Tobago party and Karl Hudson Phillips' Organisation for National Reconstruction (ONR), which had failed to win a seat even though it had got more votes that the UNC, DAC and Tapia combined in 1981, was a knock-off PNM.

Panday's reasoning was based on seeing the big picture; his focus was on getting to Whitehall. He was convinced that Robinson was the best choice to WIN the election. And his decision gave the people the confidence they needed to end 35 years of PNM rule. The people did the 'unthinkable' because Basdeo Panday stood like a statesman and removed himself from the leadership for the sake of the country.

Today, the nation is again crying out for leadership. Why then is the UNC Alliance not showing it when it has a golden opportunity to win the election? Panday and others might argue that the Robinson strategy worked to win an election but didn't solve the problem. Perhaps Panday is being cautious, having been burned once. But he also has the 1981 experiment to consider. Given the historical record, the better choice is to go with a leader. People want to know who is going to lead the nation before they cast that ballot.

It doesn't take a rocket scientist to figure out that the UNC doesn't want to damage its fragile partnership arrangements by insisting on settling the leadership issue after the election. But that fear shows weakness and a lack of confidence.

The convenient excuses we are hearing and will continue to hear will not resolve the most fundamental problem of leadership. If settling the leadership question today will fracture the coalition, so be it. Because when the voting is done and the results announced, the fracturing will indeed happen. And then the party would be guilty of a betrayal of the people.

If the UNC Alliance is serious about winning this election, Basdeo Panday must show the leadership that he demonstrated before. He must demand that the issue of a party leader must be settled now. And I am sure that the man I know will walk away if he is convinced that it is the right thing to do. He did it before because he put the country first.

People who want to lead must show the confidence it takes to win. Let the people decide who among the UNC Alliance leaders is the one who can beat the PNM and take the party to Whitehall.

Everybody who aspires for leadership does so knowing that there will always be just one leader. Each of the leaders has come into this partnership has a right to aspire to take the party into government.

Basdeo Panday has said often enough he doesn't want to lead. But he remains the pillar on which opposition unity is built. Today the challenge is for him to stand again like the statesman he is and do what Trinidad and Tobago needs. Choose the man or woman who is the most winnable leader among you, name that person and stand and proclaim to the nation again, this is your leader; this is your next prime minister.

Shakespeare's Brutus, in contemplating joining a coalition against Julius Caesar acknowledged that there is a "…tide in the affairs of men, which taken at the flood leads to fortune…" He concluded that "…upon such a full sea are we now afloat and we must take the tide as it turns or lose our ventures."

Trinidad and Tobago is now sitting on that full tide. Now is the time to end the political posturing and level with the people. They are ready to change the government. Now is time for the UNC Alliance to show them that it's is ready do the same.

(September 20, 2007)

Don't celebrate COP victory yet

Many people are impressed with Winston Dookeran and his Congress of the People (COP) anniversary rally and are suggesting that this could lead to a COP victory at the polls. And some commentators are saying the floating voters are the ones who will help push Manning back into opposition.

The problem with that analysis is the constituency. The floating voters, or the invisible 30 percent or so of the electorate, are notorious for not voting because they don't care, are too comfortable to change the status quo or are too confused to make a decision.

Securing that vote has always been the magic formula to win an election. Both the PNM and the UNC failed to get it primarily because they felt comfortable with their historic supporters. In essence, politics remained for a long time a two party affair, in spite of the proliferation of political parties election after election.

I would not be so hasty to conclude that the "Red Rally" was a turning point. Since the ONR introduced a new style of mass media politics in 1981 with music and hype, political meetings, especially political rallies, have become big fetes. It is common practice to bus people in. And it is not unknown to hand attendees a few dollars as pocket change and "for refreshments." The rum and roti politics is still there, although it has changed with the times.

At the risk of sounding offensive, I want to suggest that crowds don't win elections; the vote is won on election day by an effective election machinery that the PNM has perfected since 1956. Ask Errol Mahabir about it. I have seen that in Jamaica. I was in Montego Bay, Jamaica in 1980, when Michael Manley as the sitting prime minister staged the biggest rally that country had ever seen.

More than 100,000 people jammed into Sam Sharpe Square to hear Manley announce his "third term day." The opposition Jamaica Labour Party was hard pressed to put together 30,000 in Kingston. But when the votes were counted Manley was sent to the opposition benches with just nine of the 60 seats in the Jamaican House of Representatives. He barely won his own. Even if you accept the COP count that there were 30,000 people in Woodford Square, it says nothing about winning an election. What it says is that people want to hear what the COP is saying. And that is what was really lacking last Sunday. And that's why I am not writing Manning's political epitaph just yet.

What was lacking last Sunday, and is still lacking, is a platform for change. Winston Dookeran's speech was full of rhetoric, nice sound bites, well crafted for the media by his spin professionals. For example, he talked about a new politics with new faces. But the new faces were absent.

The dominant faces were familiar ones, people like Selby Wilson, Gerry Yetming, Clive Pantin, Ganga Singh, Roy Augustus. That's the old guard from a right-wing party that didn't excite the majority in 1981. It became a "one-love" partner with the ULF, DAC and Tapia in 1986 and the collective group won a landslide. Once it was divorced from the other partners it faded back into oblivion with even people like Winston himself, going down to defeat.

So if we're talking about a new generation of politicians, these are not the faces we need to see. I am not convinced. A day after the Red Rally Dookeran and the COP crowd moved to Fyzabad, invoked the memory of T.U.B. "Buzz" Butler and urged the trade union movement to join the bandwagon because other political leaders talk about what is to be done but are afraid to dirty their hands "in the affairs of the people."

The trouble is that Winston Dookeran and the people on his frontline are not known for dealing with the "affairs of the people," much less dirtying their hands in their business. The COP is not even a party of the people. It is an organisation formed by a group of people in a room who then thrust themselves on an electorate fed up with the opposition bickering, which was partly created by Dookeran himself with a strategy of communicating with party officials through letters that reached the media before being delivered to the persons to whom the correspondence was addressed. Such a modus operandi is counterproductive and doomed to failure.

Winston and his advisers helped create the disunity in the UNC because from the very beginning they didn't want to "dirty themselves" with the affairs of the UNC, which was formed by the people from the heartland of labour. In spite of the spin and expensive mass media campaign, I am not as optimistic as those who are already celebrating the COP's victory. I wish I could be. Trinidad and Tobago deserves a new government; Patrick Manning and his PNM have done more than enough to get the boot.

But if I had a vote in Trinidad and Tobago, the question I would be asking is why should I vote for the COP, PNM or the UNC Alliance.

That makes me a floating voter, the constituency that is supposedly going to carry Dookeran and the COP to Whitehall. In spite of the hype, Winston and the COP have not laid out a platform for change that tells me it is going to be anything but business as usual with a COP government.

It is traditional for parties to save the promises for the height of the campaign so there is still time for a lot of things to happen. But don't count on that floating and invisible voter based on the attendance at the Red Rally. The reality is that in our first-past-the-post system, numbers count. The famous 10-vote formula is the greatest threat. Three votes for each opposition party and four for the PNM gives Manning the seat with only 40 percent of the vote, making losers of the majority 60 percent. There is talent on both sides. If only the opposition could put personalities aside and focus on the big picture, there is still a very good chance that Manning will have to hand over the keys to his new $148-million mansion.

Political lessons from Canada

There is a man named Stephen Harper who is the prime minister of one of the world's most respected and prosperous nations. He presides over a minority government in Canada, which means that his party controls the support of the most members of the lower house of the parliament, but not a majority of them. If that sounds confusing it means that the three other opposition parties together have a majority and can topple the Harper government at any time on a confidence motion or by voting down a money bill.

A few years ago, nobody thought of Harper as a leader much less the leader of the country and few people outside his Alberta stronghold knew his name.

Harper was the leader of a failing party called the Canadian Alliance, boasting of new politics. Yes, new politics. Before that, he was heading a right-wing pressure group called the Citizens' Coalition that he helped form after a fallout with the leader of another right-wing party, the Reform Party of Canada, which he also helped form.

All that was happening while the Liberal Party was sitting comfortable with three successive majority governments.

So what happened?

Well, some people, who understood the nature of politics, could see the big picture and wanted to put personalities aside, decided to get together and do something about the splintered and fractured opposition.

There were two right-wing parties in the country — one, the remnant of the mighty Progressive Party that was reduced to two of the 308 seats in the House of Commons in 1993 after two back-to-back majorities; the other a right-wing party led by Harper. The question the strategists asked was this: Why are we fighting each other when we share the same basic values and why are we dividing our votes to let the Liberals run away with victory election after election?

The leaders weren't keen on the obvious answer. Unity didn't appeal to them, each wanted to stand his ground and it looked like it would be business as usual when the populist Prime Minister Jean Chretien passed the torch to his finance minister Paul Martin who was a kind of financial magician who had taken a massive debt and turned around a surplus in a few short years.

Martin looked invincible but the backroom right-wing strategists went to Harper and the leader of the Progressive Conservatives with a simple message: stand your ground and we stay in opposition forever. They insisted that enough was enough and said there must be one party. And they were not going to take no for an answer.

That one party was born out of hard negotiating and a fight for the leadership, which Harper won. It was not the prettiest thing, but it was done and the new Conservative Party of Canada was born.

The Liberals were having their own problems. Martin had coveted the leadership of the party, which he eventually got on a platter. But he had no love for Chretien and that helped the right-wing movement.

A big scandal involving misappropriating millions of dollars in taxpayers' money broke just as Martin was settling down in his new job as prime minister, but he fought back and called an election. The truth is, Martin himself engineered the scandal hoping to tarnish Chretien and come out of it smelling like a rose. The new right-wing boys were ready. The party was new, its leadership untrained in the way of the new business at hand.

But a skilful strategy and political communication team gave the Liberal party a run for its money, reducing it to a minority. One year later Martin and the Liberals were out of office and Harper was prime minister — the same Harper who was written off a few years before.

Harper would have remained a political footnote had it not been for the foresight of a few men and women who decided that Canada had to free itself from the stranglehold of a party that had somehow come to believe it had an almost a divine right to govern. They understood that no matter how noble the politics of each party was they couldn't shake the governing party, in spite of corruption and other misdeeds, without opposition unity.

Yes, opposition unity, that elusive thing that almost seems like an obscenity in today's politics in Trinidad and Tobago.

They stopped the nonsense, got together as a single party with a single agenda and they won! They defeated the invincible Liberals. Today, Trinidad and Tobago politicians would do well to learn from the lessons of Canada.

Both the UNC Alliance and the Congress of the People (COP) have people with talent and who have the national interest at heart. Both parties want to make Trinidad and Tobago a better place. On the other hand, the invincible People's National Movement, with a questionable track record and a perception of corruption worse than any previous government, is now vulnerable.

If the opposition is serious about removing the governing party, then it would be wise to look to Canada and see the light of unity, get together as one party or a focused coalition and fight the PNM one-on-one.

Time is short and the stakes are high, but political miracles can happen. But first you have to believe. It's time for opposition politicians to truly ask what is more important — their personal agendas, or the national interest.

Now is not the time to fail Trinidad and Tobago. The people are waiting and depending on you. And they won't forgive you for failing them.

(September 27, 2007)

Super weekend for TT politics

This weekend is one to watch as Trinidad and Tobago's general election campaign kicks into full gear. The two opposition parties are poised to flex their muscles, each trying to outdo the other in a show of numbers

— and class. And Patrick Manning is going to Woodford Square Saturday to rally the troops and tell them that victory is at hand.

It's almost a North-South battle with The Congress of the People (COP) in Skinner Park the same day to present its candidates. For COP, it will be its premiere event to set the tone for its campaign leading to November 5.

The next day is the coming out party for the UNC Alliance. Basdeo Panday served notice a long time ago that if Sunday's rally can't attract at least 15,000 people, he would consider it a failure. His people have been pounding the streets and have promised 40,000 will flood the car park at Mid Centre Mall.

It's not clear if supporters will see a full slate of candidates, but what is more critical for the Alliance is whether it will present a leader for the election. That has become the most contentious issue inside the political group, one that has polarised certain key people's positions.

Kamla Persad-Bissessar, one of the three UNC deputy political leaders, is making it clear that the only leader she recognises is Basdeo Panday. Kamla is no doubt sounding the alarm that Jack Warner, who is touted as the likely leader of the UNC Alliance, is bad news, so she is casting her lot with the man who is the undisputed UNC leader.

For his part, Panday has said there is no vacancy for leader of the UNC, which of course is not the question. Panday leads his party, which is the dominant member of the UNC Alliance.

That's where the issue gets fuzzy. Nobody is talking about the individual parties. The group has made a commitment to face the electorate as a single political bloc and people want to know who will lead that bloc. That's the question they want answered. And they want the answer now, not on November 6. Jack Warner's name has come up more than once.

Jack is a powerhouse within the UNC and is the man who worked tirelessly for opposition unity. He has a strong national profile and contrary to what some detractors are saying, he enjoys popular support in the Indian heartland.

He also has the right presence on the East-West corridor through his community connections and can challenge the PNM on their home turf. And if you don't know that, "you don't know Jack." It is no surprise, therefore, that there is a strong lobby for him to lead.

Thousands are heading to Mid Centre Mall on Sunday to hear what the UNC Alliance has decided. They will wave the flag, hear the speeches and enjoy the party the Alliance is throwing for the big event. But the party shouldn't count on their votes if it doesn't address their most pressing concern.

In Woodford Square the day before, Manning will have to demonstrate to the faithful that all is well, primarily because of the very public display of frustration over the nomination process. And people are going to scan the stage for certain PNM people, most notably Ken Valley, the beleaguered cabinet minister who now resides in Manning's doghouse along with other party "millstones," to borrow the term from Dr. Williams.

And if Ken is there, they will want to know what is his role and where he fits in the PNM grand scheme of things. They will be watching too for the new blood, the fresh team Manning has put together to fight the "new politics" of the COP.

Manning is going into the election full of confidence saying that he will win convincingly. But this is an election like no other and there is no certainty that if the PNM wins it will be the cakewalk Manning is promising.

The PNM's own research shows weakness in a number of key areas and the open warfare with party stalwarts like Ken Valley is a sign that there are significant cracks within the hierarchy. Some insiders are saying the party might only be able to win 20 seats, which means a formal coalition could end the Manning regime.

There is no strong evidence to point to that. But a comment from a PNM insider is telling. That person, who wants to remain anonymous for obvious reasons, has said the party may not shed too many tears over losing because it will be an opportunity to get rid of Manning once and for all. I must confess that the theory is so far-fetched, it can't be something to seriously consider. But in a society such as ours, one comment becomes two and before you know it it's a real bacchanal. So if one person is thinking it, many others are saying it.

And what of the new kids on the block?

The PNM is obviously nervous about the COP and for good reason. It is running a poll on its website asking people to comment on whether they believe Ganga Singh and Sadiq Baksh are manipulating Winston Dookeran. So far, the answer is a resounding yes. You might say, "so what?" Well, remember it's part of the party's research to develop an attack strategy.

Dookeran and the COP have a lot going for them, but the major baggage is the former ONR/NAR image in their lineup. Those people may not be on the final slate that Dookeran will present to the people. One insider has confirmed that prominent San Fernando lawyer Anand Ramlogan is the candidate for Couva South or Tabaquite. Ramlogan isn't confirming anything and he told local media that he understands why people might think he is right for politics, adding, "It's whether politics is right for me at this time."

That is really the million-dollar question. Anand is young, bright and popular. He is a jackpot for the party that can encourage him to run. He is fearless in taking on the establishment and its bureaucracy and has won constitutional challenges against the prime minister. He stands for fairness, justice and equality. He is also an advocate against discrimination and a strong voice for the little person.

As a lawyer, he is vocal campaigner for the independence of the judiciary and the rule of law. In short, Anand Ramlogan is the story-book hero that every party wants but only one can have.

And my sources insist that the time has come and he will run for the COP. For Anand, going into politics must be a difficult decision. He has a lucrative legal practice, is well respected and at the height of his career. Entering politics to sit on an opposition chair is not his cup of tea. So if he is going into politics, he is convinced that he's going into government. And five years later he sees himself on the big chair in Whitehall, if not earlier. Dookeran is in his mid-sixties and is unlikely to serve another term if he wins this election. Few people fit the successor profile better than Anand.

If my inside information is correct and he is running for the COP, then it is clear that he too, like so many others, has become disenchanted with the UNC.

Anand used to be a strong supporter of the party. For him to turn his back on them is a double blow: it sends a strong message about the weak state of the UNC, and adds strength to the COP, which is attracting much support from across the nation.

So it's a grand weekend for politics. You might even call it Super Weekend. And each rally has a star attraction.

For the PNM, it's a lookout for Valley; the COP watch is for Anand and where he sits on that stage. And in Chaguanas on Sunday, everyone will be asking, "who's the leader?"

Politics by numbers: gambling with T&T's future

The UNC Alliance is facing two foes in 2007: the People's National Movement (PNM) and the offshoot of the United National Congress (UNC), the Congress of the People (COP), led by former UNC political leader Winston Dookeran. The pending showdown is very different from the 2002 vote when the PNM won 20 of the 36 seats in the parliament.

In that election, the PNM received 50.72 percent of the popular vote with 308,807 people staining their fingers for the governing party. The opposition UNC won 283,656 votes, representing 41.66 percent of the popular vote. That was mainly a two-horse race, a straight contest between the two parties, with the only other significant contender being the National Alliance for Reconstruction (NAR) in Tobago, which was still a two-candidate affair, since the UNC didn't contest to two seats in the island.

Opposition supporters have been clamouring for unity ever since the rumblings began in the UNC following the internal executive elections, primarily because when they play politics by the numbers, they see Patrick Manning and the PNM in a relatively comfortable situation.

Manning is hoping that a month from now the splintered opposition would give him not just a victory but a special majority to allow him to change the constitution and establish an Executive Presidency.

Energised COP supporters and several columnists are saying that Dookeran's 'new politics' has captured the imagination of the so-called invisible voters and that disenchanted PNM and UNC supporters are flocking to the party. If you believe what the party is saying, it looks like more than 60,000 new members have come on board since the anniversary rally in Woodford Square.

Pontificating about politics is easy; understanding the ground battle is much more complex. So before everybody gets all emotional and starts celebrating, there's still time for some sobering reflection on what's really happening and where the focus should be if there is any chance of unseating Manning.

First, Manning controls the apparatus of state and commands a huge political war chest. Incumbency has given him all the obvious advantages and many handicaps as well. But Manning and his political communication/propaganda team are good at controlling the agenda and diverting attention from the government's weaknesses.

On the other hand, the opposition has been working hard at shooting one another and losing sight of the real target, which causes two dangerous results: voter confusion and apathy. And that's where politics by the numbers is something to watch and act on.

Let us assume that a fairy godmother appeared on the scene and made the opposition decide that whatever formula they use, there will only be 41 candidates against the PNM's 41. Suddenly the numbers start looking good and Manning might be looking at winning no more than 20 seats. Here's why.

In 2000, the UNC won 54.89 percent of the popular vote in a two-way race with the PNM, which won just over 46 percent. In San Fernando West Sadiq Baksh defeated the PNM candidate by 943 votes. In Tunapuna, Mervyn Assam won by 336 votes and in Ortoire/Mayaro Winston "Gypsy" Peters by more than 1600 votes. Those three seats and the Tobago East, which NAR won, went back to the PNM in 2002 to change the power balance to 20-16.

But what is significant in the 2002 figures is that the UNC held its support in the south, losing an average of 200 votes per constituency, and in Tunapuna it actually increased its support. All this in spite of a vicious sustained anti-UNC campaign by the PNM, which began as far back as the 2000 campaign and got worse in 2001 with Ramesh L. Maharaj and his "holier than thou" Team Unity, which did enough damage to cause Prime Minister Basdeo Panday to lose the government to Patrick Manning through a presidential edict following the 18-18 tie.

So here's the bottom line. With all the negative imagery against the UNC, it still commanded the support of 283,656 voters in the last election. That's a net gain over 1995 — when it won 17 seats and formed the government in a coalition with the NAR — of 43,165 votes. In fact the biggest loss of support was in 2001 following the fallout with the Ramesh L. Maharaj "gang of three," who were ready to do a deal with Patrick Manning and usurp the government. Support fell from 307,791 in 2000 to 278,871 a year later, still 19,421 votes more than the PNM, which formed the government.

By 2002, in spite of all the negative propaganda, including the legal prosecution of its leader and the demonisation of Basdeo Panday from inside and outside his own party, the UNC support remained strong.

So where are we in 2007?

The COP has taken away some of the UNC support. It would be entirely foolish to believe that it's drawing its support only from the 30 percent of people who never vote. And there's little evidence to suggest that it has made inroads into PNM territory. It would be equally foolish to believe that the 283,656 people who voted for the UNC have all turned against the party. Even a phenomenal shift of 50 percent would still leave it with nearly 150,000 votes.

Karl Hudson Phillips and his Organisation for National Reconstruction (ONR) didn't win a single seat in 1981 with 90,000 votes.

In fact, it seems that the COP's main target is the UNC Alliance and vice versa. And that's why Manning is happy with diverting attention from the real national issues that everyone should be debating. Instead he has shifted the agenda to front-page headlines about disenchanted supporters threatening to move their vote to the COP. The hope is that COP will fall for the basket, which would make and Manning's plan work. Manning is aware of the numbers and he loves the three-way contest, especially since the COP and the UNC Alliance are courting the same voters.

Take San Fernando West for example. The PNM candidate who beat Sadiq Baksh has been dropped for a popular panman. The COP is running their "iron lady" Marlene Coudray and the UNC Alliance is yet to say who will be on the ballot for them. In the Baksh-Seukeran contest, the PNM won by 249 votes. Sadiq Baksh polled 8842; Seukeran got 9091. The voter turnout was 77.9 percent in that constituency, nearly 10 percent higher than the national average. That means the "invisible vote" was just over 20 percent.

In 2007, the PNM could lose San Fernando West in a two-way race. But it won't because the opposition is deluding itself into believing that it will steal votes from the PNM and win. Well consider this: if there is a 20 percent defection from the PNM that would mean a loss of just over 1800 votes, leaving it with 7200 votes. That gives the opposition 10,660, a clear victory over the PNM. But wait: it's not that simple because there are two opposition horses in that race, meaning the only way the PNM can lose is if one of the opposition parties polls fewer than 3,000 votes. What do you think? All this is assuming that there will be a 20 percent shift away from the PNM, which is highly unlikely. But even with a minor shift, a two-way race is almost certain to give the opposition the seat if we extrapolate from the result of 2002.

And play the same numbers game using 2002 statistics in places like Barataria/San Juan where Fuad Khan won by 905 votes, Tunapuna where Eddie Hart (now discarded by the PNM) won by just under 700 votes, St Joseph (1228 votes gave Gerry Yetming the seat), Ortoire-Mayaro where Frankie Khan beat Gypsy by just over 300 votes. And there are five new untested constituencies. Those results are from a two-way contest: PNM vs the UNC. In a three-way race, you don't need a crystal ball to predict the result.

If the opposition parties do the math and focus on the real goal in the next few weeks, they could defeat the PNM. If they stay on the present course, Manning will be the happiest man in town and all the ol' talk about him being emperor will come to pass.

(October 05, 2007)

Panday is not dead yet; UNC support still strong

Selwyn Ryan and John La Guerre both say anyone who was under the impression that the UNC-A was a dead force should think again after Sunday's mass rally at the Mid Centre Car Park in Chaguanas.

Some time ago — on May 28 to be precise — I wrote a column entitled "Is Basdeo Panday irrelevant?" Like Canadian Salmon, I was swimming against the tide because at that time Panday had become the national political whipping boy.

However, the former prime minister has demonstrated once again that he is a political master and in spite of those who had all but written his epitaph — and not in flattering tones — he has fired up his United National Congress (UNC) and is battle-ready to go into the election to win.

Ryan was one of those who had little hope for the opposition group mounting a credible challenge to the People's National Movement (PNM) of Patrick Manning. Now he has changed his tune and is saying that

Sunday's rally could very well be the surprise of the election race. He told local media he certainly sees a three-way race.

Until Sunday, the feeling among many analysts and commentators was that it was a two-way affair between the Congress of the People (COP) and the PNM. Now many of them are wondering whether it is the COP that is the wounded and terminally ill member of the opposition forces.

COP had a feeble turnout at its public rally in Skinner Park to announce its candidates, who include well-known national figures like Selby Wilson, Gillian Lucky, Ganga Singh, Prakash Ramadhar, Anand Ramlogan and the leader himself, Winston Dookeran.

By comparison, the UNC-A rally attracted thousands, representing not just the traditional Indian heartland but also a cross section of the people who make up Trinidad and Tobago's rainbow nation. It looked like 2000 again when the UNC in government launched its campaign at that same location for re-election and went on to win 19 of the 36 seats in the House of Representatives.

In spite of Panday's legal battles, turmoil inside the party that led to the splintering and the birth of the COP, his own differences with Jack Warner, Panday was able to cobble an alliance and bring competing political interests together.

That is the kind of achievement one expects of Panday and Jack Warner. Throughout the storms and dark days, both Panday and Warner held strong to their beliefs and their vision. On Sunday they told supporters that were right: Trinidad and Tobago is worth fighting for. And the message to the electorate — especially anyone who had looked across the street to the new kids on the block — it's time to come home.

Ryan told the Trinidad Express, "The UNC's display of force and energy must have come as a shock and surprise to many people who assumed that it was dead. It is clearly not dead. Panday is clearly not dead."

And La Guerre agreed, saying, "I think a lot of people were surprised." He credited Warner for the success of the event, adding that it has justified his selection by the leadership council as the chairman of the UNC Alliance.

The big question now is where does the UNC-A go from here?

One of its members has quit, suggesting that Panday is power-hungry. Really? Who hasn't heard that before? And how many have come back to embrace Panday? Ask his former attorney general.

In announcing his resignation Stephen Cadiz, leader of the YesTT group, pledged to still support the alliance and continue working in Diego Martin East, although he no longer wants to run as a candidate.

The reality of first-past-the post politics is that it still favours the PNM in spite of Patrick Manning's troubles within his own party and his misdeeds in governance over the past six years. The PNM is wounded and its decision to discard party stalwart Kenneth Valley is adding salt to the wound. While Valley says he will continue to work with the party, he is warning the nation to stop a budding dictatorship.

In fact, he has gone so far as to urge people to put country before party when they vote. A similar call has come from Michael Williams, the former President of the Senate in the Robinson National Alliance for Reconstruction (NAR) administration.

There is no ambiguity in what Valley is saying. What he is telling the nation is Manning is a dangerous leader and should be stopped, but the PNM is worth salvaging. He, like many disenchanted PNM supporters, is hoping that Manning will lose, giving them a chance to rebuild the party of Eric Williams. Valley knew that confronting Manning publicly is political suicide but he's likely banking on breaking Manning in the election and getting a new lease on life.

That raises the more fundamental question of whether a splintered opposition can hurt Manning at all. All things being equal, Manning could very well lose the election if he were facing 41 opposition candidates in 41 constituencies. The math of politics is easy to follow.

Take the Couva South seat, which might to go to Ramesh L. Maharaj, replacing Kelvin Ramnath, who is recuperating from cardiac surgery in Canada. The PNM polled 6099 votes there in 2002, almost double what it received in the 2001 election when it got 3463. Ramnath won in 2002 with a very comfortable margin of 12,584 but the dynamics are different in 2007 in this traditionally safe seat.

PNM inroads aside, the COP candidate, Devant Maharaj, is going to use his influence as the folk hero who took on the prime minister and won, with the full backing of the Maha Sabha and the organisation's Jagriti Radio station, which it fought for and won in a major discrimination lawsuit.

The COP is hoping it can pull in the Hindu support. So it's likely Maharaj vs Maharaj and the PNM could sail between them with a minority vote and take the seat. And the scenario could be repeated over and over in all the marginal seats.

The real threat to Manning will come from Kamla Persad-Bissessar's clarion call for an opposition accommodation and the pledge of Ramesh Maharaj to campaign on the premise that a vote for the COP is a vote for the PNM. And don't underestimate the skills of Warner to broker a deal, especially working with Panday.

So don't take anything for granted. November 5 is a long way off. Anything is possible, especially since Panday is alive and well. And the lion is still king in his political jungle.

(October 9, 2007)

Time to focus on T&T's future; tomorrow is too late

Whatever you may say about Basdeo Panday — and after 40 years in politics you can say a lot — if you look at the most recent developments in the politics of opposition in Trinidad and Tobago objectively, you'll have to agree that he is not the one blocking unity.

Panday himself admitted on WINTV this week that people who get into politics make mistakes. He admitted to making many and said he is likely to make more. Politicians, he said, are usually disappointed people because they want too much, expect too much and can never have it all. But the problem today, he explained, is that people are losing focus on the most important thing in this campaign — that is the removal of the PNM from office. The people to whom he was referring are the politicians, not the hundreds of thousands who are ready to change their government.

The Congress of the People (COP) clearly understands that, but the point it is missing is how to make the change. And there lies the greatest tragedy in this campaign. Ganga Singh, whom the COP identifies only as the candidate for Caroni East, is making fun of the most serious issue that has faced the nation in decades.

Here's what he has to say: "Panday has only 12 candidates for this election, so he has only 48 hours to find more candidates to fight the election. Furthermore, he cannot find representatives to match the competence, caliber, moral fortitude and sense of loyalty to Trinidad and Tobago that we possess. That is why he is issuing these ridiculous deadlines; he is hoping to have a complete political party ready for the General Elections and the only way he can do this is if some other party unites with him."

And here's the COP's campaign manager, Gerald Yetming: "We at the Congress of the People do not respond to ultimatums, especially when it is issued from a person and party that cannot be trusted; as such we will ignore it."

Taking basket is a bad thing, and if people like Ganga and Yetming are serious about removing the PNM, they better drop the wholesale propaganda and focus on the target. The target is not Panday or Jack or the tens of thousands who still support the UNC Alliance; the target is the PNM and the goal is to get to Whitehall. Where is Winston Dookeran in all of this? He, too, seems to believe his own propaganda and is charging that Ramesh Maharaj is a PNM spy hired to try to destroy the COP.

It's time to trash the rhetoric.

Yes, the COP has some really good people, but it doesn't have a monopoly on that. So do the PNM and the UNC Alliance. And Ganga is blurring the lines between reality and propaganda. The UNC-A has already named 20 candidates and it certainly doesn't have to hang on a wait for the brain thrust from COP. It's not for me — or Ganga — to judge the competence or lack of it among any of the political candidates. That's going to happen on Nov. 5 when the people mark their ballots. What Panday is saying, and what COP is ignoring, is that time is running out. He's not giving ultimatums and creating deadlines.

Patrick Manning did that when he shut down parliament and called the election. And even he is saying to the opposition "don't blame me, I gave you enough time to unite." What is really at stake here is the future of Trinidad and Tobago. Even PNM people like Ken Valley are saying to the nation "do something about it, stop Manning." Michael J. Williams, the respected former President of the Senate is saying do something now or face a Manning dictatorship. Panday and Jack have been begging people to work together. Local and international mediators have tried and given up. The people at every level are crying for opposition unity.

Why are we listening to our own voices and not hearing the screams from the masses? Is the whole world wrong and COP alone right? Are Ganga, Yetming and Dookeran really that naïve to believe that they are really going to wipe out the UNC Alliance, beat the PNM and march to Whitehall?

I know all of them and have worked with each of them. They are not dumb and they are not politically naïve. They are brilliant men who have a problem with Panday and Jack. Panday and Jack have a problem with them. All of them have pride; all of them have big egos. All of them are human. All of them have made mistakes. Jack and Bas are ready to move on — for the national good.

Panday said the other night if you keep looking back, you can't move forward. That's why he is embracing the man he once dismissed as the worst "neemakharam" ever. Let's be truly honest. Nobody but the PNM is going to win the election unless the opposition unites.

And Panday would be wise to stop the pejorative references to the COP as the "corpse." People have pride and they do silly things when their pride is hurt. It's time for Winston Dookeran to stop the grandstanding, to tell Ganga and Yetming that Trinidad and Tobago is more important than their personal problems with Basdeo Panday.

And it's time for Winston to tell himself the country is worth fighting for, that it's OK to swallow pride and stand up for Trinidad and Tobago. Now is the time to unite. The deadline is now, not tomorrow or the day after.

Think of the crime, the mismanagement of the economy, the arrogance, the discrimination, the lack of accountability, the patronage and nepotism, the absence of sustainable development, the disdain for agriculture, the real possibility of an Executive President with too much power, a "budding dictatorship."

This is where we are heading. Think of all this. This is why you are fighting this battle. This is why the people are asking you to unite. The people of Trinidad and Tobago have no one else to turn to at their greatest time of need. Panday is the man who said, "When you see me and a lion fighting, feel sorry for the lion." He has won countless political battles and lost many. His political instinct over 40 years sent him from oblivion to Whitehall. This is his final battle in a war that will determine, forever, the direction of Trinidad and Tobago.

And the people will not forget those who let them down. They don't want to give Patrick Manning and the PNM another five years. And they're depending on you to stop them.

(October 10, 2007)

The trouble with polls

Polling organisations worldwide have developed a reputation for using small samples to accurately sample public opinion on any number of issues from food tastes to political choices. But it is politics that generates the most interest.

Since the November 5 Trinidad and Tobago election was called there have been at least five polls, each with very different predictions about the results.

One commissioned by the Trinidad Express newspaper wrote off the UNC Alliance, giving it five percent of the vote while putting the governing People's National Movement (PNM) at 34 percent and the new opposition Congress of the People (PNM) at 30 percent, literally placing the two of them in a statistical dead heat within the poll's margin of error. One done earlier for the COP put the party at the top with 30.5 percent, the PNM at 23.5 percent and the UNC Alliance at 10.5 percent.

Two surveys done by an organisation that says it operates independently and has no political affiliation give victory to a combined opposition but says the PNM will win a comfortable majority in a three-way race.

And the latest one done for the Trinidad Guardian suggests that the PNM and COP are in a dead heat at 28 and 30 percent respectively, with the UNC-A gaining momentum and coming in at 19 percent. But the sample size of 512 leaves a huge margin of error of about four percent.

The common denominator in all the polls is the undecided factor, which runs in double digits. Another is the low interest in voting.

The trouble with polls is that they are not and cannot be accurate in a volatile political atmosphere such as the one that exists in Trinidad and Tobago today. Any survey that suggests that there is a lack of political interest is dead wrong. Just take a look at the newspapers, listen to the radio broadcasts and watch television, and you'll find the highest degree of political interest since 1986, when the National Alliance for Reconstruction, NAR, swept the PNM out of office.

The other flaw in polling is that each survey reflects the voting intention of the people at a given time and does not and cannot accurately predict the intentions of voters on election day, especially in a society such as ours.

For example, one poll conducted from Sept. 29 to Oct. 6 suggests that only five percent of respondents said they would for the UNC Alliance, a full 25 percent behind the COP and 29 percent behind the PNM. And the latest poll is suggesting that both "leading parties" have dropped support and are now under 30 percent, with the UNC-A gaining a full 14 points in less than two weeks. If that is a true reflection of what's going on, then it would suggest that not only is the UNC-A gaining support — at least 5 percent — from among the undecided, but it is also taking support from the PNM and COP — a full 6 percent from the COP and four percent from the PNM.

What is significant about the first poll is that it sampled public opinion up to the day that both the PNM and the COP had mass rallies to present their candidates. It did not consider the events of the day after when the UNC Alliance held its first mass rally, which attracted three times as many people than the PNM and six times as many as the COP. In addition, during the period of that survey there were rumblings of a leadership crisis in the UNC Alliance and an announcement by one of the members of the Leadership Council that he was leaving the Alliance.

In such an atmosphere, it is logical to expect the kind of result that the poll delivered and perhaps if an election were held on October 6, that might have been the result.

The NACTA poll that came out on Saturday is suggesting that there is going to be a PNM majority, but that could be reversed for an opposition majority if both opposition parties united. And it suggests that the COP would not win a single seat.

What a difference a few days makes!

From being the leader at 30 percent in one poll, seven points ahead of the PNM, the COP moved to neck and neck with the PNM, still at 30 percent, to a position where it would lose every seat.

So what should the electorate believe? Each organisation stands by its reputation. The one that writes off the UNC-A has been off in its predictions more often than it has been correct, another has no track record of measuring public opinion in the country's politics and the third has accurately predicted two of the most critical and keenly contested elections.

Polls do well in large societies where they become media props to tell people what the popular opinion is on a particular subject. In the United States and Canada, they are fairly accurate because people depend on them to give a sample of public opinion upon which they can act.

But they, too, are flawed because they operate within a defined timeline and can only make forecasts based on what people are thinking and considering at that time. And sometimes they have been dead wrong. Like the time every polling organisation in Britain was embarrassed when the Conservative Party under John Major won a clear majority while everyone was predicting that the party would lose the election.

In Trinidad and Tobago polling organisations are handicapped because of the nature of the society where people might tell pollsters what they believe to be the "politically correct" response. It's also because of the structure and style of the mass media and the size of our society. Our culture of gossip also plays a significant part in shaping public opinion, which is why polls are not a true reflection of the public pulse.

Pollsters and communication experts will tell you that polls do not influence public opinion. But the records show that such a premise is wrong. Polls are part of a party's propaganda machinery and all parties use them internally to gauge their performance and plan or change strategy. When a poll appears in the mass media it generates public discussion and becomes central to the public debate.

It can and does make people consider and sometimes change their voting intentions. For example, a voter might say "if my party is suddenly losing by a very big margin I might decide to 'invest' my vote elsewhere or stay at home or go to the beach instead of wasting a vote for a losing candidate."

That scenario, multiplied by a few thousands, can change the result.

The real poll — as every politician will tell you — is on election day. Political parties will pay attention to what the various polling organisations will say and predict, but in our small society, where everyone hears what's happening, where people attend meetings and rallies across the nation, the best public opinion barometer is what the ground is saying.

And the true poll is conducted daily by those who pound the streets, knock on doors, stop at the rum shops, meet people and ask for their vote. They know who will vote for their party and who will not.

It is politically naïve to believe that the polls are always wrong; it is equally naïve to trust them to guide a campaign.

(October 21, 2007)

Basdeo Panday and the politics of opposition

For those who don't know him, Basdeo Panday is a convenient whipping boy for many of the ills that plague his party and the other political movements in which he has been involved. The warfare in the party that led to the splintering and the departure of its leader, Winston Dookeran, leaving to form the Congress of the People (COP) is one example.

Dookeran and his supporters still blame Panday for the fallout, ignoring the fact that it was Panday who signed Dookeran's nomination papers for the party's internal elections and requested that no one oppose him. It was Dookeran who wanted nothing to do with the old structure and attempted to discard everything and everyone who didn't agree with him, including Panday.

Now there's a re-invigorated Basdeo Panday and a UNC Alliance that is challenging the People's National Movement (PNM) of Patrick Manning and the COP, threatening its very existence.

Panday's supporters had remained dormant and confused, perhaps even depressed, during the bickering that went on for most of the five years following the last election in 2002. And for a while, it seemed that they were buying the wholesale propaganda of new politics. The PNM's persecution of Panday, his sentencing for failing to declare a London bank account and the propaganda surrounding the case, contributed to dampening the enthusiasm. But the Supreme Court's decision to throw out the case on the grounds of political interference marked a turning point. Anand Ramlogan, who is now running as candidate for COP in the 2007 election, had this to say about the case and his client:

"Panday was not charged with corruption, and for those who know him he is virtually incorruptible. His personality and traits have no leaning towards materialism and ostentation, and his primary concern and love is politics...The PNM had persecuted Panday for a technical offence that has been committed by dozens of public officials over the years with impunity."

Panday's insistence on unity and his coalition with smaller parties and pressure groups exposed the COP's insincerity and made people rethink their decision to migrate to the new party. In the end, many returned and the evidence was clear when the alliance was launched at a mass rally in Chaguanas on October 7, 2007, which the party immediately dubbed the "orange revolution."

And the final rally at Aranguez, which attracted the largest turnout any political party has ever seen in the country, has helped build a momentum that few even in the party expected one month ago.

Today, Panday has risen from the political ashes like the legendary phoenix. And now, polls — which must be taken with more than a little suspicion in this country — are suggesting the UNC Alliance has a chance of winning a majority and forming the next government. The latest one by NACTA is suggesting a PNM/UNC-A race, allocating 16 seats to the PNM, 14 to the UNC-A and none to the COP. It says the rest are too close to call and can go either way.

Panday entered electoral politics in 1966, at a time when the PNM was well entrenched in government. He shunned racial politics, ran for a social democratic party in an Indian constituency and lost to the DLP candidate. But he didn't disappear from the national scene. In the early seventies, he returned to service with the death of Hindu leader and trade unionist Bhadase Maraj and became the new leader of the Indian heartland in the sugar belt.

Panday skilfully used the sugar union as a base to build support for a political movement. While he believed in a new type of politics based on equality and respect for one another, regardless of race, religion or social standing, he would inevitably have to lean heavily on ethnic voting. Still, he believed national unity was the way to go. As an opposition senator in 1972, he placed on record a reality that was to guide his politics throughout his career.

"Ours is too small a country," he told the Senate on September 15, 1972, "to try to discriminate against each other. We are too dependent on one another and once you discriminate against one another you damage the entire country."

In 1975, Panday's sugar union joined the country's major trade unions in a rally of solidarity from which emerged a new political party, the United Labour Front (ULF). In the General Election of 1976, the ULF made a significant breakthrough with 10 of the 36 seats in parliament, replacing the Indian-based Democratic Labour Party (DLP). The victory was also a major disappointment for Panday who did not get the support of the black working class, especially those in the oil industry.

Five years later, he formed an opposition alliance with his ULF, Tapia, led by economist Lloyd Best and The Democratic Action Congress (DAC) led by A.N.R. Robinson, which had won the two Tobago seats in the 1976 parliament. In that year a new conservative party — the Organisation for National Reconstruction (ONR) — led by former PNM Attorney General Karl Hudson Phillips became the main opposition challenger.

With the Alliance and ONR as the opposition, the PNM scored an easy victory. But it was Panday who went to parliament as opposition leader, although his Alliance had fewer votes than the ONR. From there, he continued his efforts to build a national party based on embracing people of all races, classes and religions. The result was a unitary party comprising all the other opposition groups.

Panday, as the leader with the largest block of MPs in parliament, could have easily emerged as the leader of the new National Alliance for Reconstruction (NAR). However, he was convinced based on his earlier political losses that the nation was not ready to accept an Indian leader as prime minister. So he handed the leadership of the infant party to the DAC leader Arthur N.R. Robinson.

In the general election of December 15, 1986, his dream became a reality when the NAR won a landslide with 33 of the 36 seats in parliament, sweeping the PNM out of office after 30 consecutive years in power. But the dream soon turned into a nightmare as conflicts based on race and policy developed within the "one-love" movement.

The overwhelming majority gave Robinson the clout to ignore Panday, knowing that he would keep a majority even if Panday left. And that is what happened, although some of the seats giving him the majority were rightfully those of Panday's ULF.

Panday and some of his loyalists quit. The others stayed, including Winston Dookeran, who later came back to Panday's political camp, then left again and is now leading a new party — the Congress of the People (COP) in the 2007 election.

The break with the NAR led to the formation of CLUB 88 (Committee of Love, Unity and Brotherhood) and the birth of the United National Congress (UNC), which Panday described as a movement that would attract people not because of the "colour of their skins but the content of their minds." Panday's nationalism — unlike that of Eric Williams, Robinson et al — had always been based on embracing Trinidad and Tobago's diversity and celebrating its plurality.

Panday has survived the political roller coaster and continues his struggle for democracy, freedom and justice on behalf of a constituency that still yearns for these fundamental human rights nearly fifty years after Trinidad and Tobago's leaders pulled down the Union Jack and gave birth to a nation, seeking God's blessings for a land forged "from the love of liberty," promising equality for every creed and race.

Today, six years after he was removed from office, as murderers and kidnappers roam the streets fearing no one, Panday is again leading a chorus clamouring for unity among all those who share a common concern for peace, stability and good governance. And as always, his constituency comprises mainly those whose voices are muffled in the din of political expediency.

Panday was the man who called the nation's attention to the injustices that workers suffered under the Williams PNM administration. He walked shoulder-to-shoulder with George Weekes, Raffique Shah, Joe Young, other labour leaders and politicians on Bloody Tuesday — March 18, 1976 — to demand justice for the working class. And though he was brutalised and jailed, he remained committed to the same cause for which he fights today: freedom, equality and justice. His detractors like to paint him with a general racist brush. But political scientist Dr. Selwyn Ryan, who is no fan of Panday, had this comment in 1991:

"His constituency comprises those elements whom he considers social and political underdogs in a society. His rhetoric is flowery and emotional. That rhetoric may annoy those who do not share its premises and values. To call it racist is, however, a gross falsehood, and those who do, say more about themselves that the person they label."

Indeed, it may very well have been his commitment to building a nation where everybody would be equal that undermined him and led to his fall from power. Some people from within his party exploited discontent among the UNC heartland with the false notion that Panday deserted his Indian supporters.

Panday frequently reminded his inner circle that "his people" comprises everyone, people of every race, religion, class and colour, in every village and town. "Hunger doesn't have a colour," he once said, adding that poverty doesn't have a religion.

His greatest passion is for uniting the people, for building a meritocracy in which everybody would be a first-class citizen unlike the one that the late Lloyd Best once described, where "everyone felt like a third-class citizen."

Many commentators who try to explain the national politics of Trinidad and Tobago society summarise everything in simplistic racial imagery. Two main founding groups built Trinidad and Tobago: slaves, most of African origin, and indentured workers, most of Indian origin. Panday inherited the Indian base; Williams led the Africans. But there were crossovers in both parties as there are today.

Panday's philosophy has always been the same: that any party that chooses to represent only one group is doomed because the plurality and diversity of Trinidad and Tobago make it necessary for a government to include everyone.

When Patrick Manning assumed office in 2001 by presidential decree, he tried unsuccessfully to push the UNC back into oblivion by taking the cane fields away from the UNC, leaving it without its primary constituency in the hope that instead of rising from the ashes, the UNC would retreat to a "comfort zone" of marginal politics.

But Panday has refused to ride into the sunset and go away; today, at 74, he continues his struggle with a renewed urgency and an even deeper sense of national unity. He wrapped up the 2007 campaign at the birthplace of the UNC in Aranguez, announcing that it would be his last political battle. He urged everyone to remain united and asked for a victory for the UNC-A to send him off in a blaze of glory. "Stand all!" he declared, "bow to no one."

(November 4, 2007)

The result of the 2007 general election was not a great surprise. The UNC Alliance had invested enormous amounts of money on the campaign, including an attempt to get Nelson Mandela and Jesse Jackson to endorse the party. Movie star Salman Khan even made an appearance at the final rally when 70,000 showed up. In the end, the chasm between the two opposition parties proved to be too wide and Manning and the PNM gained the advantage, winning 26 of the 41 seats with just over 45 percent of the popular vote. The system had defeated the people and the political bickering had saved the day for Manning. When Basdeo Panday addressed the people on learning of the election result he accepted no responsibility for the loss, blaming only one man.

Basdeo Panday: look in the mirror

"My brothers and sisters, soldiers of the UNC-A, the unofficial results seem to indicate that the PNM has won 26 seats, the UNC-A has won 15 seats and the COP no seats. We will accept these results when they are confirmed by the EBC. Assuming that they are correct, then the PNM has won the elections. If it is in fact so, it is the mafia that has won.

I wish to congratulate all the candidates of the UNC-A, the agents and supporters, the UNC-A's several campaign teams, for your support.

I want to thank also all the people who have contributed financially to this struggle and otherwise for their generous support. If I were to start mentioning names of all those who have made this tremendous performance possible, it would take all night, and I would still leave out so many of you to whom I owe a great debt of gratitude. Thank you all and God bless you.

If the PNM is really going to be a yoke around your necks for another five years, it is because of some of those who voted for the PNM, those who voted for the Corpse and those who did not vote at all. They are the ones that are responsible for the PNM and the crime and corruption, incompetence, malice and discrimination, which this country has to endure for five more years. I want to say to every one of you who voted for Corpse, every time one of your family or friends is murdered, kidnapped, beaten, robbed and raped, I want you to go in front of a mirror and look at yourself. And I want you to confess to yourself because you are responsible because you voted PNM or you voted COP or you did not vote at all. Winston Dookeran, not all thy tears and all thy regrets shall wash away an inch of what you have done to yourself and your country. Shame on you! And shame on the Corpse!

To my loyal and devoted supporters of the UNC, I say do not bow or cringe before any man but stand tall! We have no intention of lying down, rolling over or dying. The struggle goes on. We must not abandon the thousands of persons who have supported us, giving us their blood, sweat and tears.

Since we cannot abandon these people, we must let them know that we shall never give up the fight for the creation of a society in which all peoples are treated equally, where there is freedom and justice for all, where there is no discrimination and victimisation. In the new dimension of our struggle, we may have to resort to other methods of struggle to preserve our freedoms and liberties. We may have lost this round but we shall never abandon our people. I ask you to go home in peace and on the morrow we shall chart a new course of dedicated struggle to bring happiness to all our people. Thank you and God bless you all."

(Verbatim, 11.30 pm, November 5, 2007)

Section 2
The aftermath of 2007

My son, Ajay Parasram, followed the 2007 election campaign closely and we spent many hours in the aftermath of the PNM victory discussing the politics of Trinidad and Tobago and the defects in the political model we inherited from Britain. As a student of political science now working on his doctorate at Carleton University, I convinced him to write an analysis for my blog. This analysis first appeared on Jyoti in February 2008.

Analysis by Ajay Parasram

Democracy in Portions?

The Congress of the People (COP) won nearly 150,000 votes and 23 percent of the popular vote in the Nov. 5 general election, yet none of its members sits in the national parliament. On the other hand, the United National Congress Alliance (UNC-A), with just over 50,000 more votes, captured 15 seats. And the People's National Movement (PNM) with double the COP votes won a clear majority of 26 seats.

What's wrong with this picture?

Logically, if 300,000 votes give you 26 seats, half of that should give you 13 seats. Right? Wrong!

And what about the other 199,000 votes? The math is messed up just like the logic. So let's get back to the question: what is wrong with this picture?

The party with the minority support wins the majority. It feels wrong, sounds wrong and looks like the tyranny of the minority. Damn, it is wrong and undemocratic too!

But in reality there is nothing wrong; the constitution and the law allow it. And people have become slaves to a system that usurps their right to be heard.

Such a feat is possible under Trinidad and Tobago's archaic, colonial structure of governance: first-past-the-post (FPTP) is a servant to the status quo. FPTP was designed to be a cheap and easy way to elect MPs and was introduced at a time when people could believe that their MPs were fulfilling their theoretical goal of representation.

It's based on the premise that free people from across the country will elect a representative among themselves to speak on behalf of their entire constituency. These free minds would then assemble in the national legislature (the House of Representatives or lower House), and from their debates, negotiations, and politics, some would come together to form "parties" of like-minded people.

From these organic parties would emerge spokespeople and the individual who controlled the loyalty of the House of Representatives (i.e., controls the party or parties which hold the majority of seats) becomes the prime minister, and appoints a cabinet.

But is this really how it works in Trinidad and Tobago, or anywhere in the world?

In Canada, for example, the current Conservative government's political base is in the western province of Alberta. Although 25 percent of Albertan voters marked an X for the Liberal Party of Canada, the Conservative Party holds all 28 seats in the province; the Liberals, zero. Sound familiar?

The similarity in Canada's and Trinidad and Tobago's politics is only in the sense that they share the same dated loyalty to the British Westminster model of electoral politics.

So let's get back to Port of Spain. In a country with the demographics of Trinidad and Tobago, it is easy to politicise race and though many have resisted this temptation, every political observer knows that the country's elections are essentially a mad dash for a few marginal seats. This might lead one to the conclusion that, within those constituencies that are deemed "pre-determined," there is no dissent.

The FPTP system leaves no room for dissent; it's based on winner take all and losers go home. Even the prime minister of Trinidad and Tobago barely received the majority of votes in his own constituency, although he has been the representative for San Fernando East since 1971.

The opposition parties took 45 percent of the popular vote in San Fernando East. That means out of every 100 voters, 45 said they didn't want Patrick Manning to represent them. By extension, they said they didn't want a PNM government.

But in our FPTP system they have no choice; they have got Manning and the PNM and they can't do anything about it. What chances do they have of having their views, beliefs, or interests represented?

Go over most of the other 41 constituencies and the picture is almost the same. The one indisputable fact about the Nov. 5 general election is this: a majority of the voters rejected the People's National Movement, its leader and the party's policies.

Yet with a minority vote, Manning governs with no moral or constitutional obligation to consult the "dissenters" or anyone. He has a majority and can do as he pleases.

And what of the 55 percent of the electorate who voted against the governing party? They can wait for five years, then on an appointed day, repeat the whole exercise. Under the FTTP system, the majority may yet again be denied representation.

Of course, FPTP is predicated on the belief that stability and predictability are more important than democracy and representation. The 45 percent of San Fernando East that rejected the prime minister and his party are now forced to believe that he will represent them, as he has promised to.

The problem with this system is that the power is centralised in the MPs (more specifically, the party leaders and executives), and not in the constituents that they claim to represent.

If the goal of FPTP is to elect free thinkers to come to the House of Representatives and forge alliances to represent the best interests of their constituents and their nation, why do we even have parties to co-opt their minds and ambitions?

Trinidad and Tobago is not a country devoid of dissent; it is a country that lacks the ability to make a choice because of its archaic, colonial system of electoral politics, which was designed to install inflated majorities.

Today, the MPs who speak for constituencies almost never get a majority mandate, and they are forced to balance their consciousness with their party loyalty and career ambition. The theoretical "free thinkers" of old have thus become under-representative of the people they claim to give voice to.

One need only look at the figures in nearly every constituency in the 2007 elections to see that most sitting MPs do not command the majority of support within their constituencies. Under a different system of electoral politics, the composition of the House would look quite different. And that's where we should be looking — the "dreaded" system of proportional representation (PR) that the country's first prime minister, Dr. Eric Williams, dropped like a hot potato before anyone could even read its merits or relevance, as stated in the Wooding Commission report on constitution reform.

The system can be complex and convoluted, but it can also be simple and representative, depending on how you look at it and what model you adopt.

Canada, for example, may not be a good place for a system of PR because of its massive size and regionalised polities.

On the other hand, Trinidad and Tobago fits the bill rather well. It is a small country with a small population. It is full of dissenting voices struggling to be heard and systemically being undermined by an electoral system and centralisation of power that is designed to prevent today's minority from ever becoming tomorrow's majority.

All the sitting government needs to do is ensure there is more than one opposition party contesting the election and they can nearly guarantee a victory. Trinidad's political history speaks to this. Under Dr. Eric Williams, the PNM remained the party of stability while opposition parties, with a few exceptions, were mostly stillborn.

The respected Trinidad and Tobago political scientist Dr. Selwyn Ryan describes it well: "Caribbean islands are littered with the carcasses of political parties which have materialised and then faded into oblivion without leaving much by way of a footprint on the landscape, however, much they might have influenced the political narratives that other parties have appropriated."

The politics of opposition in Trinidad and Tobago has been greatly constrained by the FPTP system that refuses to acknowledge dissent and respects only the will of the "winner," even when the vast majority of the people in one constituency reject that person.

That's why the country should adopt as its new year's resolution a determined effort to change the political status quo by demanding constitutional reform based on some form of proportional representation. The voice of the people would be heard in the hallowed chamber of the national parliament, and hopefully effect change for the benefit of everyone, not just those who are beneficiaries of party favours from the governing establishment.

During the November 5 election campaign, Basdeo Panday outlined what could best the described as a teaser on the subject. His idea is for an executive president elected by universal adult franchise using the FPTP system, providing the winner captures more than 50 percent of the popular vote. That leader would preside over a people's congress elected by proportional representation.

Such a system would allow the greatest national representation in the legislature from where members would be chosen to sit in cabinet, on committees and other bodies to conduct the state's business on behalf of all the people.

Such reforms are always difficult, because they essentially require the governing parties to advocate a system that will almost always weaken their results in the polls. If we take the 2007 election result as an example of what PR might have achieved, we would find the PNM still holding the largest block of seats, but with fewer seats.

Under a simple system of PR, where percentage of votes equals number of seats, the UNC-A would have 12 seats, the COP 9, and the PNM 18. Since no other party won at least 2 percent of the popular vote, the system described above would have only 39 seats and the system would have to adopt a measure to determine how to allocate the two other seats based on the surplus votes.

Suddenly the Manning majority would have disappeared and the system would have given a voice to the 148,000 COP voters, who have none in the parliament as currently constituted. Surely it is a better system if it doesn't shut out the opinion of 148,000 citizens.

The political structure would have been radically different. Manning would have to govern through consensus. Or the opposition could have formed a coalition and unseated the government. But the radical difference would be quite interesting.

Under a PR List system, each party contesting elections would provide a list of candidates, organised in descending importance. The percentage of the popular vote they receive would determine how far down the list they go; that is to say, if they receive 30 percent and 30 percent = 12 seats, then the top 12 people on their list become MPs. The electorate would have an opportunity to peruse the list, which would be made public before the vote. This is but one of many ways a state might organise its electoral system in accordance with proportional representation.

Another system, the single transferable vote model, allows the constituency system to remain. The ballot paper would allow the voter choices, based on preference for parties. For example, a person might vote National Alliance for Reconstruction (NAR) as number 1; COP as 2; UNC-A as 3; and PNM as 4.

The purpose of this system is to ensure that whoever wins the constituency would have the majority of support of the voters. So when it becomes clear that NAR will not win, the ballot above would be moved from NAR to COP. If it became clear that it would be a race between the UNC and the PNM, then the ballot would move from the COP to the UNC-A.

Instead of casting one ballot that is thrown away, voters under this system could vote for the party of their choice without having to gamble on the fact that their vote is wasted. Such a vote gives the individual control, turning the system upside down.

The common criticism of PR is that it is divisive and makes government slow to effect change. This view of PR is quite unfair, as small countries tend to excel under systems of PR; many — particularly in Western Europe and Scandinavia — enjoy some of the highest living standards in the world.

Making space for dissent is not divisive. Blocking people from the House of Representatives who have mandates by the electorate is divisive. Indeed, it seems tyrannical. The people spoke in 2007 as they have done in every election since the 1920s. Why is the government so unwilling to lend an ear to the people they claim to represent?

Let 2008 be the year for change. Make it your new year's resolution. You might be pleasantly surprised at the power you hold!

Ajay Parasram, M.A. Political Science (Carleton University)

Soon after the PNM won, re-election trouble began developing within both opposition camps. The United National Congress (UNC), which had just made a stunning recovery to win 15 of the 41 seats in the House of Representatives, demanded a leadership review and the holding of long-overdue internal elections. That eventually led to the Movement for Change led by Jack Warner and the rise of Kamla Persad-Bissessar to the leadership of the party.

In the Congress of the People (COP) there were also strong rumblings that threatened to undermine the party. Some members openly challenged the leader, others left and the issue of a united opposition took root again.

The commentaries in this section address some of these issues.

Griffith challenges COP leader

There is open warfare building in the Congress of the People (COP), with political leader Winston Dookeran facing a challenge from one of the party's frontline members, Gary Griffith.

Dookeran, the unelected leader of the COP, left his post as leader of the United National Congress (which he won unopposed) to form COP, saying he wanted to introduce "new politics" in Trinidad and Tobago. He refused all attempts to work with the United National Congress Alliance (UNC-A) in the Nov. 5, 2007 General Election, even an eleventh hour plea from UNC-A leader Basdeo Panday to unite and defeat the governing People's National Movement (PNM).

The result of the election demonstrated that people were ready to change their government but were torn between which of the two opposition parties to support. In the end, the PNM was returned to power with a majority of 26 of the 41 seats in the House of Representatives, with the UNC-A getting the other 15. A majority of voters had chosen the opposition, but in the first-past-the-post system, it didn't matter. Dookeran's gamble didn't pay off. His party won 148,000 votes but no seats; Dookeran lost his own St Augustine seat to political rookie, Vasant Bharath. He won it easily in 2002 as the UNC candidate.

Even during the election campaign, there was talk among COP insiders that something was not right. But the powerful Public Relations unit headed by former UNC communications and media adviser Roy Boyke glossed over the problems and painted a picture of a confident party heading for victory.

Shortly after the election campaign, chairman Gerry Yetming, a former UNC cabinet minister, announced that he was retiring from politics. And reliable party sources reported that Dookeran himself was considering ending his political career and emigrating. Dookeran has denied that and he insists all is well in the COP family and that the focus now is on winning the upcoming local government elections expected in July this year.

"We are proceeding very well and there are lots of people who are working and working at all levels, from the bottom level to the top level of the COP all over the country," Dookeran told the Trinidad Express in a weekend interview. He said the COP is continuing to build on its founding principles of integrity "in all our institutions, transcending all divisions in the society and advocating serious social reform. We are working to keep that alive and I am doing my part to ensure that happens," Dookeran told the paper, while declining specific comments on the challenge to his leadership.

Griffith isn't buying that. He insists that things are moving well only in Dookeran's imagination. He claims that Dookeran has become "a law unto himself" and has set up several parallel groups that are taking their instructions from him without any input from the executive. Griffith and other COP executive members, including the political leader, were appointed on an interim basis because of the urgency of the general election. The former army captain has told Dookeran he will no longer chair COP's national security council until the party holds internal elections. Griffith said he is angry because of Dookeran's style of leadership.

While he openly expressed concerns about the leader, he said the party is not imploding. But he added that with Dookeran as leader, the party would not be able to build on the support it had in the last general election.

(January 28, 2008)

COP bickering exposes vulnerability of opposition politics

The Gary Griffith broadside at Congress of the People (COP) leader Winston Dookeran has generated an emotional discussion about the politics of opposition in Trinidad and Tobago, raising questions about whether the country can sustain a third party operating "in the wilderness."

It has also piqued the interest of rank and file members of the United National Congress (UNC), with some members openly hoping that it's the end of COP and the return of the prodigals, while others totally oppose discussions with the party.

"Yes, we have no choice but to accept those who will be returning to the folds of the UNC, and there will be many," wrote one UNC member on a party Internet chat site in response to another who questioned whether that is the way for the party to go.

"Didn't we take back Ramesh?" asked another, in reference to the former attorney general whose break with the party caused the fall of the UNC government in 2000.

Yet another UNC member was not that forgiving. "Please note that historical evidence indicate that those COP traitors cannot be trusted," he wrote. "Instead, these men of 'integrity' have to be politically destroyed… (Gerald) Yetming and company have proved that characteristics such as loyalty, respect and commonsense are not part of their personality."

His position was that many of the frontline COP people are political opportunists who "will destroy and humiliate anyone that does not agree with them. They are not team players and hence cannot survive Trinbagonian politics."

The point is, UNC members are suspicious of COP leaders but are happy to embrace those who were seduced by COP's message of new politics and all the other trimmings of its "newness." The focus of the scores of letters — those who like the idea of discussions with COP as well as those who oppose it — was clear: be cautious, don't let us down again.

The "again" is an interesting signpost and goes back to 1986, when Basdeo Panday dissolved his United Labour Front (ULF) to merge with other opposition parties to form the National Alliance for Reconstruction (NAR) and handed the leadership of the new party to A.N.R. Robinson.

The "one-love" movement degenerated into an orgy of hate and acrimony once Robinson realised that he could dispense with the Panday faction in the party and still keep a majority in the lopsided 33-3 parliament.

He was right.

Panday left with his "tribe" to form CLUB '88 under the chairmanship of Dr. Rampersad Parasram, which gave birth to the UNC as a populist people's party dedicated to the proposition that people would join the "crusade," as Basdeo Panday put it, not because of the colour of their skins but by "the content of their minds."

The UNC embraced everyone and eventually reached Whitehall in a coalition with none other that Robinson and his NAR, which had been reduced to a rump Tobago party. Politics makes strange bedfellows indeed! Or as Panday explained when Gillian Lucky walked out on him following the infamous teacup brawl between Keith Rowley and Chandresh Sharma, "Politics has a morality of its own." Perhaps that political pragmatism explains the longevity of both Panday and the movement he heads.

The UNC remains the only party other than the PNM that has withstood the test of time in the country's politics both in and out of government. Today, the question is whether the COP can survive in a game where only two parties have dominated — the PNM and the UNC and its various predecessor organisations. And whether any third party can be useful in representing the views of those opposed to the governing party given the confines of the first-past-the-post electoral politics.

Political analysts, pollsters, and the man-in-the street welcomed the infant COP and wrote off the UNC and its allies. But the campaign and the result on November 5, 2007 General Election demonstrated that the UNC was alive and well, and that it was capable of co-opting other political elements.

Indeed that is the trademark of Panday. His earliest flirtation with politics in 1966 as a candidate of the Workers and Farmers Party (WFP) was a disaster. He belonged to the wrong "tribe," although he had all the other credentials. When he re-emerged as the new messiah in the plains of Caroni following the death of Bhadase Maraj, the charismatic Hindu/Indian leader, he inherited a constituency that has remained loyal for more than 40 years.

Maraj and Dr. Eric Williams had set the political rules as far back as 1956 and polarised the country between the two founding races. It remained that way, despite the efforts of high profile members that crossed the racial divide on both sides.

Panday lost his deposit to the candidate of the Democratic Labour Party (DLP), the successor party of Maraj's People's Democratic Party (PDP), the only party that survived from the lineup of 10 that faced the PNM in 1956.

The unwritten rules were clear: us and them, us being the governing PNM, the so-called black party, and them being the DLP, the Indian party. In 1976 when Panday re-entered electoral politics ready to do battle with Eric Williams, he knew the idea of an Indian party winning government was as remote as a snowstorm in hell.

As the leader of the Indian base through his inheritance of the sugar workers union from Bhadase Maraj, he saw labour as the vehicle to get him to Whitehall — and it eventually did, 19 years later.

Unrest in the sugar and oil industries became the catalyst for the formation of a mass movement with the mantra "Let those who labour hold the reins." The experiment brought all the major labour groups together and race and ethnicity was to be buried with the DLP, which was the significant third party in the 1976 general election. The DLP disappeared in the Panday phenomenon but the national unity he had hoped for was a mirage. It was not until 1986 with the NAR that it almost happened.

But NAR was an aberration. While the people were ready for change at all cost — and the PNM under George Chambers had given up the fight — the political philosophies were too far apart for it to happen. When Panday and Robinson squared off, the atmosphere was almost identical to the bloodbath in the UNC that led to the creation of COP. But there was a fundamental element missing in the equation.

Trinidad and Tobago politics was always based on populism. Eric Williams, Bhadase Maraj and Basdeo Panday each possessed widespread appeal within their constituencies primarily because of their respective personalities. They also commanded their base in a way no other political leader has ever done.

Robinson pulled off the 1986 victory over the PNM not because he commanded the majority; he didn't. But the country was ready for change and each leader brought his constituency — Panday, Best, Hudson-Phillips and of course, Robinson. And there was no other party. It was a script that could not fail.

The miscalculation in the COP was that Winston Dookeran, with no onerous political baggage, an excellent track record as governor of the Central Bank and a former deputy prime minister, could appeal to the invisible voter and the disaffected UNC tribe.

The party built its communication message around that theme but Dookeran lacked the "rootsy" touch that had been ingrained in the national political psyche. And the tribalism emerged to knock the COP off its pedestal.

There is a long list of political parties and their leaders in Trinidad and Tobago's electoral archives that point to the fact that it takes more than a symbol and a message to establish a true presence in the political landscape.

So where does it go from here?

Panday still insists — as he has done all through his political life — that a true national party in opposition is the only one that can make it to government. And he has said over and over again that the first-past-the-post-system is designed to keep one party in power. It is that "politics of opposition" that the PNM has kept alive to its great benefit, as was demonstrated in the last election. Eric Williams even encouraged people to create political parties so there would be a splintered opposition vote. Ashford Sinanan and his West Indian National Party (WINP) was an example. I know because Sinanan told me so.

In fact, the PNM established such strong roots during its initial 30 unbroken years in government that it "remains in office" even when it was in opposition. Robinson and Panday both discovered that there was a PNM governing bureaucracy in place that frustrated their efforts at every turn. And at the ground level whenever there was a third or any number of other parties, the PNM was very comfortable because it had the advantage of incumbency to maintain its hold on power.

The only real challenge to the PNM was from the Organisation for National Reconstruction (ONR) in 1981. Karl Hudson-Phillips was fishing in the PNM pond but in spite of the strong support he got, the PNM remained unshaken and was returned to office with the strongest majority ever up to that time.

The ONR became the NAR and later died; so too have all movements and parties.

What has survived is an advanced political model of the original Indian party. There are two political bases in Trinidad and Tobago. And it leaves no room for a splintered opposition. In 41 years, no opposition politician or party has challenged Panday and won. And there is a reason.

He built a people's movement from the ground up. He worked with the people in the trenches. He marched to demand a better deal and was brutalised and jailed, the only national leader who has gone that distance. That is why the constituency he built refuses to desert him.

"You can't just hand over this constituency to someone," Panday said during the 2007 election campaign. And the evidence is there as Ramesh L. Maharaj, and now Winston Dookeran, have discovered. Not even Panday's fall from power took away his sheen.

But Panday is ready to retire. Even if his heart tells him no, his body is showing the fatigue after 42 years. And Dookeran is finding out that voters are fickle and unforgiving. So the implosion in the COP — though hushed after the initial public outbursts — is natural, based on the history of opposition politics.

Sustaining a vibrant political movement requires money, which the COP now lacks. And existing in the political wilderness for five years has been fatal for all opposition parties except the UNC and the PNM.

Yet, new opposition parties emerge each election season, much to the pleasure of the governing establishment. Like the Shakespearean actor, they come on stage, "Full of sound and fury, signifying nothing." And then they die. Once "the revels are ended," they consume themselves and disappear.

And so it is today in the COP. Manning and the PNM will remain secure because they control the superior political machine. And until those who find the PNM brand of politics unpalatable agree to unite and dethrone them, the historical machinery cannot be dismantled to allow for a healthy multi-party democracy.

The best starting point for the opposition is what Jack Warner has engineered, an alliance of the opposition. If the COP takes a seat among the others in that alliance, there is hope that from among them a new leader will emerge who will create a new national party in the vision that Panday has had — a coalition of people, coming together for the national good, a tribe based not on gender or ethnicity, but for the "content of their minds."

The people, I believe, are ready. But the nagging question that remains is whether those who lead are ready to take them in the right direction. For now, the politics of opposition remains as it has always been. And Manning and the PNM like nothing better. And who can blame them?

(February 5, 2008)

Dookeran says deal with the UNC-A is an option

Winston Dookeran says an accommodation with the UNC Alliance (UNC-A) is an option for his Congress of the People (COP) for the local government elections. And for the first time, he has revealed that COP had considered a similar arrangement for the general election. With regard to the general election the COP political leader says the party voted against doing a deal with the UNC-A.

It's the first time that Dookeran has mentioned that. All through the campaign for the Nov. 5 general election, Dookeran and his political colleagues rejected the UNC-A's overtures out of hand. There was never any talk of discussions on that matter.

Some COP members even derided Basdeo Panday's invitation to merge the two parties, saying that the UNC-A only wanted to do it because it was unable to survive alone and find candidates to fight the general election. And Dookeran had stated publicly that there would be no deal with Basdeo Panday as the head of the UNC-A. The COP said it would discuss a merger if Kamla Persad-Bissessar were the party's leader. When that failed, COP pleaded publicly to Bissessar to leave the UNC-A and join them; she rejected that, stayed with her party, and won back her Siparia seat.

Dookeran is now saying that the idea of a deal with the UNC-A for the local election has been raised at party meetings, adding that no decision has been made. At the same time he is saying COP will maintain its integrity and "offer the country a real alternative and will not compromise our position." He said there is a committee looking at the strategy for local government elections and the party was engaged in dialogue with the public. With regard to dissent within the party, Dookeran said anyone is free to challenge him for the leadership. "We have a party with a procedure for the election of leader. Anyone is free to challenge the leader via the council," he said.

Dookeran himself has never been elected leader of the COP. He was acclaimed leader because of the urgency of preparing for the general election. He said the COP remains a legitimate political player although it does not have a seat in parliament. "We have received 23 percent of votes in the general election and came second in 22 of 41 constituencies," he said.

(March 28, 2008)

With all that was happening and the growing frustration among citizens over the government's performance, the Manning government needed a distraction. They found it in what might have been a minor incident if it were not for how the matter played out. It seemed like another faux pas by the government. But in reality the expulsion of Basdeo Panday from parliament for using his laptop without proper authorisation was a calculated political strategy. That issue took over the headlines for a while in 2008 and kept the heat on the former prime minister.

Panday expulsion is a brilliant strategy of distraction

"Politics and partisanship aside, using a computer can suspend a member? We must be in the dark ages."

Monica Pollard | Toronto

"This is far too serious to overlook. We have to move to the next level. Shut down the blasted country!"

Richard Hosein | Tunapuna, Trinidad

"The government's eagerness to suspend a mostly silent Panday is instructive. Why is he so feared?"

Senator M.F.Rahman | Trinidad

So Bas is out again! But this game of political musical chairs is not necessarily as it seems. Based on the reports in the media, it's a straight case: he was in breach of the rules set by the Speaker; he disobeyed the presiding officer of the House, so he was kicked out. Simple.

And members of the government side of the House were quick on the draw, condemning the opposition leader for his recalcitrance in not respecting the Speaker and the appropriate standing orders. One suggested that it was a continuation of Panday's "bad manners" that started when Panday shook hands with the prime minister at the opening of the 9th parliament and promptly took out his handkerchief and "wiped his hands clean."

Well, sorry to disappoint you, but it's not that simple.

I agree with the Newsday editorial that this was a case of "much ado about nothing." And the glee with which the whole issue was greeted by members of the People's National Movement (PNM) and the subsequent fete at the prime minister's residence certainly taints all the justification that we are hearing from voices opposed to the Couva North MP. And it sends an ugly partisan signal.

In the business of political communication, distraction is a powerful weapon. The rule is simple: when the going gets tough, create a distraction. And what could be better than to interfere with the man who epitomises opposition defiance?

Friday March 29, 2008 was private member's day. The House was scheduled to debate the escalating food prices. Flour up 39 percent, rice to soon cost 100 percent more and *dahl* (yellow split peas) also up 100 percent. It was a splendid opportunity to engineer an event that was bound to abort the debate.

The distraction strategy goes beyond that one day. The national agenda today is so crowded with issues that negatively impact the government's standing that Prime Minister Manning has been musing about postponing the local government election for a third time.

Just take a look at what is happening. Food prices going through the roof, crime reaching new historical highs, serious questions about accountability in the billion-dollar mega-construction projects, health and other services falling about, a $400-million private jet, the media glaring its teeth as the fourth estate.

Why not shift focus? Get the media and the people talking about something else, something about politics with lots of emotion and hype. Speaker Barendra Sinanan, Panday and a computer did the trick. And it is working. The issue has got people talking and has recast the national agenda.

And the opposition is reacting predictably. Panday and his colleagues plan to return to parliament next Friday, each armed with an "offensive" computer. And if Sinanan stands his ground, the issue will get cranked up with emotion and political rhetoric from both sides — a bonanza of "news" for the ever-hungry reporters and editors. And who can blame us? We report the events that reflect the national agenda, although we can — if we try — also help shape that agenda.

So what has happened so far is that people's anger has shifted away from the national problems they face and directed at an issue that doesn't change the price of rice. It works well for the government and if the opposition and its supporters do as I suspect they will, it will strengthen the strategy of distraction and, with effective management the government could come out smelling like a rose.

It's working. And the MPs on the government side are already massaging the message. Keith Rowley, Amery Browne, Esther le Gendre and House leader Colm Imbert, are all pointing to disrespect for the chair being serious enough to expel a member in keeping with parliamentary protocol. And as the debate progresses, the national conversation will shift in that direction. It will become clear that Panday was wrong and the Speaker did what the rules stipulate. And yes he was, if you want to take a black and white view of the issue. But it's always necessary to also analyze the shades of gray.

The issue at hand has to do with the use of a laptop computer. Basdeo Panday has used it before in parliament without any objection from the chair, so the opposition leader was following established precedence. It would seem that Sinanan wanted to make a point and he certainly did by provoking an argument with Panday.

But we need to ask what is so wrong about any MP using a computer in parliament. Didn't all members of the Senate recently (March 18) agree that members would be provided with computers and access to wireless Internet services? In our modern world with our nation boasting of heading to developed world status the Speaker's original memo and his attitude Friday are counter-productive and downright silly.

The computer and other mobile electronic communication devices have become part of everyday use by leaders and the average person. So why is it so offensive when a member of parliament uses it? The Speaker might argue that it shows disdain for the proceedings of the House and we're already hearing the "bad manners" spin from the PNM. But didn't Eric Williams display the worst case of bad manners and arrogance in the House during his decades as government and PNM leader?

He made a habit of turning his back against members of the House, making a show of opening the broadsheet, Trinidad Guardian, and switching off his hearing aid whenever he pleased. No Speaker dared question him or censure him for his actions. Not a damn dog bark, to use Williams' own words.

Panday was not going that far.

Could he have been scanning electronic files for data for use in the debate? Perhaps he was researching something relevant to the issue at hand in preparation for the debate? It's no different from checking through stacks of hard copy. Perhaps Panday's sin was to keep in tune with the 21st century. Perhaps that's why his parliamentary colleague Roodal Moonilal was quick to dub the House of Representatives "Jurassic Park."

It didn't have to be this way. This was a non-event, even less significant that the ridiculous Rowley-Sharma teacup brawl. But the Speaker over-reacted, though he was well within his jurisdiction. And Panday did what Panday does best — fight back. We will hear all kinds of debates on the issue over the next few days and perhaps week. Depending on what happens next, the issue could dominate the national agenda, pushing every other issue to the sidelines.

And that would be wonderful news for the government. Patrick Manning knows what he is doing. It would be a good idea for the people of Trinidad and Tobago to start paying attention before it's too late.

(March 29, 2008)

Leave the laptop; get on with the people's business

It is clear how the political divide in the "laptop affair" will be played out. Prime Minister Patrick Manning has drawn his line in the sand by stating that he won't tolerate lawlessness in the parliament; Basdeo Panday has suggested that his expulsion had little to do with his computer and a whole lot to do with Speaker Barendra Sinanan flexing his muscles to whip MPs into following to his rules.

The affair has caused a distraction from the real national issues and the people's concerns about high food prices and rising crime, to name the top two. The focus is on whether the Speaker was in fact within the rules of the House. And based on what the relevant standing orders say, it appears that he was on firm ground.

But perhaps we need to take a close look at the real issue at hand — the use of the computer and the narrow guidelines established by the Speaker in his memo, which was the root cause of the drama that unfolded in parliament last Friday, with police being called to escort the former prime minister out of the House of Representatives.

We live in a modern world and the Trinidad and Tobago parliament has recognised the relevance of computers and similar electronic devices. A resolution passed only this month allows Senators access to computers and wireless connections to the Internet. Why then this rigid rule about the circumstances under which a Member of the House may use a laptop computer?

Manning and the Speaker are standing firm on the provisions of the standing orders, which were written and accepted back in 1961 when we were in the dark ages with respect to modern technology. The portable computer and the Internet didn't exist then. Perhaps Speaker Sinanan should have been guided in drafting his memo by Section 91 (1) of the same standing orders that states:

"In any matter not herein provided for, resort shall be had to the usage and practice of the Commons House of Parliament of Great Britain and

Northern Ireland, which shall be followed as far as the same may be applicable to this House, and not inconsistent with these Standing Orders nor with the practice of this House."

That is indeed a critical point. It would suggest that since the rules drafted in 1961 did not provide for the use of computers, the matter should be based on what is acceptable in the British Parliament today. Sinanan, as an experienced Speaker, should know that there is something ethically wrong with cherry picking from the standing orders to suit his own convenience.

Had he followed the relevant standing order, the whole mess would never have developed in the first case because he would have discovered that English MPs are allowed to use laptops, cell phones, blackberries and other similar electronic devices in the parliament chamber. The rules in the Parliament of Westminster allow MPs to use their portable devices for a variety of purposes including sharing emails or "doing other work." In fact, the use of electronic devices is encouraged in the legislative halls of the modern world.

Had Sinanan bothered to keep in touch with reality, he would know that his memo of February 25, 2007, which became the straw to break Panday's back, was retrograde and a denial of a member's right to information.

Closer to home, Jamaican legislators have been using computers in their Parliament since 2006, so why should a progressive nation such as ours working toward making Trinidad and Tobago a developed nation establish such archaic and backward rules? Is this a case of the Speaker's determination to assert his authority or his ignorance of what's taking place on this planet?

If anyone wants to draw lines then it is clear that Panday disobeyed the rules laid down by the presiding officer of the House. But for Manning to describe this as "lawlessness" in Parliament is really taking it too far. Perhaps Manning should focus on lawlessness in the land, where homicides this year have crossed 100. I would not go so far as to say that Panday was right; he was not.

But then, following the Gandhian principle of resistance to an unjust law, he might have a strong case for standing firm against what is obviously an unjust and backward rule. To labour the argument is like trying to solve the riddle of the chicken and the egg. However, returning to Parliament for the next scene in this drama is not going to solve the problem.

Panday is known for taking national issues directly to the people. And that is where he should be headed to explain why Sinanan's law is wrong.

To engineer a confrontation next Friday is not going to settle the matter. And it will fall well within the PNM's agenda of distracting the nation from the issues that affect the lives of the people.

Panday has an obligation to represent his constituents and the citizens. He can do it best not by forcing his arrest and possible imprisonment for contempt of parliament, but by taking on the Manning regime from outside, raising the real national issues and encouraging the people to raise their voices and demand solutions.

That's what the opposition and Panday need to do: leave the laptop and focus on what really is of importance to the people and the nation.

(March 30, 2008).

Speaker's agenda lost in propaganda over laptop affair

I made a point over the weekend that the whole laptop affair in the Trinidad and Tobago parliament was a farce. The spin that is already taking shape will have nothing to do with the computer and everything to do with "Basdeo Panday's recalcitrance." I use that term guardedly because of the emotive connotation going back to a livid rant by a premier in Woodford Square in 1958.

The Trinidad Guardian has already set the tone. In an editorial, it noted that Panday was out of line and he should follow the rules. Bishop Abdulah is also sounding off on it. And Prime Minister Patrick Manning is talking about lawlessness in the House, which he says he won't tolerate. (He seems content enough to tolerate it in the country. But that's another matter.)

And lest you think that Manning used that word off the cuff, think carefully. His mission since Panday was running the government was to paint the man in a corner with allegations of corruption. He has succeeded — with the media's help to some extent — in shaping a public image of Panday as a corrupt man, even a criminal. There's no need to labour the point; we know the story.

So when Manning talks about "lawlessness" he is saying "that criminal Panday." He's crafting his imagery very carefully. It's the way spin works. So unless Panday and his colleagues expose what's happening, and point out why Manning threw a fete for his people right after kicking Panday out of the House, the "laptop affair" will go down in the country's political history as another incident of Panday throwing a tantrum and a responsible parliament dealing with him appropriately. Period. Matter closed.

I know you're asking, "what's the point?" Didn't the Speaker kick Panday out for not following instructions? Wasn't Panday out of place not to follow the Speaker's ruling?

Well, that's the point of the propaganda. Don't fall for it.

Parliament is governed by a set of rules called standing orders. The speaker can't make them up and neither can any MP. The ones that apply now have been there since 1961, the dark ages when you think of modern technology. These standing orders set out rules, guidelines and procedures for the operation of the nation's parliament.

And they are different from any letter that a Speaker might want to send from time to time. So if the Speaker wants to issue directives about the conduct of parliament and the behaviour of members, he must do so in accordance with the standing orders.

That means if Speaker Barendra Sinanan wanted to make a ruling on the use of computers, then he should consult these same standing orders to be guided as to how to go about writing his directive. And if he had done so, he would have found no reference to laptop computers or any of the modern communication devices in the standing orders, because they didn't exist in 1961 when they were adopted.

Then he would have to be guided by the relevant standing order that said when there is doubt, you must follow what the British parliament is doing, in which case he would have known that in the United Kingdom, parliamentarians are not only allowed to use their computers, blackberries etc., they are encouraged to do so. After all, this is the 21st century.

So the point is that Speaker Barendra Sinanan is trying to establish an autocracy in the people's parliament. His actions are a clear and present threat to our democracy.

By sending out his memo on when and under what circumstances an MP can use a computer, he is saying he can change any rule to suit his pleasure or the whims of those pulling his strings.

A computer is really an electronic library, filing cabinet, communication tool and a million more things. The Speaker's break with ethical parliamentary conduct and established standing orders illustrates contempt for the democratic process, and is a first step to a parliamentary dictatorship in which free speech is a casualty.

The late Guyanese President Forbes Burnham told me once that his regime never censored the press. When I pressed him with examples he explained it this way: "We just tell them what not to print. We are a developing nation and when the press prints stories that are inimical to the interest of the state and our development process, then we tell them they can't print such stories."

That was in 1975. But the danger lurks everywhere. And a government determined to suppress free speech and undermine democracy and citizens' rights will, like Burnham, change all the rules unless the people stop them. Suppose Mr. Speaker sends out a memo saying MP's can't criticise government policy without first submitting notes to the House? If we accept the legitimacy of the memo on computer use, then we accept that the speaker can do this, too. If you follow the logic that was used to expel Panday, you will see that Barendra Sinanan — or any Speaker — can make any rule, regardless of what the standing orders say, by sending out a memo. That's a violation of parliamentary procedure.

The danger is that the Speaker, in attempting to redefine the parliamentary protocol, is arbitrarily establishing rules without reference to the standing orders. If we let that happen, we abdicate our freedoms.

And take it another step.

Can he not send a memo telling MP's they can't have their briefcases in parliament? A computer is an electronic briefcase. In effect, his memo was saying MPs could use a briefcase only under rules established by the Speaker.

Barendra Sinanan's actions are a threat to parliamentary democracy. And it's a pity that the whole nation will be fed the trash about Panday being kicked out because he didn't "respect the chair."

The media and the public are falling for the propaganda and the spin and not seeing what is really happening. We are keeping our eyes on the spider and getting tangled in the web. And when Panday returns to Parliament, as he says he will, the real story will remain untold.

If I were in Panday's shoes, I would leave Sinanan and the parliament alone and walk a mile with the people. I would tell them what is really going on.

Why? Because in a real democracy, the people are more powerful than those who govern them.

(March 31, 2008)

Don't save face, save the nation

Basdeo Panday and opposition members of parliament demonstrated Friday that they have a clear agenda for now on how they will conduct their affairs. Panday stated categorically earlier in the week and again Friday that the "laptop affair" was not about the computer, suggesting that it was a conspiracy to silence opposition voices and undermine democracy.

The question now is: where does it go from here as the next acts unfold in this political drama?

As the politicians dig into their respective positions the national agenda has shifted from such critical issues as rising food prices, escalating crime and the myriad other people's issues, to constitutional and parliamentary semantics that would not feed hungry bellies or calm the fears of a nation living in fear.

Over the next week, Panday and his colleagues will go to the people to explain what has happened and what, in their view, is about to happen. For six consecutive nights, the opposition will state its position on the "laptop affair" and attempt to paint the current administration as one that is intent on suppressing people's rights, ignoring their concerns and undermining democracy.

Perhaps they will also offer some solutions to deal with the pressing needs of the people and justify any prolonged absence of the other 15 members from the opposition benches. For the other side, Panday's suspension from parliament is just the first act in a continuing campaign to discredit the former prime minister.

The next will be to try to rob him of his seat as leader of the opposition. Here's how: section 83. 3. (b) of the Constitution states that the office of the leader of the opposition shall become vacant if "the holder thereof ceases to be a member of the House of Representatives for any cause other than a dissolution of parliament."

Panday might fall into this category by virtue of his expulsion. If the president agrees that his expulsion means that he has "ceased" to be a member of the House, even temporarily, he has the constitutional authority to fire him. And therein lies the storyline for legal and constitutional battles that will follow. It is a matter of interpretation.

Panday is already arguing that the Speaker breached standing orders to suspend him because his memo on the use of laptop computers was improper. Therefore, if the rule was wrong, then the Speaker was out of line to suspend him.

For his part, Speaker Sinanan — and members of his governing party — argue that the standing orders under which Panday was suspended were clear and the matter of the "legality" of the Speaker's memo is irrelevant. If the president moves to fire Panday, the Couva North MP will follow the same line of argument that his suspension is illegal. He will also argue that he has not "ceased" to be a member of the House.

But in the meantime, what about the people's business?

Panday cannot return to the House during his suspension and his colleagues made a bold political statement Friday that they are standing with their leader. For the next week, they will play to the masses and gauge public opinion before making their next move.

But they cannot — and must not — continue their boycott indefinitely. By all means, they must tell the people their version of the story and shout it as loudly as they can. That's what democracy is all about. But when the shouting is over the people's business must come first. The people elected them to represent them both inside the parliament and within their respective constituencies. That is their primary responsibility.

Here's another interesting note. If the boycott continues, each of the MPs (except Panday) would be liable to expulsion and/or dismissal for non-attendance without the authorisation of the Speaker. What are the real opposition options?

- They can carry on with all the sound and fury, but in the end, Panday will remain expelled until the end of the year (even if he mounts a legal and constitutional challenge);
- Panday will likely be fired as opposition leader, thereby creating a vacancy which the UNC-A would have to fill, possibly opening old wounds and creating new ones;

- by not attending parliament, the other MPs would automatically vacate their seats;
- breaking the boycott just to retain the legitimacy would be seen as hypocritical and opportunistic;
- they can all resign and demand an election.

Perhaps now is the time for the opposition to make a bold play on behalf of the people of Trinidad and Tobago and go for the final option. Of course, Manning would scoff at the idea and refuse. He has a five-month old majority of 26. Why seek another mandate?

And constitutionally, he can continue to run the parliament with his members only because the section 60:1 states that "a quorum of the House of Representatives shall consist of twelve members of the House and a quorum of the Senate shall consist of ten Senators..." That's based on the House of Representatives having 36 members; the expanded House of 41 puts that at one third, which is 14.

It is a tremendous political gamble with serious risks. However, under the constitution, a by-election must be held within three months of a seat becoming vacant. If 15 seats become vacant at the same time, it would be a strong enough statement to demand a general election. The opposition would be treading on political landmines.

If they quit and challenge Manning to a new political duel, their chances of victory today are better than they were in 2007, especially with people seeing that the Congress of the People was a political mirage.

The number of national issues crying for attention, the disdain for the people shown by the Manning administration, the reckless expenditure and the serious allegations of corruption in Manning's administration are enough to lift people out of complacency.

Although Manning will refuse to call a general election he would have to call 15 by-elections in 90 days. In those 90 days, the opposition would have the opportunity to meet the people one-on-one and challenge the People's National Movement (PNM) on opposition-friendly turf.

Manning and his PNM would have to fight the 15 by-elections or they will lose face as an arrogant, discriminatory party that doesn't care about people in the opposition heartland. Manning cannot take that chance, so he would have to fight. And if the people are as fed up as I believe they are, they will return all the opposition members to parliament.

The opposition loses nothing, and gains credibility. And it would have three months to showcase itself as a government in waiting by putting all the national problems on the front burner and by offering solutions. But perhaps Manning's arrogance will tempt him to call a general election. Stranger things have happened.

(April 5, 2008)

One critical issue that the Manning administration failed to address in its new term was food inflation. As it had done previously, the government focused on mega projects and ignored the most basic needs of citizens.

Food prices and survival back home in TT

I often sit at home here in Canada and wonder how on earth people back home in Trinidad can survive with their meagre wages and the escalating food prices. And I wonder if I can ever go home and feel comfortable again — or just manage — on the small pension that I would get from Canada on retirement.

I write about these thoughts today because I looked at the Trinidad and Tobago papers and can't believe some of the things I read. Pholourie is now two for a dollar, doubles $4.00 and in some places $5.00, the same for saheena, baiganee and aloo pies.

I refer to these because it's the common breakfast tradition to stop by the roadside vendor for what used to be an affordable meal before taking on the day. And while the temptation is to blame the poor vendor for gouging the consumer, the reality is that she or he is not making any more profit. It is a case of covering the cost of production.

All of these food items are flour-based. Flour just went up again in the country, now retailing at around $5.00 a kilo. Supermarkets are trying to cushion the increase to stay in business and retain customers. But they can't do it for long. Like everybody else, they have to pay higher costs for electricity, water, rent, wages and every other item associated with doing business.

And in the midst of all this, the labour unions are asking for a minimum wage of $20.00 an hour. It's a real catch 22. People can't survive today with what they are making so they need a higher wage, businesses cannot sustain a higher wage because it will pull them under.

I know that international factors are partly responsible for what's happening, but that's little comfort for people who just need to eat and feed their kids every day, buy books and clothes to send the children to school, pay for doctors and medicine. And when I think of these things, I wonder if anybody in office — past and present — really gives a damn about the little people whom they exploit election after election.

The country has the capacity to feed itself 10 times over if those in charge would just think of people for a change. If they would just come out of their offices or just park their BMWs and Mercedes and walk among the people, they'll see the potential.

For generations, farmers have suffered from flooding and poor access roads.

Fixing just these two problems could cause a greater supply of fresh produce to the markets at lower prices. Yet every government has paid lip service to the farming community and the problems remain.

I remember working as a consultant for Caroni (1975) Limited and being privy to a whole lot of confidential information (which I can't reveal even now) for structural change leading to profitability. But what was the answer? Shut it down. In one short-sighted, politically motivated move, the Patrick Manning government shut down the industry, tossing an entire community of nearly a quarter million into an economic tailspin. I will write about Caroni and its socio-economic role another day, but I want to stick with the food issue today.

Caroni owned 75,000 acres of arable land. The company was producing rice in a fully mechanised operation. It had a thriving dairy and livestock sector, citrus and much more. It had viable plans to make these profitable but as a state corporation, its decision-making was in the hands of the Whitehall elite.

Today, some of the best agricultural lands are being converted into ghettos that the government is passing off as housing communities, while men and women capable of farming these lands have no work and still have to provide food for their families. It just doesn't make any sense.

Tobago used to be a food basket. The island has the potential to produce more than enough for the whole country, but the land is just sitting there.

Food security is more important than everything else to maintain a nation's independence. Today, we are seeing the folly of an import culture. I agree that globalisation has changed the rules dramatically and we must somehow "pay" for that. But common sense tells us that we can do better. We can invest some of the energy windfall in agriculture and food production. We don't need to go to Guyana to grow food; we have enough land and human resources in Trinidad and Tobago to do it. We are blessed with everything — land, climate, people and money. Why can't we solve the most basic problem of feeding ourselves?

I ask myself this question everyday and wonder if any one of the people who govern the nation is doing the same. I know it's easy for them to afford everything because they have the money. But certainly each of them knows at least one family that didn't have breakfast this morning. They must know that at least one mother today went hungry so she could buy medicine for her sick child.

Today, new high rises are reaching into the sky, the prime minister is flying high in private jets, he lives in a 148-million dollar mansion built with the people's money and has his own private security. The government boasts of a robust economy and a Vision 2020 strategic plan to make Trinidad and Tobago a developed nation.

I must be an idiot, but honestly, I cannot figure out how they can believe this when tens of thousands of people have no future, when kids go hungry every day, where doctors live in mansions and drive the best cars and people can't get the most basic health care without handing over their week's grocery money.

Something is wrong with the country that nurtured me and made me who I am. I am deeply hurt by what I see and it pains me most because I know that it doesn't have to be so. We can do better.

I really want to go home again and plant a rose garden in my front yard. But I'll have to wait and hope that things will change. For now I have to be content with buying doubles at Drupati's roti shop here in Toronto.

(April 2, 2008)

TT minister calls for supermarket boycott; blames grocers for high food prices

A Trinidad and Tobago government minister has shifted all blame for high food prices to supermarkets, which he claims are gouging consumers. And Consumer Affairs Minister Peter Taylor is advising people to boycott supermarkets and buy from suppliers instead.

Taylor told reporters supermarket owners are unreasonably marking up food prices to fatten their pockets. He accused some of them of marking up basic food products such as rice by between 35 and 40 percent. He said they can make a decent profit with a mark up of 15 percent.

"This is the same society that we all have to live in, that we all have to exist in, there has to be some basic humanity. There is no need for the volatility in certain prices...but yet still you are seeing unreasonable increases every week and we are saying it has to do with a lack of social conscience," Taylor said.

The minister said suppliers are willing to hold prices down and urged supermarkets to do the same. He said consumers have an option of buying directly from suppliers and advised them to do so. "The options are, you can access the cooperative at NFM on Wrightson Road, you can go directly there and purchase flour." He said they could do the same for other commodities.

Taylor stopped short of denouncing supermarkets as "some sort of cartel." However, he said "the market is being influenced in a certain way, we all have the social responsibility to move away from that sort of practice."

Taylor admitted that government's hands are tied with respect to the situation. "The whole issue of regulations is not really the purview of the government. Price controls are not recommended in pure economic sense because what it will tend to do is open the door to black marketeering," he said.

Grocery owners quickly called the minister's statements "irresponsible." While there has been no formal response from the Supermarkets Association, many grocers denied that they were fixing prices to fleece the public. They suggested that the minister was trying to shift responsibility from the government and stir up anger among consumers against groceries. They explained that they were victims of high prices just like everybody else and the minister was acting irresponsibly in suggesting that some kind of cartel is exploiting the situation. They said wholesale prices of most items have been steadily rising and they are just responding to the reality.

One of them wondered if Taylor was trying to incite kidnappers to go after grocery owners.

(April 3, 2008)

Looting, assault and robbery a routine affair in TT

When a government minister calls the looting of foodstuff and the brutal attack on a citizen a "normal and habitual" thing, it is time to be very worried about the state of affairs in Trinidad and Tobago.

The comment came from Consumer Affairs Minister Peter Taylor Friday about an incident on the Beetham Highway Thursday, a day after he accused supermarkets of gouging consumers and advised people to boycott the groceries and buy directly from suppliers.

Taylor was talking about an attack by bandits on two vehicles transporting flour, milk and juice to supermarkets. These are high-priced commodities that are in short supply. Looters savagely beat the driver of one of the delivery vehicles before relieving the truck of most of its cargo. While police were trying to deal with that case, bandits were looting another vehicle. All this was happening in broad daylight, in full view of people driving along the Beetham stretch just outside Port of Spain.

Taylor told the Trinidad Express he "would not read anything" into the incident, calling it "an isolated incident," and then added this gem: "I am sure that you have experienced, on many occasions, that in times of heavy traffic, persons would routinely get looted on that Beetham Stretch... Yes, of course it has happened before...Persons have had their jewelry snatched...So I would not attribute that to any trend."

In other words, it was business as usual. Taylor advised the nation not to panic.

Not to panic?

These community members come out of their urban ghettos, attack people routinely, steal their personal belongings, brutally attack citizens and go about their merry way. And you tell people there's no reason to panic?

It is no wonder that the nation is under siege by criminals. Gangs roam freely knowing that their activities would be considered "routine and habitual."

Peter Taylor's casual dismissal of a serious criminal matter is consistent with the way the authorities treat crime. His ministerial colleague responsible for national security has repeatedly said outside of gang activity, there is no real crime problem. And their boss, Prime Minister Patrick Manning, while admitting that crime is at an "unacceptable" level, is content to see it as being influenced by drugs. Manning is content to breed criminal activity through his pandering to "community leaders" and appeasing of criminals by offering them jobs and government contracts.

When a Cabinet minister calmly dismisses the looting of vehicles and the assault of honest, hard-working people, there is indeed every reason for law-abiding citizens to be very concerned.

Sorry Mr. Minister, there is reason to panic, especially because of your disturbing acknowledgement that criminal behaviour is part of the normal lifestyle in Trinidad and Tobago and that we should just accept it and not "read anything" into it.

(April 5, 2008)

Revenge of the stepchild

UN Secretary General Ban Ki-moon opened the United Nations conference on Trade and Development (UNCTAD) in Accra, Ghana on Sunday with a warning to delegates that higher food prices risk wiping out progress toward reducing global poverty and eventually hurting world growth and security.

Ban pledged to use the full force of the world body to tackle the price increases, which threaten to increase hunger and poverty and have already sparked food riots in Asia, Africa, the Middle East and nearer home, in Haiti. "I will immediately establish a high-powered task force comprised of eminent experts and leading authorities to address this issue," he announced.

His speech far away on the African continent sounded familiar and similar to what the people of Trinidad and Tobago have been hearing from the Patrick Manning government for months. The prime minister keeps promising measures to deal with the problem while at the same time shifting blame to anyone but those who must take responsibility — members of his government.

Now a head honcho of the governing People's National Movement (PNM) is talking about buying food from "sources" in Latin America at one third of the current cost. John Donaldson was short on details, saying only that Consumer Affairs Minister Peter Taylor would have the details Tuesday. That's the same Peter Taylor who urged people to boycott supermarkets and brushed off looting as "routine" practice along the Beetham Highway.

And from London where he is at the bedside of his ailing spouse, Basdeo Panday is calling for a people's revolt against the present regime. "You don't have to wait five years for change, you can bring the government down by demonstrations and marching, but the people must have the courage...If they do nothing, then they must simply be prepared to suffer the consequences," he said in an interview with the local media.

In the end, the reality remains the same. People are hungry and cannot afford food in a nation that is awash with billions of dollars from an unprecedented oil boom that has seen the price of oil rise beyond US$115 a barrel.

Many years ago, Professor George Sammy warned Trinidad and Tobago to nurture agriculture because a nation can never be independent unless it can feed itself. "You can walk naked," he told an agriculture conference, "but you cannot go without food." But nobody was listening. Nobody important, that is. Agriculture remained, as it did through every administration, a stepchild and a pariah.

Every year, farmers begged for help to arrest the problems of flooding and access roads. Every year, they implored those in authority to create the mechanisms to make agriculture attractive and profitable. And every year, they were left with an empty begging bowl. Today, that neglect is showing. Food prices are steadily climbing, the government keeps making promises and the army of the hungry grows. And Dr. Sammy's predictions have come true. Part of the food problem is that nations that grow food for export are hoarding it for themselves or selling it where they can get the best price in the new globalised world. The other part of the problem is a failed agriculture policy.

Every Trinidad and Tobago government has refused to help the struggling small farmer cope with flooding, access roads problems, technical expertise, funding and marketing. For the most part, farmers provided a service. And nobody was listening when they asked for help because despite their problems, the food reached the market.

Today, we are hearing about hundreds of small farms, allocation of lands for a demonstration farm, mega-farms with Cuban experts and an ambitious Caricom food plan proposed by Guyana. But it's all talk. And the most fundamental and basic problems remain. Even if some of these things happen, it would take years to see the result. And many of the same recurring infrastructure, economic and logistical problems would continue to undermine agriculture.

And then there is the politics of agriculture.

"We try to bribe dem by keeping Caroni open, but dey still aint vote for we." That's a direct quote from the late PNM Cabinet Minister Ronald J. Williams, who called his boss, George Chambers, "a damn fool" for not shutting down the sugar company that sustained a community of nearly a quarter of a million people, most of whom were perceived to be pro-opposition.

Two decades later, Manning did it, ostensibly to save the plundering of the treasury by a company that existed on a subsidy averaging one million dollars a day. He called it the best decision he has ever made. But he is yet to demonstrate the wisdom in taking that decision. Thousands of former sugar workers are still waiting for the land his government promised them, land that would have been producing food today. Even a court judgment has not accelerated action on these farms. And I would wager that we are not going to see those farms soon.

There is a reason for the disdain for agriculture: politics.

Manning once told me that a state enterprise did not exist for profit. "It is there for social stability, social stability," he insisted. If that is so, why close down a state industry like Caroni (1975) Limited? If any state enterprise qualified under Manning's definition, it was Caroni. Manning did it for political spite in an irrational move that was not based on economic or social planning. It was an opportunity to crush the opposition base and destroy its leadership.

It didn't work.

In fact, Manning could very well have been on the opposition benches if Winston Dookeran and his tribe had heeded the call of the United National Alliance (UNC-A) to fight Manning in 2007 as a united team. So much for dispossessed sugar workers.

That is why those farms for former Caroni workers will remain a promise and an illusion. That is why agriculture remains a stepchild. And that is why the nation is unable to feed itself. If you look at Caroni alone in the context of a national agricultural strategy, you would be amazed at some of the truth that got smothered in the spin about the company being a drain on taxpayers and the economy.

First, it employed nearly 10,000 people directly and a further 6,000 cane farmers produced cane for the factories. That's 16,000 people and their dependents — a total of about 64,000. These people supported the shops and other businesses that grew up in the agricultural communities. The essential trade provided tens of thousands of small entrepreneurs who worked and lived, looked after their families and upgraded their standards of living.

In other words, that state enterprise that Manning shut down provided the "social stability" that was so important to him.

The spin only portrayed Caroni workers as illiterate cane cutters and field workers. In reality, Caroni was much more than that. It was also a community of mechanics, drivers, heavy machine operators, clerical workers, computer technicians, managers, engineers and doctors. Here are some other facts Manning didn't tell anybody:

- Caroni represented 44.7 percent of the GDP in the agricultural sector;
- Caroni injected TT$680 million into the national economy every year, including guaranteed foreign exchange from sugar and rum exports;
- Caroni workers earned $447 million a year and paid $32 million in direct taxes to the government;
- Caroni subsidised the state medical services by providing FREE medical services to all its staff and its dependents — more than 60,000 people — and provided free prescription medicines to them;
- Caroni subsidised the local government authorities by providing land for cemeteries, parks and recreation grounds and assisted by maintaining these facilities;
- Caroni subsidised the state housing plans by providing land and loans to its workers;
- Caroni subsidised the business sector — particularly the soft drink industry — to the tune of $60 million a year;
- Caroni operated profitable beef, rum and citrus subsidiaries;
- Caroni had a fully mechanised rice subsidiary capable of providing domestic needs;
- Caroni owned assets valued at more than one billion dollars.

In short, the company that was a drain on the economy and a burden on taxpayers was taking one million dollars a day and giving back nearly two. It was not an economic parasite. And more important, it provided social and economic stability to an entire community and the nation.

It was the golden goose of agriculture that Manning killed. And contrary to what Manning said in the last general election, keeping Caroni open did not condemn the children of sugar workers to remain in "slavery." Yes slaves and indentured labourers built the industry, but their children have moved on. The lawyers, doctors, politicians, white-collar workers and leaders who run the affairs of the nation in the public and private sectors are children or grandchildren of sugar workers. Sugar built the nation.

And while sugar cane may have lost its economic appeal, the land and the expertise existed to create a revolution in agriculture that would have been the envy of the region and the world. From the ashes of sugar, Trinidad and Tobago could still build a sustainable agriculture sector.

But will it?

Trinidad and Tobago's wealth has been its curse. It has generated waste and avenues for corruption while failing to address the most basic human need — food. It has created an army of "dependents" whose gratitude would provide the political muscle for those in power to remain there. And the reality is, there is no need to keep agriculture in the dark ages or to fear those who would benefit from a sound agricultural strategy. It's not too late.

The floods are coming, the roads need fixing, and the lands need to be cultivated. The people are ready. But is the government ready to help create a revolution in agriculture, or is it content to just throw around its energy windfall and nurture its import culture? That's a question the politicians have to answer. If they don't, people will have to eat the money. And that means the masses would continue to starve.

Instead of cultivating the land and encouraging farmers to do so, the Manning administration treated farmers with scant courtesy and often entered the lands unannounced, destroying crops and displacing people.

(April 21, 2008)

What agriculture incentives?

Trinidad and Tobago's Finance Minister Karen Nunez-Teshiera told reporters last week that government spending is aimed at taking the country forward "to the realisation of Vision 2020" and boasted that agriculture is getting the most incentives. She was clear that it was not spending "that has no end," but rather a medium term necessity to meet government's objectives of diversification of the economy away from energy.

The minister was putting spin on the runaway spending that has caught the eye of the Central Bank and international financial institutions. The World Bank has said Trinidad and Tobago needs to watch its spending on mega-projects.

And the central bank governor has cautioned government about its expenditure. Ewart Williams told journalists last month it is imperative for the government to slow down the public spending both by the central government and quasi-government institutions. He predicted that unless government "cools it," inflation would remain in double digits. In January, it reached 10 percent, and dropped slightly by the end of March. Williams said governments all over the world are watching inflation closely and developing monetary policies to keep it in check.

But the finance minister wanted to make it clear that if the country is expected to diversify away from energy it must spend money on dealing "creatively" with traffic congestion, education, skills training and health. "To achieve developed status, we have to raise the Human Development Index, therefore we have to attend to education, health and infrastructure. Expenditure is intended to diversify the economy and to take the country to the realisation of the 2020 vision. It is not expenditure that has no end, it is an expenditure that is medium term to meet those objectives," she told reporters.

She dismissed criticism of public expenditure on mega-projects, noting that Williams was speaking of liquidity, consumerism and the need to encourage a culture of savings. She said government is aware of the inflationary pressures, which she attributed to the high cost of food. "Government has given the most incentives in the area of agriculture. What government is doing, and doing apace is increasing food supply and food production," she told reporters.

What incentives?

Apart from a food consultation that was more than an election gimmick prior to the 2007 poll, very little has been done to help develop agriculture. All the historical problems remain and the promise of small farms created from thousands of acres of former sugar lands remains a promise. The fortunate few who have started farming on these lands are faced with soil problems created by excess acidity from many years of sugar cane cultivation. Irrigation is also a major problem.

The solution is simple. Provide the funding — estimated about $140 million — to fix the twin problem. After all, the government had no problem finding the same amount of money to build a mansion for the prime minister and has been spending recklessly on other projects, like the Lara Stadium that is running up a cost of more than half a billion dollars.

The minister's boast of the most incentives for this pariah sector in the economy is dishonest. If spin could put food on the table, everyone in Trinidad and Tobago would be feasting at the Hyatt hotel like the prime minister and there would be no crisis.

Why, for example didn't the minister explain why the government has failed to accept an offer of $360 million from the European Union (EU) to help agricultural development for former sugar producers? The EU did not make the gesture overnight. The opposition was asking about it during the 2007 election campaign. And Kamla Persad-Bissessar produced documents that she claimed was evidence that the government did not care for the EU money. It turns out that she was right.

The Manning administration did not cash in on the first tranche of $40 million two years ago and there is no sign that it will meet the mid-2008 deadline to apply for the second. The EU doesn't just give away money. It had asked for serious proposals on the government's strategy to make use of the human resources formerly engaged in sugar cane production. So why was it so difficult for the government to produce a strategy when it had been saying for years it has one? Instead, it missed the boat on that first $40 million.

There is talk that the Ministry of Agriculture is working on a document that outlines strategies to retrain and re-employ sugar workers as part of its plan following the closure of the sugar industry. That's a prerequisite for applying for the EU grant. But it's not clear if the government wants the money. The real issue is whether the government is honest about what it wants to do with the former sugar cane workers.

It is all well and good to pontificate about it as it has been doing for years, but spin and empty promises don't convince international institutions. So far, the administration has failed to act on its own proposals to transform the abandoned cane lands into alternative, valuable employment.

And if the government remains unwilling or incapable of making a credible case to the EU, the country would miss out entirely on a grant of millions of dollars that could have fixed the many problems. That EU money could make the difference between success and failure for struggling farmers.

But who cares?

They are just former sugar workers "who doh vote for we," to quote the late PNM head honcho, Ronald Jay Williams. And there are much more important things on the government's agenda, such as private jets, new hotels, parking lots and other infrastructure that are demanding billions while the poor remain hungry.

(May 5, 2008)

Has Rowley's time come?

Keith Rowley should know that he is wasting his time and effort sounding off about a probe into the Urban Development Corporation of Trinidad and Tobago (UDeCOTT), or any organisation for that matter. What does he expect? And if the shoe was on the other foot and another cabinet minister was out the door shouting for accountability, perhaps Rowley would have been a part of the Cabinet chorus singing "all is well" just like Lenny Saith, Colm Imbert and the others. Rowley is no saint, but people should pay attention to what is happening. And if Rowley was genuinely concerned, he would do something about it.

It's interesting how it all developed. For quite some time now, influential people have been asking why the government handed so much power to Calder Hart and UDeCOTT. And people were also asking for some serious accountability over the mega-projects that are consuming billions of dollars. The government, which included Rowley, remained silent and did nothing. But Rowley knew a long time ago that something was wrong. And when he became the target of an Integrity Commission probe, he knew that he had to make a play. So he did. And he did it knowing that the boss would not be amused. He was gambling that he might have an ace. It turns out — for now at least — he had a jack, and it was Patrick Manning who had the ace. But the game is not yet over. He can pass the jack and win.

When the so-called Rowley affair gets off the front pages with some other "distraction," it will be business as usual. Calder Hart will still be doing what he has been doing all along.

Politics is about power. Manning holds it now, and he's going to make sure that nothing will change that. The rule has always been the same: "Not a damn dog bark." And Senator Hazel Manning reiterated it quite clearly last week when she announced to the media, "The prime minister has spoken."

That's why Ken Valley's "crusade" against Manning and his call for Rowley to fight for the leadership of the party will not achieve anything. In the end, both Valley and Rowley risk becoming political footnotes, irrelevant men who dared to challenge the absolute power of the leader. And don't believe for one moment that if the PNM's constitution allowed a one-member-one-vote system to choose a leader, Manning would be at risk of losing his job.

You see, the PNM has survived for more than half a century not because it is a democratic institution but because it is a disciplined one that demands conformity to certain rules and patterns of behaviour that keep the tribe together. "One for all, and all for one," to borrow a line from the Musketeers who put their lives on the line to protect the King of France.

So when the bedlam erupted over the UDeCOTT matter, Rowley broke the rules and stepped into the line of fire. And look how quickly he became the outsider! From senior cabinet minister to pariah in one day. Look where he was: he was the man who "efficiently managed the PNM's ambitious state housing programme which has resulted in 26,000 housing starts since 2002."

And there's more: "The PNM believes that Keith is the embodiment of our Vision 2020 philosophy that advocates equal opportunities for personal growth, self-expression, enjoyment of life and participation in the development process." That's straight from the PNM's website.

So what happened?

The party muzzled its members and cabinet is now fully behind UDeCOTT. It turns out, after all, that cabinet had approved the hotel that Rowley questioned. It's just that a few people didn't know about it, were not told that they should know about it or had forgotten.

Rowley's biggest mistake would be to challenge Manning for the leadership of the party. He is not an idiot. Manning made sure Rowley's earlier attempt failed and with so much more at stake today, Manning would pull out all the stops to make sure he retains power. If Rowley goes up against Manning and the tribe, he would be committing political suicide. The tribe would make sure of it.

But if Rowley is really interested in standing for integrity, accountability and the rights of the citizens of Trinidad and Tobago, he can fight another fight and win. Now is the time for him to rise above partisan politics and stand up for the nation and its citizens.

He can do it by hanging up his PNM political hat and standing up for what is right. If Rowley is genuine — and today I give him the benefit of the doubt — he would get together a citizens coalition and scrutinise everything the government has been doing since Manning usurped power in a presidential coup in 2001. People would volunteer their time and talent. And he would get invaluable support because people are tired and frustrated with the current regime. That citizens' coalition would conduct research and produce facts about what's wrong.

(May 9, 2008)

Now is the time to stand up for T&T

One of Basdeo Panday's famous lines is, "If you see me and a lion fighting, feel sorry for the lion." And in his more than four decades in politics, he has fought many intense battles against heavy odds to demonstrate that he is indeed a warrior who doesn't run away from a fight. Or as he himself says, "I don't duck and run."

And those who have engaged him in battle know that, in the end, Panday wins. Raffique Shah, Kelvin Ramnath, Ramesh Lawrence Maharaj, A.N.R. Robinson, Winston Dookeran and Patrick Manning have experienced Panday's wrath.

In the political bloodletting that threatened to destroy his United National Congress (UNC) Panday stood firm as he watched his anointed successor Winston Dookeran walk away with many UNC "loyalists" to create a new political organisation while the political pundits wrote him off as a spent force.

The political pundits put their bets on the new kids on the block; they were wrong. The pollsters scoffed at Panday; they were wrong. The people drifted away for a while and then they came back, as they always do.

From the ashes, Panday emerged once more to prove that no one could keep him down. With his trusted friend and ally, Jack Warner, he put together a powerful alliance that comprised smaller political parties and included his former political foe and former Attorney General Ramesh Lawrence Maharaj, and his deputy leaders Kamla Persad-Bissessar, Jack Warner and Wade Mark.

Panday and Warner led the UNC Alliance to a stunning victory that few expected. Had Winston Dookeran and the Congress of the People

(COP) heeded Panday's calls for a united opposition front, the political history of Trinidad and Tobago would have been altered dramatically and Patrick Manning and his People's National Movement would likely be sitting on the opposition benches today.

Now, Panday is back home from a sojourn in England where he was at his wife's bedside during her illness and surgery. And he's ready to do battle against Manning. Panday has everything on his side. For the first time since 1986, the nation is united in a common cause that is not tied to political partisanship or ethnic rivalry.

The reality in Trinidad and Tobago today is that Prime Minister Patrick Manning is blinded by his own arrogance and so obsessed with power that he considers himself invincible. But he isn't; no one is. And if Panday is serious about mobilising the nation, Manning should start getting worried. Here's why.

Manning is unpopular even in his own party. The purge of people like Ken Valley, Eddie Hart and Fitzgerald Hinds before the last election was a sign that he was cleaning house to expand his autocratic rule. He reluctantly kept Penny Beckles and he seems to have Colm Imbert right where he wanted him. The only remaining thorn in his side was Keith Rowley. And when Rowley touched Manning's sacred cows — UDeCOTT and Calder Hart — it was too much. Rowley had to go.

So much for the inside story.

In the public eye, he is also losing support. His oath of office in Woodford Square, his refusal to fire Martin Joseph and find a new police commissioner, his coziness with criminal "community leaders," the escalation of violent crime, the reckless spending — including a plan to buy a $400 million private jet that's still on the agenda — his inability to deal with rising food prices, his failure to develop agriculture and so much more provide the script for Panday's next big political act in the country.

Manning had created all the right conditions during his 2002-2007 administration for the opposition to remove him; they failed because they refused to unite. Now Manning is at it again, showing disdain for the nation and running a government that appears to be accountable only to him.

His outright refusal to consider an effective probe into UDeCOTT creates doubt and makes people wonder what he is hiding and why is Calder Hart so important. The enquiry he announced Friday is aimed at bringing down the heat, but it is a far cry from an enquiry into UDeCOTT.

Tens of thousands of people cannot afford shelter. Their children are hungry; they cannot afford medical care; bulldozers are mowing down their crops and destroying their shacks. Yet, the nation has money to construct billion-dollar white elephants that feed Manning's ego, doing nothing to develop the economy and insulate it to deal with the bust that's coming after this boom.

Today, the nation has an opportunity to rise together and speak with one voice and tell Manning he must serve the nation or be fired. And Panday is ready to lead. It is a common political premise that a people get the government they deserve. Perhaps that's true.

But in a democracy, the people are more powerful than those who govern them. And that is why Panday has one final golden opportunity to unite the people — all the people, including those who helped put Manning in office. Ken Valley and Keith Rowley must join Panday. They cannot have their cake and eat it too. The trade unions, the private sector organisations, the NGO's, the concerned individuals like Mary King must all put nation first and stand up and fight this battle.

This is not a UNC or UNC Alliance issue. This is a national one. Manning is on a destructive course that is taking Trinidad and Tobago down a path of no return. Trinidad and Tobago is in great danger. And everyone must stand up for the nation.

Manning has the full resources of the state at his disposal and more money than any administration has ever seen, yet he refuses to solve the country's most basic problem, while squandering billions. But the power of the people is stronger. Panday can provide the leadership, but only if the nation will stand up for justice, equality and freedom.

We are still a democracy where the will of the majority is supreme.

Manning claims to be a man of morality and spirituality, yet despite presiding over a period of surging oil prices, he has proven himself incapable of serving the interest of his people. There is no moral or spiritual reason for Manning's failure; he cannot even blame his party because he has proven his distaste for any form of responsible dissent.

Incompetence and self-indulgence cannot be tolerated from a prime minister, and it is time for a united opposition of citizens to speak out for the future of this country. This is not a soliloquy of political parties; this must be a national movement of Trinidadians and Tobagonians, regardless of their race, religion, or political allegiances, to transcend the confines of politics and struggle for the welfare of the nation's people.

If we are "forged from the love of liberty" then now is the time for us to show it.

(May 2, 2008)

Failed state or failing?

If you look at the 2007 Failed States Index compiled by a group called the Fund For Peace, you might be tempted to say there is nothing to worry about. But there is cause for concern.

The index classifies nations in one of four groups — Alert, Warning, Moderate and Sustainable — with Alert being the worst. Trinidad and Tobago falls in the Warning group and is rated at 116 out of 177. The index measures social, economic and political indicators classified in 12 sections. These are:

- Mounting Demographic Pressures
- Massive Movement of Refugees or Internally Displaced Persons Creating Complex Humanitarian Emergencies
- Legacy of Vengeance-Seeking Group Grievance or Group Paranoia
- Chronic and Sustained Human Flight
- Uneven Economic Development Along Group Lines
- Sharp and/or Severe Economic Decline
- Criminalisation and/or Delegitimisation of the State
- Progressive Deterioration of Public Services
- Suspension or Arbitrary Application of the Rule of Law and Widespread Violation of Human Rights
- Security Apparatus Operates as a "State Within a State"
- Rise of Factionalised Elites
- Intervention of Other States or External Political Actors.

The definition of each is interesting and worthwhile reading. For example, under the political heading it lists:

- Massive and endemic corruption or profiteering by ruling elites

- Resistance of ruling elites to transparency, accountability and political representation
- Widespread loss of popular confidence in state institutions and processes
- Growth of crime syndicates linked to ruling elites.

Does that describe what's happening in Trinidad and Tobago Today? How about this: "Fragmentation of ruling elites and state institutions along group lines"?

Under Social Indicators, you'll find these points:
- Specific groups singled out by state authorities, or by dominant groups, for persecution or repression
- Institutionalised political exclusion
- Public scapegoating of groups believed to have acquired wealth, status or power

And under the economic indicators group:
- Group-based inequality, or perceived inequality, in education, jobs, and economic status
- Group-based impoverishment as measured by poverty levels, infant mortality rates, education levels
- Rise of communal nationalism based on real or perceived group inequalities

It is clear that these indicators and definitions are present in some form in Trinidad and Tobago today. Whether they are real or perceived is debatable, depending on who you ask or which group responds.

For its part, the government has said repeatedly that the country is in no such danger and these concerns, expressed mostly by the opposition, are without merit. But ask the average apolitical citizen and you will find disagreement with the state's view of things. And that is why it is important to consider the dangers we faced as we sit in that second group, titled "Warning."

It is indeed a warning that we are heading into the "Alert" group of 32 states, which includes Sudan, Somalia, Nigeria, Zimbabwe, Ethiopia, Uganda, Iraq, Afghanistan, Haiti, Burma, to name a few.

The "Warning" group of 97 states is headed by Colombia and includes the CARICOM nations of Antigua and Barbuda, Belize, The Bahamas, Grenada, Guyana and Trinidad and Tobago. It also includes India and China.

Here's how Trinidad and Tobago scores on the index on a scale of one to 10, with one being the best and 10 the worst:

It gets a score of 5.2 in the areas of the "state or dominant groups singling out specific groups for persecution, institutionalised political exclusion and public scapegoating of groups believed to have acquired wealth, status or power."

Its highest score is in the areas of "group-based inequality, or perceived inequality, in education, jobs, and economic status and rise of communal nationalism based on real or perceived group inequalities." It is rated at 8.1 out of 10, which suggests this is the most disturbing issue. Overall the country gets a score of 67.5. It gets a failing grade in 10 of 12 categories, including crime.

Norway, which is the most secure of the 177 nations, has a score of 17.1; Canada 25.1 and the United States 33.6. On the "failed" end the highest score Sudan, 113.7; Iraq, 111.4; Somalia, 111.1 and Zimbabwe, 110.1

While Prime Minister Patrick Manning is right to say Trinidad and Tobago is not a failed state — and the statistics support his view — he and the other power brokers must indeed accept that there are alarm bells going off in critical areas. And unless the government makes a genuine effort to fix what's wrong, the nation will continue the downward trend and eventually take its place among the world's failed states.

(May 13, 2008)

The Albatross around Manning's neck was a man named Calder Hart and Manning's seemingly endless efforts to defend Hart. The prime minister fired Keith Rowley for complaining about Hart's influence and for acting as a law unto himself. Rowley and the opposition pounced on Manning and demanded an enquiry in the Urban Development Corporation of Trinidad and Tobago (UDeCOTT), which Hart headed as Executive Chairman. Manning resisted but, in the end, appointed an enquiry to look into UDeCOTT and the construction sector.

Manning announces enquiry into construction sector, UDeCOTT

Prime Minister Patrick Manning made an about turn in parliament Friday (May 23, 2008) and announced the establishment of a Commission of Enquiry into the construction sector, which would include UDeCOTT. Manning made the surprise announcement as parliamentary debate on the appointment of a Joint Select Committee (JSC) to investigate UDeCOTT neared its end.

Manning told the House of Representatives when he proposed the JSC there were no specific allegations against UDeCOTT. "Today for the first time, someone got up in this House and made a clear and specific allegation, as a consequence of which I am authorised by the government to announce the establishment of a commission of enquiry into the construction industry," Manning told the House.

He was referring to comments made by Tabaquite MP Ramesh Maharaj, who spoke just before him. Maharaj alleged that a locally-incorporated subsidiary of Sunway, a Malaysian company, had links to the wife of UDeCOTT chairman, Calder Hart.

"I am also authorised to say that the commission of enquiry which will comprise four persons and will be chaired by Mr Gordon Deane, a former chairman of the Integrity Commission," Manning said. "We hope that at the end of the day, truth will prevail and that Trinidad and Tobago will have a new system of operation in the construction sector...and that we will move inexorably on to the achievement of developed country status by the year 2020," the prime minister said.

(May 24, 2008).

(Note: Deane was replaced following widespread objections and replaced as chairman by Prof. John Uff)

All things being equal, Patrick Manning and the People's National Movement should have remained in office until the end of 2012 or early

2013, having won a convincing 26-seat majority in the November 2007 general election.

However, there was discontent within his party even before it was returned to government and, for the first time, the rumblings inside the People's National Movement (PNM) were spilling beyond the confines of Balisier House.

Among the many issues that hurt Manning and his government were the expulsion of Keith Rowley from the cabinet for what Manning called "wajang" behaviour unbecoming of a cabinet minister, Manning's continuing defence of Calder Hart (the Canadian who had become a top bureaucrat, allegedly with more power than the cabinet) the flirtation with buying a private jet and the blatant disregard for fiscal responsibility, accountability and transparency.

Manning had also been trying to create an opportunity to write a constitution to create an over powerful executive presidency, which he would inherit without getting the approval of the electorate.

Manning's missteps gave the opposition an opportunity to bury him politically. However, the United National Congress (UNC), after a spirited showing in the 2007 election, seemed to lack the muscle to fight back. That led to a revolt within the party that saw Panday ousted in an internal election and the emergence of a new executive led by Kamla Persad-Bissessar as political leader and Jack Warner as chairman.

The reinvigorated UNC rode the wave and, within months of the change of leadership, forced an election that the UNC and its coalition partners won with a 29-seat majority. Within months, two of the country's maximum leaders fell and a new dawn emerged.

This section deals with some of the issues of that period that impacted the governance of Trinidad and Tobago. The re-election of the People's National Movement, led by Prime Minister Patrick Manning in 2007, provided the administration an opportunity to develop the country further and focus on the needs of the people. However, Manning was determined to do things his way without any regard to what the citizens or the opposition thought.

In August 2008, the Indian High Commissioner to Trinidad and Tobago confirmed that the Manning administration was trying to woo Indian farmers to Trinidad to help develop mega farms. The diplomat said his office passed the idea to the relevant authorities in India and it would be up to the companies and farmers to decide whether they want to come to Trinidad.

A Times of India report on July 30, 2008 about the Trinidad and Tobago government's proposal to the Indian government stated:

"The government of Trinidad and Tobago has recently sent a proposal to the government of India inviting farmers and corporates to take up farming in their country...The Caribbean government has decided to lease out to Indian farmers seven plots, each measuring 100 acres, for 30 years...Indian investors can undertake 'investment, development, management and operation of agricultural farms' in the earmarked plots.

"Through the Indian mission in Port of Spain, the Trinidad government wants to reach out to all interested farmers, cooperatives and organisations interested in such ventures.

"But the lack of proper policy to undertake such ventures at the international level has become a stumbling block in sending farmers overseas," it added. The news raised some interesting questions and also triggered racist, anti-Indian sentiments from some quarters.

Why does Trinidad and Tobago need a new form of indentureship?

It is an interesting coincidence that on the day the nation took a holiday to commemorate Emancipation Day 2008, we were hearing about the possibility of Indians being encouraged to leave their homeland (again) and come to Trinidad and Tobago to develop the country's "mega-farms."

A report in the Times of India alerted the local media to the story, which was confirmed by the Indian High Commissioner to Trinidad and Tobago, Jagjit Singh Sapra, who pointed out that there is no firm proposal yet.

But there might be. And that's why this story is worth noting.

At first glance, it seems like a good idea since Indians are an agrarian people. They created India's green revolution and they rescued the dying plantation economy in Trinidad in the post-emancipation period. So perhaps they can do it again.

But times have changed.

The Indians who saved agriculture in the 19th century remained in Trinidad and made the British colony their home. And their descendants have gone on to keep agriculture alive for more than 150 years. The state has an able and willing agricultural work force, so why does the Manning administration want to bring Indians to Trinidad and Tobago to run mega-farms?

In the 19th century after Britain set the slaves free, the plantations suffered a dramatic decline because of the absence of a reliable source of cheap, effective labour. Slaves refused to work for their former masters for good reason — the plantations symbolised degradation, abuse and servitude. Slavery lacked any measure of humanity and was the worst injustice "civilised" society inflicted on fellow humans. And indentureship was not much better.

In fact, according to Lord John Russell, British Secretary of State for the West Indian colonies, indentureship was "a new system of slavery." He was not exaggerating the issue. Indians were treated like leased animals, herded into plantations and jailed if they strayed from their designated places of work. They were abused, flogged and treated as new slaves. Many were murdered. Their children were denied an education. This is how one planter justified it to a committee of the Legislative Council:

"This is an agricultural country. Unless you put their (Indian) children to working in the field when they are very young, you will never get them to do so later. If you train them to work in the fields you'll never have any difficulty...if you decide to educate the whole mass (of Indians)...you will be deliberately ruining the country."

It took the efforts of Canadian missionary, Dr. John Morton, to free the children from forced bondage by setting up Canadian Mission Indian schools alongside Presbyterian churches. That was the beginning of the upward mobility of the Indians and their first step to move from the periphery to the centre of society.

This digression in history is important.

In the 19th century, Indian labour brought the plantations out of decline and Indians remained close to the land for generations. And their commitment to agriculture is what has kept the markets supplied. And it continues today.

So going back to India might give agriculture the boost it needs, but why go to India when you have a strong agriculture-based work force in the country today clamouring for farmland so they could feed themselves and their families?

What about the mass of Indians who are citizens of Trinidad and Tobago who have spent their lives feeding us? Why can't they run the mega-farms and develop agriculture? Why can't the government give local Indian businessmen leases to land under the same terms that would be offered to Indians from India? The answer is this: it's bad for Manning's politics.

He closed the sugar industry and put 10,000 families on the breadline, calling it the best decision he ever made. That was a political decision aimed at destroying the opposition base. It's been more than six years since he promised the former sugar workers small farms to develop agriculture as part of their severance agreement. In spite of a court ruling ordering the government to hand out the farms, the former Caroni workers are still waiting.

Yet we keep hearing about the need to develop agriculture. We hear about investing in Guyana; we hear the Cubans are coming. And now the Indians might be coming.

For generations, the local farming community, dominated by descendants of the indentured Indians, has suffered neglect from every government of Trinidad and Tobago. Manning cannot give the farms to locals because he might offend his "constituency" while strengthening a voting block that has traditionally supported the opposition. He fears that former sugar workers might become a powerful army of agriculturalists and vote him out of office.

He cannot take that risk.

He told me in 1999 — and has said the same thing publicly — that his greatest mistake in his first administration (1991-1995) was that he didn't take care of his people. When I asked him what he meant, he explained that "his people" were those who had been loyal to him and his party, not necessarily people of any one ethnic group. It amounts to the same thing.

He is determined to take care his "tribe," which comprises people from the two founding groups. Political tribalism is not race-based, but built on blind loyalty. That's the constituency Manning can't offend. They might pull back their support for him. So he cannot and would not employ the ready, willing and able agricultural work force to create his mega-farms. Instead, he must keep them down. It's a matter of political expediency. They are not from his "tribe."

Manning has done everything to frustrate efforts of the farming community, including the mass of sugar workers who lost their jobs in his first strategic move after taking office following the 2002 general election. And in the 2007 general election while the opposition campaigned to re-open the sugar industry as the base for a major agro-industrial thrust, Manning said the industry would only be revived "over my dead body." He justified it by saying that the sugar industry would keep the children of sugar workers in servitude, that his vision is for them to move out of the agricultural sector and improve their lives.

Where does Manning live?

The Indians who slaved on the plantations worked hard to free their children from that scourge. Their children and children's children are the judges, lawyers, doctors, teachers, engineers, farmers and fishermen; they are the leaders and role models in every facet of national life. They did it while their parents lived off the land, feeding them and the nation.

Perhaps somebody needs to tell Manning that Basdeo Panday, Noor Hassanali and Satnarine Sharma are products of sugar and agriculture. Manning's false notion that the plantations would condemn the children to "slavery" is bogus and dishonest. In fact when he closed the sugar industry he was working hard at creating a community of dispossessed people. He was robbing them of their self-respect, their independence and their pride. And that is why he will not give them the land that is rightfully theirs. And now he talks about importing Indians to do the same thing that nationals can do and are willing to do. It's hypocrisy!

He's doing it because expatriate Indians are not rooted in the community; they don't have political allegiances and they are transients. They would have to live according to contractual rules and go home when they are no longer needed.

Why do you need a foreign work force and entrepreneurship class when you have them at home? It sounds like indentureship all over again. And it feels like history is repeating itself — first the Chinese, now the Indians.

Here are some questions that people must ask:
- Will Manning import individuals or families?
- Where are they going to live?
- Will their children go to school or be condemned to live like those who arrived in Trinidad under indentureship?
- How would you deal with the language barrier?

- What happens to them when they have toiled and created a vibrant agricultural sector?
- Who will inherit the farms they would build and nurture?

Manning probably knows the answer to all these already, but he's not going to tell you. Perhaps you could look to Zimbabwe and Robert Mugabe for some of the answers. When Mugabe took charge as a populist former freedom fighter, he inherited a nation that was the breadbasket of the region. He allowed the white farmers to develop their holdings and create food stability. Then he moved against them. He took their farms and handed them to his supporters, "his people."

His shortsighted political strategy destroyed agriculture and the economy. Today Zimbabweans are starving; eight in every ten people have no work. The economy has collapsed and inflation at more than one million percent is the highest in the world.

I am often puzzled by the complacency of the citizens of Trinidad and Tobago and the silence of the politicians and other primary definers of society on critical national issues such as this one. But perhaps I am wrong. Or maybe "we like it so."

(August 2, 2008)

One important part of Patrick Manning's political strategy was to extend his influence within the Eastern Caribbean and create a strong political and economic union with some of the lesser developed Caricom states. And he was particularly close to Grenada, which raised the question about the prime minister's intentions.

Is Manning making Grenada a colony of Trinidad and Tobago?

A report in the Trinidad Express says former Grenadian Prime Minister Keith Mitchell offered Prime Minister Patrick Manning a proposal about a year ago to make his island a "virtual colony" of Trinidad and Tobago, with Grenada getting free access to the country's education, health and transportation systems among other benefits. The offer was in a letter signed by Mitchell.

"The only thing that the letter didn't speak of having access to was the Trinidad and Tobago treasury. But, of course that was an unspoken word. But clearly we would have been in effect minding Grenada," the Express quoted one former minister as saying.

The report said certain cabinet ministers were of the opinion that Mitchell was trying to cut a deal for Trinidad and Tobago to pay its bills.

Now the same issue is on the table again.

Two weeks ago, Manning initialed a memorandum of understanding with the new Grenadian prime minister, Tillman Thomas, and the prime ministers of St Lucia and St Vincent for an economic union by 2011 and a political union two years later.

And Manning has been flying around the region, knocking on the doors of his regional counterparts to tell them about a deal that is still a big secret in Trinidad and Tobago.

At least two prime ministers — Bruce Golding of Jamaica and Dean Barrow of Belize — have told Manning they don't like the union idea.

But outside of that memorandum of understanding (MOU) involving Trinidad and Tobago and the three countries of the Organisation of the Eastern Caribbean States, Manning signed bilateral deals with Thomas during the Grenadian leader's recent two-day visit to Port of Spain.

Manning went out of his way to be cozy with Thomas, the man who had dethroned Manning's friend, Keith Mitchell, in a general election in July. Manning had openly supported Mitchell and went as far as suggesting that Thomas had planned a coup against Mitchell.

Manning sent a private jet for Thomas, who was more than eager to say there was no bad blood between him and his host. The $400,000 plane fare was not the only thing Thomas got during his 48 hours in Trinidad. In two separate MOUs with Thomas, Manning agreed to many of the things Mitchell wanted. Scholarships for Grenadians and access to Trinidad and Tobago's health care system to Grenadians, to name two.

Shortly after Thomas went home, Manning flew to Grenada, picked up Thomas and made a lightning one-day visit to three OECS states to sell the union matter. The trip also gave the two leaders an opportunity to discuss other matters of "mutual concern."

Then Grenada's finance minister announced that the country was broke. Nazim Burke said there was no money to pay civil servants and finance government operations. The treasury was bare like Mother Hubbard's cupboard and the island would have to go cap in hand for overdraft facilities to pay its way.

Neither Burke nor Thomas has said who will provide the funds for a bail out and under what terms. Which leaves the question about whether Manning and the Trinidad and Tobago taxpayers would be the benefactors.

Burke did say he has been talking with the International Monetary Fund (IMF), which is an international agency with very strict and binding rules. Few governments that want to stay in office court the IMF.

So are Manning and Thomas are now singing from the same song sheet that Mitchell wrote, offering to pawn Grenada and the future of all Grenadians to Manning for "a few pieces of silver"?

And it raises questions, too, about what really is in that larger MOU with Trinidad and Tobago, Grenada, St. Lucia and St. Vincent that Manning is hastily trying to ram through the parliament.

Government has an obligation to make sure the people of Trinidad and Tobago see that document in its entirety so there can be a public debate, not just the rushed limited exposure in the legislature where it will pass with Manning's majority regardless of what the opposition says or thinks. And it will pass in the Senate, too, because of the government's majority there as well.

The opposition has an obligation to demand that there is full disclosure and that the people of Trinidad and Tobago get a clear picture about what we are getting into and why. What is it that these countries have to offer than others don't have? And why the great rush?

Manning is on record as saying that the majority of people in Trinidad and Tobago are behind him on this, but that comment within days of signing the MOU and without the public seeing the document raises the question about the basis on which Manning is making such a judgment.

Now he is embarking on a public information exercise, which is essentially a marketing drive to sell a product that people have not seen, hoping that the fancy public relations would trap the citizens into buying "cat in bag."

Trinidad and Tobago is still a democracy. And the politicians and the media have an obligation to the citizens to do everything they can to preserve and protect it. Political and economic union might be a good thing. But it could also bad for Trinidad and Tobago. The people have a right to know the facts so they can weigh them and decide.

(August 28, 2008)

While the Manning government was moving from one misstep to the other creating the best opportunities for the opposition to benefit, the two parties — COP and the UNC — remained far apart, still going after each other instead of seeing the value in getting together to try to defeat what had become one of the most arrogant and corrupt administrations ever.

Why is the opposition giving the government a free ride?

I have asked myself over and over again why the opposition in Trinidad and Tobago remains calm while the nation burns. I have heard all kinds of lame and unfounded excuses, including a media bias. But I am always totally confused when there are critical national issues at stake and those elected to serve the people and protect their interests remain silent.

Take the latest bacchanal between Keith Rowley and his former boss, Patrick Manning. I have heard some opposition advisers dismiss the whole affair as another PNM scheme to distract attention from the real national issues.

What nonsense!

Let's look at what is happening and why the opposition should be pouncing on Manning and demanding answers.

Manning stood up parliament and admitted that there was a discrepancy involving $10 million in the Cleaver Heights Housing Development in Arima and suggested that there was some kind of collusion between the then housing minister Keith Rowley and the contractor, NH International. That is corruption no matter how you cut it, unless, of course, Manning was lying through his teeth. And if he was fabricating the story just to malign Rowley and NH boss, Emile Elias, then he is guilty of contempt of parliament.

But Manning has letters, which he says prove his case about that $10 million. Therefore, by his own admission, Manning indicted himself and his government in corruption. It is corruption because the prime minister, who presides over cabinet, who is the captain of the ship, is saying some years ago he discovered that $10 million was missing and he then promptly shut up and did nothing about it.

It is corruption because the prime minister never disclosed this to the public, never asked for a forensic audit or demanded answers from his minister, who was at time a member of the PNM tribe. See no evil, hear no evil, speak no evil. Protect the tribe.

It is corruption because $10 million of taxpayers' money remains missing and has been missing for several years. And if Rowley had remained in the club, shut his mouth and refrained from attacking Manning, the nation would have never known about it.

And here's another question. Why did Manning reappoint Rowley to his cabinet knowing that under Rowley's charge, $10 million was missing? That is the context in which the opposition needs to present this issue to the nation. And I'll bet that journalists would be more than happy to cover the story if those who run the communication and media affairs of the party are willing to do their jobs and deal with the issue.

The role of the opposition in a parliamentary democracy is to be vigilant on behalf of the people, to keep the government in check and to represent the interests of those constituents whose voices are silenced by the majority. It means taking control of the national agenda and putting critical issues on the front burner. The vigilance must not and cannot be a flash in the pan, a quick response to a singular issue or a vague press release.

It must be a continuous battle to demand accountability and transparency in government affairs, and fairness and equality for all the people, all of the time.

The opposition must also be pro-active in providing solutions to national problems and demonstrating that it is an alternative to the governing party. Sadly, with some exceptions, the opposition in Trinidad and Tobago continues to abdicate its responsibility.

And the current fiasco is a good example.

Why, for instance, is the opposition not seizing the opportunity to revisit other matters of alleged corruption and discrepancies?

Manning has opened a door for the opposition through his own vendetta with Rowley and the opposition is looking the other way. They have files on Manning and evidence of discrepancies and alleged corruption. And they have staff paid by the state to do the necessary research. So why leave Manning alone?

It is easy to blame the media for not running with the opposition agenda, but much more difficult to develop effective communication strategies to make the media notice and act. That's where the opposition is falling down and disappointing those who look to it for leadership.

Roodal Moonilal told me last year that Manning and his team of political novices is no match for the power of the opposition and predicted that Manning's government would fall long before another election is due. I have heard the same boast from Ramesh Lawrence Maharaj.

But so far, that opposition power has not rattled Manning and he continues to command the agenda while the opposition watches and waits. Like Nero, they fiddle while Rome burns.

George Bush didn't get to the White House by accident. Bill Clinton got re-elected in spite of the damning Republican inquisition about his personal financial dealings and his affair with Monica Lewinsky.

Somebody should ask why. And the opposition should wake up and do its job. To do less is to betray the nation.

(October 2, 2008)

Free speech at risk in TT?

The talk around town is that Prime Minister Patrick Manning is behind the suspension of two radio broadcasters from 94.1 FM, one of two radio stations owned by the Gillette Group of Companies. The station's Vice President of Operations denies that. O'Brian Haynes confirmed that he received a complaint from Manning but insists that the radio announcers and newscaster were suspended for breaching station policy, not for offending the prime minister.

On October 25, Manning heard a broadcast on the station while he was at a barbershop in San Fernando. The broadcasters commented on the budget and the rise of the price of premium gas. They also criticised Manning for suggesting that people should convert their cars to CNG, noting that there are serious risks associated with that.

Manning returned to Port of Spain, went to the 94.1 studios and demanded to see the manager. He subsequently telephoned Haynes and complained about the broadcast. Haynes said the management suspended the two men because they were unprofessional and breached the station's policy about news and opinion.

"A lot has been said about it. People are saying they were suspended because the PM made a report. That is not so. They both broke protocol over the manner in which the radio station delivers the news," Haynes told the Trinidad Guardian adding, "We never supported the delivery of news with commentary and opinion."

He said the men should have known better than to present their opinions within a newscast. "We were especially concerned about commentary that is highly-opinionated, since it taints the integrity of the newscast," he said. He told the Newsday newspaper he supports Manning's position that the newscast had been unprofessional journalistic behaviour. "He is right," he said.

The Media Association of Trinidad and Tobago (MATT) issued a statement on the matter saying Manning acted improperly when he went to the radio station in person to complain. In a news release, MATT president Marlon Hopkinson expressed concerns over the prime minister's actions saying it deems Manning's visit to the radio station "as inappropriate in light of the fact that it can be perceived as an attempt to intimidate or to stifle freedom of the press...The Association feels the prime minister has available to him many avenues of redress and should have perhaps considered the perception of his actions."

Hopkinson added, "MATT values, above all, an independent media operating without interference or fear, however, the association as well notes that standards of journalism must be adhered to at all times."

Opposition leader Basdeo Panday said Manning was out of line in going to the station to lodge a complaint. He said, "Such behaviour by a prime minister is undemocratic, arrogant and dictatorial at best since it tramples on the freedom of the media to perform its functions relating to scrutinising government's conduct and policies without fear."

Panday, who as prime minister didn't have the most cordial relations with the media, said Manning's behaviour was unwarranted and was an attempt "to intimidate the media for performing their role and duty of demanding accountability — particularly crucial when one considers that this government has gone to great lengths to evade accounting to the public for the $250 billion that it has spent in the last seven years."

Panday noted that there are proper avenues and methods for lodging objections to material published in the media, including writing the media house management, the media complaints council, and the Telecommunications Authority. "But speeding into Port of Spain from San Fernando to personally storm into a media house is beyond what is reasonable or acceptable. If this kind of behaviour is tolerated from the prime minister it will signal to other persons such as ministers that they too are free to assault the media whenever anyone criticises the government, and soon the media will be muzzled," Panday said. He added, "In countries where democracy has fallen, it is not uncommon for dissenting voices to be dragged out into the streets and executed. Is that where Mr. Manning proposes to take our country?" And he urged the media and the public at large to resist all attempts by the government to muzzle and intimidate them "in the pursuit of truth and free responsible expression."

(November 4, 2008)

Improve media standards, but don't curtail freedom

The government of Trinidad and Tobago is taking a professional approach to dealing with the media fiasco created by a visit to a radio station by Prime Minister Patrick Manning to complain about what he considered "unprofessional conduct" by two broadcasters who were subsequently disciplined by the management of the organisation. It has asked media icon Ken Gordon to chair a review committee on the media, primarily because of Mr. Gordon's stature not only in Trinidad and Tobago, but in the Caribbean and the wider global media community.

While I still hold the view that Mr. Manning was wrong to personally "drop in" on the radio station, I also acknowledge that media have a responsibility to be fair and accurate and, in Trinidad and Tobago, that quality is wanting among many media practitioners. However, the media must be free from fear and in that, Mr. Manning's visit sent all the wrong signals.

It is no secret that governments everywhere become uncomfortable when they are the subject of severe criticism. It's a natural reaction. But Mr. Manning's insistence that he did nothing wrong and that he was exercising his rights just as any other citizen is something the media cannot accept. He is not an ordinary citizen and whether he intended it or not, his visit sent a clear signal that he would not tolerate criticism.

Media must ensure that they accept their professional responsibility. Unless truthfulness, responsibility and a commitment to fairness and balance guide their work, the government would justify the introduction of regulatory measures to keep the media in line. And that's what media must worry most about.

Without a doubt, there is a fair amount of irresponsibility in the Trinidad and Tobago media. Too often, citizens are exposed to unprofessional conduct from a new generation of media personnel who have no regard for truth, fairness, balance or common decency. Some of what passes for journalism borders on obscenity and hate.

The government, the opposition, businesspeople, ordinary citizens have all been victims of the media onslaught; the biggest culprit in the media is talk radio. But an analysis of media content would demonstrate that there is still a fair level of professional journalism and little evidence for a government minister to suggest that the Trinidad and Tobago media are the worst in the world.

The proliferation of radio stations has caused a significant decline in broadcast and journalistic standards; some media managers are content to put anybody in front of a mic without any consideration for the tremendous responsibility the job demands.

In this context, I fully support any measure for media to improve their standards if media are to continue to be the guardians of democracy or a fourth or fifth estate. However, no government has the right to take away or infringe in any way the right of the media to operate freely. The Trinidad and Tobago constitution enshrines the right to a free press and the freedom of expression; media must accept no less.

And the government of the day must face media scrutiny of its affairs. In a democracy, the media are there to seek out the issues on behalf of the people and report on them as fairly and objectively as they can so that the people can form an informed opinion on which they can act. That's how democracy works.

Democracy can only flourish when there is a free and independent media. Every government — especially in small emerging nations such as ours — owes a responsibility to the people to ensure that they have access a free and unfettered media.

Journalism's first obligation is to the truth and its first loyalty is to the citizens. Its practitioners must maintain an independence from those they cover and must at all times serve as an independent monitor of power. Media must also accept that their role in a democratic society is to provide a forum for public criticism and compromise while maintaining a fair and accurate picture of the community they serve. And they must never forget that while they have a right to operate without government hindrance, citizens too — including politicians and the other primary definers of society — have rights that they will defend.

Media mirror society, perhaps even define an agenda, but they must never shut out dissent or allow anyone to manipulate media in such a way to prevent today's minority from becoming tomorrow's majority.

One year after Manning's 26-15 victory, do we like it so?

The world is in euphoria over the election of Barack Obama as the first African-American president of the United States. And for good reason.

This is an event that few thought possible in a nation that had defined itself, just a few decades ago as one based on racism and hate. Obama's rise to the highest elected office is the realisation of part of the dream of which Martin Luther King Junior spoke.

In the celebration taking place in Trinidad and Tobago even the media seem to have lost sight of our own political situation and the re-election of Patrick Manning one year ago.

On November 5, 2007 the people of Trinidad and Tobago voted for a change but instead handed Manning and his People's National Movement (PNM) a commanding majority, which he has used to advance his personal agenda while showing disdain for the people.

A majority of the electorate voted against the PNM, but because of the nature of the country's electoral system, Manning was returned to office with a 26-seat majority with the alliance of the United Nation Congress (UNC) and a few smaller parties winning the other 15.

Indeed, although it was officially a UNC-Alliance victory, it was the resurrection of Basdeo Panday and the UNC, aided by Jack Warner. For all the sound and fury, the new Congress of the People (COP) of Winston Dookeran, failed to make a parliamentary breakthrough.

Today, one year later, it is still chasing the dream of taking on Manning and winning. And Panday is doing the same. But beating Manning any time soon is not on the horizon, even if all the opposition forces unite.

There are many reasons for this, but perhaps the most fundamental one is the cynicism that exists today based on past experiences, particularly the quick collapse of the NAR one-love movement that swept the PNM out of office in 1986. In a way, 1986 had a tinge of the Obama rise to power. In 30 years, under Eric Williams and later, George Chambers, the PNM had come to believe that it was invincible. Divide and rule politics in our first-past-the-post, winner take all electoral system had worked well up to then.

But the grand coalition formed out of political necessity coupled with the bust from the oil boom changed the dynamics and while Arthur Robinson was no Obama, he offered the nation the simple message of hope and change. The people responded and the rest, as we know, is history.

Five years and a short-lived coup later, the PNM was back in office with Patrick Manning as prime minister. He was clearly not up to the task, making blunders and missteps that pulled down his government within four years. That sent Basdeo Panday and his UNC to Whitehall in a coalition with Robinson. Panday and Robinson got along only out of political expediency. And Panday tried to pull himself out of the political quicksand by making his coalition partner president, a move that Manning in opposition rejected outright.

By 2001, after a feud in the UNC forced fresh elections within a year of winning a majority, Robinson had his revenge and handed the government to Manning in breach of all Commonwealth parliamentary conventions. He justified his presidential coup by saying the country needed change, so he made a decision based on "morality and spirituality".

It was the opening that returned a PNM government to office with a clear majority after Manning governed for nine months without convening the 2001 parliament. Five years later, on November 5, 2007, Manning won a second majority.

So how have we fared in the past year?

Manning campaigned on a platform of continuity, presenting himself as a caring leader who put people's concerns first. He would take the country forward, he pledged, making his Vision 2020 a reality. Even before he launched the campaign, it was clear that something was wrong in the house of the PNM. Manning dumped some of his party's stalwarts, most notably Ken Valley, who went on to accuse Manning of working hard to set up a dictatorship. He kept his nemesis, Keith Rowley, out of necessity, but held him on a tight leash.

The opposition latched on to the fear of an impending dictatorship and mounted a strong campaign. In the end, the system favoured Manning and he returned to government determined to do things his way with his fresh team. His first signal to the nation that he would follow his own agenda happened in Woodford Square, the PNM sacred ground where Eric Williams "put down his bucket" and launched the party in 1956.

Manning took his oath of office in a public ceremony, ostensibly to allow the people to participate. But the people were really his people. The sea of PNM red that flooded the square had no room for the rest of the nation. It was the first of many issues in the first year of Manning's administration that sent a clear message that Manning would pave a new political path according to an agenda that put him and his priorities first.

That first act was a breach of the constitution, which states that a cabinet comprises the prime minister and an attorney general. Manning took the oath alone, and for a few hours the country technically did not have a legally constituted cabinet. Manning ignored and dismissed all criticism. And he continues to do it everyday. The most glaring example was his recent personal visit to a radio station to complain about two broadcasters who had dared to criticize him and his policies. While he has a right to complain, his commanding presence at the station with his full security detail sent a message intended to intimidate the media.

But Manning doesn't seem to care about public opinion when he controls all the apparatus of state and a treasury overflowing with windfall energy revenues. Over the past year, Manning has treated the opposition with contempt and ignored the people's concerns on crime, social services, health and public expenditure to name a few. And as the world struggles with its worst economic crisis since the Great Depression Manning and his government refuse to heed calls by the private sector and the Central Bank to show restraint.

His PNM predecessors showed the same contempt for economic advice and drove the nation to near bankruptcy following the end of the 1980's oil boom. But Manning is intent on having his way.

He refused to appoint a police commissioner selected through a rigorous recruitment process. Crime continues to plague the nation, with more than 450 homicides so far in 2008, and government's latest response is to join with evangelical preachers to cuddle criminals who choose God and pledge to give up crime. And there's more:

- He refuses to take commercial flights and travels by private jet. He even toyed with the idea of buying his own jet for half a billion dollars, backing down under public pressure although the purchase is still on the agenda.
- He is creating a political and economic union with Eastern Caribbean nations and refuses to give the people a say in the matter.
- He has built a mansion for himself for more than $140 million, has put aside $13 million for his personal entertainment budget while poverty climbs and families have no food and shelter.
- Inflation is running into double digits and he continues with business as usual.
- He is trying to impose a constitution on the nation that no one takes responsibility for writing, yet he says it's not his. Some of the measures appear to threaten the independence of the judiciary.
- He refuses to take responsibility for escalating food prices, blaming farmers and grocers. His agriculture minister went as far as saying farmers plant crops in flood-prone areas to fleece the treasury when crops are washed out.
- He refuses to address concerns about high levels of corruption under his watch and kicked out senior government minister Keith Rowley from cabinet for asking questions about government expenditure.

That's not even the tip of the iceberg. There's more. Much more. But perhaps "we like it so." And what is the opposition doing? That's a subject for another day.

(November 6, 2008)

Section 3
Challenging the status quo

Jack Warner, the rookie MP for Chaguanas West, had hoped that Panday would retire following the 2007 general election and allow the party to choose a new leader. In fact, Panday had made that pledge publicly to tens of thousands of supporters and to the country on the eve of that election. "Send me in a blaze of glory" he told an election rally in Aranguez as he asked people to elect the UNC Alliance.

However, he reneged on that and Jack was not amused. Panday reacted by accusing Warner of corruption and insisted that he would not hold long overdue internal election until after local government elections, which Manning had already postponed several times.

The rift between the two caused a breach in the party and eventually saw Jack leading a movement for change that forced the election that ousted Panday and installed Kamla Persad-Bissessar as political leader of the UNC.

Time to change, unite and save T&T: Jack Warner

UNC deputy political leader Jack Warner is determined to change things in his party and face whatever consequences follow. In a letter to supporters following Wednesday's meeting of the party's national executive, he also called for opposition unity. "It is time to change the way things are in the party so that we can change the way things are in the country," he wrote.

Warner's letter is printed below:

I attended a Natex meeting last night and my disappointment at what transpired continues to be profound. But there comes a time in everyone's life, I believe, when he or she, must make an account of himself or herself. That time has come for me in the context of what is happening in my country, the constituency I represent and the party of which I am deputy leader. My silence would not just condemn me but would also condemn the very representation I swore to uphold for the people who put their faith in me in the last general election.

I entered the realm of politics for no personal gain, since politics could give me nothing I did not already have nor sought after, neither fame nor fortune. Fame I seek not even though I am well known enough due to my dedicated efforts in the field of football and fortune has not been unkind to me as a result of a lifetime of hard work and a sound education.

But there are two features of my life that define me — a strong sense of nationalism and a genuine concern for the underprivileged. Both of these principles prompted me to enter politics as I saw the dangerous course on which Patrick Manning's PNM had placed the nation.

Since the day I made that decision, I have dedicated every fibre of my being, every ounce of my energy, every penny I could donate, all the tolerance I could muster, all the abuse and ridicule I could sustain, all the sacrifice I could make, all towards one end, to see my country back on track, saved from the precipice of disaster under the dictatorial and inept Manning administration.

But there are challenges within my own party as well if we are to regain government and rescue our beloved nation. There must be an understanding of the political dynamics playing out now. We must come to terms with the urgent need for a unification of all political forces to effect the changes so urgently required.

We must settle our own political leadership issue by the holding of internal elections so long overdue. We must come to terms with our failings that have kept us in opposition.

This is not just about the future of the party I represent, it is about the very survival of our democracy, it is about the day to day existence of every man, woman and child. There must be an alternative to what our country endures today.

Within the United National Congress we must embrace the kind of changes necessary if our goal of saving the nation is to be realised.

There is an advisory on some fire equipment encased in glass that reads "In case of emergency, break glass." That is the point we have reached. It is time to break old patterns, to formulate instead breakthrough initiatives, to recreate ourselves as a political organisation, to become more relevant, to respond to the urgency taking place in our country.

The situation has reached crisis proportions and action commensurate with the prevailing circumstances must be adopted now. I am prepared to accept the political consequences of challenging the status quo within the UNC. I have no choice.

These are desperate times we face as a nation that require desperate measures.

I will not fail the expectations of the people who trust me to do the honourable thing, I will not shirk my responsibility to my country and my constituents who ask me daily, "When are you going to unite as an opposition force with all groups opposed to the conditions in the country under Patrick Manning?"

Well, the short answer to that is that we have to confront the stumbling blocks to this and decide as a party what we must do to change our thinking and our structure. There is no time left.

I am going to personally do what I can to initiate the changes necessary. I will take the message across the length and breadth of this country. The UNC is the only political vehicle through which the changes necessary to be wrought now can be effected, but we will not achieve it alone and we will get nowhere if we continue along our current path. The world around us is changing while we remain static. It is time to move on. It is time to change the way things are in the party so that we can change the way things are in the country.

There is nothing wrong with this admission. No matter how great any movement, the need to examine and question positions and the state of being is what essentially ensures perpetuity. That process of self-examination assures that greatness is truly achieved. And it is what will assure us all that Trinidad and Tobago is finally saved.

Regards

Jack Warner | Deputy Political Leader United National Congress

(November 27, 2008)

Jack ready to hit the road if UNC refuses to change

Jack Warner is sticking to his guns on his call for change within his party and has said he is ready to walk away from the party if it refuses to make changes. The outspoken Chaguanas West MP and UNC deputy leader believes that his party is not taking the initiative to change in order to confront the governing PNM.

Warner wants the UNC to hold internal elections, stop dealing with politics of the past and move into the 21st century. He also believes opposition unity is a necessity.

However, he has made it clear that he has no quarrel with UNC leader Basdeo Panday, who has said the party will hold off on the internal election until after the local government election, which has been postponed twice and is now scheduled to mid-2009. Warner wants the election sooner rather than later but Panday insists that the party's national executive has taken a decision to defer the vote, which is generally held every two years.

Panday disagrees with Warner's contention that the party is stuck in the past and not responding to change. "In politics, when you have what is called a mass democratic party, it attracts all kinds of people, the good, the bad, the ugly, the brave, the cowards, the greedy, the hungry...it attracts everybody so you learn to live with that," he told the Trinidad Express. Panday said he will die fighting for the people and when the time comes for internal party elections, the people will decide.

Warner has never suggested that Panday should leave or that the former prime minister is the problem within the UNC. He has always been a great admirer of Panday whom he describes as the best politician in the country. But he wants Panday to use his experience to reform the party. "Let me make it very clear. I have no strife with Mr. Panday, neither inside nor outside of the party. This is not a Jack Warner versus Panday issue," he explained in an interview with the Express.

Warner said the youth of the party have been clamouring for change in the party that they see as a "dinosaur." He is convinced that the UNC's future is in attracting the youth of the nation, not just with members over 50 and 60 years of age. He claimed other UNC members share that view but prefer not to speak out publicly about it for fear of offending Panday. Warner believes a secret ballot would show an overwhelming call for change in the UNC.

Warner also dismissed rumours that he and opposition chief whip Ramesh Lawrence Maharaj are plotting to take over the party. He insists that Panday must take charge and begin the restructuring of the party before the local government elections.

"Friday after Friday I sit down and watch these boys and girls who cannot even run a parlour run this country and inside I weep. It need not be so. We have many bright people in our country and yet we have a foreigner [Calder Hart] heading major institutions in this country," he lamented.

He said he is not prepared to let that continue. "At the end of the day I will continue to call for change throughout the length and breath of the country and if my cries for change are not heeded and go unanswered, I will simply walk away into the sunset, I have no problem with that, but I will not sit down and knowingly participate in an organisation that refuses to reform itself," Warner said.

(November 30, 2008)

"Send me off in a blaze of glory"

The political Pandora's box that has brought confusion, acrimony and all manner of strife within the United National Congress (UNC) in the past is ready to be opened again. And the same manner of venom and uninformed opinion that characterised the last episode of bloodletting is making the rounds again.

Jack Warner, whose money and political savvy took the party out of intensive care just before the 2007 election and made a stunning comeback with Basdeo Panday, is the centre of attention these days. Warner has tried to effect change within the party of which he is deputy leader, without much success. He is also lobbying for unity.

In a television interview last month he laid out his concerns about what he felt was stagnation within the UNC and a reluctance to embrace change. He called for internal elections and for the party to work on uniting the opposition. His assessment was that the party has not kept pace with the changes needed to compete in the 21st century. The UNC risks becoming irrelevant if it does not embrace change, Warner cautioned.

Having read the entire transcript of that interview, I find nothing offensive in his statements. His opinions were based on his experience within the governing structure and it was clear that he was neither seeking office nor suggesting that his leader, Basdeo Panday, should go. He even reiterated his admiration for the man whom he described as the best politician in the region.

However, he was very clear that there are some people who are holding back progress and suggested that Panday should be using his experience and political acumen to guide the party forward and into the 21st century.

But suddenly, the man who single-handedly pulled the UNC out of the deep depression caused by internal bickering and the fracturing following the last internal election has become the UNC's latest neemekharam. Internet chat groups are now littered with baseless accusations ranging from ingratitude to political opportunism.

Much of what is making the rounds sounds so familiar, almost like they have come from a single template of hate and vilification. There seems to be no end to the name-calling and partisan posturing.

And the real tragedy of it all is that the two men at the centre of this contrived political battle are not at war with each other. Both men want the same thing: a better, stronger UNC ready to confront the political challenges that face the country today. And both of them have said on numerous occasions that the only way to wrest power from the governing People's National movement (PNM) of Patrick Manning is to unite the opposition.

There is a difference of opinion between them on how to get there and the pace at which the change needs to happen. Warner believes things are moving too slowly and he feels internal elections would settle the leadership issue so the party can move on. Panday is not convinced about that and has said the national executive put the internal election on hold until after the local government election which is due around the middle of 2009. But unless I missed something, I have not heard Warner call for Panday to step down or announce his intention to challenge Panday for the leadership of the party.

Panday has said repeatedly that he is no longer able to carry the torch. In the last election he announced to tens of thousands of supporters that the 2007 general election would be his last. "Send me off in a blaze of glory," he told supporters as he pleaded for a mandate to govern.

So what then is the problem?

If Panday, by his own admission and statements, has stated clearly that he is no longer interested in running, then any member of the party has the right to run for the leadership, including Jack Warner or other high-profile members like Ramesh L. Maharaj, Kamla Persad-Bissessar, Roodal Moonilal, Vasant Bharath and Kelvin Ramnath to name a few. Any floor member can do the same.

The problem is this: everyone wants change and nobody but Warner feels comfortable seeking it unless Panday himself demands it. And even when Panday seeks it, few are willing to make it happen. It seems like everybody wants to go to heaven but nobody wants to die.

That is the cancer that has eaten into the UNC over and over again. And unless it is rooted out it will emerge again and again and eventually deal the party a fatal blow. And those who say Panday is the problem have it wrong. Some people in the UNC feel that they cannot have an opinion that conflicts with Panday's and to hold an opposing view is somehow disloyal to "the chief."

But anyone who knows "the chief" also knows that he would listen to constructive ideas and consider workable solutions. What he detests is whining and negativism. That's why he and Warner brought together an alliance for the last general election. While the pundits were writing an unflattering epitaph for Panday and the UNC Panday and Warner demonstrated that the party was the most powerful opposition force in the country and that as a team they could command tremendous support.

Panday is a pragmatist and understands politics better than any politician in Trinidad and Tobago today. He has done his duty ten times over and people should let the man have the retirement he has earned, that says he craves and deserves. But they won't let him have it because his commanding presence gives them comfort.

Following the 2002 general election, he made it clear that he was leaving; he even appointed a team from within the parliamentary caucus to deal with the transition and his retirement. I know because I was present at that meeting as a member of the national executive. But nobody on that team was prepared to even discuss the change that Panday was seeking. And nobody was willing to stand up and lead. People preferred to remain stuck in their comfort zones and later even announced publicly that no such transition team was ever appointed.

Panday anointed Winston Dookeran who became UNC leader and Panday became chairman of the party. There was every reason for it to work, but it didn't.

Dissident UNC and former NAR elements immediately hijacked Dookeran and helped dictate an agenda that was in conflict with the direction in which the UNC wanted to go. Panday fought back. Warner walked away from Dookeran's side and worked with Panday to create the UNC-Alliance, which they led to a convincing victory on November 5, 2007, in spite of the new Congress of the People (COP) led by Dookeran.

People who are trying to drive a wedge today between Panday and Warner are neither ignorant of the history of the party and the relationship both men share nor just committed to creating political mayhem; they have their private agendas, which do not include the vision of both men.

Both Panday and Warner know that Panday will not ride away into the sunset. Panday remains today a most powerful fixture in the national political landscape and must help guide the UNC or a new united political movement born out of the UNC. Warner wants that too and understands Panday's role; all he's asking is for things to move more swiftly, for the party to re-brand itself in a manner that is acceptable to the nation as a viable alternative to the PNM. And he's asking for the UNC to keep its "big tent" open to embrace all those who want political change.

There is no conflict between the two men. They share the same values, the same dreams for Trinidad and Tobago and the same concerns for the nation. And they both know that a political party is built through hard work and dedication; it is not a commodity that can be traded or handed over.

In the end, the people always decide. But the people who must ultimately decide must know the truth and that, unfortunately has become the latest casualty in this partisan propaganda campaign that is doing no one any good.

And the greatest losers are the citizens who continue to look for hope and find none.

(December 07, 2008)

Can Couva North be Panday's Waterloo?

When Jack Warner's Platform for Change bandwagon rolls into Jerry Junction Friday (14 August 2009) afternoon, it would be the strongest challenge yet to Basdeo Panday and the first time Panday has ever faced such a powerful broadside from one of his own. Friday evening could be Panday's Waterloo.

Panday has been the MP for Couva North from the day he entered the House of Representatives in 1976 as the leader of the United Labour Front.

In 2000, when he was prime minister, Panday polled 14,383 votes with 79 percent of the popular vote. A year later, in his fight with Ramesh L. Maharaj and his Team Unity he dropped two percent but rose again to

14,157 votes in the 2002 election, although with a smaller percentage of the popular vote.

By 2007, however, following a prolonged internal battle that saw his anointed leader Winston Dookeran leave to form the Congress of the People (COP), Panday's support declined dramatically in the constituency that he held for decades.

He dropped nearly 6,000 votes, getting only 8,428 votes with PNM rookie Nal Ramsingh coming a close second with 5,249 votes and 29 percent of the popular vote. In the absence of the COP's Hulsie Bhaggan, who polled 4,409 votes, Panday's safe seat was at risk for the first time; he won with less than 50 percent of the popular vote.

It was a clear sign that Panday was becoming a shadow of the political warrior who fought and won countless battles on behalf the masses; the "Bloody Tuesday" hero, it seemed, had started to lose his sting. It is against this background that Warner is challenging Panday on his own turf.

In 2007, the party had risen out of intensive care thanks to the efforts of a powerful united alliance that included Kamla Persad-Bissessar, Ramesh L. Maharaj and Warner. Together with Panday, they mounted a credible campaign, proved every pollster wrong and won 15 seats. It was a remarkable recovery for a party that had risen from the ashes. But the fighting that had plagued the UNC for more than a year took a heavy toll and chased away nearly 90,000 loyal supporters.

The party lost 89,231 votes and dropped 16.9 percent in the five years between the elections. And all of it went to COP. It certainly didn't go to the PNM, which also lost 8,994 votes over the same time.

And COP did something more. Its campaign of new politics attracted a hidden constituency in addition to the disenchanted UNC and PNM supporters. Of the 148,041 votes it received, 49,816 were from "others" — those who didn't care to vote before and the young, upwardly mobile who had lost faith in the old politics of the PNM and the UNC, and were looking for a viable alternative. There were also first time voters who felt COP offered hope.

That combined constituency is still there and it's growing. And that's the one Warner is targeting, hoping that he could get the UNC to change in order to meet the challenges of the 21st century and unite all the opposition — including COP — into a single, viable alternative to the PNM. It is the UNC's ticket to Whitehall and Warner is convinced that he is holding it in his hand with the people standing with him.

Warner has taken his cue from the message in the statistics, a clear signal that something had changed in the demographics and the traditional loyalties. COP had appealed to that silent constituency as well as nearly 90,000 traditional UNC voters. He tried without success to register that message inside the party and when the UNC refused to pay attention he went public, drawing the wrath of his leader and those loyal to Panday. That has led to the current warfare, which is more intense than any political battle Panday has ever fought. Rather than walk away, Warner is going for the jugular and challenging Panday in the UNC heartland.

He already controls Chaguanas West and now he is moving in with full force into neighbouring Couva North with Panday unable to do anything about it. And if his Friday launch can attract the thousands, he expects it would send a clear signal that the 8,424 people who stained their fingers for Panday in 2007 might be having second thoughts about their MP's ability to continue to represent them and, more importantly, to lead the party.

For the first time, Panday could be facing defeat from inside.

It would be a tragedy for him and a most humiliating fall for a man who fought a valiant campaign from the trenches to Whitehall for four decades on behalf of the ordinary, dispossessed and disadvantaged.

It would be a double tragedy because when the political history is written, Panday's legacy would be obscured by the final battle for the soul of the party he founded and launched on a rainy day in 1989, inviting all to join a crusade to which people would flock not because of the colour of their skins but by the content of their minds.

(August 14, 2009)

Panday, Dookeran want independent inquiry into Bakr's affidavit

Opposition Leader Basdeo Panday wants an independent inquiry into allegations by Jamaat-al-Muslimeen leader Yasin Abu Bakr about a deal to help the People's National Movement (PNM) win the 2002 general election in return for a list of favours, including the forgiving of millions of dollars that Bakr owed the state.

The former prime minister, whom President Robinson kicked out of office in 2001, has said there is public perception of political interference in the Office of the Director of Public Prosecutions and only an independent probe would be acceptable. Panday said the opposition must be allowed to have input in selecting the people who would conduct the investigation.

He told the Express newspaper he was happy to learn that a high court judge had asked for the contentious Bakr affidavit be forwarded to the DPP, calling it "a tremendous example that gives us courage that there are some people in the judiciary who are still independent."

The Couva North MP pointed to Manning's action in blocking the appointment of the current acting DPP, who will be sworn in as a judge this week, and said it is clear that the prime minister wants to control the DPP. He said under these circumstances where Manning's conduct is being questioned and "because I know that the confidence of people in the judiciary has fallen very low" there must be an independent inquiry.

The political leader of the Congress of the People (COP) has also commented on the matter. Winston Dookeran told the paper he wrote Manning four months ago, calling on him to refute allegations contained in Bakr's affidavit. He said he got a reply from Manning saying the matter had been referred to the attorney general but since then he had heard nothing about it.

"I am very much encouraged that the matter has come back into the public focus," he said, adding that if Manning does not speak out on this, then it will create further doubts in the minds of the people. "We support the need for a probe. We look forward to it and hope that this matter would not be swept under the carpet."

Here's some of what Bakr alleges in his affidavit:

- The Jamaat-al-Muslimeen would work within the crime-ridden area to bring about a reduction in crime.
- The Jamaat would work within the poor areas in the marginal constituencies to mobilise the voting persons to vote.
- In the "ghetto" the Jamaat and its members would be responsible for developing strategies to ensure a high or higher-than-usual turnout of voters in the marginal constituencies.
- The Jamaat would publicly come out in favour of the ruling party in government and endorse the PNM party for re-election.

- The Jamaat and its members would work actively in campaigning for the PNM party in the marginal seats.
- The Jamaat would "go to the people" and ensure that they voted for the PNM party.
- The Jamaat would be responsible for ensuring the orderly implementation of social programmes in the targeted marginal constituencies.

It said the PNM leader accepted the plan and agreed to a list of Muslimeen demands, which included a promise to write off debt to the state amounting to several million dollars. Bakr claimed that once Manning won the election he reneged on the deal.

(September 13, 2009)

Time to defend our freedom

Chief Justice Ivor Archie sounded alarm bells Wednesday about the implications for the independence of the judiciary in the draft constitution that Prime Minister Patrick Manning has been selling across the country.

That alone is enough for citizens to be deeply concerned. But looking at the immediate situation, there is even more reason for worry.

The Judiciary requested $349 million to carry out its work, which includes administration and maintenance of its physical infrastructure; it got $42.5 million. What it means, according to Archie, is that many of the things that were supposed to happen in terms of improving the judicial system will have to be put on hold. "There will be no family court roll out this year without a significant supplementary appropriation ... and our ability to deliver on the refurbishment of physical facilities, especially in the magistrates' courts, is severely restricted," he noted. "We will just do the best we can, as always," Archie promised.

I find it unbelievable that the Manning government, which is spending $116 million to buy and refurbish diplomatic properties, and many millions more for state propaganda and ego-boosting mega-projects, is short-changing one of the most important arms in the administration of the nation.

A glance at where the money is going in the $44 billion budget suggests that the Manning administration is deliberately undermining the judiciary.

There are many ways to destabilise any institution. One way is to starve it of vital funds. And this is exactly what the government is doing in Trinidad and Tobago today.

The allocation of $42.5 million is small change compared to other expenditure. For example, the recent summit of the Americas cost nearly one billion dollars. The November Commonwealth Heads of Government meeting (CHOGM) will likely cost ten times what the government is giving the judiciary. Then there's Manning's $12 million entertainment allowance.

And on Tuesday the government paid $24.6 million for a property in Toronto for its consulate in Toronto — more than half of what it is giving to the judiciary. And it is yet to explain why the 2010 estimates show $46.2 million for the purchase, when the final price of $24.6 (Cdn$4.25) was set since July.

Money has been tossed around "like it going out of style," yet the one place that needs it most isn't getting it. Can this Manning government be serious about dealing with the administration of justice?

In the present constitution, the judiciary is one of three equal but separate branches of government and is independent of political influence. That is under threat today. And citizens must raise their voices to defend the one institution that offers protection for their rights and freedoms; to lose judicial independence is to lose freedom itself.

The administration's underhand method of destabilising the judiciary by providing only financial crumbs for its operation is the clearest signal yet of Manning's disdain for the judicial system and the rule of law.

And the worst is yet to come, unless the citizens of Trinidad and Tobago, the media, politicians and other primary definers in our society unite for once to defend our freedom and democracy itself.

Now is not the time to sit on the fence. Now is the time to act; tomorrow is too late!

(September 17, 2009)

Does Jeremie's "Friend or Foe" exclude PM Manning?

John Jeremie deserves no applause for his performance in the Senate on Wednesday (September 22, 2009), when he promised to go after white collar criminals and anyone who breaks the law. It's because his oratory smacks of hypocrisy.

In his quest to hunt down law breakers, be they "friend or foe," the Trinidad and Tobago attorney general promised that he would scrupulously investigate all allegations of wrongdoing. "There will be no sacred cows, Mr. Vice-President. The rule of law demands nothing less," Jeremie assured the parliament.

And he seemed so deeply concerned that two crime-busting agencies under his jurisdiction have been lethargic in dealing with white collar crime that he pledged to immediately wake them up and get them to work. Jeremie suggested that some of the nation's white collar criminals are "the very elite in this society" and appealed to citizens — patriots he called them — to show "goodwill and support...and we shall need your prayers."

Yes, he remembered to invoke the Almighty. After all, the Manning administration is one of "morality and spirituality." That's why President Robinson gave the nation Patrick Manning as a Christmas present in 2001.

While Jeremie was pontificating about his noble intentions, Jeremie was also censuring the Law Association for defending a judge who has asked for an investigation of the nation's highest elected official. Certainly the prime minister cannot and must not be above the law.

It has to do with an affidavit that was rejected by the country's highest courts. But there is one court that still needs closure on that matter and Jeremie, while talking of going after "friend and foe," is shielding his boss from public scrutiny.

Let's forget all the legal semantics and accept that the controversial affidavit is dead. But still, Manning should not be hiding behind some technicality that makes the Abu Bakr Affidavit legally irrelevant. What he should be doing — and Jeremie should be telling him this, instead of shielding him — is confronting the matter and demonstrating once and for all to the public that Bakr, an insurrectionist, is no friend of his and he doesn't have any deal with him. The nation needs to be sure of that!

We know that both men met during the 2002 general election campaign; what we don't know is what both men discussed behind closed doors. We want to give Manning the benefit of the doubt that Bakr's allegations are baseless. However, consider some developments that took place and you'll see why Manning owes the country an explanation. Getting Jeremie to shout down a judge is not good enough.

Consider the following, which have been in the public domain for years:

- Didn't Manning grant the Jamaat-al-Muslimeen land, then under pressure rescind that decision on the eve of the election?
- Didn't the Jamaat openly campaign for Manning and the PNM?
- Didn't the UNC complain of intimidation of their supporters by Muslimeen operatives during the election campaign?
- Didn't Bakr say at public meetings that he would be the PNM's security minister?
- Didn't Manning meet with gang leaders — or community leaders — and offer to appease them with lucrative government contracts?
- Didn't a judge say the URP was infested with criminals?

The list is long — very long.

Manning needs to explain all this to the people. And Jeremie would do well to end the hypocrisy and finger his boss as well. Anything less would be unacceptable.

(September 24, 2009)

Ramesh might challenge Panday for UNC leadership

Ramesh Lawrence Maharaj might be getting ready for the biggest political gamble of his career — taking on Basdeo Panday for the leadership of the United National Congress (UNC).

The former attorney general has never gone this far but his political battles with Panday led to the fall of the UNC administration in 2001 within months of the party winning its first ever election against the People's National Movement (PNM).

That came after Maharaj and UNC cabinet ministers Trevor Sudama and Ralph Maraj walked away from Panday and held discussions with then opposition leader Patrick Manning in a bid to topple the government and install Manning as prime minister.

Panday pulled the rug from under their feet and asked President Robinson to dissolve parliament and hold fresh elections, which led to the historic 18-18 tie and the installation of Manning as prime minister.

And the rest, as they, is history.

Maharaj had been unhappy with the way Panday was running things long before the 2001 election. And in the internal elections, which saw his Team Unity taking control of the national executive of the UNC, he slammed his own party's leadership for ignoring the needs of its constituents.

Panday grudgingly installed Maharaj as deputy leader, but never gave him the respect the post deserved, which only widened the growing rift between the two political heavyweights. By the time Panday announced the date of the 2001 general election Maharaj was ready for battle with Team Unity mounting a political challenge to the UNC.

Maharaj's purpose was never to win the election. He knew from the beginning that was an impossibility. What he set out to do and achieve was to cause significant damage to Panday and the UNC. He caused the UNC to lose the critical marginal seat of Tunapuna to give the PNM the extra seat for the 18-18 tie. Panday has never recovered from that although he has remained a powerful political force in the country.

After the loss of the 2002 general election, Panday reluctantly agreed to step aside and hand the leadership to Winston Dookeran who was seen as a strong uniting force with an untarnished image. But that failed because Dookeran demanded dramatic changes immediately, which Panday, as party chairman, felt were too draconian. Dookeran, who had Jack Warner as his deputy leader, eventually walked away and formed the Congress of the People (COP) and Warner embraced Panday.

The near death experience of the UNC from the internal bickering over Dookeran caused the defection of thousands of UNC loyalists to the COP. But Warner, Maharaj and a few others came together with Panday to stage an incredible political recovery that most political pundits had called impossible. However, once the UNC Alliance won 15 seats, the grumbling and bickering resumed, leading to the current Movement for Change led by Warner, which includes Maharaj and MP Winston "Gypsy" Peters.

That movement has caused former allies to draw political swords against each other and it's that demand for change that is driving Maharaj to consider a run for Panday's job.

Panday, of course, has not said if he will run in the election tentatively set for January 24, 2010 subject to final ratification by the party's national assembly.

But he has always said he responds to the people and if that is what they want, he'll run. It's interesting that Warner has never said Panday should not run and he has never suggested that he would want the leader's job. In fact he is on record as saying he would run for the post of chairman, which Panday now holds in addition to the leadership. And Warner has always said if the people choose Panday — or anybody for that matter as the UNC leader — he will work with him.

There are several possible contenders, but few Panday loyalists will consider running against the "chief."

There have been calls for some of them to do it, particularly Siparia MP Kamla Persad-Bissessar, who is one of the UNC's deputy leaders. She and Maharaj have never got along ever since Panday gave her the attorney general's post when he fired Maharaj in 2000 and subsequently appointed her as acting prime minister instead of Maharaj.

So it's possible that party insiders would push her to run if Maharaj tosses his hat in the ring. That would make an interesting race.

There is also Roodal Moonilal, who is bright and smart enough to keep his lips sealed on the fighting in the party. Deputy chairman and St Augustine MP Vasant Bharath and Caroni East MP Tim Gopeesingh are all possible contenders.

But it seems that nobody is going to make the move if Panday is running. Nobody except perhaps Maharaj, who is only "thinking" about it for now, although Kamla has been thinking about it since 2001. Maharaj has been very vocal on the need for change and has insisted that in its present state the UNC cannot win an election. But he is adamant that his fight to reform the party is not personal. "I do not regard this as a personal issue between Mr. Panday and myself. I am prepared to take on the issues in the party to ensure that the party is put in a position to win a general election," he said in an interview with the Trinidad Guardian.

The leadership of the UNC is perhaps the most critical issue facing the masses who are opposed to the PNM and the Manning administration. It is clear that Manning has given disaffected citizens more than enough reasons for a change in government, but he remains strong because of the lack of a united opposition.

Today, there are three competing political forces that have the potential to become a single, powerful entity that can topple the PNM in a free and fair election. That's why settling the UNC leadership is front and centre in deciding whether opposition unity is possible.

Panday still commands strong support among loyalists in the UNC heartland and has the backing of 11 of the elected opposition members. But there are strong divisions in the general membership about whether Panday should continue to lead. On the national level COP, which is the second major opposition party, has made it clear that it will never do business with the UNC with Panday as its leader.

That hard position is in conflict with democratic principles since it is insulting to tell the UNC membership it does not care about what they believe. They may very want to elect Panday. Warner, who leads the Movement for Change, remains a member and deputy leader of the UNC and despite his sometimes open verbal clashes with Panday, remains respectful of his leader and recognises his contribution to the nation. And he has always been careful to predicate all his calls for change with a pledge to honour the wishes of the party's membership.

No matter what happens in a UNC leadership vote, a fragmented opposition would be Manning's return ticket to Whitehall whenever he chooses to call an election, which could be much earlier that 2012.

Maharaj is not well-loved in the UNC heartland and beating Panday in an election would be extremely difficult, if not impossible. That's why he is still being cautious. The only hope for the unity is for a reconciliation with the dissidents in the UNC in an arrangement that would recognise that Panday cannot disappear from the political scene.

At the same time, Panday must accept that while his leadership might guarantee a few heartland seats such a situation would do nothing to help the very dispossessed constituents he has represented for four decades. Panday must now behave like the statesman he can be and step aside as leader and let the party nominate and elect the best man or woman to represent the UNC. Armed with such a mandate the new UNC leader can then work to unite the opposition and challenge Manning and his PNM and win.

It means a break from business as usual. People like Panday, Maharaj or Dookeran continue to have powerful roles to play. But it is an insult to the nation to suggest that there is no one competent, smart enough and willing to serve as a national leader and the next prime minister. That person is waiting and the people are ready to make their choice.

(October 10, 2009)

Who will lead UNC?

The United National Congress (UNC) is planning its much anticipated internal election for January 24 next year, having changed its rigid stand on holding the vote after the Local Government Election. There is no local election for a while so there is no justification to delay the vote any longer.

Basdeo Panday's refusal to hold the internal election was the single issue that precipitated the fallout with some key party members including deputy leader, Jack Warner, who went on to form a Movement for Change within the party with a view to preparing it to beat the People's National Movement (PNM) in a general election. But with two factions in the UNC party members would have to think carefully about their choices when it comes to casting a ballot for the leader and other party officials.

Today, it's not even clear whether the RamJack members, who are facing disciplinary charges, will be able to participate in the election or whether Panday will run for the leadership. The UNC founder, who was elected UNC Chairman in the last internal election, also holds the post of Political leader, which was handed to him by the executive after Winston Dookeran left and formed the Congress of the People (COP).

Panday has said repeatedly that he will respond to the wishes of the UNC members. If they want him to lead, he says, he will run again against anyone who wishes to challenge him for the post.

But the real issue that UNC members will have to face is whether the leader they choose will be able to topple the PNM in a general election? Sadly, Panday might not be that person. There are many who might run if the "chief" is not in the race. However, the culture within the UNC is that no one challenges Panday for control of the party and the executive. The records are clear on that. When Ramesh Maharaj and his Team Unity won control of the executive ahead of the 2001 general election, Panday was able to woo back members of the executive and take control. But winning on that score didn't return him to government. Then as it is now, there were two UNC factions. And the result was disastrous. Will 2010 be different or a repeat of history?

So the starting point in this race is not who will run but whether there can be a reconciliation before the starting gun is fired.

Warner believes reconciliation is the most sensible thing, because common sense shows that a divided opposition is a gift to the PNM. Just look at the history of Trinidad and Tobago's politics, especially the 2007 general election, when the PNM won a strong majority with fewer votes that the combined opposition.

Panday is a coalition builder. He got into Whitehall in 1995 with a formal coalition with his political foe, A.N.R. Robinson. He is a pragmatist who believes that politics has a culture of its own and he is on record as saying that he would "sleep with the devil" if necessary. The fact that he has survived in politics for more than four decades — including six years as prime minister — is testimony to his political brinkmanship.

So what really would be Panday's move? He must know that a fractured party is not a winning option. Yet he is holding fast to his position on the "dissidents" and insists that there is nothing to reconcile. His position is that Warner et all have broken the party rules and that they and others who violate those rules must face the consequences. In that context, he believes that people like Jack Warner and Ramesh Maharaj cannot continue to be members of the party unless they accept the UNC's disciplinary process.

He said the same thing about Ramesh in 2001 and embraced him again in 2007.

The RamJack group doesn't buy the legality of the disciplinary action against them, which could lead to their expulsion. Warner is not worried about the charges against him because as far as he and his legal team are concerned, they are without merit.

That would suggest that Maharaj could be considering the biggest gamble of his political career — challenging Panday for the leadership of the party. The Tabaquite MP has not said if he will do so, only that he might consider it. His past deeds as leader of Team Unity is a blemish that would make his bid extremely difficult if not impossible.

What of the others?

There is a strong lobby for deputy leader and Siparia MP Kamla Persad-Bissessar to run for the leader's job. And there are others who might think their time has come — people like Roodal Moonilal, deputy chairman and St Augustine MP Vasant Bharath and Caroni East MP Tim Gopeesingh. But they are unlikely to get in the race with Panday trying to reach the finish line too.

And that's why the party needs to call a truce among its leaders and become one party again. That is, if it is serious about returning to Whitehall. If it can't do that, the whole internal election issue could be a charade that won't get the party any closer to removing the PNM.

Why?

Because there is a substantial following for the RamJack movement and because the other strong political party — the COP — wants nothing to do with a UNC under Panday's leadership. The leadership of the UNC, therefore, is perhaps the most critical issue facing the masses who are opposed to the PNM and the Manning administration.

It is clear that Manning has given citizens more than enough reasons for a change in government, but he remains strong because of the lack of a united opposition.

Today, with three competing political forces that have the potential to become a single, powerful entity that can topple the PNM in a free and fair election, there is a splendid window of opportunity for change.

A united opposition is indeed a strong possibility if the UNC can behave in a mature and professional manner that would demonstrate to all that it can be an alternative government. Panday still commands strong support among loyalists in the UNC heartland and has the backing of 11 of the elected opposition members. But there are strong divisions in the general membership about whether Panday should continue to lead.

It is time to look forward not for political expediency, but for the future of Trinidad and Tobago.

(October 13, 2009)

Warner, Dookeran keep unity flame ablaze

Jack Warner and Winston Dookeran are getting closer, following their recent breakfast "love-in" in Port of Spain to rekindle their political relationship. In a media release on Wednesday (October 13, 2009), Warner's office said the Chaguanas West MP and the leader of the Congress of the People (COP) will share a platform on Sunday at Divali celebrations in Felicity. Dookeran will deliver the feature address at the event.

The relationship between both men had been strained for years. The problems started shortly after Dookeran and Warner ran on a single ticket in the last internal election of the United National Congress in which Dookeran was elected UNC leader unopposed and Warner won one of the three posts of deputy leader.

UNC leader Basdeo Panday had stepped aside and personally nominated Dookeran for the top party post, but tension between Dookeran and the national executive led to a formal break, with Dookeran leaving the UNC and forming the COP.

Warner disagreed with that move and embraced Panday instead and in the 2007 general election he and Panday ran a joint campaign as leaders of the UNC Alliance. But since then the relationship between Panday and Warner had grown cold.

Last month, Dookeran and Warner met in Port of Spain for what Warner called "a love scene". It was the first time in three years that the two men embraced each other publicly. They agreed to meet again in an attempt "to fashion a common understanding on certain key political issues."

The release said Warner, who is in Cairo, Egypt attending the FIFA Under 20 World Cup, was elated to learn that the COP leader had accepted his invitation to deliver the feature address. "When my constituency decided to host the third annual celebrations, I immediately contemplated on having Mr. Dookeran deliver the feature address. Subsequent to my first meeting with him last month, scores of my constituents had urged me to continue talks with him as they felt that positive political objectives could be derived. He was therefore the obvious and instant choice to speak to the people of Chaguanas and wider Trinidad and Tobago on the auspicious occasion of Divali," Warner said.

He noted that it would be "something of a homecoming" for Dookeran who was MP for the area before the UNC's Hulsie Bhaggan defeated him. In 2007, Warner ran against the Manohar Ramsaran, who had defected to COP, and won a landslide.

Warner believes it's time to put past battles behind and move on. "I am positive that his message would be well received and that it could lead to bigger and brighter things in the future," Warner said adding that he intends to speak to Dookeran about scheduling future meetings to begin to "strategise on a political formula to defeat the PNM in the next election."

(October 14, 2009)

Warner urges constituents to work for unity to destroy Ravanas of T&T

Jack Warner told his constituents on Sunday (October 18, 2009) the cultural diversity of Trinidad and Tobago's plural society constantly serves as a reminder of the many opportunities that exist to build a great and powerful nation. And he said he is privileged because he sees the potential in the diversity "which can be used to unite us."

Warner was speaking at a Divali celebration in Felicity in his Chaguanas West constituency and sharing the stage with Congress of the People (COP) leader Winston Dookeran, who delivered the feature address.

Warner noted that the key message of Divali is one which celebrates the victory of good over evil, right over wrong, light over darkness and wisdom over ignorance.

He called them themes that offer "courage, hope and confidence as we anticipate a brighter tomorrow" and told his constituents their greatest contribution to nation building has been the refining of the moral fabric that is provided in Hindu folklore.

"From your own teachings, it is clear that you have understood that to educate a man in mind without morals is to create a menace to society. So patiently, through your teachings and your scriptures you have provided stories and images which have influenced behavioural patterns not only within your religious enclave but also throughout our national community," he observed.

The UNC deputy leader said there is a need in Trinidad and Tobago today for a spiritual awakening, "a renaissance that would give birth to many Lord Ramas...[to] rid our society of the Ravanas of Lanka who are among us to plunder, pillage and rob us of a good life." He noted that the "Ravanas" are in different forms causing mayhem and death on the nation's highways, depriving citizens of "the basic amenities in life like water, a roof over our head, food to place on the table and a secure nation in which we can live."

In a clear reference to the Manning government, Warner said, "The Ravanas rape our treasury and create debts which our children and our children's children would never be able to repay, sentencing them to long periods of poverty; our future is threatened."

He said if ever there was a need for a Lord Rama to emerge again it is now. "Lord Rama was that beacon of hope who fearlessly challenged wrongdoing and the darkness that covered the land. And though it seems as though darkness always preceded light, what is clear is that when light appeared darkness was removed; today as we celebrate Divali it has to be with the hope that the victory of light over darkness will continue to remain a constant struggle for us until we win."

He urged the nation to "ask Lord Vishnu, of whom Lord Rama was an avatar, for wisdom and knowledge to be the light not only in the communities where we live but the national community of Trinidad and Tobago."

Warner said, "As a nation, we can no longer be content to eat and see our brother starve. As a people, we can no longer be satisfied because crime is not on our doorstep but in someone else's home. As true Hindus, we can no longer participate in breaking down others and building up our own. These motifs are not located in the celebration of Divali and it is your dharma, your duty to ensure that the message of good, light, wisdom and righteousness is never left isolated but becomes the clarion call that will influence our people to move to higher ground."

He added, "Lord Rama is on his way, moving among us and through us, to be beacons of light to illuminate this darkness which has engulfed us. Let the lights provide a vision for change. It is for us to accept the challenge and make the change. It is for us not to be a part of the problem but the solution that would bring an end to ignorance, expel the darkness and allow good to reign over evil."

(October 19, 2009)

Dookeran praises Warner, launches new search for political unity

Congress of the People (COP) leader Winston Dookeran said on Sunday (October 19, 2009) Jack Warner is an exemplary politician and a true patriot who loves Trinidad and Tobago.

He was speaking at a Divali celebration in Warner's Chaguanas West constituency. Warner had invited the COP leader to share the stage with him and deliver the feature address.

In acknowledging Warner's gesture, Dookeran said he was humbled by the invitation and reminded his audience that it was in Chaguanas 25 years ago that he started his political career, winning a seat for what was then the United Labour Front (ULF). He said while Warner and others spoke at the function on behalf of their constituents he would speak for the entire country since he holds no seat in parliament.

But first he showered praise on his host. "I salute him [Warner]as an exemplary parliamentarian and a true patriot of our country. I know Jack Warner loves Trinidad and Tobago." And then he shifted to his message of unity, saying Divali offers the ideal opportunity to talk about such a subject. He said Hindus believe that there is a bit of the Divine in each one of us in the form of the soul or the Atma.

"My message to you tonight is to use the bit of divine power inside each one of us to sustain harmony and unity of purpose among our people, and in the politics of our land," he said, adding that he found the true search for unity in the pages of the Ramayana. "In this epic poem, we see how the structure of unity and character leads to a decisive victory of the divine man. It took fourteen years, and was at all times sustained by truth," he said, referring to Rama's banishment from his kingdom and his triumphal return after exile.

"The Ramayana centres on the principle of unity in diversity, arguing that otherwise there will be constant restlessness in society. The restlessness in the politics of our society today is because our leaders have severely violated the principle of unity in diversity," he said. Dookeran added, "We see this visibly in government, in our parliament and in our political parties. This is why the COP is founded in unity in diversity and is opened for all of the people of Trinidad and Tobago."

The former central bank governor said citizens must never fear the future but must instead work together to shape it through unity. "Our politics must not promote racial divisions, nor must we, the people become victims in our own society. It is unity of purpose and unity in diversity that protects the world, and secures an enduring freedom for our nation," he said.

The COP leader said the restlessness in the nation's politics must stop, adding that "the recklessness must come to an end, and reason must now come to the fore, with a sense for the future. Tonight, I start that journey with you again, for yet another time, as we tap that bit of divinity in each one of us to bring a oneness between unity and character in the politics of our country. I know the road is dangerous ahead, but I also know if we do not take it, the danger ahead will be even greater as the nation plunge into permanent crisis." Dookeran offered guidelines for taking charge of the future:

- we must not fear the future
- we must be brave and courageous
- we must create that future

He said, "Unity of the people we can. Unity of the people we will. Unity of the people we must. For the unity we seek, we must find common ground, but common ground is not all we need."

He explained that in seeking unity "we must also seek higher ground" and reiterated that the nation and its leaders must remove race from politics so that "the unity we seek would move the nation into action." Dookeran said he looks forward "to starting the journey of unity" for yet another time. "Once it was at Reinzi complex, then it was, in the midst of booing at Centre Mall, Chaguanas on February 19, 2006, and now it is here at Marchin Village, in the constituency of Chaguanas West," he said.

(October 19, 2009)

It's time to end battles and unite to win the war

Anyone who believes Tuesday's (October 20, 2009) decision to drop all charges against the RamJack trio did not have the blessing of Basdeo Panday must be truly naive. Nothing happens in the United National Congress (UNC) without his approval.

I have worked with him as a communication consultant when he was prime minister and when he was outside of government. And my experience is that he listens to valid suggestions and acts on them if he can see good value. He also knows when it's time to close the book.

In this context, while he is silent on what took place, it is clear that certain power brokers and advisers would have sat down with him and convinced him that this is the way to go. His sojourn overseas always allows him to sort out such matters.

And if this is indeed what has happened, then there is hope yet that the UNC can rise again in partnership with other opposition parties to be the vehicle to remove the People's National Movement (PNM) from office.

The danger, however, is that some people can see this as an opportunity to pounce on the UNC leader and continue a campaign to kick him out of the party that he and a few dedicated supporters launched more than 20 years ago.

Panday is a good deal maker, and after more than four decades in politics — both in government and in opposition — his political smarts are needed in any movement. He is no doubt ready to retire, but if people push him, he will fight back as he has done in the past.

When his party lost the 2002 general election, he made it very clear at a caucus at which I was present that he was tired and needed to retire. He went so far to establish a committee to handle the transition and select a new leader. But that committee never functioned and never made any attempt to carry out its mandate. One member told me that I was foolish to believe that the "chief" was serious about leaving. However, despite the non-performance of that committee, the "chief" did leave and literally handed over the party to Winston Dookeran. And my guess is he may be ready again to trust someone else to carry the torch, if he is sure that person is the right leader.

Today, the best political move that the UNC can make is to embrace the platform for change, clean up its membership list, court new members and have an open election in which anyone can run. In these days of unprecedented accusations of corruption, transparency and accountability are qualities that would attract hordes of new members.

There is nothing in Jack Warner's Platform for Change that is in conflict with the UNC's mission and vision; indeed, it is written as a UNC document and praises the leader for his contribution to nation-building. And it urges unity with other political movements. Tuesday's move by the party's national executive is a quantum leap forward. Now it needs to take the second giant step and unite for the significant battle ahead.

On the other side, the RamJack team must also show its willingness to stand by its declared aim of rebuilding the party and returning it to Whitehall. The most unproductive development from this would be for RamJack to trumpet it as a great victory and to allow its supporters to try to demonise Panday. Whatever anybody might say or do, Panday still commands support among a small, but dwindling constituency of the UNC heartland.

Those who support him are watching and won't allow anyone to trample on the only leader they have known and supported for 40 years.

The people are ready to change their government, if only because of the UDeCOTT scandal which is the worst to ever surface. It's so bad, we are seeing today an open confrontation between the prime minister and a former senior PNM cabinet minister who is appealing to his own party to fight against corruption.

It's almost a perfect political storm waiting to sweep away the PNM, but only a united opposition can hope to benefit from it. The Congress of the People is ready to talk unity and change. The signals from Rienzi are also positive. The only matter that needs to be settled is who will lead.

Warner has said he would stand with any leader so long as the membership elects that person in a free and fair election. If the politicians and their supporters truly want to work to save the nation, then they have to seize this opportunity and move forward. It's time to summon the troops to prepare for victory.

(October 21, 2009)

PM Manning says Rowley was not fired over UDeCOTT

Prime Minister Patrick Manning told the House of Representatives on Monday (October 19, 2009) that he fired Diego Martin West MP Dr Keith Rowley for his behaviour, not because he was critical of UDeCOTT, the Urban Development Corporation of Trinidad and Tobago. When he fired Rowley he used the term, *wajang*. "It is behaviour. People must learn how to behave. That's the problem," Manning said.

Manning made the statement in response to a claim by Tabaquite MP Ramesh Maharaj, who had said the prime minister fired Rowley and former Arouca South MP Camille Robinson-Regis because of their criticisms of UDeCOTT.

The exchange came during debate in the House on a bill to validate the work of the Uff Commission of Enquiry. Manning said he wants to stay clear of "the ole talk" on the matter. "If there is a commission of enquiry, the attitude of the government is to let the commission do its work and when the commission makes its findings, the government will take whatever action it considers appropriate. That is the position of the government," Manning said. And he insisted on correcting "the mischief of the member for Tabaquite, and that is that the government was taking a particular position vis-a-vis UDeCOTT."

The prime minister said, "What the government was saying was that on the basis of no evidence at all, individuals in this parliament were calling for this enquiry when there was no basis for it." He said once the government determined that there was a basis for an inquiry, he agreed to establish the probe, noting that his government has been consistent on the matter.

Manning had used parliament as a platform to cast aspersions on Rowley, asking him to explain a $10 million discrepancy in the government's Cleaver Heights housing project, which was handled under Rowley's watch when he was housing minister.

In his contribution to the debate, Rowley demanded that the Uff commission fully examine the controversial project so that he could get his "good name back from the prime minister...The PNM is on trial." Rowley noted that it was one of his lawyers who discovered that the government had failed to gazette the inquiry as required by law. It was because of that omission that the validation bill was before the House. The former cabinet minister said he wants the inquiry to be saved so it could complete its work and in particular, examine the details of the Cleaver Heights project. He also wants to know how the personal fax number of UDeCOTT executive chairman Calder Hart ended up on the rubber stamp of the contractor who first won the $368 million contract for the Ministry of Legal Affairs Building-CH Development.

(October 20, 2009)

Manning calls Rowley "a raging bull"; defends UDeCOTT

Prime Minister Patrick Manning launched a scathing attack on Diego Martin West MP Dr. Keith Rowley in parliament Wednesday (October 21, 2009), saying when Rowley faces opposition he behaves like a "raging bull." Manning was on the floor of the House of Representatives for the debate on the UDeCOTT validation bill, which passed with unanimous support.

But it was Rowley who was on his mind. And his contribution was a direct attack on the MP, who on Monday made an impassioned plea to members of his own party to stand up against corruption in the People's National Movement (PNM). Rowley told the House of Representatives his mission is to break the mould of corruption in the PNM, adding that those who defend UDeCOTT are adding to the damage to the PNM.

"There are strong forces that are making it their duty to make sure this Commission of Inquiry does not succeed," he charged. He said that by passing a validation bill "we are validating the hope to save the PNM. We of the PNM, other than anybody else in this country, have a particular interest in this matter...the PNM is on trial!"

In his response to Rowley, Manning said he had to "suffer" from his cabinet colleague's bullying for 12 years, going back to the time Rowley ran against him for the leadership of the PNM. "The minute you oppose my good friend, he gets very, very angry. And if you oppose him strongly, he becomes a raging bull...You don't know the trouble I have seen. I have had to live with that for 12 years," Manning said. The prime minister said he had enough of it and fired Rowley last year for that kind of behaviour. That decision, he said, also served as a lesson to the new cabinet members.

"Mr. Speaker, we do not tolerate bullying in the secondary school system. And we not tolerating bullying in the cabinet. And if the member for Diego Martin West wishes a cabinet in which bullying is the order of the day, he is going to have to form that cabinet himself. It ain't going to happen in this one. We not tolerating it!" Manning declared. He presented the House with a photo of Rowley, saying it was a snapshot of a man full of hate. "I see hate, bitterness, acrimony, animosity and, Mr. Speaker, I see a man completely out of control."

Rowley sought permission for the prime minister to give way so he could ask a question: "I would just like to ask him the name of the brand that he was drinking, so that I could avoid it," Rowley said.

Manning was quick to reply with biblical references.

"Mr. Speaker, the brand from which I was drinking was the Holy Bible... If I appear to be drunk, I am drunk on God and love," as he snapped at Rowley for suggesting that Manning's reference to the Bible was blasphemy. "Yuh believe you are a God? Yuh not God, yuh know," Manning said. He insisted on quoting from the Bible, saying when the PNM was preparing its candidates for the last general election, it discussed Corinthians, chapter 13, which speaks of the power of love. He said the only candidate absent from that session was Rowley, so he seized the opportunity to preach to Rowley and the House.

"Since he didn't hear it then, I want him to hear it now... 'If I could speak all the languages of earth and of the angels but didn't love others, all I would be is a noisy gong or a clanging symbol.' How did my friend sound on Monday? Noisy gong, clanging symbol?" Manning asked. He said hate is impairing Rowley's judgment as he went on to defend Calder Hart and UDeCOTT.

He relied on two UDeCOTT media releases, in which Hart and his wife denied any interest or involvement in a $367 million contract awarded to CH Development. He said UDeCOTT also stated that no member of the Hart family was involved in the award of the contract. Manning said both Rowley and the opposition have ignored the denials and are claiming there is a relationship between Hart and CH Development based on the word of a jilted lover, a reference to Carl Khan, the former husband of Hart's wife.

"It is not really Calder Hart and UDeCOTT. They want the prime minister and the government of Trinidad and Tobago. That is what they after. And they cannot understand how we ain't fall yet. And let me tell you, we shall not fall."

(October 22, 2009)

UNC delegate tells Panday step aside and let Kamla lead

Kamla Persad-Bissessar got an enthusiastic endorsement on Sunday (October 25, 2009) from members of the United National Congress (UNC) at the party's national congress at the Rienzi complex in Couva, Central Trinidad.

One member from the floor called on UNC political leader Basdeo Panday to step aside and let Persad-Bissessar lead the party. The delegate, who was identified only as "Abdul," told Panday to hand the leadership over to deputy political leader Kamla Persad-Bissessar on an interim basis until internal elections are held.

"There is only one person who I think could take this party to victory," Abdul said. "Mr. Chairman, I am sure that almost everybody in this hall today supports what I am saying. I think it is high time that we give Kamla Persad-Bissessar a chance... If there is any doubt, because, Mr. Chairman, you always say that you would listen to the wishes of the people, if there is any doubt about what I am saying, you could pass a ballot here today and let there be a secret vote and you would see what I am saying.

"It is not that I love Mr. Panday less, but I love this party more...this has nothing to do with you or Mrs. Persad-Bissessar. This has to do with... the members of the party, and getting into government," Abdul said.

Panday thanked him for his comments and promised that his observations "would be taken into consideration."

The UNC Congress later endorsed a resolution for internal party elections to be held on January 24, 2010 and Panday told reporters the vote would present the opportunity for all party members to say who they want for their leader. He was still ambiguous about whether he would seek the leadership, only stating that he would run if he gets nominated but added, "I may not get nominated."

Persad-Bissessar was careful not to say much about the support she got from the floor. "That is the view of one member here today," she told reporters, "Certainly it is not the view of everyone out there. This is a democracy."

She acknowledged that there was hearty applause from the audience, but the UNC deputy leader was not making a big deal of the endorsement. "I'm sure I have some fans," she said.

Like Panday, she was not saying if she would run, adding that she would leave that decision for later after consultations with her constituents. She seemed to offer a compromise on unity somewhere between Panday's rejection of COP's call to dissolve the UNC and join COP and a move for a united opposition. Persad-Bissessar said a united opposition is the only vehicle that would allow the country to go forward and remove the PNM.

"As Mr Panday said today, unity doesn't mean one party dissolving ... into the other. There are various forms of unity," she said, adding that there can be unity on the issue of property taxes and crime. "There would be obstacles. We would go backward and forward, but we would never stop trying to unite everyone together to defeat the PNM," she stated.

Persad-Bissessar is one of three deputy leaders of the UNC and heads a special committee appointed by the UNC national executive to try to unite all the opposition groups. In that regard, she has already made a deal with one political grouping headed by former UNC Alliance candidate for Chaguanas East, Dr. Kirk Meighoo.

In July, with the executive's blessing, Persad-Bissessar attended a meeting of the Congress of the People (COP) at the invitation of COP leader Winston Dookeran, but during her speech, some COP members booed when she mentioned Panday's name, saying "No Panday, no Panday."

COP's deputy leader Prakash Ramadhar subsequently apologised on behalf of the party. The UNC invited Dookeran to Sunday's congress as a reciprocal move, but Dookeran sent two senior members of the party to represent COP.

One week ago, he appeared on a joint platform with Chaguanas West MP Jack Warner at a Divali celebration in Felicity and pledged to reopen his mission to unite the opposition. Commenting on the unity process, Persad-Bissessar said a dialogue with opposition groups is continuing, adding that there is common ground that is being explored.

(October 26, 2009)

Dookeran slams gov't; talks of Panday-Manning alliance

Winston Dookeran delivered a powerful speech Tuesday night (October 27, 2009) at a Congress of the People (COP) public meeting at Asja Boy's School in San Fernando, in which he delivered a scathing attack on UNC leader Basdeo Panday and drew a political connection between Panday and Prime Minister Patrick Manning.

The COP leader referred to Panday's comments a few days ago about COP not having any seats in parliament and used it as an opportunity to present COP as the political vehicle to speak not for a single constituency but for all of Trinidad and Tobago.

And he also offered a report card on the Manning administration's poor performance since it was returned to office in 2007. Dookeran also gave a political lesson on governance and the role of a prime minister, who he said must:

- preside over the development of the country;
- preside over steps that will improve the quality of life for the people;
- preside over the provision of basic amenities so that the people would have a decent life;
- preside over creating a civilisation that is better than the one that existed before taking office.

He said on all scores Manning has failed and instead of getting a better, more progressive society, Manning has given the nation a criminal industry "that is larger in its growth than the whole economy." Dookeran said, "Today we know we cannot walk the street with any sense of comfort... So this prime minister has presided over the escalation of criminality in this land and the breakdown of law and order in this society and you know what makes it worst, he is happy about it."

The former planning minister offered a glimpse of what he would offer the nation as prime minister:

- create a better society to make sure that the underprivileged have a better deal;
- start to end the cycle of poverty;
- a programme of action to increase the empowerment opportunities for the young;
- opportunities for large and small businesses.

Dookeran accused the Manning government of stealing people's pensions while allocating more and more money for so-called poverty reduction programmes. "They are using the money in the name of poverty in order to create clients of the state and vote banks for all times," he said.

The former Central Bank governor pointed to World Bank statistics that show Trinidad and Tobago at number 81 in business competitiveness among 183 countries and at the bottom — number 183 — when it comes to enforcing contracts. Dookeran said contrary to what the government preaches, its policies are creating under development, not taking the country forward.

The COP leader saved a portion of his speech for dealing with former Prime Minister Basdeo Panday. He said Manning and Panday are "gatekeepers" of two traditional political groupings. "One of them holds the view that their main support, which is mainly Afro-Trinidadians, will always vote for them regardless, because they have the power of the treasury in their hands and that is what they hold on to.

"And the other gatekeeper who believes, not that the Indians support him but that the Indians owe it to him to support him, that he must get their votes because they are now the victims of what the government does," he said.

He said anyone who pays close attention to Manning would hear him defending "the PNM and UNC against the attack of RamJack and Rowley." He suggested that Manning betrayed himself and the secret is out that he wants to prop up the UNC because "the presence of the UNC is important for the retaining of power by the PNM."

He continued the connection by referring to Panday's support for an executive president. "He used some words about conditions under which he will support it, which we know can always change — but there were some coded messages that were passing through parliament and Rienzi.

"In parliament the prime minister was saying that I will defend you in the UNC and I will defend the PNM; we shall not fall — meaning the UNC and the PNM. And Mr. Panday returns the favour and says thank you very much, I will now support the executive presidency in Trinidad and Tobago," he said, calling the charade high level diplomacy.

"Their interest now is the preservation of their gatekeepers' position. So they are saying, you give me this and I will give you that and we will stay together," he said.

Dookeran said Trinidad and Tobago is a dynamic country and the arrival of COP on the political landscape increased that dynamism, moving it to a higher level.

He said, "The gatekeepers cannot hold back their flocks — whatever flocks they feel they have — because there is now a new political organisation that is expansive, open and flexible that is bringing all the flocks together under the COP for a new Trinidad and Tobago."

He dismissed as a "myth" suggestions that COP cannot win the support of the grassroots supporters. He said COP has been meeting the people, helping them through clinics and other outreach programmes, demonstrating that "we want to bring people together, not divided by race, not divided by geography, not divided by anything else."

He predicted that COP will bring about a renaissance in the politics of Trinidad and Tobago.

(October 29, 2009)

Manning and Panday meeting because they need each other

Basdeo Panday's meeting with Patrick Manning Tuesday (November 3, 2009) has raised eyebrows across the political spectrum and some commentators are wondering why the two are meeting now.

There are good reasons. Both men are facing revolt from top members of their own parties and both of them have been talking publicly about constitutional reform, which ostensibly is the subject of Tuesday's consultation between the prime minister and the leader of the opposition.

On first glance there is nothing unusual about it. The constitution allows for regular consultations between the holders of the two offices and Panday and Manning have met before to discuss law and order, following which the opposition supported anti-crime legislation.

Would Tuesday's meeting bring a similar deal, this time on the constitution? That's hardly likely, given their respective positions on the issue. If each holds firm on his positions on constitutional reform there is bound to be deadlock.

For instance, Panday wants a unicameral parliament, proportional representation (PR) and an executive president elected by the people in a one-person-one-vote system. Panday also wants a guarantee that the judiciary would remain independent of political influence and he rejects the Caribbean Court of Appeal as the country's final court.

Manning refuses to even think of PR, insists on a Justice Ministry — which, critics say, would compromise judicial independence — and he wants an executive president elected on a system similar to the U.S. electoral college model. There is little room for compromise, but then again it depends on how badly they need each other. And that could change the situation dramatically.

The worst kept secret is that Manning is facing a revolt in his party, which has been building since he kicked out Keith Rowley from cabinet. That dissident movement is growing bolder daily and Manning is worried that a palace coup is in the making. The only way to smash it is to go back to the people for a fresh mandate, leaving out all those who are fighting him. But can he risk that?

In the opposition camp, Panday is facing his own revolt from the RamJack team that is gaining strength and seems to be moving toward an alliance with COP, the Congress of the People.

Both Manning and Panday seem to be rapidly losing political friends, so perhaps the best deal is for them to become best friends, which is what COP leader Winston Dookeran has been saying.

But what can they offer each other? Plenty.

Manning can cut a deal to help out the Hindu Credit Union (HCU) with the hope that tens of thousands of HCU depositors, who are in the heartland of Panday's United National Congress (UNC), might be grateful and embrace Panday.

Panday can return the favour by supporting a modified constitution with an executive president. The dilemma, however, is that some of his faithful MPs are dead set against Manning's constitution and there's the risk that he could lose their support. Most notable among them is deputy leader Kamla Persad-Bissessar, who is being touted as Panday's successor.

If both men can make a deal, Manning could gamble with a snap election and hope to win enough seats to get close to the magic number of 32 MPs, and Panday could deliver the other votes to make the constitution pass.

The catch is this: Would Manning go to an election under current conditions? If he does, would the Rowley team fight him and not an election? Can Panday find the funds to mount a campaign and can he convince voters that he's their best hope?

No matter how you look at it, both men are on the ropes and they need each other badly. The problem they both face is what formula they can find to survive and fight another day. And that is the only reason why they are meeting.

How I wish I could be a fly on the wall!

(November 03, 2009)

Opposition political games hurting T&T

I have followed Trinidad and Tobago politics as closely as I can from Toronto, relying largely on media reports and to a lesser extent on the political connections I have maintained since leaving home many years ago.

And I get the impression that while there is obvious discontent in the Manning government, there is very little anger or desire to upset the status quo beyond much of the predictable political rhetoric.

While a perfect political storm has been building for a long time that could sweep the Manning administration out of office, the opposition seems oblivious to that reality. And apart from random bursts of enthusiasm to demonstrate that its elected members are not comatose, there is little to give the citizen hope that change is on the horizon.

The United National Congress (UNC), headed by its founding leader Basdeo Panday, its offspring, the Congress of the People, led by former UNC political leader Winston Dookeran, and the RamJack group, led by Chaguanas west MP Jack Warner, are all presenting themselves as the logical alternative to the People's National Movement (PNM). But none has demonstrated a clear agenda for change that is attracting mass excitement or presenting hope for the suffering masses.

In other words, there is nothing on the political horizon to suggest that Manning is in any imminent danger of losing his mandate. If fact, if he were to call an election soon, he might very well get the constitutional majority he so desperately craves.

It's because there are mixed signals from the COP and the UNC. On the one hand, Panday is saying he is ready to talk about uniting all the groups opposed to the PNM and has even sent letters inviting Dookeran to meet. But at the same time he has told COP it is impertinent to suggest that the UNC must merge with the UNC.

For his part, Dookeran, who initially re-launched his "unity" effort to do what he once failed at, is now connecting the political dots to draw a picture of intrigue involving Manning and Panday in an endgame destined to deal a fatal blow to COP and install Manning as an executive president without even giving the people an opportunity to have a say in the matter.

Another part of the equation is the dissident UNC group led by Warner that insists that it will stick with the UNC and re-invent it as the political vehicle to save the nation. Warner hopes to reestablish himself and his change agenda in the UNC and from there, build a strong united opposition alliance to crush the PNM.

But Panday and the UNC establishment are keeping the RamJackers out for now, while Warner is keeping the threat of legal action in his back pocket for use if necessary.

There are those who still believe that simple arithmetic would have changed the political equation and they still point to the results of 2007 to explain their theory that had COP heeded Panday's eleventh hour call for an alliance, the combined effort would have put Manning out of office.

That argument doesn't stand up for one principal reason: the bulk of defectors from the UNC to COP were tired of the way the UNC was running its affairs under Panday's leadership, and the new and hidden voters that COP attracted were also no fans of the UNC and Panday.

A merger of COP and UNC would have likely created a devastating blow to the opposition and probably handed Manning a stronger victory since many of the 148,000 who voted for COP would have either stayed at home or considered voting for the PNM.

Panday is going to run again to be the leader of the UNC, and if those who support him behave like they have always done, the "chief" would be re-elected unopposed.

All the talk about Kamla Persad-Bissessar challenging Panday is just talk. While she would love nothing better than to lead the UNC, she is smart enough to know that she cannot challenge the "chief". It's just not done. Nobody has ever done it.

So voters who want an alternative to the PNM will get Panday leading the UNC because the RamJack team, with all its advertised muscle and professed good intentions, seems unable to topple the UNC machine.

That leaves COP, which is still led by Dookeran, at least until his present term ends in 2011. As for Warner and his team, they could soon be left without a party.

Warner has always been very clear that he is not leaving the UNC, but if the party continues to frustrate his efforts to run for and get elected as a member of the national executive, he would have no choice but to move on.

But where? That's the mammoth political headache that still leaves the unity question unsettled.

Warner has kept the door open for a union with COP, but the door isn't wide open and there is talk from very reliable COP sources that some of COP's backers would be more comfortable if Warner is not a part of their "tribe."

Then there is the huge socio-economic chasm separating COP and the UNC. Some of COP's most influential backers want nothing to do with the UNC. They have made it clear that UNC tribe doesn't belong in COP. On the Panday side, there is no enthusiasm to unite with COP and lose its identity.

The UNC's founding base is dwindling, but it remains significant enough to make a difference in the country's political fortunes. And those who continue to sustain the UNC are not going to walk over to COP.

If I were to guess, I would say even if Panday and Dookeran want to do business, they could very well find it nearly impossible, because their respective memberships have no love for one another. Despite all the platform rhetoric and posturing in the media, there is no real sign of any united opposition in the near future. And that leaves Manning as secure as he ever was.

(November 29, 2009)

Section 4
A new dawn
for the rising sun

On December 12, 2009, Kamla Persad-Bissessar did what most people in the United National Congress (UNC) considered the "unthinkable." At a media conference at her Siparia constituency office, she announced that she would run for the leadership of her party. It was a strategic move for the former cabinet minister who served in the Panday UNC administration (1995-2001) in the portfolios of Education Minister and Attorney General. It was the first time that anyone had challenged the leader, and those who stood with Panday predicted that she would become another of the many Panday casualties.

They were wrong. In a campaign that was as intense as a general election campaign, Kamla rose above the mudslinging and demonstrated that she was fit and ready to be a leader while the "chief" was no longer up to it. The Kamlamania she created with her dignified campaign propelled her from MP to prime minister in five months.

This section deals with the campaign for the UNC, which created a new dawn and new hope for Trinidad and Tobago.

Kamla to take on Bas, Ramesh for UNC leadership

Kamla Persad-Bissessar ended the speculation Saturday and announced that she will seek the leadership of the United National Congress.

In a brief address from her constituency office at Penal Junction, the Siparia MP said she agonised over the decision and was torn between loyalty for her "mentor and guru, Basdeo Panday" and her obligations and duty to her constituents and the nation. The announcement ended a week of intense lobbying by her supporters, friends and advisers who pushed her to take the plunge, arguing that she has the best chance of winning against the incumbent, Basdeo Panday, uniting the opposition and defeating the People's National Movement in a general election.

In her speech, carried live on national radio and television, Persad-Bissessar outlined some of the problems facing the country, blaming the Manning administration for neglecting the nation.

"Our country is going through its darkest hour through the lack of good governance and disdain for you the people who live in fear, confined to self-imposed jails in your own homes while thugs, kidnappers, rapists, and murderers walk freely.

"The wealth of our nation is being plundered daily by a governing elite obsessed and intoxicated with power and delusions of greatness while you struggle to live off the crumbs.

"Our leaders can find more than two million dollars for a state banquet while tens of thousands of children go to sleep hungry every night; they can do this while hospitals lack beds and medicine and gangs fight for turf in our nation's schools," she said.

In an address full of emotion, Persad-Bissessar spoke about difficult times when she felt discarded, but remained focussed on her mission of service.

"My brothers and sisters, you all know all too well that I have been on floor before, but I remained loyal to our cause, remained focused on the vision and with your help, your faith in me I am here, standing again. And no one is ever going to keep me down again!" she said.

There was tension, as more than once it seemed that she might endorse Panday. "We have had a leader with vision and foresight in Mr. Basdeo Panday. This is a man who led from his heart, with equality as his guiding light. This is the leader who recognised the value of women as we fought, and continue to fight, for the equal place we deserve in our nation, and in our world," she said.

She described Panday as "the greatest leader" the country has ever had, but then argued that the bickering in the party had reduced the UNC to a poor shadow of its former self, incapable of undertaking its most important duty to the nation — defeating the People's National Movement (PNM).

"Self interest and bickering have deformed us and restricted our ability to move forward and take on the most pressing task ahead — that of purging our nation of the PNM blight that has taken root, destroying our self-respect as a people, plundering our treasury and dividing us," she stated.

"When there is a lack of leadership, society stands still. That is where we are today in Trinidad and Tobago. Now is the time to shake this nation out of its slumber. And to do it requires courageous, skillful leaders who can seize the opportunity to change things for the better," the former attorney general declared.

And she rallied the troops to stand up with the UNC and rise against the evil that has taken root in the society. "I am asking you to rise to the challenge of restoring our party to the greatness it once had.

"I am asking you to rise up with the UNC to show the PNM that it does not have a divine right to plunder and rape this nation and keep all our people in perpetual misery. I am asking you to rise up with the UNC to build a nation where gender, race, and class do not divide us," she said.

She said her decision was the most difficult she has ever had to make, noting that the election on January 24 will be the most important in the UNC's history. "To run or not to run became the most difficult question to answer. I asked over and over again whether my duty was to personal and dear friendships or to our nation.

"Was it more important to maintain the status quo while mothers struggled to choose between medicine for their sick children and putting breakfast on the table?" she asked. Persad-Bissessar said she questioned whether it was right to engage in battle with friends and political kinfolk and said there was one overriding issue that sealed the matter.

"The guiding principle that helped me arrive at a final decision was this: can we save this nation if I shut my eyes or looked the other way while Patrick Manning and his thugs continue to hold all of us to ransom, keeping us in perpetual fear," she said. "I said, Yes, we can! And I am determined that we must! With your help, we'll do it!"

Then she ended the tension and speculation.

"And so, my dear friends, I am pleased to tell you, with the greatest humility, I will stand as a candidate for the leadership of the United National Congress."

(December 12, 2009)

Kamla's gamble

Up to the last moment, Kamla Persad-Bissessar seemed unsure that she really wanted to make the boldest move of her political career — to take on the mighty Basdeo Panday who has said famously that "if you see me and a lion fighting, feel sorry for the lion."

It was a difficult decision, she explained, but she did it for the party and for the country. Now it's left to see how her gamble plays out.

For weeks, she was hearing the same words from friends, supporters and advisers: Your time has come, only you could do it. Even her estranged political colleagues, Chaguanas West MP Jack Warner and Mayaro MP Winston "Gypsy" Peters, were saying she is fit to lead.

While Peters made it clear he would choose the Siparia MP over his colleague Ramesh L. Maharaj, who is also running for the leadership, Warner was careful not to burn bridges. He had said Persad-Bissessar was eminently qualified to lead the party and he stands by it. For him, the election is something the membership must decide.

So the starting gun has fired and there are three powerful figures in the race. It is the first time ever that someone has dared to challenge "the chief" head on. That in itself is a sign of the times and a signal that the UNC is accepting that it cannot be business as usual — or at least some members are accepting that.

Panday still has the support of most members of the parliamentary caucus, but his detractors say that's all he has and that he would lose in a free and fair vote on January 24, 2010.

But those who support the former prime minister say Persad-Bissessar is taking too much of a gamble and she is destined to be a political footnote, another casualty in the long list of people who have confronted Panday, going back to the earliest ULF days.

However, Persad-Bissessar's gamble has some logic to it, and even if she does not win the coveted leader's job, she would have demonstrated that she has the courage that leadership demands, the courage to stand up against friends and allies and say, we have to change the way we do things.

And she would have demonstrated the same commitment to the vision of the UNC that attracted her to it following the 1991 election when she was a member of NAR. Even as she told supporters that she was going after Panday's job, she was praising her "political guru and mentor" as the best leader the country ever had.

So why make the drastic move?

That, she explained, was because times have changed, and Panday no longer has the support to take the party back to government. There is national consensus on that, although Panday's closest allies are saying that is not so.

In fact, former UNC Senator Robin Montano is of the opinion that despite all the venom from Panday haters, the former prime minister might still be able to command strong support and possibly win back office if he could woo back some defectors to the infant COP back to the UNC.

However, some of Panday's own people are worried that Panday could be pulled under by the tide in favour of Persad-Bissessar. And they are saying rather than shake things up, they'll go with the flow and retire to a comfortable pension after the present Parliament is dissolved.

Popular opinion seems to suggest that if she were going into a one-on-one fight with the PNM today she would defeat the party and become prime minister.

And that really is the gamble.

At 57, she knows that she has limited fighting days ahead. To sit this one out would have meant never having a shot at it again. On the other hand, if she pulls it off there is a very strong chance that she could immediately unite the opposition, which is a proposition to make Patrick Manning shudder. And then go the next step and remove the PNM and become Trinidad and Tobago's first female prime minister.

But even if she can't beat Panday, there is a chance that she would have signalled her intention to unite and lead a strong opposition. And that would be an important statement — not only about her determination to lead, but as a strong representative of her gender.

She set the tone that she was not fighting a personal battle, but a principled one in which there would be no mudslinging to gain cheap political points. While she made it clear that she still respected the man she is setting out to dethrone she also pointed out without saying it directly, now is the time for him to hand over.

"We have had a leader with vision and foresight in Mr Basdeo Panday. This is a man who led from his heart, with equality as his guiding light," she observed. But then she declared, "Now is the time to shake this nation out of its slumber. And to do it requires courageous, skilful leaders who can seize the opportunity to change things for the better."

Courageous and skilful were the buzzwords.

She is the one, she was saying, with the courage and the skill to do what Panday had done before but can no longer accomplish, which is "to return this nation to the glory that once defined it before it was abused and polluted by Patrick Manning and the PNM."

It is early days yet. There could very well more challengers and the leadership candidates are yet to say how they will achieve the lofty goals of uniting the UNC and the rest of the opposition into a battle-ready army to defeat the PNM.

But Kamla has made a decisive step forward from which there is no turning back. Whether she wins or not, she would have made one bold move for her party and the nation and a quantum leap for women.

(December 12, 2009)

Don't celebrate Kamla's victory yet

There is a kind of euphoria sweeping through Trinidad and Tobago as Kamla Persad-Bissessar positions herself to take over the United National Congress (UNC) and then lead the party in a general election against the People's National Movement (PNM).

Her supporters are hoping she'll create a political tsunami as powerful as the one that swept the PNM out of office in 1986. The mood is so charged that if this were a general election, she might have easily done it.

But it isn't. This is an internal affair to be decided by financial members of the UNC. According to party officials, there are about 34,500 eligible electors, although that could increase by a few thousand by the time registration closes on Friday (December 18, 2009).

What that means is that while the public might consider the incumbent leader, Basdeo Panday, unpopular or not capable of returning the party to government, the membership that will vote on January 24 might have other ideas.

Jack Warner, who is running for the chairmanship of the party, is putting his trust in the membership and hoping that the wave of support across political lines for Persad-Bissessar would influence even committed Panday supporters to embrace change and look forward.

The issue that UNC members have to consider when they mark their ballots on January 24, 2010 is the future of their party and the nation, not loyalty and emotion. The question they have to honestly answer is this: who is best able to achieve the long-term goal: Panday, Persad-Bissessar or the other contender, Ramesh L. Maharaj? Which of the three leaders courting them today can achieve the colossal task of healing the wounds, uniting the opposition and beating the PNM in a general election?

That is the only question they should consider, because in our system of parliamentary democracy, a party with a majority can govern as it pleases, without even the courtesy of pretending to pay attention to the opposition.

Panday is without doubt a powerful and influential politician who commands popular support among a dwindling base in the UNC heartland. Outside of that, however, his support has been waning ever since Maharaj conspired with Patrick Manning to paint Panday and the UNC government as a bunch of crooks.

The PNM is today one of the most unpopular administrations in the history of the country. The latest public opinion poll suggests that only 16 percent of those surveyed believe Manning is fit to govern and 70 percent consider the PNM government corrupt. Manning's billion-dollar expenditure on two international summits, while tens of thousands live below the poverty line, has struck a chord with the average voter; most people — 72 percent — blame the Manning regime for squandering the nation's windfall revenues.

With all this in its favour, the opposition just has to get its act together and wait for Manning to call an election.

But getting there is easier said that done, as we have seen with the UNC in the past. Now that Warner is backing Persad-Bissessar, the tide has turned and there is a chance that Panday could be swept under. The task at hand is to find a formula to convince UNC members that they hold the future in their hands. They must choose between living in opposition, or having the best chance ever of returning to government.

Panday is counting on another political resurrection like the one that came in 2007 when everybody — including the pollsters — were already writing his and the UNC's epitaph and crowning the new kids on the block, the Congress of the People (COP).

But a few pieces are missing from the political jigsaw. Warner was part of that political resurrection, as were Maharaj and Persad-Bissessar. And there is the critical issue of funding a general election campaign, not to mention the splintered opposition.

Perhaps more important than all of that is the perception that Panday is well past his prime and cannot win another election, which is what prompted Persad-Bissessar to choose between loyalty to Panday and a duty to the party and the country.

The political arithmetic is very clear in the first-past-the-post system. Manning and the PNM won the last election with a strong majority of 26 seats in the 41 chamber House of Representatives with 45.85 percent of the popular vote.

What the opposition needs as a first priority, therefore, is to find a formula to unite, but it must be a genuine marriage, not the kind of shotgun arrangements that came apart as soon as the votes were counted in 1986.

That requires a UNC leader who is willing to compromise, who can earn the respect of all opposition groups and command support across party lines. Persad-Bissessar could be that leader. First and foremost, her gender brings strong support from that constituency as is evidenced from the endorsements from strong national figures like Hazel Brown, Diane Seukeran, Diana Mahabir-Wyatt and Dana Seetahal.

She carries no baggage like Maharaj, who is marked as the man who brought down the Panday government and is reviled among UNC supporters for making deals with Manning. And she has a pretty decent track record in public office.

Panday's handicap is his hostility to the idea of change within the UNC that has alienated many of his most loyal supporters and friends, including Warner. And while he talks of unity, he also shows contempt for those who do not subscribe to his views.

The challenge for Persad-Bissessar is to get a majority of eligible UNC voters to understand that settling the leadership issue is only the first step in a very long journey to government.

It is very easy to be seduced by opinion polls and non-voters who attend political meetings. The nightly random People Meter poll on TV in Trinidad Wednesday night showed 95 percent support for the decision that Warner made to back Persad-Bissessar.

That could be cause for dancing on the streets. But hold the celebration! How many among those who voted in that poll can vote on January 24? That is the critical question.

The signs are pointing in the right direction, but there is work to be done. And unless the Persad-Bissessar campaign gets on the road one-on-one and spreads her message strongly enough to convince the voters that now is the time for change, Panday could very well be back and get his wish to "die with my boots on."

(December 17, 2009)

The future is ours to control

On an overcast winter morning in Toronto one might argue that I am too far away to feel the warmth of the (rising) sun in Trinidad and Tobago or to understand the critical issues that face our nation.

I say "our", because although I live and work in Canada and am a Canadian citizen, I am and will always be a Trini. Trinidad and Tobago never stopped being my home and it will always be home.

That's why I created this blog as a non-profit effort to try to make sense out of what's happening at home, so that others like me would read and understand the critical issues taking place back home. And who can say that what's happening in Trinidad and Tobago's politics is not important? That's why this blog devotes so much space to politics and politicians.

And the story with which I am preoccupied these days is the state of the United National Congress (UNC) and its convulsions as it tries to redefine itself and reposition itself as a government in waiting.

In 2007, the party rose from its near death experience, proved all the political pundits wrong and won 15 of the 41 seats in the House of Representatives; the infant Congress of the People (COP) won none.

That should have been a signal to move on quickly, to seize the opportunity to re-brand itself as the people's party and work towards challenging the government every step of the way to do its job. Instead, the party engaged in its usual narcissism and set itself on a path of self- destruction. Ego and self-interest became the order of the day, while Patrick Manning went on an orgy of maladministration, plundering the treasury, and showing absolute disdain for the citizens and their legitimate concerns.

In short, like Nero, the UNC fiddled while Rome burned. The central issue has been whether the party would be doomed to exist in opposition in perpetuity or whether it could return to Whitehall. The consensus was that it had to change, but the man who pushed that idea soon became demonised and a pariah for daring to challenge the UNC status quo. While some of his parliamentary colleagues silently agreed with Jack Warner, only two dared stand with him.

Today, that so-called RamJack group has been disbanded, having achieved its principal aim of getting the party to hold long-overdue internal elections. And one RamJack member and another MP have not only agreed that change is vital, they are doing the unthinkable; Ramesh L. Maharaj and Kamla Persad-Bissessar are challenging Basdeo Panday for the leadership of the UNC.

Warner is seeking the chairmanship, hoping that in that role he could use his local, regional and international expertise to reorganise and create a highly effective and professional organisation and move on to plan a strategy to win an election, not get a few seats and remain in opposition. So far nobody else, as far as I know, is running for that post.

In past party elections, the common strategy has been to have parties within the party with the campaigns becoming so caustic and divisive that cliques developed that hurt the organisation later.

Just look at the Team Unity slate that Maharaj mounted in the 2000 election that saw him being elected as deputy leader. I was in Trinidad during that campaign and on reflection cannot believe that the people who opposed one another were of the same party with the same mission and vision. It was just a race for who could win.

Today, the party is engaged once more in an exercise to elect members of a new executive and a political leader. Panday has said he wants to run with a slate of people with whom he could work comfortably. That's his right, as it is the right of the two other leadership contenders, Persad-Bissessar and Maharaj. But will such a strategy build a better UNC?

A leader or a chairman of the UNC must immediately get to work to heal wounds and rebuild the party. And no matter who wins, the task will be an extremely demanding one. However, a series of competing slates will be unproductive if those who seek office insist of each getting "a pick-up side" for the election.

The best strategy for the party today would be individuals who feel they are competent to hold office and have the capacity to make a difference to put their names on the ballot. Each person running for office would in effect be an independent. It does not mean one person cannot endorse another. For example, Warner has endorsed Persad-Bissessar but both she and the Chaguanas West MP have stated publicly that their campaigns are independent.

That makes sense, because when the campaigns are over there will only be one leader, one chairman, and one person holding each of the other posts. All of these men and women will have to work together to heal wounds, unify the party and develop strategies to make a new UNC that would be strong and capable of undertaking its responsibilities of making the government accountable to the citizens and eventually taking charge of the government in a general election, which could come long before it is due in 2012.

The UNC cannot pretend that if there are two or three "slates" running in this campaign there won't be the usual nastiness that we have seen before; we are already hearing it.

The party must avoid at all costs the risk of the election creating pockets of interest groups that would become cancerous and threaten the very existence of the UNC. That is why Panday, Warner, Persad-Bissessar, Maharaj and all those who want to lead the party must stand up for the people, the party and its vision for Trinidad and Tobago. They must do all they can to avoid the kind of campaign that we have seen in the past, with the resulting bitterness and divisiveness that have caused the party to reach the point of implosion more than once.

The UNC must be bigger than the individual and must stand up for justice, fairness, equality and accountability. It must do it in its own house before trying to fix the nation's problems.

The past is gone forever, and it is the duty and responsibility for UNC politicians running for office to understand that it cannot be business as usual. Now is time to look to the future and to focus on the task at hand, which is to build a national party, unite the opposition forces and take on Patrick Manning and the People's National Movement (PNM) and win.

Now is the time to renew and rebuild. The past is gone forever but the future is ours to control.

(December 27, 2009)

Challenging the UNC status quo

It should come as no surprise to anyone that the majority of the parliamentary caucus of the United National Congress (UNC) is supporting Basdeo Panday in his quest for the leadership of the party.

While the Panday camp will trumpet this a "stunning" development and a political coup, this endorsement is really the worst kept secret within the party and in the public domain. All of them had said at one time or another that they would stick with the status quo and support Panday. One senator even said that it would be "disrespectful" to go against the chief.

It is, however, a master stroke by those running the campaign to capitalise on the agenda setting. The motive is to grab the Sunday headlines and offer a hot political subject for the talk shows and commentators in the days ahead. The hope is to generate enough hype to call the election a done deal.

The next stage of the strategy would be Panday's triumphant return from London with "hordes" of loyal fans and supporters congregating at Piarco to welcome home the chief. In reality, many may not even be UNC financial members.

It's a good mass media strategy to try to launch a coup by dazzling the voter and obscuring the real issues in the Panday-mania all of this is expected to create. But in reality, as noted by both Jack Warner and Kamla Persad-Bissessar in their reaction to the announcement, nothing has really changed.

Both of them are pressing ahead with their respective campaigns, with Warner planning to publicly launch his in Felicity on January 9, 2010. Persad-Bissessar and Ramesh L. Maharaj are running against Panday for the leadership of the UNC and Warner is running for the post of chairman.

What is happening today is what Warner predicted when he launched the Movement for Change with Maharaj and Mayaro MP Winston "Gypsy" Peters.

At that time, Persad-Bissessar was still a Panday loyalist, but she decided to challenge Panday because, as she says, he cannot take the party back into government. For Warner, this is just a manifestation of what is wrong with the UNC and what he has been clamouring to change — business as usual and blind loyalty to a leader who is out of touch with reality.

He is also concerned about the lack of people participation in the decision-making process. "I wonder if any of the 10 parliamentarians consulted with their constituency executive committees so as to get their views before signing such a letter?" Warner asked. Both he and Persad-Bissessar are saying they expected this kind of allegiance to Panday and are hoping the people will understand that now is the time to shake up the system and send a message to their party that it needs to pay attention to what they want and understand that it cannot be business as usual.

Persad-Bissessar, Maharaj, Warner and all who challenge Panday have a monumental task ahead that is perhaps as difficult as climbing a greasy pole. But so often the determined climber gets the ham. And that's what the challengers expect.

Persad-Bissessar is confident that she will defeat Panday. "I will win, which means the people win," she has said.

More than 35,000 UNC supporters will write the next chapter in the UNC's history with the marks they place on the ballot on January 24, 2010. Those who support Panday are determined that only he can take the party back to Whitehall; those opposed say the exact opposite. When the votes are counted and the winners announced, the analysts and commentators will have their say, but the people will have to live with their decision.

One way or the other, the Rising Sun will shine after January 24. But the lingering question is whether it will comfort an entire nation that is crying for leadership, representation and an end to the Manning regime.

(December 27, 2009)

All not well in Panday camp

Basdeo Panday must truly be fuming about this week's *faux pas* by his campaign team on the ground. The first was not as bad, but two coming back to back is unforgivable and somebody is going to pay dearly for it when "the chief" gets back to Trinidad.

Panday is no fool and after more than 40 years in the political game, he knows the rules. And rule number one is never leave room for the enemy to move in or pounce on you. His campaign personnel broke that rule at least twice this week.

The first was a letter of support for Panday from 10 MPs and four senators. Good move, but only if everybody is on board. They weren't. One legislator broke ranks, said she never signed any document supporting Panday and endorsed Kamla Persad-Bissessar, who is running against Panday for the leadership.

Roodal Moonilal's attempt at damage control put out the first fire but while people were still asking what went wrong, the campaign made the same mistake again. The women's executive put out a statement pledging full support for the leader, but it turned out that was not the real story.

Again, there was egg on the faces of the Panday campaign team.

Within 24 hours of the release of that claim, four executive members of the women's arm said they were not consulted, had nothing to do with it, and threw their support behind Persad-Bissessar.

The response from Jennifer Jones-Kernahan, the head of the women's group, compounded the problem by trying to discredit her own people. She said those who objected were not "functioning members" and that "others" were called in to do their job. Even a fool would find that hard to digest. How can an executive be changed overnight without a vote? And who are the "new" executive members? On what basis did Jones-Kernahan arrive at the claim that the UNC women were behind the leader?

But there was more.

Vasant Bharat called up his friend, Jerry Narace, for Christmas drinks at his house. Just two old business friends getting together, they both claimed. But that meeting between Patrick Manning's right hand man and the UNC's vice chairman left even Panday supporters scratching their heads and wondering what was going on. Certainly Bharath wasn't meeting his ol' pal to sell him Cheekies diapers! Then Bharath started sounding like his leader was about to give up the fight. He was almost saying Panday could be a loser.

Even if Persad-Bissessar won, Bharath said, she won't be in charge because the parliamentary caucus is fully behind the leader and the majority in parliament would determine who's the opposition leader: 10-5 means Panday remains leader even if he is not leader of the party.

It was another bad move. And no doubt Panday was unimpressed. It might have been an attempt to show that it would be pointless voting for anybody but Panday, but it sounded like blackmail and people don't like that.

Then Suruj Rambachan announced that maybe he would be on Panday's team or maybe not. In any case, he wants to be a deputy leader — with or without Panday's blessing.

If this is how the Panday camp plans on running a serious campaign, then the other side should be delighted. But they should not bring out the champagne yet. Panday is no novice and he loves a good fight. He is the man who said politics is war and fighting a political battle is better than sex. He is not about to give up this fight.

There's time to recover. And he has already promised to launch "an aggressive" campaign to make sure that no one would topple him.

Persad-Bissessar has been getting lots of face time on local media, while Panday and the other leadership contender, Ramesh L. Maharaj, are on holiday abroad. And while the three leadership candidates prepare for battle, the man who has led the campaign for change is getting ready to launch a high energy campaign.

Chaguanas MP Jack Warner is advertising the biggest event of the campaign with his official launch on January 9. But Warner knows as well as the other guy, Trinis love a party and crowds don't win elections.

Amid all the hoopla, there is the chance that the campaigns could get seduced by mass meetings and media coverage, with all kinds of opinion polls and surveys — most unscientific and lacking credibility — announcing winners and losers.

In the end all that matters is what each financial member of the UNC thinks and does. And the smart politician would look in that direction if she or he wants to win. That's why nobody can call this election yet.

This election is about the future. UNC members have a choice. And they have to take responsibility for their actions. How they mark their ballots will determine the next chapter in this political drama. The vote on January 24, 2010 is a choice between riding a wave of change or maintaining the status quo. Patrick Manning is paying attention.

2010 is upon us, a new decade of the 21 century.

Happy New Year!

(December 31, 2009)

The will of the majority must prevail in UNC election

Members of the United National Congress (UNC) are looking for clear signals from party leader Basdeo Panday when he launches his re-election campaign on Saturday (January 9, 2010) to hear if he will stand up for freedom and democracy or follow the strategy already marked by some of his people on the ground.

Panday has been in England and is expected home on Wednesday. In his absence, his campaign team has been working on preparing the groundwork for what Panday has promised would be an "aggressive campaign."

But one aspect of the strategy seems to be at odds with Panday's own political and personal philosophy. Panday has always been an advocate for freedom and democracy, although his critics say that's only for public consumption.

He is on record as saying that if voters reject him and choose a new leader in the January 24 internal election, he will leave "with joy in my heart." But that's not what MPs Roodal Moonilal and Vasant Bharath are suggesting. They seem to have an opposite position. They have said even if Panday loses, he would still have the support of the legislators who signed the recent pledge of support and would therefore continue to be opposition leader although he won't be leader of the party. Ten MPs and four of the six UNC senators signed that document.

All along, Panday has welcomed competition and has boasted that the UNC is the most democratic political party in the country and the region because of its policy of electing its officials — including its leader — through a system of one-member-one-vote.

This election is the first in which he is facing a direct challenge to his leadership. And it's coming from two of his MPs — Ramesh L. Maharaj and Kamla Persad-Bissessar. Still, his public pronouncements so far have not in any way indicated that he would stand against the democratic will of the people. He insists that he will win and he has charged that there is some sort of conspiracy with former UNC members who defected to the Congress of the People (COP) to steal the UNC base. But there is no sound basis for that, in much the same way as there is no sound basis for allegations that Patrick Manning is helping out by getting CEPEP workers to sign up as members only to vote for Panday.

UNC deputy leader Jack Warner, who is running for the chairmanship, has expressed deep concerns about the delay in publishing the preliminary membership list, which should have been available since last Saturday. And he is not buying the argument that the workload is causing the delay.

The party is saying it has to be careful that it scrutinises each new membership application "with a fine-tooth comb" to ensure that there is nothing bogus and that people don't hold dual membership in political parties. That issue of the list is causing some members to ask if there is truth in allegations that the membership committee is "sanitising" the list to make it acceptable to the Panday camp. Committee chair Kelvin Ramnath has dismissed that outright.

But people are still skeptical and are looking to Saturday for clear signals from Panday about how this battle would be fought; UNC members want to hear from "the chief" that he remains committed to his public statements about democracy. They are waiting to hear his pledge that if he does not win the vote, he would not subvert the democratic will of the people by remaining opposition leader, while there is a legitimate leader of the party elected by the membership.

This would be different to the time when he had anointed Winston Dookeran as UNC leader and remained opposition leader. The membership voted in that election too, but there was no challenger, so in principle, Dookeran was the leader even before his name appeared on the ballot.

In this election, it is an open contest involving three candidates who are free to campaign and seek the support of each member. In such a case, assuming that the process is free and fair, whoever wins must be accepted by all within the UNC as the leader both inside the parliament and in the party executive. Panday must insist on that and he needs to tell the people that. That in itself would win him support from "confused" members. Any other plan would amount to an attack on freedom and democracy, which is against Panday's political philosophy. Even if the 14 decide that they want him to be the leader of the opposition, he must tell them no because the party should rally behind its leader.

If he wins, nothing changes. He is already party leader and leader of the opposition. But if Maharaj or Persad-Bissessar win, he must step down and tell those who support him to stand firm with the new leader and help unite the party.

It would demonstrate that he is indeed a leader and that he respects the will of the people. Any other decision would not and must not be acceptable to the general membership of the UNC.

No one can have an argument with Moonlilal and Bharath or any of the others who have publicly pledged their support for Panday. That is their right and they should campaign aggressively to have their leader re-elected.

But in the end, they must accept the verdict of the people. If Panday does not win, it is their duty and responsibility to support the new leader. That is the democratic thing to do. A minority of 14 MPs and senators must not be allowed to overturn a decision of the majority. That would be a dictatorship and a betrayal of everything the UNC has ever stood for since its inauguration in 1989.

(January 5, 2010)

Nomination day marks start of home stretch in epic UNC election battle

In the 37 years that I have worked as a journalist, I have covered political parties, general elections and political scandals on my beat. But never have I reported on a local event, a party election, that has generated as much interest as the internal election of the United National Congress (UNC) that takes place on January 24.

I expected that the media would pay attention, but it has gone way beyond that, even pushing aside Carnival into the inside pages as a news event, along with the national scandals and government activities. There are good reasons for it. One reason for the extensive news coverage is because of the players and the manner in which the UNC chooses its leadership.

Unlike most other political parties that have a leadership race and a nominating convention at which they select a leader, the UNC has an open election at which every eligible financial member has a vote. This one-member-one-vote policy is similar to the general election in which a first-past-the post vote determines a winner. But the UNC goes further and elects its entire 18-member national executive in this manner.

In past elections there have been rival slates, each operating like a party within the party with campaign slogans, literature, rallies and motorcades aimed at attracting voters. Another attraction is that for the first time there is actually a leadership race.

The incumbent, Basdeo Panday, is the founder of the party and has always led unchallenged. Most of his MPs have endorsed "the chief" again in this contest, although one of them admitted that it is only out of "respect for the old man."

The "old man" is 77 and still in a fighting mood, with his famous slogan, "If you see me and a lion fighting, feel sorry for the lion."

In this fight he is taking on a lioness in Siparia MP Kamla Persad-Bissessar who sat at his side for more than a dozen years, always loyal and dedicated to the leader and the party.

But she has done the "unthinkable" and decided to run for the leadership, saying she has put the nation ahead of personal loyalties. Persad-Bissessar is presenting herself as the only candidate who is capable of ending the divisiveness in the UNC, unifying the party and preparing it to win an election.

And if the groundswell of support in the national community were an indication of how she would fare in a general election, she is likely to win a landslide. But it is not, although the intense media attention is fooling many people. On radio talk shows, people who are not members of the party are pledging support, saying they will vote for Kamla only to find out they can't.

The other challenger is Tabaquite MP Ramesh Lawrence Maharaj, who has a checkered political history and the unholy distinction of cutting a deal with the PNM in 2001 to help topple the Panday government. He is saying all that is irrelevant and is marketing himself as the only one of the three who can actually fix the party problems, deal with the national concerns of the people and beat the PNM.

Despite his confidence, that's not what others are saying. What is peculiar about Maharaj's campaign is that he is only attacking the lady who wishes to lead, not the "chief." In fact he is saying only "Bas and I" are fighters for the people and only they can "save" the party.

That is adding another dimension in the political drama. Maharaj was a member of the so-called dissident RamJack group led by Jack Warner, a UNC deputy leader, MP for Chaguanas West and internationally known for his work as vice president of FIFA. Warner, Maharaj and another MP, Winston "Gypsy" Peters (Mayaro) broke ranks with the party and established a Movement for Change to educate the membership of what was wrong within the party and offer solutions to rebuild and strengthen the UNC to win an election. Their chief concern was that the party needed to hold elections for a new executive whose shelf life had expired.

Warner disbanded the movement after the party announced elections and stood by his principle of putting nation first and endorsed Persad-Bissessar, not his RamJack colleague. While Maharaj is saying that is Warner's right, he is not amused that his friend and ally is supporting someone else.

Some of the 18 posts could be won unopposed on Monday after nominations close. That's because Warner, Maharaj and Persad-Bissessar are running independent campaigns with no team. That means anyone who opposes members of the Panday team will be running an independent campaign.

The next episode of this drama is about to unfold. And judging from the coverage it has generated so far, we could expect to see and hear a lot more before the ballots are marked on January 24.

Just over 34,000 people have a critical choice to make. And for now, no one knows for sure how it will end.

(January 11, 2010)

Warner fought for Mark to get senate leader's seat

Wade Mark is one of the most loyal supporters of United National Congress (UNC) leader Basdeo Panday. In fact, when Panday first announced that he would seek reelection to the post of party leader, Mark was the first to back Panday and offered to sign his nomination forms.

Mark, who is one of the UNC's three deputy political leaders and a former party chairman, also strongly opposes Chaguanas West MP Jack Warner. He is convinced that Warner has been one of the people who tried to squeeze him out of the senate. Mark was the opposition senate leader in the previous parliament and was reappointed to the post in the current parliament.

But the irony of all this is that he owes that not to his political leader but to Warner. So if Mark wants to hold a grudge about who tried to steal his thunder he should be looking at Panday.

Two days after the general election of 2007, a small group of party officials met privately to discuss, among other things, who would get the six senate seats in the new parliament.

Panday proposed Congress of the People (COP) leader Winston Dookeran and was promptly shouted down. But he stood his ground and argued that such a move would be consistent with what he said on the eve of the election — that he wanted to mend fences and unite with COP. But the others who were there, including Warner and Ramesh L. Maharaj, said it was also inconsistent considering the fact that the election night "look in the mirror" speech was not on the theme of uniting with Dookeran. In that speech, Panday blamed Dookeran for the PNM victory.

Panday argued that it would be a good strategic move, because Dookeran would turn down the offer and then he, Panday, would be able to say it was Dookeran who didn't want to unite.

Earlier in the meeting, the officials made a unanimous decision to appoint Maharaj as Chief Whip in the House of Representatives and his main task in and out of parliament would be to reorganise the party to get back in government. So when Maharaj insisted that the Dookeran idea was a bad one, Panday backed off.

But Panday had another idea that seemed to be popular among most of the UNC officials present. The idea was to fire Mark and hand the job to Dr. Carson Charles, who was the leader of the National Alliance for Reconstruction (NAR), which was one of the parties that contested the elections as part of the UNC Alliance (UNC-A). Charles had contested the St Joseph seat, which he had held in the NAR government, but lost to the PNM's Kennedy Swaratsingh.

It was Warner who intervened and suggested that it was wrong to dump Mark. He disagreed strongly with his colleagues who were saying Charles would be better suited to lead the senate, because he was more articulate than Mark. There were even some pejorative statements about Mark.

But Warner argued that Mark had been a strong voice for the party in the senate, was a fighter and campaigner for the party and that nobody should deny him his rightful seat in the senate.

He knocked down the suggestion that he had just been beaten by the PNM's Christine Kangaloo in what was a UNC seat held previously by Gillian Lucky. Warner said that was irrelevant, since Charles was also a defeated candidate and in any case, Panday had established a precedent as prime minister to appoint as senators members of the party who had been defeated in general elections.

After a lengthy discussion, the group conceded and accepted Warner's recommendation to keep Mark as senate leader. Both Mark and Charles showed up after the discussions and nobody told Mark about the heated arguments that had taken place ahead of his arrival.

It was not the first time that Warner had stood up for Mark.

In previous election campaigns in 2001 and 2002, communications adviser Roy Boyke wanted to discard Mark entirely from the political platform. He argued that Mark was not presenting "the right image" and should not be chairing important national meetings during the campaigns.

But Warner and certain "lesser" communication advisers disagreed and Boyke grudgingly agreed to leave Mark alone. Still, Boyke was able to push Mark aside for a few meetings.

Boyke also wanted to squeeze out Kelvin Ramnath, especially in the 2002 campaign, when he and Gerry Yetming, who was the campaign manager, argued that Ramnath represented an "Indian constituency" that was ok for the cottage meetings in the UNC heartland, but not for the national stage. Even Roodal Moonilal agreed that Ramnath should not speak on the major platforms, suggesting that Ramnath's politics was no longer relevant.

Panday was not privy to those discussions, but when he learned about it, he put his foot down and demanded that Ramnath speak on the national platforms.

Boyke also had problems with Kamla Persad-Bissessar. She was the designated "law and order" spokesperson in the 2002 campaign, but he wanted to sidestep her and push Gillian Lucky, who had become a very forceful platform speaker.

Lucky got some vital face time on the national platforms, which helped her win her seat in Pointe-a-Pierre. She later walked out of the UNC over a disagreement over Panday and others on the infamous "teacup affair" involving Chandresh Sharma and Keith Rowley.

(January 12, 2010)

Media, politics and the truth

On Tuesday (January 12, 2010), the banner headline in the Trinidad Guardian screamed: "From RamJack to Kamjack." The Trinidad Express had another take on the Monday's events: "I'm no drunk" and Newsday, the third daily newspaper in Trinidad and Tobago, went with "Kamla bids for total control".

Each paper was reporting on the same event — the political story of the year, the internal election in the fragmented opposition United National Congress. It was nomination day for the January 24 vote, which is based on a one-member-one-vote system to elect its political leader and members of the national executive.

Each was looking for "the story," which was quite obvious, but since the UNC leader was not giving reporters what they wanted they had to get what they could — even if the truth was a little twisted in order to sell papers.

Take the Guardian for example.

It was wrong on all counts. First its headline suggested that there was an alliance between two independent factions in the election when there was none. Both Kamla Persad-Bissessar and Jack Warner had made it clear in several public statements that they were not part of any team (Kamjack). But the rumour had been around for days. Can it be true? The Guardian made it so without checking with the two people who would be the most important players in such an alliance if it were true: Warner and Persad-Bissessar.

The paper also reported as fact that there was a Warner team when Warner had stated that he had none and there would be none. The Chaguanas West MP had to write the editor to set the record straight and he reiterated the point when he spoke at a public meeting on Tuesday night.

Was somebody up to mischief or was it just a combination of irresponsibility and incompetence? Certainly the reporter could have asked the man himself. That's what reporters do — ask questions, ascertain the facts and report them.

But that didn't happen.

The two other papers liked the "rum" story that UNC leader Basdeo Panday had put on the agenda. Panday had suggested that Persad-Bissessar, who is challenging him for the leadership of the party, had a drinking problem and was therefore "vulnerable" and unfit to lead. The former prime minister had descended into gutter politics and nobody seemed to care that he was avoiding serious discussion on why he should be re-elected leader.

All day reporters were hounding Persad-Bissessar to react, in effect seeking to change the lady's agenda and shift it to the one set first by Panday and then embraced by the media. It didn't matter that she had more important issues to discuss. The juicy scandal of a drunk seeking to unseat her leader (another drunk?) had greater appeal.

And what about Ramesh L. Maharaj, the other leadership contender? No front page for the former attorney general, although he did get some face time with his comment that the election is a two-man race for the leadership.

And Panday didn't get anywhere in the media agenda, other that his rum talk. The day's coverage provided an interesting example of the power of media to influence public opinion and to set the agenda. And the tragedy of it is that the efforts of the leadership candidates to explain why people should elect them to run the country's opposition party became secondary.

Such issues were lost in the gossip. And the voter who might have been looking for useful information about the election, was left with nothing more that an incorrect story about an alliance that didn't and never existed and an accusation that one candidate might have a drinking problem.

With 11 days to go perhaps we might hear the real story.

We can hope. After all, this is Trinidad and Tobago. And anything is possible.

(January 13, 2010)

Kamla praises Panday but says he's too wounded to lead

Kamla Persad-Bissessar went into a stronghold of the United National Congress (UNC) Thursday night (January 14, 2010) to ask devoted and loyal supporters of UNC leader Basdeo Panday to reject him and make her leader.

In an impassioned appeal in Dow Village, California, the Siparia MP traced Panday's struggle on behalf of the people and praised him for his love and dedication over the years. "I say without fear of contradiction that Basdeo Panday has been the greatest fighter for the people. He fought for you and for all of us," she declared. "He is a hero and will always remain a national icon. He deserves it because he fought a brave fight for you and he won many battles," she said, adding that there will always be room for Panday in the UNC.

However, she noted that times have changed and he will not lead the party back to government, which is why they must change their leader.

"The PNM and their propaganda have wounded Mr. Panday ever since they pulled down his legitimate majority government and installed Mr. Manning. Ever since then they have persecuted Mr. Panday and they will never stop," she said.

Persad-Bissessar traced the gradual decline of the UNC under Panday's leadership, noting that after winning the most votes ever for a political party — 308,000 and 51 percent of the popular vote in 2000 — the best the party could have done in the last election was 29 per cent.

And she noted that in that election 90,000 UNC members deserted the party. "They were too fed up with being in opposition and were lured away by the hope of new politics. But they are ready to come home. They are UNC 'til they ded!" she said. "But they will only come home when we welcome them with open arms. Not when we insult and abuse them at every turn. They will come home when they feel love and affection," she said as she blamed Panday for crushing the hopes of unity.

"We cannot unite when we refuse to talk. We cannot solve problems when we are part of the problem. When Mr. Panday asked me to seek unity with the opposition the message was clear from everywhere. We cannot do it with Mr. Panday," she said. She added that it is clear that under Panday's leadership the party risks remaining in opposition for life and urged the UNC membership to vote with their heads, not hearts, on January 24.

"No matter how much we love Mr. Panday, you have to admit that this nation is saying he cannot take us back to government," she said. No leader who has lost four consecutive elections should continue to lead, she added.

Persad-Bissessar admitted that she did not "stand in the rain in Aranguez" when the party was founded but she noted that she has been loyal ever since she entered "the house of the Rising Sun". She said, "I have learned from him what service means and I have learned from him the value of hard work and commitment. I have learned from him that I must stand up for the people, that I must stand up for what is right. I am the pupil who is ready to graduate...And I am here to claim my rightful place in our party."

She pledged that she will always remain loyal to the UNC and will protect its interests. "I am here to tell you that the party that you built with love and sweat will remain UNC. And nobody is going to change that... This is our party and it will always remain our party."

However, she said it is time to stop living in the past and look to the future. The country, she said, is under the yoke of an oppressive regime that needs just one more electoral victory to introduce a dictatorship. And she said so long as Panday remains leader, it would happen. "Stop holding on to false hope, stop believing our own propaganda that we will hug and kiss and Mr. Panday will lead us back to Whitehall. It not going to happen! It not happening!" she declared.

In pleading for their votes to make her leader, the Siparia MP said, "You want a prime minister not a leader of the opposition. You have been in opposition for too long. It's time to move on."

She told supporters they hold the future in their hands and that they are the only ones who can make the difference to save the nation from ruin. "You can squander it or you can shape the future," she said.

(January 15, 2010)

You are a loser, Kamla tells Panday

Siparia MP and UNC leadership candidate Kamla Persad-Bissessar, took off the gloves Saturday (January 16, 2010) as she went on the attack against Basdeo Panday saying there is no way he will ever get the party back into government.

After praising Panday in a speech earlier this week, putting him on a pedestal and gently chipping away at it to show that Panday can't win again, she went on the offensive Saturday night in El Dorado. She called Panday a loser, saying it is a lie that he led the UNC to three victories against the PNM. "The UNC only win one election under Mr. Panday. Only one...For 44 years he has been fighting elections and only for six years of those he was in government, and a few months in 1987 as a foreign minister under Mr. Robinson," she said.

She walked with electoral figures to support her argument, saying a tie is not a win, no matter how you spin it. And she said the facts show Panday lost four successive elections since 2001. "If you are a party leader that cannot win then you are a failure. When you lose four elections in a row you are a loser. You have to win...the leader of our party can rant and rave as much as he wants and try to drag people down with his slander but he cannot change one fact. He is no longer capable of winning an election," she said.

She also took issue with statements made by Panday during his campaign stops. On Friday Panday asked for a "disciplined team" and pledged that with it he will take the party to government. She said it is not going to happen. "The team he is running now is the same one he had in 2007 — with a few cosmetic changes and the loss of three powerful members — and he lost. "Now three of your best players are gone and you telling me that same old team going to win. WIN WHAT?" she demanded.

"We started out with 19 seats, drop to 18 and ended up with 15... and 114,000 people run away. And then what happen? You had a disciplined team and lost. You chased away the best of them, you chased away all our supporters, you chased away everybody. How are you going to win?" she asked. "What are you going to win when you can't even walk in Couva North?"

Persad-Bissessar also took issue with a statement attributed to Panday in which he is reported to have said that the Siparia MP is the least liked among UNC MPs. Again she pulled out the electoral figures to dispute Panday.

"In 2007 of the 41 constituencies we won 15. And of the 15, only four had more than 10,000 votes. The highest votes in Trinidad and Tobago for the UNC was in Chaguanas West — 11,140; the second highest was in Naparima and the third highest vote of 10,338 was in Siparia.

"So if in political terms we talking about love the three best loved people are Jack Warner, Nizam Baksh and Kamla." She said the reverse is true of Panday. "And you want to know who are the least loved? Caroni East, Caroni Central, Couva South and Couva North. The least votes came from these constituencies — and you want to know who are the MPs? I will tell you. Tim Gopeesingh, Hamza Rafeeq, Kelvin Ramnath and Basdeo Panday," she said.

She also dealt with Panday's criticism that she was using her gender to win votes. "Don't insult women and suggest that they are dotish to vote me because I am a woman. Mr Panday I offer hope when you offer failure. I am a woman and I am proud of it; I am a leader and you are not. And that is why people will vote for me," she said.

She urged supporters to make sure they vote, because only their vote will make the difference. And when I become leader of the UNC the whole country will be in safe hands. Because we will fix our internal problems and we will win the government," she said.

(January 17, 2010)

Is there life after the election?

Where will it all end?

That is the question that many UNC supporters are asking as the internal election campaign heads down the home stretch. While there are 18 posts at stake the real interest is in two positions — political leader and chairman.

Basdeo Panday is confident of victory and so are his two challengers, Tabaquite MP and former "RamJacker" Ramesh L. Maharaj and Siparia MP Kamla Persad-Bissessar. The chairmanship might have been an insignificant affair were it not for who is running. It's a contest between Chaguanas West MP Jack Warner and the current UNC vice-chairman, St Augustine MP, Vasant Bharath.

In the leadership affair, it seems that the strategy is anybody but Persad-Bissessar. Maharaj has made it clear that he supports Panday and will let him continue as opposition leader if he wins the leadership. And Panday has totally ignored Maharaj, training his political guns instead on his Siparia MP, whom he has described as unfit to lead by virtue of her "weakness," which is the euphemism he has used for calling her a drunk. His focus is on Warner as well, trying to connect both of them although each has an independent campaign.

Warner has reciprocated with frontal attacks on Panday, while Persad-Bissessar began her campaign almost apologetically. However, she has maintained that while Panday was a great leader and a fighter that is in the past. And she seems to have now taken off the gloves and has been confronting Panday with the label "LOSER."

She has been using electoral statistics, to show that contrary to what Panday has been telling everybody, he led the UNC to only one election victory against the PNM — in 2000 when the party won 19 seats to get a clear majority. Panday has insisted that he won three, but the official statistics confirm Persad-Bissessar's argument.

Reality in politics is perception, and those who support Panday will go along with his story and vice versa. The statistics and the truth have become major casualties in this epic political struggle in which Panday, for the first time ever, is facing a challenge for the leadership of "his" party.

And it is coming from a woman, who sat at his side for more than a decade. Indeed many had labeled her Panday in a skirt. At the end of the day on January 24, the real story begins to unfold.

If Panday is back and Bharath wins the chairmanship, it might seem like business as usual. But it cannot be. Panday would have been severely wounded in a brutal campaign and the divisions in the party won't go away. Warner and Persad-Bissessar will become instant pariahs and the Panday loyalists at Rienzi will withdraw the welcome mat for good.

That would settle the immediate matter of who is boss. But it won't settle the real issue, which is that the UNC is stuck in the opposition and has been in a steady decline since 2000. And the leader must accept the responsibility for that.

Can Panday and his loyal MP's, some of whom are not as loyal as Panday would expect, reshape the party and defeat the PNM? That is the message in this campaign from those opposed to Panday.

Panday has been unable so far to show that he can win, except to say once he will restore discipline in the party and he will beat the PNM. The party's last election showing was dismal with only 29 percent of the popular vote as opposed to the 51 percent in 2000. But even more significant is that the infant Congress of the People (COP) received 148,000 — only 50,000 fewer votes than the UNC, which amounted to 22 percent of the popular vote.

The UNC's rejection of newcomers in the internal election — about 16,000 of them, allegedly COP members who wanted to return to the party — has already sent a signal that despite all the talk of unity the UNC is a private political club and newcomers are not going to enjoy the special privileges of those who were there when the struggle began. Even Persad-Bissessar is singled out as an "outsider" for her former NAR allegiance although Tim Gopeesingh, who also came from NAR, is embraced lovingly, especially by the Pandays.

Persad-Bissessar and Warner cannot run off and join the COP because it would damage their credibility since both of them have campaigned as "UNC til a dead." So would they try to crawl back home and say, "Sorry, chief, we made a mistake?" Hardly likely because that is not their style and even if they did "the chief" would not be forgiving after all the mudslinging.

So there are only two alternatives: accept two plots in Panday's political graveyard or stand up take the fight to the people. My guess is that the gravediggers can take a holiday.

This election has generated a kind of political revivalism that few thought possible. And Persad-Bissessar and Warner are the primary beneficiaries. The citizenry appears to have come to the conclusion that under Panday they have reached the last page and it is time to close the book on the UNC, although for many, there is an understandable sentimental attachment to the party and its leader. But that alone will not get the UNC out of opposition.

No matter how this campaign ends, it seems that the UNC is mortally wounded.

There is life after January 24. The people appear to be battle ready but unless those who oppose the Manning regime figure out a strategy to remove the current administration this battle would have all been in vain.

But it doesn't have to be that way.

This election has offered hope. Where there is hope, there will be a way forward. And the spark that this election has ignited could grow into a political inferno that has the potential to change the politics of Trinidad and Tobago forever.

(January 18, 2010)

What is the UNC protecting?

The internal election in the United National Congress (UNC), that reaches its climax in the next few days has been an eye-opener for many. Not because of some of the expected campaign talk but for the messages in statements on platforms and in media interviews.

There is no doubt, that in its glory days the party represented the widest cross section of interests in Trinidad and Tobago and people of every group gravitated to it. It was primarily because the UNC had a vision of equality and justice and was born out of a desire to make life better for everyone. Its liberal democracy philosophy and the bottom-up approach to leadership helped create the movement that took Basdeo Panday to government in 1995 in a coalition with his political arch-enemy, Arthur N.R. Robinson.

The UNC's performance in government, brought it its first and only true electoral victory, the majority in the 2000 general election. But under the weight of allegations of corruption the government fell and the party has never been able to rise again. In the nine years since the 2000 victory, the party has continually lost support among its own membership and those non-members who supported the UNC's vision and its performance in government.

The figures are alarming and not getting any better. Here's what the statistics show for the 2000 general election, which was a two-party affair with 36 seats at stake:

- UNC — 307,791 — 51.7% — 19 seats
- PNM — 276,334 — 46.4% — 16 seats
- NAR — 007,409 — 01.2% — 01 seat (Tobago)

By 2007 the PNM was back in office with a majority, but only with minority support. And a third party had emerged, born out of dissent within the UNC. There were 41 seats:

- PNM — 299,813 — 45.85% — 26 seats
- UNCA — 194,425 — 29.73 % — 15 seats (UNC and a coalition of smaller parties)
- COP — 148,041 — 22.65% — no seat

The figures show what might appear to be an illogical imbalance but it is a well-known anomaly in multi-party political systems.

While a majority of the electorate rejected the governing party, the PNM returned to Parliament with a stronger majority than in the 2002 election primarily because those who opposed the government were not united in a common cause.

The message from the current internal election campaign from those trying to unseat Panday and his loyalists, is that the UNC has lost its "winnability" and the party has declined steadily since it lost government in 2001. They blame it on the erosion of democracy, the demise of party institutions and a lack of accountability and professionalism. And they are saying the fragmented opposition won't work with the Panday UNC so returning to government seems to be a lost cause.

Panday and his team dismiss the charge, saying those who want to take control of the party — people like Jack Warner and Kamla Persad-Bissessar — are political opportunists who have no regard for those who laboured to build the UNC.

In this context the UNC faithful are "protecting" the party from interlopers whose mission, they say, it is to dismantle the party and hand it to others. The "others" is code for the Congress of the People (COP) that stumped the UNC Alliance in the 2007 election, taking away 90,000 of its supporters.

Many of those prodigals have become disenchanted with the COP's new politics and its disdain for the rank and file members and have tried to return home to the UNC only to find the doors closed. What's worse, high-ranking UNC MPs and officials are maligning them as outsiders and even thugs trying to storm the UNC to steal it from those who are die-hard, loyal founding members.

On the campaign platforms, Panday has made impassioned speeches pleading with those who love the UNC to "protect" it. "It is not my party," he has said, "the UNC is your party that you laboured to build," noting that only those who were present at its birth can appreciate the need to be protective of the "baby" that will turn 21 this year.

In that context he is appealing to a small group, while excluding the youth and those who have been attracted to the UNC's vision and want to be a part of it but were not there at the beginning.

If only those who witnessed the birth of the movement understand and are welcome, where is the room for growth, especially to include young men and women who are seeking membership in a movement that invited everyone in 1989 to join a crusade for justice, equality and freedom?

Panday and the UNC have not addressed that and they have dismissed concerns that after nine years in decline there is no hope for the UNC ever getting back into government.

"Give me a disciplined team," Panday said this week, "And I shall give you government." That's a tall order for a party that has been so fractured from this campaign that healing, if at all possible, will take a painfully long time. One prominent UNC MP has made it clear that those who are "undisciplined" have no place in the UNC, which suggests that dissenters will become pariahs as the new executive gets down to business.

And this raises the question of what is the UNC today and what is the party protecting and what is its future?.

If, as Panday says, only those who have been around since the Aranguez declaration of 1989 that founded the UNC are welcome, then he is at the same time condemning the UNC to stagnation and a permanent place in opposition.

This is not to suggest that Panday and his loyalists have no political currency, or that they lack the skills needed to move the party forward; rather it is a signal that the UNC will remain a closed shop for a privileged few who fanatically follow the leader. Such an attitude means the UNC is missing the best opportunity ever to get back to Whitehall.

The present government is perhaps the most unpopular ever and there is a clamour for change that no serious political party should ignore. The interest this internal election has generated is unprecedented. Tens of thousands who cannot even vote are saying they are ready to move the government, but the question today is whether the UNC is too wounded to answer the call.

When the shouting is over, this party will remain the official opposition. And it will remain there unless it emerges with a determination to change the way it conducts its business. It has no other alternative because those founding members alone, those who belong to the privileged group, are too few to win an election.

The UNC has to court the general electorate and present the country with a clear alternative or suffer the humiliation of greater defeats. The tragedy for the UNC — and for the nation — is that if a new leadership emerges after Sunday's vote, it will meet intense hostility from the party's loyalists and its Parliamentary caucus.

On the other hand, if the status quo remains and Panday and his team are returned to office, those who opposed him will feel his wrath and will likely be banished.

Either way, the party will continue to lose its attractiveness. And the message of protecting a privileged political few while excluding the majority will tell the nation that the masses have no place in the UNC, especially the youth who are tomorrow's leaders.

The UNC, it seems, has become a poor shadow of the serious political movement it once was and if it fails to manage its affairs professionally and with transparency it will witness an exodus of members and supporters. And that would be the greatest gift that anyone could hand to Prime Minister Patrick Manning and his PNM.

(January 12, 2010)

Ajay Parasram
Has the UNC lost its way?

When a movement stops moving, by definition, it dies. The UNC elite believe they are still a party in motion, but they are moving side to side at the highest levels of the party while people below them are being ignored.

I was born a Trinidadian. My country and its people remain in my heart and mind every minute of every day. Circumstances led to my family being transplanted to Canada, but it was clear to my three brothers and I growing up with our parents in near cultural isolation from our homeland that Trinidadian politics was the issue of the day, whether we liked it or not. (I liked it.) It was how we connected with home.

Even though I am not a resident of Trinidad and Tobago, I feel personally betrayed by the political machinery of its bureaucratic, anti-democratic nature across party lines.

I have a tremendous amount of respect for Basdeo Panday, and his leadership established over decades of struggling with the people to fight for a better country. When I first met him, I was an idealistic 18-year old, volunteering with the UNC for the summer before starting my undergraduate degree.

My experience with the UNC influenced my decision to study Political Science. I met with Panday at Rienzi in 2002 and was very inspired by this leader who carried such charm, charisma, and experience with ease. He listened carefully, he thought thoroughly, and he planned strategically.

We talked about lots of things, but one conversation in particular stands out in my memory. He told me that I was young and radical today, but as I aged, I would become a little less radical. As I got a little older still and took on more adult responsibilities, I would become a little conservative. I would have to worry about things like bills, or looking after children, and eventually, by the time I was middle aged or so, I would find it hard to remember being a young 18 year old radical who wanted revolutionary change.

I've never forgotten that conversation, and it occurs to me almost eight years later, just two days before the UNC will hold an allegedly free vote on leadership, that what Mr. Panday was saying is autobiographical.

He was a young radical, he fought hard and long to build an opposition movement that could challenge the 'divine right' of the PNM. And he succeeded, for a while. But as his movement, his party, got older, it started taking on more bureaucratic responsibilities. It started worrying about self-preservation rather than social change. Panday and his posse have said that only those who were there for the birth of the UNC in 1989 can understand and criticise it. My apologies, I was 5 years old.

But I would wager my tuition fees that when Panday was walking door to door in constituencies through the 1970s and 1980s, he wasn't talking about party discipline, hierarchy, or the need to exert strict control. He was probably talking about building a movement together that would empower people to exert influence over the governance of their own lives. This is a message that crosses racial boundaries, it crosses class boundaries, and it crosses gender boundaries.

A party that jealously seeks to preserve its own status quo because it believes that only the anointed ones can move us forward, can criticise us, is a broken party and failed movement.

I understood the UNC in 2002 to still be a party of mass movement, and it is for that reason that the party stayed in my heart. I understood the political dynamics that led to President Robinson arbitrarily and erroneously dismissing the incumbent UNC government in 2001 on the basis of "morality" to disguise his personal vendetta.

Throughout my undergraduate degree and into my graduate degree, I would produce reports, write articles and analysis on Trinidadian politics, and generally do all that I could from abroad to help advance the movement I believed in so strongly as an impressionable 18 year old. As my studies advanced, I was witnessing the slowing down of the movement I was so proud to be a part of, but never lost hope that it would re-energise itself once more.

As recently as 2007, I remember fighting passionately with another member of the Trinidadian diaspora at a party I hosted. She supported COP, arguing that the UNC dream was dead and gone. I would not accept this, and I certainly was not willing to turn my back on the leader who had inspired me so much. The movement had come to a grinding halt though, and I was stubbornly refusing to admit this.

It is not entirely the fault of the political leadership; it is also a function of the dirty politics in Trinidad, and a function of the process of party-institutionalisation. The party had grown older, but it had not matured.

The same material constraints Panday warned me about in 2002 — that as I got older, I would become bogged down by things that would make me less radical and more conservative — had happened to him and his party.

I never saw that young woman again, and this microcosm helps put into stark focus the brokenness of sticking to our traditional guns as we try to build a movement. You don't build a movement with sticks and stones; you build it with humility, service, and action.

When Panday called on us to send him into retirement in a blaze of glory in the last elections, I wanted to help him because I was grateful for his lifetime of service. But this hubris, seeking a capstone in his career (which he had already achieved through being the Prime Minister) badly compromised the real objective of removing the PNM and healing our bleeding country.

Looking back at my fight with my Trinidadian comrade, why did I, a UNC supporter, and she, a COP supporter, drive each other away when we are chasing the same goal of struggling for a better Trinidad and Tobago for everyone?

This is when I abandoned all romanticising of party loyalties, and realised that true social change does not come from the institutions of political parties. It comes from people who are united to resist oppression and fight for their collective freedom. The structures of electoral democracy are far too easy to hijack.

When the practice of state-democracy becomes the system of oppression, people are forced to self-organise and render the structures of partisan politics irrelevant. A real democracy would not require party loyalty and discipline — it would require an informed and compassionate population of peers.

A party must never shun new members, and it should never, never, shy away from criticism that will only help it mature. Democracy is people power, but representative democracy as is being practiced today is elitist hypocrisy. The UNC today is barely a shadow of the party it was when I was 5 years old.

Rather than staying true to the radical proposition that all those who seek a better Trinidad and Tobago could find an equal place in a mass movement of the people, the party has instead stayed true to the dogma of conservatism and self-preservation, grasping at the nostalgia of battles long-since fought.

I applaud Panday's unwavering fighting spirit, but it is misplaced and misguided today. Vicious attacks playing on divisive race politics or harmful gendered stereotypes is unbecoming of a leader and devastatingly disappointing to the now 26-year old radical, who still wants social change.

The rising sun of the UNC was meant to shine on all Trinidadians who wanted a better tomorrow. Today, conservatism ensures it only shines on the privileged few. The people of Trinidad and Tobago who dared to believe in a mass movement are being denied what they so desperately deserve. If the party continues to block the light of its own rising sun, it will condemn itself to the bitter resentment of everlasting night.

(January 23, 2010)

Kamla beats Bas; says it's people's victory

Kamla Persad-Bissessar was gracious in victory Sunday night (January 24, 2010) and opened her arms to welcome all those who campaigned against her in the internal election of the United National Congress (UNC).

In a brief address, she said: "I am your servant. I accept the assignment you now place in my hands. And I pledge that I will never let you down." She said she was deeply humbled and told UNC members a new journey begins now. "And I call on everyone tonight to unite as one family — because that is what we are, one family — and let us begin the crucial task of rebuilding our party. And then we will extend our loving hand across the nation and embrace everyone and invite them to join our crusade for justice, equality and love.

"I know some of you have lost hope, but I am here to tell you that the flame you kindled today with the trust you have placed in me and my colleagues will grow into an inferno that will burn away the darkness and let the rising sun shine again.

"I have always told you that I put the Lord in front and walk behind. Today we have walked with the Lord and we have done the righteous thing.

"Let us work together to build a fairer, more prosperous Trinidad and Tobago where all of us can live in harmony; no matter what our backgrounds, this is our home. We are one nation with one destiny.

"I have said it before and I repeat it: There is no PNM Trinidad and Tobago; there is no COP Trinidad and Tobago and there is no UNC Trinidad and Tobago. There is only one Trinidad and Tobago.

"Our nation is going through its darkest hour and we must come to its rescue and do what is right to arrest the continuing decline.

"I say to you tonight, there is no PNM way or UNC way to heal a sick child; there is no partisan way to help a single mother who is working day and night to feed her hungry children. There is no them and us; just US.

"All of us make up one nation, one family. That is how God meant it to be and that is how it will be under my leadership.

"To my opponents, I say again, this was not about us but about the future of this nation. And I invite you to join us in the revolution that begins now. We need you as much as we need every member to spread the message of hope for a better tomorrow. Let us embrace change and we will get out of opposition and remove the Manning regime whenever Manning chooses to call an election.

"All families have differences and in the heat of political campaigning people say things that offend. But as a mother, wife, sister and daughter, I know how to forgive. And I want you to know that I hold no animosity toward you. Let us embrace for the national good and work together to rebuild our divided party and win the next election.

"I do not know all the answers and none of us does, but together we will meet and talk and hold consultations and we will bridge the gaps and present a winning platform that will benefit everyone in this country. Because I know that none of us is as wise as all of us; none of us is as strong as all of us.

"We all have the same concerns and the same dreams. We want to rid this country of the plague that has descended on it, and we want to create a new society in which each of us can blossom and grow.

"This victory is your victory and the nation's victory," she said.

(January 24, 2010)

Kamla takes charge of the UNC; praises media

Kamla Persad-Bissessar on Wednesday (January 27, 2010) formally took over the leadership of the United National Congress (UNC) from Basdeo Panday, the man who founded the party in 1989. And in speech to mark the occasion she said Sunday's vote marked the initial step towards reconciliation, reunification and rebuilding of the nation.

"This is a victory of the people, wherever they happen to be, man or woman, of every creed and race and space and place," she said.

She said the election was a very important part of the democracy in the UNC and praised those who had the foresight to create a system that allows every member to participate in the process of electing a leader and other members of the national executive.

"My message this afternoon goes beyond lines and other boundaries, real or imagined, and the message simply is that change is no longer just in the air, it has arrived at your doorstep.

"On Sunday night a few thousand people ensured that politics in Trinidad and Tobago would begin to take on a whole new meaning and that what before separated us would now bring us together.

"That the old way of doing things would now be replaced by the ONLY way of doing things, with tolerance for each other, with the greater good in mind, where personal political ambitions are secondary to nobler, national pursuits in the interest of every citizen."

She said the UNC must never again betray the trust of its membership and the nation. "The political tribalism that once divided us will now give way to a nationalism and patriotism for the hunger of a child in Laventille is the same as that of one in Penal, and the fear of a father for his family's safety in Tobago is the same as the ones in Toco.

"And the pleas for water in Cedros is the same as those in Diego Martin, and the cries of a patient for proper medical attention in Port of Spain is the same as the ones in San Fernando," she said.

She praised the new chairman, Jack Warner, his perseverance and dedication in demanding accountability and change, and for taking the issue to the members across the country. "And so we congratulate Mr. Warner and the Movement for Change for challenging the status quo and helping bringing us to where we are today.

"Had it not been for their untiring and selfless dedication to the cause of democracy in our party, the voices of our membership may have remained silenced and our nation would have suffered the result," she said.

Persad-Bissessar also pledged to make the new UNC a government in waiting. "I shall recommend to our executive that we should immediately establish a shadow cabinet that will have responsibility for monitoring the day to day activities of the government. She promised that "we will become the national watchdogs on your behalf. And we will not allow the Manning regime to get away with anything."

She invited everyone to work with the UNC and join the new revolution for change. "Today I want to invite all of you to come home and bring the rest of the family. There is room in the house of the Rising Sun for everyone.

"And my arms are open wide to embrace each one of you as we begin this revolution of change that will sweep the Manning administration out of office."

She also expressed her deepest gratitude to the media who contributed to keeping the issues alive during the campaign for the internal election and for keeping on the national agenda daily, the issues that affect our people.

"You are the guardians of democracy and you have never abdicated your responsibility to the people and the country," she said, adding that, "You have my word that I will at all times defend your rights to freedom because without a free media our democracy would be deformed."

The new leader said, "Free speech allows for a marketplace of ideas in which our citizens would be able to judge for themselves — as they did in our just concluded election — what is right and what isn't.

"We must never allow organisational pressures to get in the way of that freedom. You carry a great burden of responsibility to this nation to report without fear or favour to ensure that today's minorities are not prevented from becoming tomorrow's majority."

Kamla Persad-Bissessar's victory was a turning point in the history of the United National Congress and the country. However, the next steps were difficult and Basdeo Panday refused to accept the people's verdict. And for a while, MPs who should have responded to the changed political reality and join the new leader still held on to Panday's coattails.

Panday's control of the UNC is a betrayal of the people

Over the years since 2000, the United National Congress (UNC) had grown lethargic and had become a poor shadow of the democratic, people movement that Basdeo Panday launched in 1989, predicting that people would flock to his crusade not because of "the colour of their skins but because of the content of their minds."

That bottom up movement propelled Panday into government in 1995, but his inability to deal effectively with dissent within his cabinet and caucus caused his fall from power within months of the UNC winning a majority in the 2000 general election.

Panday and the UNC never recovered and instead of going through a process of self-examination and rebuilding, a small group of men and women huddled together at the Rienzi complex week after week, ignoring the people and refusing to admit that it was time to wake up and get serious about winning an election.

Jack Warner, the rookie MP from Chaguanas West, dared to challenge the status quo and earned the title of *neemakharam*, but he was determined to effect change. And he did. He started the revolution for change that saw Panday and his loyal team wiped out in the January 24 internal election, except for Roodal Moonilal.

There were a few significant things about that election:

- For the first time Panday faced a challenge for the post of leader of the UNC

- Panday stated that he would respect the verdict of the people and leave with "joy in my heart" if he lost

- Panday promised never to be a "yoke" on the necks of UNC members

- Panday predicted that if he lost the election the UNC would be dead in six months
- The unprecedented support for the new team that won, led by Kamla Persad-Bissessar and Warner

Now three weeks later, Panday remains leader of the opposition and he is acting as if he is still leader of the party. And public pronouncements from some pro-Panday legislators and Panday himself suggest that they are in charge of the party, not Persad-Bissessar. The reason is clear: some MPs elected by people in 2007 have refused to accept the people's right to choose and insist on keeping Panday in office through their continued support. And today the members of the Senate represent views of a single MP, not the party.

At a time when the party should be engaged in a process of healing and planning for an election, it remains a home divided. An energised Panday is now talking about a divided party with "them" and "us." "I'll just let them wallow in their mess," he was quoted as telling the Trinidad Guardian, adding that Persad-Bissessar is "misleading the nation and tarnishing the names of all the MPs if she does not say specifically who is supporting her."

That should never be an issue.

Once the members of the party had made a choice through a democratic process established by the party, there should be no question about loyalty and support for the leader.

Panday is the one who has always boasted about his respect for democracy. In a statement shortly after learning of a challenge to his leadership, Panday said he was supremely proud of his achievement of introducing a UNC constitution that allowed "any person in good standing to go up for elections." And in a speech in 2000, he urged citizens to stand up against tyranny. "Never surrender your freedom to those who have no respect for democracy and freedom," he said. And he has said more than once if the people rejected him he would leave "with joy in my heart," vowing never to be an albatross around the necks of UNC members.

So why is Panday taking comfort from a constitutional anomaly that allows him to remain the official leader of the opposition when the majority of the members of the opposition party rejected him?

Panday must stand up for democracy and respect the people's decision. A total of 1,359 UNC members voted for Panday; Persad-Bissessar won the support of 13,493. If you divide the votes among the 41 constituencies in the country only 33 people per constituency voted for Panday as leader.

Even Panday's Couva North constituency turned against him during and after the vote. One of his most loyal lieutenants, constituency chairman Orlando Nagassar had this to say:

"We found it very difficult to mobilise people for the internal elections to vote for Panday. Although we transported people to the polling stations, they went and voted for Kamla," he said on Monday (08 Feb. 2010) when the whole executive offered the new leader their resignations.

That statement alone should be the signal for Panday to summon his MPs and tell them that they must respect the people's verdict, support the new leader and get the party in shape to win an election. And he should get involved in using his political experience and skills to make it happen. Instead, he is gathering his few loyal troops to "mash up" the party that he founded as a people's movement, ignoring the very ideals for which he fought for decades only to hold to power that is not rightly his.

Panday has no moral ground upon which to stand. Today he cannot even rely on the people whose support so often sought when he was down. Despite the optimism of some of his supporters, the people have made a clear choice. So it would seem that the only result that Panday can hope to achieve from his political tantrum is to inflict serious injury to the party since there is no way he can be leader.

And the puzzling question is why? Why would a man like Panday, who has fought all kinds of battles on behalf of the people, deny his own party a chance to continue the struggle he started and get back into government?

Panday appears to be working hard to make his own prediction come true — that the UNC would not last six months under the leadership of Persad-Bissessar. There must be some other hidden agenda. And the members of the UNC must demand some answers, and do it now.

But I also blame the new UNC leader for letting this state of affairs continue. She has the support of a strong chairman who has demonstrated that he has the ability to mobilise the people to stand up for what is right. Why doesn't the leader give Jack his jacket and let him fix this problem today? If the MPs are refusing to do the democratic thing, then it is time for the people in their respective constituencies to demand that they do. They are in office because the people put them there to do a job. And part of the responsibility of an MP is to recognise the party's legitimate leader.

The people deserve better. They voted for change. And the leadership has an obligation to the people to create the change. Anything less would be yet another betrayal of the people.

(February 14, 2010)

Kamla unseats Panday

Kamla Persad-Bissessar on Thursday (February 24, 2010) took the oath of office to become Leader of the Opposition, succeeding Basdeo Panday whom she defeated in the party's internal election on January 24 to become leader of the United National Congress. President Max Richards, who administered the oath, said it was a historic event to appoint the country's first female opposition leader.

The Siparia MP has held the post before, but it was in an acting capacity while Panday was banished from the House of Representatives.

It took a month of negotiations before she was able to secure the support of the majority of opposition MPs to remove Panday and take office. In a brief statement following the event, Persad-Bissessar said she is now one step closer to getting into government. She added that a UNC government would return peace to Trinidad and Tobago.

"Our party now speaks with one voice. We will chart a new way forward to deliver on the hopes and expectations of our citizenry, desperate for a way out of the crisis which the Manning administration has led this nation into," she said.

"I oppose the arrogance and self-glorification of the current leadership in the PNM. I oppose the lack of compassion and concern for the well-being of our citizens, so many of whom are ironically supporters of the ruling party. I oppose the trampling of the rights of workers. I oppose the view that people will vote only along tribal and ethnic lines regardless of whether they are being properly represented or not," she said.

The UNC leader said she represents change and opposes those who believe that things cannot change. "I pledge to the nation that Trinidad and Tobago will be returned to the peaceful, stable and progressive society it once was," she said. Persad-Bissessar told the media she is ready to take the party forward and invited everyone to come on board.

In a message that seemed to be directed to some members of the party who still refuse to accept her leadership, she said the UNC "is not in the business of running anybody out of the party" and promised to try her best "to hold everyone together."

The holdouts include, St Augustine MP Vasant Bharath, who attended the ceremony although he did not sign the letter endorsing her for the post. "I never pretended to support Mrs. Persad-Bissessar and I thought I would have been hypocritical after she was appointed leader of the Opposition for me to then jump and endorse her," he told reporters. Bharath had said he would accept Persad-Bissessar's leadership under certain conditions. He wants the party to have a discussion "to facilitate a graceful exit" for Panday. "I think we as a country and as a people will always be judged by the way we treat our elders and leaders and our children," he said.

However, Panday himself refuses to be graceful in the new political landscape. In a media statement Thursday he said he would accept Persad-Bissessar's leadership although he still has reservations about the election in which she defeated him. And he said he would not sit on the front bench while UNC Chairman Jack Warner is Chief Whip. He has demanded, as he has done in the past, that Warner account for "millions of dollars." He wants Persad-Bissessar to fire Warner and has said he would sit in the back bench until she does that.

For his part the Chaguanas West MP has again dismissed Panday's allegations.

Don't let Panday stand in the way of progress

As things "fall in place" and Kamla Persad-Bissessar takes over as the official leader of the opposition, there remains a divisive element within the United National Congress (UNC) that will be a continuing headache for new political leader and UNC Chairman, Jack Warner.

Persad-Bissessar has now completed the journey from MP to leader, having waited a month for colleagues Roodal Moonilal and Tim Gopeesingh to heed the people's call for change. However, others like Vasant Bharath, Ramesh L. Maharaj, Kelvin Ramnath and the Pandays (Basdeo,

Subhas and Mickela) continue to remain in denial. What is sad is that while the membership of the UNC and the nation rallied behind the campaigns of Persad-Bissessar and Warner, seven people seem determined to divide the opposition only because they refuse to accept that they were rejected by the membership in favour of a new team led by Persad-Bissessar and Warner.

Panday still refuses to accept the legitimacy of the new leader and continues to mouth his flowery rhetoric of saving the UNC, which he built with his "blood, sweat and tears," while insisting that the party would die within six month. The reality is that he himself wants to be the executioner because he cannot let go.

I have followed Panday's career from the day he entered politics and have worked closely with him both in and out of government. Without a doubt he has contributed to the country's development, but the UNC and the nation cannot continue to rest on Panday's laurels while the nation groans under the weight of the Manning regime and cries for help.

Panday cannot offer that help and the people made that very clear when they voted him out on January 24. The task for Persad-Bissessar in the days and months ahead is mammoth; she cannot continue to allow detractors to stand in the way.

So far she has demonstrated leadership and I have no doubt that she will continue to do so and take the party back to Whitehall. But she must be careful not to let her guru and mentor get in the way. She must recognise that Panday appears unable to overcome his political *tabanca* and under these circumstances he cannot be an asset to the UNC. He will remain an obstacle not because he is incapable of helping but because he refuses to accept change. That attitude caused his break with so many men and women with whom he had been associated politically over the decades and remains his Achilles heel.

Panday loyalists, including members of his family, will remain committed to a resurrection although it is clear that Panday's time is up and he must either work with the new political dispensation within the UNC or be left out. It is all well and good to say and do all the politically correct things such as depending on the wisdom of the former leader and handing him a seat on the front bench. But Panday doesn't want that.

His failure to send Persad-Bissessar and Warner to his famed political graveyard continues to haunt him, so those who expect positive contributions from Panday today are deluding themselves. Now is the time for the UNC to move on with its agenda without Panday, whose old politics will retard the party's growth and its ability to return to government.

The campaign that propelled Persad-Bissessar into the leadership, proved that the UNC membership wanted nothing to do with Panday and his few allies. Except for Roodal Moonilal, every member of the Panday team was wiped out. The message was clear. Even political unknowns beat UNC stalwarts who chose to be counted with Panday. This is why the new leadership must be wary of how they proceed in the unity and healing that is now necessary. Persad-Bissessar and Warner promised that to the membership and UNC they are waiting for them to deliver.

The membership and non-members alike, expect the UNC to rebuild itself as a vibrant political force and government in waiting. They asked for a revitalised party that would offer hope. Handing Panday any front line position now would work against what the people expect. In fact it would be a betrayal.

Persad-Bissessar is the new leader of the UNC and Leader of the Opposition. That is what the UNC membership demanded with their vote. Everyone in the party — including Panday — must accept that unconditionally.

(February 25, 2010)

Section 5
Kamla rises

With Kamla Persad-Bissessar firmly in control of the opposition and clear signs that the other parties were ready to do business with her, her focus shifted to the leadership of Patrick Manning and his PNM administration.

Her first decisive strike was a motion of no confidence. It was the straw that broke the back of the Manning regime and led to fall of the government. It also heralded the creation of a coalition of interests led by Persad-Bissessar that would win a decisive victory and take charge of Trinidad and Tobago. She fought on the theme WE SHALL RISE!

Kamla files no confidence motion in government

Opposition Leader Kamla Persad-Bissessar on Monday (8 March 2010) filed a motion in the House of Representatives seeking to have the Parliament approve a no confidence vote in Prime Minister Patrick Manning.

In a media release, Persad-Bissessar said the motion expresses "the lack of confidence held by the population in the Prime Minister arising from the questionable conduct of the Prime Minister in a number of controversial matters." It noted that the latest is Manning's "Hart" failure.

The opposition leader said, "The startling revelations and documentary evidence laid before the public showed the family ties between former Chairman of UDeCOTT, Calder Hart, and that of CH, the company that was awarded contracts worth several hundreds of millions of dollars.

"That the Prime Minister over the years and recently as one month ago had stoutly defended the integrity of Calder Hart and his relationship with him makes him culpable to the dubious dealings which have now been placed in the public domain," she said. She added that following Hart's resignation UDeCOTT must place on hold all of its the current multi-million dollar projects pending a forensic investigation into all the activities "of both that organisation and its former Chairman."

Persad-Bissessar said, "Prime Minister Patrick Manning must be held accountable for his actions. He has even gone as far as removing one of his senior ministers, Keith Rowley, from his cabinet because he dared to question the lack of Cabinet oversight on UDeCOTT and raised the prospect of the corrupt practices at UDeCOTT through the irregular procedures and flagrant violation of ethics by Mr. Hart."

She added, "The population is reeling from the questions which now hang over the head of the Prime Minister whose close relationship with Calder Hart, his lavish praise of his work and shameful defence of all charges against the former Chairman, even when so much evidence became known during the John Uff Commission of Enquiry, all combine to making Patrick Manning answerable to the people.

"The Prime Minister no longer enjoys the confidence of the people to honour his oath of office and to serve the people of this nation in their interest without fear or favour."

The motion:

March 8th, 2010
The Honourable Barendra Sinanan
Speaker of the House of Representatives
Office of the Parliament
The Red House
Abercromby Street
Port of Spain.

Re: Private Members' Motion

Dear Mr. Speaker,

In accordance with the Standing Orders of the House of Representatives I wish to have the following motion placed on the Order Paper for the next sitting of the House. I beg to move: Be it resolved that the House of Representatives declare that it has no confidence in the Prime Minister, Patrick Manning.

Respectfully, (signed)
Kamla Persad-Bissessar MP
Leader of the Opposition.

Who shot Calder Hart?

When Calder Hart resigned on Saturday (March 6, 2010) and promptly left the country with his wife and daughter, the news spread like wildfire. It was because Hart had become a kind of symbol for the political assault on Patrick Manning and the Urban Development Corporation of Trinidad and Tobago UDeCOTT, which Hart headed.

He had been under extreme pressure following startling revelations before the Uff Commission of Inquiry that linked Hart's wife to directors of a company, CH Development, that won a lucrative UDeCOTT contract, awarded while Hart presided over UDeCOTT.

Hart had always denied the allegations but before the Uff Commission closed its hearings, his lawyers decided not to cross-examine the witness who provided the information, Carl Khan, a former husband of Hart's wife.

The opposition UNC had also raised the matter while Basdeo Panday led the party. Jack Warner provided the resources for the research in Malaysia and it was Tabaquite MP Ramesh L. Maharaj who first raised the matter of Hart's alleged family connection to the multi-million dollar contract to build the government's legal affairs tower. Just days before Hart's sudden departure from UDeCOTT and Trinidad, the Congress of the People (COP) produced documentary evidence that confirmed what had been known for several months.

COP is trumpeting its move as the straw that broke the camel's back. Perhaps it is so but then again it may very well have been the weight of all the overwhelming evidence against Hart that had come before. For COP it was a master public relations coup. The timing of the release of the COP report was perfect, coming in the same week that the High Court was to rule on whether it would allow the Uff report with the UDeCOTT details go to the president.

It turns out the court decided against Hart and UDeCOTT, clearing the way for the report to get into the hands of the president. What better timing to spill the beans on Hart and connect the dots to try to paint a picture of corruption! And like all good politicians, the party's leaders have been saying COP's investigation was key to the latest developments.

COP leader Winston Dookeran hailed members of COP's legal team at a weekend unification forum noting that they blew the whistle on some of Hart's business dealings.

It's true that the team had made connections with a Malaysian law firm, which was able to access birth and marriage certificates of persons who are allegedly involved in several local projects and to make the family connection. Hart's defenders are still suggesting that the documents might be bogus.

So the truth is nobody has anything that could stick to Hart or Manning or UDeCOTT ... not yet at least. For now Hart is a free man and there is no evidence today that will change that. As far as his former colleagues are concerned people are hounding Hart "without justification" and one of Hart's lawyers has said his client is returning home and is within reach with just a phone call.

What is clear, is that opposition politicians collectively contributed to the fall of Hart. And if they are wise they will keep the pressure on Hart, Manning and UDeCOTT to get to the bottom of the matter.

It makes no sense to try to score political points instead of doing more to get the hard evidence that could make a case for corruption.

However, it would be useful for Trinidad and Tobago if COP's leaders pool their legal and other resources with the official opposition and work to dig deeper and unearth real evidence that can prove some of the allegations about corruption that have been making the rounds since the day Patrick Manning fired Keith Rowley for ostensibly behaving "like a *wajang*".

The truth is nobody has shot Calder Hart, who remains a free man. He has fallen from his pedestal, but he isn't even wounded. And for now, there is no sign that the political grandstanding will change that.

(March 9, 2010)

Opposition unity is good news but at what price?

The good news coming from UNC Political Leader Kamla Persad-Bissessar, is that she is keeping her campaign promise of uniting the opposition. The better news is that she is putting the party's three deputy leaders to work on a unity strategy. And the best news is that she would ensure that party members are involved.

The team, which is led by Oropouche East MP Roodal Moonilal, is in the process of working on a report and Kamla has promised that when it is submitted, the national executive and all arms of the party will have their say. She said once that is done she intends to engage the broad membership and the general public "in our deliberations on this very important issue" on national unity.

Kamla told supporters at a political meeting in Barataria Monday (March 15, 2010), that the UNC's vision includes objectives and strategies to address the wider problems of the society, which is why there is an urgent need for unity.

"The Unity that our party desires, is a unity that will be based on principles, integrity in the process, a commitment to good, honest and effective governance, and most importantly a unity that will not only be embraced by the electorate…but one that is sustainable.

"I have tremendous faith in you and your patience…the nightmare we have been enduring will soon be over."

The nightmare of which she spoke is of course, the Manning administration's failure to effectively govern and the mounting allegations of the worst corruption to ever surface in the country's political history. What is even more interesting is that the anti-PNM movement is stronger because of the conflicts within the PNM at this time.

There is without doubt a vibrant "dump Manning" movement within the governing People's National Movement (PNM). For the first time, the party is challenging a sitting prime minister and suggesting that he quit.

That provides the greatest opportunity for unity among those political forces that want to see genuine change. But the challenges are also enormous, which is why Moonilal and his team have to be careful about how they approach this assignment.

Kamla has been careful to define the broad terms of any political nuptials, noting that it must be sustainable. That is critically important because unless there are strong base fundamentals on which the parties can agree there is no point in having a flawed unity.

The Congress of the People (COP) continues to position itself as the alternative government, while ignoring the seismic change that has shaken the UNC at its roots and established an entirely new approach to doing business. In the new political order it is the UNC that is in command primarily because COP's initial strength was from disenchanted UNC members who wanted nothing to do with the old guard led by Basdeo Panday.

Kamla campaigned on a promise to unite the party and the opposition and do what Panday had failed to do: beat the PNM. The people took her at her word and now she is demonstrating that she plans to keep her promise. The danger is that in the haste to form a united front, the UNC could lose its focus and, because of political expediency, compromise its identity as a people's party.

It would be better for the Moonilal team to fail, than to succeed in a unity venture that would eventually crumble as the NAR "one love" experiment turned out in 1986-7.

There is today a perfect political storm in favour of the opposition. While the two main opposition parties have a common goal, each has its own guiding principles and philosophy. Each has its own constituency and it would be a fatal error to assume that an agreement to unite will solve the problem.

The UNC is today the strongest it has been since it won its first general election in 2000. The people are ready for change and see the new leadership as offering the best hope for that change. There is, therefore, no great urgency to have a shotgun marriage that would fail.

A formal coalition, based on the recognition of the individual identities of the parties, is a far better and more honest approach than unity deals which force each to give away too much. The electoral formula that would see Manning swept out of office is simple: one to one contests in each constituency. And that is the point on which the UNC must keep its focus today.

If the COP claims to have strength outside of the traditional UNC heartland, then that is where it needs to focus if it genuinely wants to unseat the Manning administration. All it would take for an opposition victory is for the UNC to keep its 15 seats and take the six marginals that were within reach in 2007. That may not be an attractive proposition for COP, which would likely demand some of those "safe" seats as part of a unity formula.

But the UNC must stand firm. Here's why: COP knows that it cannot win an election alone and history has shown that a divided opposition in our electoral system benefits the governing party. So whatever happens, the starting point must be a unity plan in which the opposition parties agree that only one opposition candidate will face the PNM in every one of the 41 constituencies.

If COP refuses to agree to that, it would be wise for the UNC to seriously consider building its strength with its other allies because if the mood in Trinidad and Tobago remains as it is, the UNC alone can win a majority against the PNM.

(March 17, 2010)

COP, UNC agree on two-way contest in next election

The next general election in Trinidad and Tobago will be a two-way fight between a united opposition and the governing People's National Movement (PNM). The leaders of the United National Congress (UNC) and the Congress of the People (COP) have agreed on such a political formula although they have not worked out the details of the structure of a united opposition.

Winston Dookeran and Kamla Persad-Bissessar met Friday (March 26, 2010) at the opposition leader's Port of Spain office to discuss unity and elections. It was their second meeting since Persad-Bissessar won the leadership of the UNC. Dookeran had previously made the suggestion of a two-way race in any future general election but it is the first time that he and Persad-Bissessar have agreed on the matter.

The COP has its own ideas about governance and leadership and a UNC committee headed by Dr. Roodal Moonilal is working on a draft unity strategy for consideration by the party's executive and membership.

There are several unity proposals under consideration, including a plan for a formal coalition in which each party will retain its identity and its leadership. Such a plan would mean that each would have to negotiate which seat it will fight in a power sharing arrangement. Dookeran prefers such an arrangement.

"COP ... has established a permanent place in the political landscape of Trinidad and Tobago. I have no doubt about that and I think that will continue to be so. But for the purposes of the challenges ahead of us we have to find the right formula to have the one-to-one contest," Dookeran told reporters Friday. He called the discussions with the opposition leader "interesting, inspiring and useful," noting that they agreed on three principles. "That is, we are both very much interested in and will work towards charting and drafting and crafting strategies for unification within and between and amongst our parties.

"Secondly we've agreed in principle that we will work together for the purposes of the Local Government election which is constitutionally due by July.

"We have had agreement and consensus that we both would want to engage in any electoral contest on a one-to-one basis against the PNM." Dookeran stated that he and the UNC leader have "in principle agreed that we will work towards a sustainable unification not only between our two parties, but with other political groups in the society."

He said such a plan would, "offer to the nation, at the appropriate time, something that will be purposeful and will in fact have the competence to tackle the various problems we are facing in our society." He added, "We will, in addition to that, be able to agree in principle at this stage that whatever elections are held in Trinidad and Tobago, we will strive to find the right formula and model to agree on a one-to-one contest against the ruling party."

The two leaders plan to meet again in a month, but Persad-Bissessar is confident that there will be a unification and a one-on-one contest. In the 2007 general election PNM won a minority of votes but won 26 of the 41 seats in the House of Representatives with the other 15 going to the UNC alliance. COP and UNC together won a majority of votes but because of vote splitting, the PNM won and COP failed to win a single seat although it got more than 22 percent of the popular vote.

(March 27, 2010)

Manning tells PNM get ready for election

Patrick Manning told members of the governing People's National Movement (PNM) Saturday (March 27, 2010), to get ready for a general election. Speaking at a special convention in Chaguaramas, the PNM political leader instructed each of the party's constituencies to immediately commence the screening of its candidate for an election. Manning advised delegates to start the screening in his own San Fernando East constituency. And he said since the opposition has been calling for an election he might just give them their wish.

"Since they feel that the time has come for a general election, then I will agree with them. As a consequence of which I now direct the party to commence the nomination of candidates exercise for the general election immediately. Screening begins on Wednesday, April 7, in the constituency of San Fernando East," Manning declared.

The screening coincides with an opposition no confidence motion in Manning that opposition leader Kamla Persad-Bissessar will move in the House of Representatives. Manning told the convention the party would apply to the Commissioner of Police for a permit to hold a public gathering on April 9, in Woodford Square, Port of Spain on the day of the debate.

The parliamentary convention is that if a prime minister loses such a vote the government falls and fresh elections are held. But the president also has the discretion to appoint another member from the House who in his opinion is best able to command the loyalty of the majority of MPs.

The PNM has a strong majority and it is unlikely that the opposition vote will get anywhere close to passing, so Manning's position is not under threat. Last week all 41 constituencies passed a resolution supporting Manning's leadership.

What the opposition hopes to do with the motion is, to place on official records what it considers are the misdeeds and shortcomings of Manning. The debate itself could be very embarrassing for Manning. What will also compound Manning's problems is the negative fallout over the resignation of UDeCOTT boss Calder Hart, who is under criminal investigation. Hart was under scrutiny at the Uff commission of inquiry into UDeCOTT and the construction sector.

Commission chairman Professor John Uff is expected to hand over his final report Monday (March 29) to President Max Richards. Persad-Bissessar is already demanding that Manning lay the report in Parliament. In a media release Friday she stated that all the evidence presented during the inquiry is already in the public domain. She said Manning should follow the protocol and make the report public.

Manning told delegates, he is fully aware of what is going on in the country and better informed than the media about what people are saying. And he said he is never going to make the mistake of not sufficiently taking into account the views of the people. He spoke of his administration's successes. And he suggested that by putting the opposition UNC in office the country would be taking God out of government.

When President Robinson appointed Manning as Prime Minister on Dec. 24, 2001 following the 18-18 tie, he justified his action by saying the country needed a government of "spirituality and morality." Manning said, "Don't put God out of your thoughts by putting them back into office."

Speaking at a Voice of the People rally as Manning made his election announcement, the leader of the UNC responded to Manning. "Let me answer you, Mr Manning, don't back back on that promise, you know, Mr. Manning. Don't back back at all because Mr. Manning knows he cannot stop the wave." She called on the thousands gathered for the rally to say whether they had confidence in Manning and got a thunderous, "NO!" in reply.

(March 28, 2010)

Manning makes a gamble but is the opposition ready?

Mark April 9 on your calendar. That's the day the opposition in Trinidad and Tobago will try to document all Patrick Manning's misdeeds in a motion of no-confidence in the prime minister.

The opposition — and Manning — know the vote will not succeed, but the revelations likely to come out will be enough to make Manning's already waning popularity get worse. But the motion is not what will make that day important. What makes the date special is what the prime minister intends to do on that day to pre-empt the opposition motion. And all my political instincts tell me that Manning will announce that he is dissolving Parliament for a general election, most likely on May 3 or shortly thereafter. May 24 is a likely date because it is the date in 1971 when he formally became the MP for San Fernando East for the first time.

Once he does it, he will march out to Woodford Square where thousands bussed in from across the country would embrace him in a well-orchestrated rally to launch the election campaign. It would be a brilliant stroke to steal the opposition's thunder and walk away with a winning hand in the opening round of the election game in which he hopes to hang a "Jack" and make a clean sweep — high, low, Jack, game.

Manning doesn't have to call an election until 2012. But the events of the past few months have signaled clearly to him that he is losing ground both inside his own party and at the national level.

Some of his advisers are therefore telling him, he could score a double victory in an election now by killing off the dissent in the party and getting re-elected, leaving an unprepared opposition right where it is — in opposition. Manning is gambling on the opposition remaining splintered, so he could have a majority victory without winning half of the popular vote as happened in 2007.

However, if the opposition is truly focused on winning government it would put aside its differences and mount a joint campaign now in which the two parties — the Congress of the People (COP) and the United National Congress (UNC) — would not fight each other in any constituency. In effect, the PNM under Manning would be facing one strong opposition candidate in each constituency, thereby preventing vote splitting. But there is no time to lose.

Apart from the cosmetic announcement last week, that the COP and the UNC have agreed in principle to field only a single candidate per constituency, there is no real progress in moves for meaningful unity.

The UNC, energised by the rise of Kamla Persad-Bissessar, is firm in its commitment not to give too much to the COP; for its part the other party is equally adamant that it is strong and commands a significant constituency. But those issues will become irrelevant if Manning pulls the plug and calls an election. All that would matter then is whether the combined opposition would see the big picture and make the necessary compromises to win an election.

The big picture, of course, is winning government. But achieving that goal is easier said than done. Manning has a plan and he has the resources to hire the best in the business to make it happen. When he went to the Senate Monday, to make what are obviously grand electioneering promises, he was sending the clearest possible signal that he is ready to take his chances with the electorate.

What he tossed into the mix were two of the most controversial issues today: the proposed Trinidad and Tobago Revenue Authority (TTRA) and the hated property tax. Now after defending both, he is ready to back away.

And here's the reason. The Public Services Association (PSA) has always been part of the PNM's vote machine. The TTRA had put that at risk and with the association consorting with the opposition, Manning realised that it was time to halt the TTRA bill for now and bring the PSA back home to the PNM. With regard to the property tax, Manning was aiming at business people and the middle class, some of whom he met last week at the hastily arranged meeting with members of the Syrian-Lebanese community. Those insiders who say Manning didn't win many hearts when he met the group should pay attention to the signal he is sending with the rethinking of the same tax that he and his cabinet had staunchly defended while the business and middle class denounced it.

Manning also sent another signal. On the day that the president received the Uff report on the UDeCOTT inquiry, he announced that the health ministry was giving mega contracts to the agency for a major hospital development initiative.

The PNM leader is gambling on getting his troops back on board and winning again without any of the "dissidents" like Keith Rowley, who has been a thorn on Manning's side for the longest while. There is no doubt that there is a splendid opportunity for those opposed to the Manning administration to get together now and defeat the PNM. The revolt within the PNM spilled over Monday night (29 March) with anti-PNM demonstrations at a PNM rally in Valencia in northeast Trinidad. That and the grumbling from inside the party provide the opportunity that the opposition can exploit.

However, a united opposition is still not in sight and that is why Manning appears willing to take the risk. But a day is a long time in politics and anything is possible. Manning could be stronger than ever when it is over or he might just have to take up the Bible and move to a different pulpit to begin his other chosen career. How it ends really depends on how the opposition responds to the best opportunity for victory that it has ever had.

(March 30, 2010)

Manning's options: prorogue or dissolve?

What is Patrick Manning really thinking?

The flurry of activities since Manning dropped the bombshell, that he might call an election two years before it is due, has convinced most people that the PNM leader will take the gamble, primarily to shut off debate in parliament. Former cabinet minister Fitzgerald Hinds seems certain that a general election now will put the party out of office.

There are two critical issues that Manning would like to pre-empt: the debate on the opposition no confidence motion that is scheduled for Friday (April 9) and the exposure of what's in the Uff report presented last week to President Richards.

The attorney general promised last week he will lay the "unsanitised" document in the Senate this week, which means that a Pandora's Box could open up, exposing all kinds of embarrassing things about Manning, his government and the dealings with former UDeCOTT boss, Calder Hart.

That would suggest that an election is a bad idea, especially since the two opposition parties — the United National Congress (UNC) and the Congress of the People (COP) have already signaled their intention not to oppose each other, meaning that the PNM will likely face a single opposition candidate in each constituency.

The other factor is that, the UNC is now stronger than it has ever been following the election of a new executive led by political leader Kamla Persad-Bissessar and chairman Jack Warner. In a general election the gloves will come off and during a campaign of three weeks — which is the shortest campaign time possible under the country's electoral rules — a lot can happen.

Manning made the mistake of calling an early vote in 1995 and ended up losing the government. So is he ready to take the risk again?

The consensus is that he is, and is hoping to use every resource at his disposal to try to convince the electorate that he is still the best choice to lead the country and that despite what he calls anti-government propaganda, his administration has done a good job. But that would not tally with public opinion. Polls show Manning has been the worst leader since independence and the latest surveys indicate that his government's approval rating is under 20 percent.

Then there is Keith Rowley, the latest PNM pariah who is refusing to accept that approval rating and is planning to run for the PNM if his constituency wants it. Manning will have the final word and Rowley will probably not be on Manning's team.

Of course, one way to shut up Rowley is to let him run. It would be a coup because a candidate running for election cannot bad mouth his own party. However, Manning's arrogance and hatred for Rowley would likely prevent him from using this tool to muzzle his fiercest critic.

But with Rowley outside of the PNM camp during an election campaign, there could be even more chinks in Manning's armour since the former cabinet minister has slammed his own party for allowing corruption to grow under Manning. Rowley has been largely responsible for exposing corruption in the Manning administration, particularly with respect to UDeCOTT. And he is on record as saying that any election would be fought on the issue of UDeCOTT and corruption.

So Manning finds himself wedged between the proverbial rock and a hard place. An election could put him out of office; waiting means the opposition will gain strength and the internal revolt will grow. And he faces the same problem with Rowley — to have him or not to have him on a PNM election slate.

Manning can prorogue parliament, in effect silencing the voice of the legislature, while under no obligation to call an election. He did it in 2002 when he was unable to elect a Speaker and convene parliament after he became prime minister when President Robinson fired Basdeo Panday. If he chooses that route he can govern with the executive arm alone without breaching the constitution. And every legislator will lose her/his voice in parliament. Manning can then manage information carefully — as he did in 2002 — and indulge in a propaganda campaign to glorify himself and his administration without having to worry about MPs and senators. All he would have to do is recall the Parliament briefly in July to either postpone local elections again or announce a date, and then prorogue again. So while everything points to a general election, Manning may show up in parliament on Friday only to announce that the parliament will be prorogued. On the other hand he could do what most people expect and what the PNM fears — tell the House that he has advised the President to dissolve the parliament for a general election. He gambled before with such a thing and lost. Will he be brave enough to try it now? Only Manning knows.

(April 4, 2010)

Kamla wants Manning to fire housing minister, UDeCOTT board

Opposition leader Kamla Persad-Bissessar on Sunday (April 4), called on Prime Minister Patrick Manning to immediately fire Emily Gaynor Dick Forde, the Minister with responsibility for both UDeCOTT and the Housing Development Corporation (HDC). Persad-Bissessar also wants Manning to fire the UDeCOTT board.

The leader of the United National Congress (UNC) was responding to the publication of the Uff report on the inquiry into UDeCOTT and the construction sector. Chairman of the commission, Prof. John Uff, presented the report to President Richards on Monday and the attorney general has promised to lay it in the Senate on Tuesday.

But on Sunday, the Newsday newspaper in Trinidad published the main points of the probe along with a list of 91 recommendations. The report recommends a police probe of former UDeCOTT executive chairman Calder Hart and the whole UDeCOTT board.

It also says there should be an investigation into the circumstances in which nine hectares of lands owned by the National Union of Government and Federated Workers (NUGFW), which had been sold to the NUGFW at subsidised rates, was purchased by UDeCOTT, at a profit for NUGFW.

In a media release Persad-Bissessar pointed to the NUGFW matter, noting that she had previously said that it was a matter for the Integrity Commission. "It is now clear that the Uff Commission agrees with me," Persad-Bissessar said. "The Members of the Board continue to shamelessly hold on to office despite the incriminating evidence presented in the report. They must be fired now!" she demanded. The Opposition Leader said the report "reveals a sordid tale of mismanagement, corruption, subterfuge and cover-ups. It is a most damning statement of Manning and his government whose ministers and board of directors should be investigated for malfeasance in public office." She added that it confirms that there is massive corruption in the way UDeCOTT was doing business and demanded that authorities immediately begin the recommended investigations.

"In addition Mr. Calder Hart should be located and returned to Trinidad. Since the members of the Board of UDeCOTT have been put under scrutiny, they should not be allowed to leave Trinidad," Persad-Bissessar said. She observed that based on the report it would seem that what is even more frightening is the fact that the prime minister kept praising Calder Hart and behaved as if nothing was wrong. She said based on the findings of the report it is a important for the Integrity commission to investigate charges made by the opposition involving UDeCOTT board members Michael Annisette and Dr. Krishna Bahadoorsingh. In addition to calling for the line minister's dismissal along with the whole UDeCOTT board, the opposition leader is also calling for:

- the attorney general to provide the human, physical and technical resources to the police to immediately begin their investigations, since reports emanating from inside the police service indicate that they are being frustrated in their work
- the DPP to examine the evidence so far collected by the police and lay charges
- the attorney general to tell the nation what he knows about the whereabouts of Calder Hart
- the relevant authorities to seize the passports of persons who the Uff Commission says should be investigated
- a review of the companies and agencies now exempt from the Freedom of Information Act in order to create transparency and public accountability
- the publication the report in all of the newspapers so that all the citizens can read of the corruption perpetrated against them by the PNM government.

(April 5, 2010)

Kamla wants Manning's resignation

Opposition leader Kamla Persad-Bissessar wants Prime Minister Patrick Manning to resign and call a general election immediately.

The UNC leader was commenting on the dismissal of the UDeCOTT board announced Tuesday (April 6) by Attorney General John Jeremie.

Persad-Bissessar said acting against the board is "too little, too late" and suggested that it is unacceptable that the government refuses to act on serious allegations against UDeCOTT, its former executive chairman Calder Hart and senior executives. "In the circumstances there is concern that evidence may be destroyed and the Prime Minister should now fire himself and call the election now," she stated.

Persad-Bissessar said she doubts that the criminal probe into UDeCOTT will result in tangible action anytime soon, and gave the assurance that a UNC government would take decisive action on the issue of corruption. "I give the undertaking that when we form the government we will ensure all are investigated and those who have to go to jail will go to jail according to law," she stated.

The UNC leader is on record as proposing, the establishment of a special court to deal with criminal trials involving allegations of political corruption against public officials. According to attorney Anand Ramlogan, "There is precedent for this is in the way the Dole Chadee prosecution was conducted. The need for an independent investigation into this [UDeCOTT] fiasco is yet another reason why this government should be removed from office as soon as possible."

Writing in a column published on *Jyoti*, Ramlogan said, "The right hand cannot investigate the left hand. History has proven that the PNM cannot be trusted to investigate." Ramlogan also suggested that the line minister for UDeCOTT be fired. In an interview with *Jyoti*, Persad-Bissessar expressed disappointment over Jeremie's failure to help police find Hart and suggested that Jeremie's statement Tuesday is just window dressing. She wondered why Jeremie is cherry picking in terms of what investigations are given priority. Persad-Bissessar said the Uff report called for:

- a full investigation of the award of the $368 million Ministry of Legal Affairs construction contract to CH Development Limited
- an audit of the conduct of all of UDeCOTT's senior staff and directors for the period 2004 to 2009 as to their "involvement in errors and omissions" concerning the Brian Lara project
- an investigation into what steps were taken by UDeCOTT's managers to control and reduce delay at the $3.2 billion government Campus Plaza project in downtown Port-of-Spain
- a review and redefinition of the roles of UDeCOTT and related state agencies.

She noted that all these appear to have been glossed over. The opposition leader also noted another significant issue raised in the Uff report — an investigation into the circumstances in which 9 hectares of lands owned by the National Union of Government and Federated Workers, which had been sold to the NUGFW at subsidised rates, was purchased by UDeCOTT, at a profit for NUGFW. That sale occurred while senator Michael Annisette was both a UDeCOTT board member and shareholder in the NUGFW holding company that sold the land.

She also made reference to another forensic probe of the Cleaver Heights project and asked why this issue continues to engage such prominence when three previous investigations have shown that there is nothing to support allegations of impropriety by former cabinet minister Dr. Keith Rowley.

(April 7, 2010)

Parliament dissolved

Prime Minister Patrick Manning announced Thursday (April 8), that he has advised President Max Richards to dissolve the Trinidad and Tobago Parliament effective midnight, April 8, 2010. The move effectively kills an opposition no confidence motion that was scheduled to take place on Friday April 9, in the House of Representatives.

Manning did not announce an election date but sources close to the opposition told *Jyoti* the election would most likely be on May 17 or 24. An election must be held not later that three months from the date the parliament is dissolved.

Manning's People's National Movement (PNM) won a clear majority of 26 of the 41 seats in the House of Representatives in elections on November 5, 2007. No election was due until at least 2012. But the government has been under increasing pressure from the opposition to call an election because of what politicians say is the Manning administration's poor record and its inability to deal with crime and corruption.

Manning told a special PNM convention last month, that he would likely give the opposition its wish as he put his party on an election footing, instructing all constituency executives to begin the nomination process immediately.

The opposition had been expecting the election. In 2007 the United National Congress (UNC) and the Congress of the People (COP) ran independent campaigns and that helped Manning win a comfortable majority although his party won just over 45 percent of the popular vote. Since then the two parties have talked about a united opposition front, but the unity process has not advanced beyond an agreement in principle that they will field single candidates in an election.

COP Leader Winston Dookeran is out of the country, but UNC leader Kamla Persad-Bissessar assured reporters this week that the unity deal is on.

Manning's gamble. Don't celebrate yet

The consensus among opposition supporters is that, Patrick Manning has just written his political epitaph and the man who plans on serving the Lord after politics might very well be on his way to starting his new career. Even many of his own supporters in the People's National Movement (PNM) are saying Manning is making a bad gamble.

But is he? Perhaps this is a carefully planned strategy to shake off some of his baggage and win a fresh mandate as a leader of integrity.

In the past two and a half years since winning a strong majority, Manning has had the benefit of great windfall revenues while presiding over an administration that has been accused of being the most corrupt in the history of independent Trinidad and Tobago. His move to dissolve parliament on the eve of an opposition no confidence motion earned him the label of coward, with the leader of the opposition calling it an admission of Manning's colossal failure. "He is petrified of the information which would have come before the parliament," Kamla Persad-Bissessar told reporters Thursday as she pledged to have an election campaign in which the opposition would expose:

- the UDeCOTT and Calder Hart issue
- the criminal probe into the Abu Bakr land deal
- the construction of a Church at Guanapo Heights
- the dangers posed by Trinidad and Tobago Revenue Authority Bill
- the unpopular property tax
- unchecked crime
- the breakdown in the provision of health, water, education
- the squandering of the nation's resources

It sounds like the making of a winning campaign. But the opposition should be careful and not start celebrating a victory just yet.

Though Manning has created his own troubles, he is counting on his political skills, the use of state propaganda and the loyalty of the PNM tribe to return him to office. Today, with the legislature silenced, Manning is fully in charge, governing only with the executive branch, which he heads. He has already put the state propaganda machine into full gear and over the next few weeks he will bombard the population with positive messages about the achievements of his government.

His failings will become virtues in the well-orchestrated advertising blitz and Manning will present himself as a man of morality and spirituality whose character is beyond reproach. Those who have broken the rules, he will say, will pay the ultimate price. "Don't put God out of your thoughts by putting them back into office," Manning told his supporters last month when he put his party on an election alert.

He is also counting on an unprepared opposition, a lack of unity and the yet unsettled internal issues in the United National Congress (UNC) that have remained simmering since the internal election in January.

The opposition is confident that it can beat Manning and the PNM. It insists that the unity matter is going to be settled, despite the rumblings of discontent from the Congress of the People (COP).

But what about the Panday factor? Persad-Bissessar fought her campaign for election as leader of her party on the promise to shake the Panday UNC from its lethargic state and win. The membership voted overwhelmingly to break away from Panday. In addition, COP sent a signal that with Panday out of the way, it was willing to do business with the UNC.

But Panday and some of his loyal MPs like Kelvin Ramnath and Ramesh L. Maharaj, who have so far refused to accept the new leadership in the UNC are now saying that they are ready to seek re-election. Can they become the albatross around Kamla's neck that could deprive her of the victory of which she is so confident?

Some UNC supporters welcome the return of the party's founders, saying if Kamla accepts them she would show magnanimity and independence, immediately providing healing and hope to consolidate the UNC base. The flip side of that argument is that the return of the Pandayites would muddy the unity waters with the COP, which had always been adamant that it would not seek unity or political accommodation with a Panday UNC.

It is no longer a "Panday UNC" and Panday would be only a candidate if he is nominated to run again, despite the rejection by his own constituency and the UNC membership at large. But it would be naive for anyone to suggest that his presence would not bring back memories of the baggage that caused the UNC to remain in opposition since it was toppled in a presidential coup in 2001. Added to that, the widespread national support for Kamla could wane if there is a perception that she is embracing Panday again.

In effect, what may very well happen is that if the UNC wins a majority Panday and his loyal MPs would be the real power. Manning could exploit all of this as he tries to convince the electorate that despite the PNM's shortcomings it has the maturity to govern.

The road ahead for the opposition is bumpy, but victory is possible. What is needed is a united opposition and careful, well-focused campaign with a slate of candidates that's acceptable not only to the UNC base but to the nation. That's a tall order and time is short.

(April 9, 2010)

Manning was facing palace coup: Kamla

Opposition leader Kamla Persad-Bissessar said Saturday (April 10) Prime Minister Patrick Manning's explanation as to why he dissolved parliament is an admission that he is a coward and that he is frightened to face the representatives of the people in the national parliament.

Manning stated Friday that he asked the president to dissolve Parliament because he did not want the opposition "on the eve of an election" to use parliamentary privilege "to slander those of us in government."

In a media release Persad-Bissessar dismissed the point stating that no election was due until 2012 so it was Manning who created the "eve" of an election by shutting down the parliament. She said there were other reasons, which Manning is not talking about. "If fact we know that Mr. Manning was facing a revolt within his own party and at least five PNM MPs were prepared to support the opposition motion of no confidence in their own leader," she stated. "Mr. Manning was facing the risk of being dethroned in a palace coup and therefore he moved to silence the parliament."

The UNC leader also took issue with Manning's statement that he would be prepared to take legal action against the opposition. Manning stated, "If they wish to make *comess*, they are now free to do it, but do so outside the parliament. I have a battery of lawyers standing by."

Persad-Bissessar made it clear that dealing with the people's business is not *comess*. "The truth is not *comess*," she said. "We in the opposition will continue to speak out against Mr. Manning and his corrupt government even though he has shut down the Parliament and is refusing to call an election."

The UNC leader said Manning cannot escape the judgment of the people and noted that he has other motives for his action in not setting the date for an election. "Mr Manning is withholding the election date because having silenced the legislature he now rules without any accountability to the people's representatives and the people's Parliament.

"We expect Mr Manning to misuse public funds to carry on a propaganda campaign and delay the election as long as he can. But he cannot delay it forever; he will have to face the people by July 8," Persad-Bissessar added. She said the prime minister has shown contempt for the people and the democratic process by shutting down Parliament for the spurious reason he has advanced. "His action demonstrates his dictatorial ambitions. The UNC warns citizens to be on guard against this oppressive regime and this budding dictator," she said.

The Rowley factor is the PNM albatross

Patrick Manning is campaigning on his integrity, urging everyone to re-elect him on that basis.

It's a long time since President Robinson inflicted Manning on an unsuspecting population on Christmas Eve 2001, declaring that the nation needed a government of spirituality and morality. More than eight years later, Manning has failed to show that he fits that mould through his personal behaviour in office and his government's programmes and policies, although if you listen to him you would hear otherwise.

On Saturday night (April 17), he was knocking down the UNC/COP alliance as a farce while boasting about what he and his government had done for the country, pointing out that it was all done with "integrity." And he has also been wearing his religious beliefs on his sleeve, suggesting as Robinson did in 2001, that the UNC would deprive the population of spirituality. Here's what Manning had to say when he addressed supporters the day after parliament was dissolved: "Don't put God out of your thoughts by putting them back in office."

The "them" he spoke of was the opposition United National Congress (UNC) led by Kamla Persad-Bissessar, a woman who makes it her business to put "God in front" while she walks behind.

And Manning has been speaking of integrity using the propaganda that worked for him in 2001, calling the Panday administration the "most corrupt" ever in the country. Perhaps it is time for a reality check.

By his own admission, Manning is the most "vilified" prime minister in the country — and for good reason. The UDeCOTT scandal alone justifies the label, especially his staunch defence of former UDeCOTT boss Calder Hart while he was aware of a police investigation of Hart.

But wasn't it Keith Rowley who called the Manning regime the most corrupt ever, saying it was even "more corrupt than the UNC"? And didn't Rowley promise that the next election in Trinidad and Tobago would be the UDeCOTT election with PNM corruption front and centre? And what about the continuous attacks on Rowley by Manning and his colleagues, painting the former minister as corrupt?

So here is the most important question.

If indeed Rowley was and continues to be so corrupt that the government has launched investigation after investigation (the latest announced by the Attorney General when he laid the Uff report in the Senate), how can Manning speak of integrity today when the same Rowley is a candidate for the PNM in the May 24 general election? Rowley, the "*waajang*" and the "*raging bull*" whom Manning had to tolerate for 12 years, is now acceptable. And Manning talks about integrity!

Here's what Manning told parliament: "The minute you oppose my good friend (Rowley), he gets very, very angry. And if you oppose him strongly, he becomes a raging bull...You don't know the trouble I have seen. I have had to live with that for 12 years." Manning was raging mad after Rowley had appealed to his party and the nation to fight PNM corruption. His mission, Rowley told parliament, was to break the mould of corruption in the PNM.

And what of Rowley the candidate?

Is the PNM administration that he described as "more corrupt than the UNC" suddenly sanitised and purged of corruption? On what basis can the candidate for Diego Martin West honestly campaign and ask the people of Trinidad and Tobago to reinstate the regime that he has fought for so many months as being the most corrupt ever?

The Rowley factor is the one every voter should use as the measure to determine the integrity of the governing PNM. It is one issue that demonstrates the hypocrisy in the PNM and Manning's false commitment to integrity and good governance.

For the PNM, Rowley had become a pariah for daring to speak out against what he saw as corruption. Not nominating him, however, was the lesser of the two evils for the PNM. Had he been rejected he would have been free to continue his attacks on Manning and the PNM while remaining loyal to the party. That would have been bad news during an election campaign.

Now that he has been readmitted to the "tribe," the party has effectively muzzled him, hoping that a gullible electorate would buy the Manning and PNM hypocrisy. Manning cannot have it both ways. Neither can Rowley. The people have a clear choice on May 24.

The PNM will try to sweep corruption under the rug, continue to boast of spirituality and morality and try to delude the population into believing that Manning is a saint who has been a victim of misinformation and sabotage. If he succeeds, the population will have itself to blame, because in the final analysis a people get the government it deserves.

(April 18, 2010)

The tide turned in favour of the opposition on April 21, 2010 when the leaders of four parties and an activist group signed the Fyzabad Declaration that created the People's Partnership. Kamla had kept her promise to unite the opposition and Congress of the People Leader Winston Dookeran also kept his promise not to dissolve his party. The declaration committed all five members to work together with a common platform for change but at the same time each would maintain its own identity with its leader. The other significant issue was the recognition that Kamla would lead the group and become Prime Minister following a victory of the coalition. The partnership members are:

Kamla Persad-Bissessar — United National Congress (UNC)
Winston Dookeran — Congress of the People (COP)
Ashworth Jack — Tobago Organisation of the People (TOP)
Makandaal Daaga — National Joint Action Committee (NJAC)
Errol McLeod — The Movement for Social Justice (MSJ)

Kamla declares victory at hand; leaders sign unity accord

Kamla Persad-Bissessar verbatim after signing Fyzabad declaration (edited):

"Tonight, friends and family all, citizens of one of the great nations in the world, let us thank these icons of leadership in our nation for joining our platform tonight...The winds of change are blowing, my friends, tonight I ask you, can you feel it? Can you taste it. And tonight I say victory is at hand...most important of all, do you want it? And if you do then together we will march...We will put God in front and we will walk behind...tonight we ask you to join in a march to victory.

From today Charlie King Junction will not only be remembered for the labour struggle (of the 1930's) ...but for the place where the declaration of unity was signed. Once more citizens rise up to fight corruption, malice and spite. Nothing will stop me because together we can be happy and together we can be sad. Tonight is a historic moment...

Tonight we have joining us a man they call Jack Warner. Where do I start to speak of Jack?...He has helped thousands of people in this country... today I am proud that he has joined us on this platform.

And so friends, tonight while we are gathered here I want you to remember that Mr. Manning and his team cannot come with performance or with anything to improve the lives of the people...they will come with bribes and character assassinations. They will come with lies but this government under Mr. Manning has been the most anti-worker government ever...so what do you do on May 24?...

We will increase old age pension to 3,000. We will increase the minimum wage...we have the solution. History is being made right here right now. I remember calling on all parties not to remain stuck in the mud but to gain traction not distraction...

My fellow citizens, I was lambasted for preaching unity. They said I would sell out my party...tonight I say to you I will preserve the integrity of the United National Congress and I will not change the logo and name of our party unless I come back to you...

We will respect everyone of our partners...we must live with unity in diversity. So there is no shame in keeping your rising sun, there is no shame in keeping the logo of the Congress of the People...this not about logos and names...A partnership is not about a quick fix...each partner must be respected and loved. If we were all one shape and size what a boring world that would be...when we look at the diversity of our people and the diversity of the rainbow then we say, O Lord, how great thou art!

And so I ask you tonight, to put your faith in God let your heart not be troubled, do not be afraid...we are now united in common purpose as we go forward to forge a new day a brave new world for Trinidad and Tobago. I invite all our leaders to witness the signing of the people's partnership...a partnership for good governance in Trinidad and Tobago...we will share this document with you."

The Fyzabad Declaration April 21, 2010

A Partnership for Sustainable Good Governance in Trinidad and Tobago

1. WHEREAS the People of Trinidad and Tobago in their Constitution -

- a) have affirmed that the Nation of Trinidad and Tobago is founded upon principles that acknowledge the supremacy of God, faith in fundamental human rights and freedoms, the position of the family in a society of free men and free institutions, the dignity of the human person and the equal and inalienable rights with which all members of the human family are endowed by their Creator;

- b) respect the principles of social justice and therefore believe that the operation of the economic system should result in the material resources of the community being so distributed as to subserve the common good, that there should be adequate means of livelihood for all, that labour should not be exploited or forced by economic necessity to operate in inhumane conditions but that there should be opportunity for advancement on the basis of recognition of merit, ability and integrity;

c) have asserted their belief in a democratic society in which all persons may, to the extent of their capacity, play some part in the institutions of the national life and thus develop and maintain due respect for lawfully constituted authority;

d) recognise that men and institutions remain free only when freedom is founded upon respect for moral and spiritual values and the rule of law;

2. AND WHEREAS

The Parliament of Trinidad and Tobago has been dissolved and the **General Election** will be held on 24th May 2010. This General Election is a decisive and a historic turning-point and watershed in the development of our great twin-island Republic and the following political parties recognise and acknowledge that our nation needs men and women of selfless dedication, firm resolve, integrity and national commitment to take our beloved country forward.

3. AND WHEREAS

The Partners herein, in the interest of the people of Trinidad and Tobago agree and subscribe to this historic Partnership and to pool their considerable talents and resources in the national interest at this critical juncture in the history of Trinidad and Tobago.

4. AND WHEREAS

The Partners believe that, the opportunity exists for the people of Trinidad and Tobago to vote for a people-oriented and participatory Government committed to social justice and implemented by an effective, results-oriented team whose national objective is to put into practice Collaborative Leadership to achieve good Governance.

5. In this PEOPLE'S PARTNERSHIP the partners are:

(1) UNITED NATIONAL CONGRESS, (*'UNC'*);

(2) THE CONGRESS OF THE PEOPLE, (*'COP'*);

(3) TOBAGO ORGANISATION OF THE PEOPLE, ('TOP')

(4) NATIONAL JOINT ACTION COMMITTEE, ('NJAC'); AND

(5) MOVEMENT FOR SOCIAL JUSTICE, ('MSJ').

6. NOW THEREFORE the Partners agree and declare as follows:

a. **LEADER OF THE PARTNERSHIP AND PRIME MINISTERIAL CANDIDATE:**

   The Partners agree that the Leader of the Partnership and Prime Ministerial Candidate is and shall be Mrs. KAMLA PERSAD-BISSESSAR.

b. The Partners agree to select candidates and only one candidate from the partnership shall contest the General Election in each constituency in Trinidad and in Tobago and such candidate shall be the standard-bearer for the Partners in that constituency.

c. The Partners commit to adopt Principles and Codes of Conduct whereby the interest of our beloved Country is and shall be put before party and individual self-interest and as a Government comprising the Partners they will implement a Public Policy Programme to improve the quality of life of the People of Trinidad and Tobago based on shared principles of National Development and national unity. Together these constitute the foundation for sustainable government. The said Principles and Codes of Conduct include but are not limited to the matters set out in the Appendix hereto attached and marked as "A".

d. The Partners have established **Collaborative Teams** to develop a common **Public Policy Programme** to be shared on a **Common Platform** and have agreed to establish mechanisms for the achievement of **Consensus**.

e. The Partners agree that they will abide by the spirit and letter of the Constitution and law of Trinidad and Tobago and to propose legislative changes as are necessary to give effect to the will of the people.

FOR and on behalf of
UNITED NATIONAL CONGRESS

Kamla Persad-Bissessar
Political Leader, UNC

FOR and on behalf of
TOBAGO ORGANISATION OF THE PEOPLE
Ashworth Jack
Political Leader, TOP

FOR and on behalf of
MOVEMENT FOR SOCIAL JUSTICE
Errol K. McLeod
Political Leader, MSJ

FOR and on behalf of
CONGRESS OF THE PEOPLE
Winston Dookeran
Political Leader, COP

FOR and on behalf of
NATIONAL JOINT ACTION COMMITTEE
Makandal Daaga
Political Leader, NJAC

Dated this 21st day of April, 2010

Manning's dirty politics won't hurt Kamla

It would seem that Prime Minister Patrick Manning is following the Panday script in trying to knock down his prime opponent, Kamla Persad-Bissessar.

As the leader of the United National Congress (UNC) continues to gain political strength and additional non-traditional allies, Manning is engaging in dirty politics, mudslinging and attempts at character assassination. Here is what he had to say this week in Tabaquite in defence of his wife, Hazel Manning:

"Let me tell you who Hazel Manning is...She does not smoke...she does not drink...get drunk and wine down to the ground...Hazel Manning is a woman whose shoe latchets Kamla Persad-Bissessar is not worthy to untie...leave Hazel Manning alone...she is the best transformational minister this country has ever seen!"

What Manning didn't say is why he saw it fit to appoint his wife to cabinet three times without ever having her face the electorate. No one has ever voted for Hazel, yet she has been sitting at her husband's side in cabinet since Manning was allowed to usurp the position of Prime Minister on Christmas Eve 2001.

In our parliamentary system we allow backdoor appointments to the cabinet through the senate. But to do it three times is anti-democratic and sends a clear message that the appointee is not fit to represent the people and by extension should not be fit to sit in cabinet. In Manning's case it smacks of nepotism. As to Hazel's competence, well that is another matter entirely. During the UNC internal election campaign in January Panday tried the same approach, going as far as calling Kamla a drunk and suggested that she cannot be a leader unless she defeats "her problem." Her problem, she admitted, was Panday. And she soundly defeated him. And now her problem is Manning and the PNM and she is set to beat them as well. Manning's Waterloo is at hand!

In January, Panday's strategy didn't work and Manning's attempts to pull a page from Panday's script will also fail. The nasty politics strategy failed in January because Kamla refused to be drawn into Panday's agenda and instead stayed on the high road outlining her vision to heal the ailing UNC, take it out of intensive care, return it to its strength and then unite the opposition to beat Manning.

And today she has delivered on all those promises and demonstrated that she is not only a leader, but a strong and effective one who is most likely going to be the country's prime minister when the votes are counted on May 24. She would be wise to stay on focus telling the people about Manning's failings and to outlining her policies for rebuilding the nation that Manning and his PNM clique have deformed through their divisiveness and misguided policies.

So far, the nation has responded positively to the UNC leader and her efforts to unite the country. She has refused to engage in tribal politics and she has enunciated clear policies about governance and accountability.

On the other side, Manning and his colleagues are digging deep to find dirt, hoping some of it would stick. And in a desperate attempt to counter the people's indictment against him, Manning is now enlisting his wife to sing his praises.

"Some people are spending a lot of money to attack my husband," Hazel Manning told supporters this week. "So let me tell you what he is really like and you don't have to pay me any money to tell you... Every night he gets only four or five hours of sleep. He works long hours, he listens to people's views and asks for advice, because he knows that being Prime Minister is not a part-time job."

The people of Trinidad and Tobago know that too.

So long as Kamla and her colleagues stay on focus, they would relieve Manning of his stress on Monday May 24.

(April 23, 2010)

Opposition team can easily win majority in May 24 vote

Much has changed since Trinidad and Tobago went to the polls in November 2007. But some things remain the same. For example, there are still 41 seats in the House of Representatives and to a large extent, there has not been a significant demographic shift.

The great challenge for the political parties is to sift through the million names, find their supporters and nail down the vote for the May 24 election. It's always the most difficult part of an election campaign and the thousands of foot soldiers assigned the task of bringing in the votes are usually the unsung heroes who do not stand on the stage in front of the bright lights on election night.

May 24 will be no different, except for who might be doing the real celebrating. In 2007, Patrick Manning and the People's National Movement

(PNM) cruised to an easy majority victory with 45.85 percent of the vote, representing ballots from 299,813 voters.

The combined opposition of the United National Congress Alliance (UNCA) and the infant Congress of the People (COP) split critical votes in key marginal seats to give the PNM the advantage. In the end, they had 342,476 votes (52.37% of the popular vote) and COP got no seat in parliament, with the UNC candidates of the UNCA winning 15. Such is the nature of Trinidad and Tobago's first past the post electoral system.

In 2010, the COP and the UNC have joined other political groups to fight the PNM in one-on-one races in all 41 constituencies, making vote splitting a thing of the past. Of course there will likely be a few independents or an insignificant party or two, but they will have no more than nuisance value.

So the fight on May 24 is between the PNM and the opposition. One on one. And if we use the 2007 numbers as a measure of what might happen, it looks like Manning might be sitting in opposition in the 10th Parliament.

Of course there is the argument that it is not simple arithmetic. Agreed. But Manning is also much weaker in 2010 than he was in 2007. And the UNC has a new leader and a new leadership, having dropped its founding leader Basdeo Panday and much of its unwelcome political baggage.

Based on figures from 2007 and assuming that the opposition has kept its support (I think it's fair to assume that it has added support), we can expect that the opposition might win nine seats in addition to the 15 that the UNC held in the 9th Parliament. The figures below are based on 2007 results:

1. Point-a-Pierre PNM — 7,427; UNC/COP — 9877 — (plus 2450)
2. Chaguanas East PNM — 6,757; UNC/COP — 9079 — (plus 2322)
3. Barataria/San Juan — PNM 7,179; UNC/COP — 9275 (plus 2096)
4. St. Joseph PNM -7,965 — UNC/COP — 9090 (plus 1125)
5. P. Town South/Tableland PNM — 8,929; — UNC/COP — 9345 — (plus 0416)

In those five seats, the opposition is starting with a majority, which equals 20 seats. In addition, seats that the UNC held previously are within reach:

1. San Fernando West PNM-7,371; — UNC/COP — 7257 — (114 needed)
2. Tunapuna PNM-8,468; UNC/COp — 7827 — (641 needed)

In Tobago East, the PNM won with 5,601, with the combined opposition getting 4722, just short of victory by 879. This is a vulnerable PNM seat, which was held by DAC before.

One other strong possibility is Lopinot/Bon Air West. The PNM won it with 8,535 in 2007 but the UNC/COP combined vote was 7067, meaning a lot of hard work and the right candidate could make the difference between winning or not. With the seat allocation announced in the unity deal, it would mean that if these are the 24 seats that give the opposition a majority government, all members of the coalition would be included except NJAC, which is contesting four seats, all of them very strong PNM constituencies.

There is talk about the making of a political landslide, similar to the one that washed the Chambers PNM out of office, dethroning the PNM for the first time in 30 years. Since then the PNM has been in an out of office and this is the first time the party has been so pressured that it called an election two and a half years before it is due.

The signals are clear. No wonder Manning was hastily building a church, because it seems that after May 24 he could begin his new career preaching the word of the Lord.

(April 26, 2010)

Political games in the PNM

When 2010 started, the last thing on Patrick Manning's mind was that within four months he would be fighting for his political life.

He had already banished Keith Rowley, had planned to push Penny Beckles aside and the prospect that Basdeo Panday would be returned as leader of the United National Congress (UNC) in the party's internal election brought comfort to his heart.

Two things happened that upset Manning's political apple cart. A revolt from within started to gain momentum and Kamla Persad-Bissessar emerged as the new leader of the UNC in a decisive landslide that pushed Panday to near political oblivion. By February 24, when Kamla formally dethroned Panday and became the leader of the opposition as well, Manning knew he had a problem.

Kamla's 10-1 victory against Panday spawned a new spirit of nationalism, unlike anything the country had seen. Even high-ranking PNMites like Beckles and Diane Seukeran (Faris Al Rawi's mother) were congratulating her; the women's constituency was fully behind her and she knew that she was standing on the threshold of Whitehall.

The opportunity came much sooner than she expected when Manning, fearing a palace coup, shut down the parliament on April 8 and set the stage for an election two and a half years after winning a strong majority.

Scandal after scandal had weakened the governing party and the inexperience of most of his cabinet — and his own blunders — made matters worse. What added salt to Manning's political wounds, was the constant war with the likes of Rowley, who refused to roll over and die; instead many within the PNM rallied behind the man who gave Manning a near fatal "Hart" attack.

Today, Manning is insisting that the race is just starting and there is a long distance to travel before the final tally on May 24. He is predicting that a "weak" Kamla would buckle under pressure and a hastily assembled coalition would come apart. He is counting on winning again, despite the heavy odds in favour of the opposition.

In 2007 victory was easy.

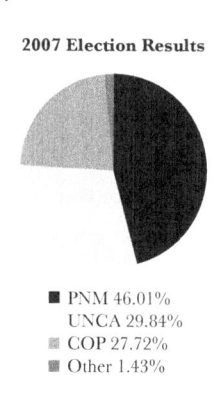

2007 Election Results

- PNM 46.01%
- UNCA 29.84%
- COP 27.72%
- Other 1.43%

General Election November 5, 2007

Parties	Votes	%	Seats
People's National Movement	299,813	45.85	26
United National Congress A	194,425	29.73	15
Congress of the People	148,041	22.64	0
Democratic Action Congress	8,801	1.25	0

Democratic National Assembly	376	0.01	0
Independents	120	0	0
Valid Votes	651,576		
Invalid Votes	2,306		
Total Votes	653,882		
Voter Turnout	66%		

(Source: EBC)

Two strong opposition parties fighting each other, provided the ideal opportunity to give Manning seats that he would have lost in a one and one fight. In the end he walked away with the prize, although the majority of electors rejected him. The repeat performance he was counting on failed to materialise when Panday was thrown out as leader of the UNC.

Kamla kept her campaign pledge to, "heal the wounds and unite" the opposition and immediately dedicated herself to sealing a unity deal with Winston Dookeran's Congress of the People (COP) and other political groups. To his dismay Manning found that the opposition he considered weak, unprepared and fragmented had found a way to unite and fight him one on one. And although there is no scientific poll yet suggesting that Manning's retirement is at hand, it is clear from what is happening on the ground that Kamla's time has come.

For Manning that is bad news. Not only does he stand to lose an election that was not due for another 30 months, he risks losing his position in the party. Rowley fought for and won his nomination as a PNM candidate not to sing Manning's praises, but to guarantee his bona fide as a PNM MP when the time comes to overthrow Manning. He had planned to launch his campaign for Diego Martin West on Thursday (April 22), but the party has now canceled the meeting, saying it was unauthorised since the party has not yet ratified Rowley's nomination.

Rowley had planned to stay within his constituency and avoid the PNM national platform — and for good reason. After his open war with Manning and his declaration that the Manning administration was the most corrupt ever, how can he in all honestly campaign for the Manning PNM?

And on the other side of the coin, after Manning's many attempts to paint Rowley as corrupt, how can he present Rowley as part of a clean, honest team? And that is where the rules of this political game change.

Rowley is not campaigning for the PNM to win this election; Rowley is campaigning for Rowley to win a seat in the next parliament as a man of integrity who helped bring down a corrupt Manning administration. His next move would be to demand that the party replace Manning for having caused the collapse of a majority government in 30 months and to offer himself as an alternative — Mr. Clean himself. And there are enough people in high places in the PNM who would dance according to that kind of music.

Once firmly in charge, Rowley's next act would be to launch a continuous attack on the new administration, hoping to inflict mortal wounds quickly that would lead to its demise in a single term. Then the PNM and a sanitised leadership would return to Whitehall and it would be business as usual for the party that Eric Williams founded in 1956.

But maybe not.

If Kamla and her team do what they promise and run a government that is above board, develop a meritocracy in which everyone is equal and treated fairly, maintain a partnership involving the state, labour and business, get the economy fixed and tackle crime at its source the PNM would find it hard to make another breakthrough.

But the race the to 2010 finish line hasn't even started in earnest. Anything can happen in the next few weeks. (26 April 2010)

(April 26, 2010)

It's worth it to dream of a united T&T

Divisive, tribal politics has been a feature of Trinidad and Tobago for so long that some people think there can't be any other way. But there is a way because we are one nation, one people.

Our origins, our religious beliefs, our customs, history and cultural traditions make us a state that defines cultural relativity in which we take the best of what each of us has to offer to create a unique national mosaic. That is the true Trinidad and Tobago.

Look at us at Carnival! One people! That's us.

Stephen Cadiz spoke of it on Monday night (April 26) in Felicity when he appeared on a platform of the United National Congress (UNC). He told supporters when the various parties met to discuss unity, the most important issue was the future of Trinidad and Tobago. He said that is a concept Patrick Manning and the People's National Movement (PNM) don't understand. And he urged everyone to stand up for Trinidad and Tobago. "We have to put aside our differences and start the business of building a nation," he said. "We put our country first and on May 25 we wake up to a brand new day," he proclaimed. "We will rise, Trinidad and Tobago!"

But that's not what you will hear from some fanatics who are still dedicated to the idea that politics is about "we and dem." These are the people who still cling to the position that has got us into the mess that we are in today.

It's difficult from Toronto to gauge the true situation on the ground, but from emails I have received and contacts with friends, family and colleagues I know, many UNC supporters are upset that Kamla Persad-Bissessar has "given away" too much. For them, "strangers" in the UNC will create problems. The strangers are people like Makandaal Daaga, Errol McLeod and even Jack Warner. It's nothing but blatant racism. What these people are saying is "How dare these Black people take over our Indian party!" And there are others who have not yet forgiven Winston Dookeran and see COP as trying to force itself on the UNC, uttering the words of the party's ex-leader, Basdeo Panday.

It's not pretty and reeks of the ugly political tribalism that has disfigured Trinidad and Tobago and will continue to retard progress, unless we as a people understand that there cannot and must never again be a "we and dem."

We came close in 1986 but the dream didn't last. Today, a new spirit of unity has taken birth with Kamla as the one nurturing it. It took a tremendous amount of struggle and swimming against the tide from Kamla and men like Jack Warner to break the tradition and demonstrate that regardless of our ethnic and religious identities, service to people, the community and the nation comes first.

Kamla fought Panday and won on the premise that her leader had lost touch with the people and reneged on the solemn pledge to put people first. Jack demonstrated that a Black man could be just as welcome in a predominantly Indian community as an Indian. For most of the people in Chaguanas West, he is just Jack, the best MP they have known.

It will take time for us to reach this level of political maturity. There are still those who are telling me that they prefer to vote for a PNM candidate than to support Jack, whom they describe as a man who has tried to steal "their party." Others prefer to stay at home rather than cast a vote for a party led by a woman who dared to fight Panday and then "cuddle" with the likes of Jack, Dookeran, Daaga and others who are not "UNC people." You would not believe some of the trash coming from these people.

For those who came in late, or who have forgotten when the UNC took birth on a rainy day nearly 22 years ago, thousands stood in the mud in Aranguez to hear the founding leader call for race and class to be banished. (The party was formally launched on April 30, 1989 at the National Stadium.) Panday invited the masses to join his crusade for justice, freedom and equality and predicted — as Martin Luther King jr. did — that people would join the movement "not because of the colour of their skins but because of the content of their minds."

Anyone who objects to the unity partnership that Kamla, Jack and others have put together to fight for the future of Trinidad and Tobago needs to revisit the history of the UNC.

And if they profess to be supporters of Panday by rejecting this alliance, they do Panday a disservice by suggesting that there is something wrong. Daaga fought for the same principles in the 1970 uprising that Panday and the UNC later adopted. McLeod fought with Panday in Oropouche in 1976 as a founding member of the United Labour Front (UFL) and went to parliament on Panday's labour platform.

The grand coalition of interests that Kamla and Jack put together, is the culmination of Panday's dream of a truly united party based on a love for our nation, freedom, justice and equality. They have done what Panday strived to achieve for 22 years. Anyone who supports Panday's ideals should welcome their efforts.

For a small minority on both sides of the political divide — including Manning — a national coalition bringing everybody together is a great loss because it marks the beginning of the end of political tribalism in which cronyism, nepotism, corruption and patronage take precedence over the rights of the people.

Trinidad and Tobago is in the midst of a great revolution. The test is whether this People's Partnership will prevail and if it wins, whether it will do what it proclaims. If it does, then I can say with joy in my heart, "My country has agreed to grow up!"

(April 28, 2010)

Jack exposes PNM conspiracy to smear him

UNC Chairman Jack Warner revealed what he said is "the smoking gun", to prove that the Manning campaign is plotting with British journalist Andrew Jennings to try to smear him. He said the evidence was contained in two confidential emails that someone left under the door at his office.

He said he found the package on Friday morning (April 30) and discovered it was an exchange between an American communications company, which he identified as SANITAS and the Trinidad and Tobago advertising agency, Valdez and Torry. Warner said the emails contained details of a plan to enlist Jennings in a scheme to discredit Warner by exposing what Jennings claims is corruption in FIFA involving Jack Warner. Warner is vice president of the international football body.

Last week People's National Movement (PNM) leader Patrick Manning, spoke about a conference on corruption in international sport taking place in Miami between May 1 and 4 at which Jennings would make presentations. He said he planned to transmit it live on television in Trinidad. Subsequent to that Warner advised Manning that he was not bothered by that and would gladly pay for the broadcast if Manning was unable to find a sponsor.

On Friday Warner connected the dots and read from the emails, which he said dealt with a number of issues including a plan to get Jennings involved in a "monstrous conspiracy involving Jennings and Manning." He said the email described him as "the project" and said time is running out to achieve the goal. The UNC chairman said the plot involved money for Jennings to be passed through the T&T agency because time is short. Warner quoted from the email he said was from the U.S. firm: "We have to move swiftly against Jack Warner."

Warner said the plan included getting Jennings to do interviews for broadcast locally on the national television service. He said the email was sent to government ministers Neil Parsanlal and Conrad Enill as well as communications specialist Maxie Cuffie.

Jenning's wrote to *Jyoti* on Friday (April 30) offering himself for interviews. *Jyoti* thanked Jennings but declined his offer, because we did not have the resources to conduct the interview.

Warner said, what he discovered exposed the dangers people face from an administration that has boasted that it had special branch officers watching a judge. He asked if people are really free. "How many others are being watched?" he wondered. "How many phones are tapped? How many computers are being hacked? How safe are you with blimps in the sky?"

He said it is no wonder that Herbert Volney felt compelled to resign as a judge and stand up in defence of the people as a candidate for the United National Congress in the May 24 general election.

The UNC chairman said the evidence before the people is clear. Patrick Manning's past performance, including his harassment of a former Chief Justice and putting a sitting judge to be a PNM candidate for the presidency (Justice Anthony Lucky), provides proof that Manning has to go.

The email that Jack Warner claims is the "smoking gun" to prove that there is a PNM conspiracy to smear him was allegedly send at 1:16 PM on April 29: "Time is clearly not on our side. Everyday goes by the project becomes ever more difficult. Regardless of the conference it is very good to get our hands on Jennings's info and use it in promotion.

"We can also help him get his research out on the street to raise the profile. I have a call and an e-mail into Jennings to discuss this and several other outstanding issues regarding the conference and his travel.

"The conference will be a good opportunity to showcase the overall FIFA corruption with Warner as the puppet master ... Every day we wait decreases the chances of success and increases the difficulty. Regardless, this is going to be tough but is critical to the campaign outcome.

"My recommendation is for us to engage Jennings, get what info he has, facilitate media at the conference for his event and manage interviews and media for him. We can also look to go live at the conference, although I have not seen his presentation I have offered Jennings help with it.

"In fact, it would be better to go live to tape and transmit the information back to Trinidad and Tobago for newscast and for replay and the Government's station. We have done this before.

"It would be interesting also to develop a separate event in T&T or make Jennings available with telephone interviews with local media from Miami.

"Time is closing and it will be tough for the client to transfer the necessary funds prior to the needs for us to be in Miami. Funds have to be transferred for Jennings from here, we may have to get creative with Valdez & Torry money through a sub-contract to Sanitas and then have the client pay you direct."

Warner said Valdez & Torry replied to the e-mail at 3:41 PM asking for a decision to be made on the conference. He said the e-mail was also forwarded to PNM chairman Conrad Enill, Information Minister Neil Parsanlal, PNM Public Relations Officer Jerry Narace and Maxie Cuffie, who is the CEO of the Government Information Services Limited (GISL).

Stand up for T&T

As the political parties gather Sunday May 23, 2010 for their respective rallies, there are going to be some disappointed people who won't be attending the events. Among them are persons who wanted to be candidates and failed to get the nod from the leadership of their parties. It is inevitable. After all there are only 41 seats available for the contest, so no party can accommodate all the people who wish to enter the race.

But how one reacts to the disappointment is a powerful statement not about the party but about the person.

A political party is bigger than any individual, including the leader or the party's elite. It is an organisation with a set of rules and a vision of what it hopes to achieve for the community and the country it serves. It expects its members, its activists and officials to accept these ground rules and live by them.

When a party wins an election, some of its elected members become cabinet ministers; others enter the cabinet through the senate. And the rules of engagement include the principle of collective responsibility. In our parliamentary system, there is a convention that members will vote as a block unless the party determines that each person may vote on conscience.

The People's National Movement (PNM) is an example of how this system works. The party rejected some high profile members during the

2010 screening process in what many supporters and activists considered clear victimisation. They mounted protests, made their point and went home. But in the end they remain loyal to their party, their party's ideals and will support the PNM. People like Penny Beckles, rejected twice, remain loyal. Ken Valley, kicked out and humiliated by the PNM in 2007, accepted the decision and supported the candidate who replaced him. And there are many more.

On the other side, Kamla Persad-Bissessar demonstrated the same commitment and resilience; she stood firm in 2007, saying she would never desert her party after being rejected for the leadership of the UNC Alliance. She came back to lead the party in an internal election that has already changed the course of Trinidad and Tobago politics forever.

Today, those who are boycotting political events because they were denied the opportunity to be candidates are demonstrating that they put themselves ahead of the party, the community and the country. If they fully accepted the party's leadership and worked on the ground among the people on the premise that the party is the right choice, then by extension they ought to accept the final decision of the party in choosing a candidate. Failure to do so means that the commitment was to self and self promotion, using the people as props to achieve the goal of getting a nomination.

In the case of the UNC, the party has had to make very difficult decisions about its candidates and it had to consider its vision of inclusion and unity. So some people did not make the cut despite being genuine about their commitment to the party and the people.

And some of the candidates may not be the best thing since sliced bread. However, a party expects that its genuine members and supporters will rally with it and help it win because of what the party represents. And it is critical for members to trust the leadership's judgment in times of stress.

In the UNC process, for example, Deputy Leader Lyndira Oudit failed to get the nomination for Couva South. She is disappointed and hurt, but accepts the decision. For her, the bigger picture is more important that being a candidate. "Is difficult to hide the hurt; I'm only human...But, I will get that over because I've begun to look at the bigger picture and tomorrow we shall see in Chaguanas," she told a reporter on Saturday.

That is what party politics is about. It is about a vision, a goal, a commitment and about working together as one team. In a democratic system there will always be dissent, but compromise and consensus must guide the decision making process and members who fail to accept that are showing a measure of selfishness that is not congruent with selfless service. If the system is broken, the membership will fix it.

Basdeo Panday did it when he broke with NAR and the result was the UNC — a party that remains committed to its founding principles of justice, freedom and equality. Jack Warner and the Movement for Change did it. Kamla's campaign for the leadership of the UNC demonstrated that when people feel let down they can change their leader. And she knows that if she fails the people, the people will move her.

Now is the time for everyone to put personal feelings aside, walk the talk and stand up for Trinidad and Tobago.

(May 23, 2010)

One million to choose the way forward for T&T

After weeks of intense campaigning, the election that shocked even the closest within the governing party is taking place two and a half years ahead of schedule. And if polls are accurate, Trinidad and Tobago will have its first female prime minister when the results are declared Monday night.

Prime Minister Patrick Manning called the snap election in April, eight days after he advised the president to dissolve parliament. He said it was to avoid a no confidence vote and stop the opposition from slandering his government. Later in the campaign he told supporters it was not so; he had planned the date since October last year.

Manning has been prime minister since he was selected by then President Arthur N.R. Robinson to replace Basdeo Panday in 2001. Panday had won a majority in 2000, but his government fell under the weight of corruption allegations. In the 2001 vote, his UNC and the opposition PNM led by Manning won 18 seats each, but Robinson chose Manning over the incumbent, who had the higher popular vote, stating that the country needed a government of spirituality and morality.

Manning soon became, in his own words, "the most vilified" prime minister ever and his government collapsed because of serious divisions within his own party over his open war with Keith Rowley, who was booted out of cabinet for raising concerns about corruption in the government. Ironically, the man who was to be the leader with integrity was facing accusations of mismanagement, squandering the state's resources, corruption, nepotism and arrogance.

And his own people — Rowley in particular — were publicly challenging him, especially for turning a blind eye to corruption and for defending the man who had come to symbolise all that was corrupt — Canadian Calder Hart.

Against this background, Manning's principal opponent, Kamla Persad-Bissessar, is confident of victory for her People's Partnership coalition that had to be hastily put together when Manning called the election.

Persad-Bissessar had just become leader of the United National Congress (UNC) in an internal election in January in which she challenged and defeated 10-1 the party's founder and her own political guru, Basdeo Panday. She had been in politics for two decades with an impressive and unblemished record. Her rise to the office of opposition leader offered the opportunity to begin the process of uniting the opposition that she promised during the leadership campaign.

Manning said during the election campaign that his surprise election call caught the opposition with "its pants down", but Persad-Bissessar surprised Manning and sealed a unity deal with the Congress of the People (COP), the new political party that robbed the UNC of more than 100,000 votes in 2007 and might have caused Manning to win. COP had been discussing unity with other political groups and once the UNC came on board, the opposition agreed to unite under Persad-Bissessar.

There are 41 constituencies at stake with one-on-one battles in each, except for a few constituencies where there are 18 independents and candidates of a fringe organisation linked to Imam Yasin Abu-Bakr, the leader of the Muslimeen sect that led a failed coup in Trinidad and Tobago in 1990.

The People's Partnership comprises the UNC as the principal partner, the COP, the National Joint Action Committee (NJAC), the Movement for Social Justice and the Tobago Organisation of the People (TOP). The New National Vision (NNV), led by Abu Bakr's son, is fighting 12 seats.

Most analysts give the edge to the People's Partnership. The PNM has had a difficult time dealing with allegations of corruption, especially since it was coming from within its own ranks as well as the opposition. Rowley told PNM supporters to vote for him but not for Manning, because what is more important is the party and what it stands for. He said an election is not the time to throw the captain overboard, but added that once the ship is in dry dock, there will be time enough for a court martial.

His campaign seemed to be courting defeat to allow him to rise as the new PNM leader. And the opposition capitalised on this and Rowley's open war with Manning over corruption.

The People's Partnership campaign was hastily put together, but it remained focused on ending crime and corruption and offering hope for good governance with a people centred policy.

The PNM suffered from the baggage of their "most vilified" leader, who tried to raise race and the fragility of a coalition as good reasons to give him a fresh mandate. It also suffered from Manning's refusal to admit that crime was the major national issue and his attempts to sweep away all allegations of corruption.

In his final pitch to voters, Manning appeared confident and asked for continuity, which could mean keeping the status quo with all the ills that caused a government with a strong majority to collapse in just over two years.

Persad-Bissessar asked for an opportunity to allow an experienced and dedicated team to take charge of the nation's affairs, pledging to introduce a government of the people with the right of the people to recall their representatives.

If old loyalties take precedence over nation, Manning could be back. On the other hand if Trinidad and Tobago wants a fresh start, voters would choose the People's Partnership and for the first time a woman would hold the country's highest political office.

(May 23, 2010)

The People's Partnership (PP) won a landslide in the General Election in Trinidad and Tobago Monday, May 24 2010 heralding a historic era in the country's politics. Kamla Persad-Bissessar, the leader of the People's Partnership, will become the first female Prime Minister of the country.

Prime Minister Patrick Manning won his San Fernando East seat, which he has won in every election since he was first elected in 1971. Here are the final unofficial result is 29 seats for the partnership and 12 for the PNM.

| *Arima:* | *Rodger Samuel* | *7,612 (PP)* |
| | *Laurel Lezama* | *7,241 (PNM)* |

Arouca/Maloney:	Alicia Hospedales	11,467 (PNM)
	Anna Maria Mora	5,476 (PP)
Barataria/San Juan:	Dr Fuad Khan	10,850 (PP)
	Joseph Ross	6,742 (PNM)
Caroni Central:	Glen Ramadharsingh	13,996 (PP)
	Sheila Nadoo-Kurban	4,719 (PNM)
Caroni East:	Tim Gopeesingh	14,981 (PP)
	Harold Ramoutar	3,724 (PNM)
Chaguanas East:	Stephen Cadiz	10,797 (PP)
	Mustapha Abdul-Hamid	6717 (PP)
Chaguanas West:	Jack Warner	18,676 (PP)
	Ronald Heera	1,471 (PNM)
Couva North:	Ramona Ramdial	16,157 (PP)
	Nal Ramsingh	5,159 (PNM)
Couva South:	Rudy Indarsingh	15,045 (PP)
	Anthony Khan	4,773 (PNM)
Cumuto/Manzanilla:	Collin Partap	12,998 (PP)
	Darryl Mahabir	7,144 (PNM)
D'Abadie/O'Meara:	Anil Roberts	9,561 (PP)
	Karen Nunez-Tesheira	8,241 (PNM)
Diego Martin Central:	Amery Browne	9,040 (PNM)
	Nicole Dyer-Griffith	8,041 (PP)
Diego Martin North/East:	Colm Imbert	8,538 (PNM)
	Gavin Nicholas	8,077 (PP)
Diego Martin West:	Keith Rowley	8,777 (PNM)
	Rocky Garcia	8,023 (PP)
Fyzabad:	Chandresh Sharma	12,631 (PP)
	Joel Primus	7,214 (PNM)
La Brea:	Fitzgerald Jeffrey	9,590 (PNM)
	Ernesto Kesar	7,121 (PP)
La Horquetta/Talparo:	Jairam Seemungal	8,712 (PP)
	Nadra Nathai-Gyan	7,633 (PNM)
Laventille East/Morvant:	Donna Cox	10,797 (PNM)
	Kwasi Mutema	3,780 (PP)
Laventille West:	NiLeung Hypolite	10,730 (PNM)
	Makandal Daaga	2,725 (PP)
Lopinot/Bon Air West:	Lincoln Douglas	9,279 (PP)
	Neil Parsanlal	8,222 (PNM)
Mayaro:	Winston Peters	12,846 (PP)
	Clifford Campbell	7,330 (PNM)
Moruga/Tableland:	Clifton De Coteau	11,628 (PP)
	Augustus Thomas	8,681 (PNM)

Naparima:	*Nizam Baksh*	*16,598 (PP)*
	Faiz Ramjohn	*2,553 (PNM)*
Oropouche East:	*Roodal Moonilal*	*17,929 (PP)*
	Christin Ramdial	*2,892 (PNM)*
Oropouche West:	*Stacy Roopnarine*	*14,188 (PP)*
	Heather Sedeno-Walker	*3,526 (PNM)*
Pt Fortin:	*Paula Gopee-Scoon*	*8,885 (PNM)*
	Nyahuma Obika	*7,959 (PP)*
Pointe-a-Pierre:	*Errol McLeod*	*10,979 (PP)*
	Christine Kangaloo	*6,685 (PNM)*
Port-of-Spain North/St Ann's West:	*Patricia Mc Intosh*	*8,088 (PNM)*
	Annabelle Davis	*5,120 (PP)*
Port-of-Spain South:	*Marlene Mc Donald*	*7,855 (PNM)*
	Gizelle Russell	*4,808 (PP)*
Princes Town:	*Nela Khan*	*14, 149 (PP)*
	Anwarie Ramkissoon	*5,051 (PNM)*
San Fernando East:	*Patrick Manning*	*9,736 (PNM)*
	Carol Cuffy-Dowlat	*6,109 (PP)*
San Fernando West:	*Carolyn Seepersad-Bachan*	*9,111 (PP)*
	Junia Regrello	*7,810 (PNM)*
Siparia:	*Kamla Persad-Bissessar*	*15,808 (PP)*
	Vidya Deokiesingh	*4,037 (PNM)*
St Ann's East:	*Joanne Thomas*	*9,283 (PNM)*
	Verna St. Rose	*6,570 (PP)*
St Augustine:	*Prakash Ramadhar*	*15,166 (PP)*
	Balchandra Sharma	*3,991 (PNM)*
St Joseph:	*Herbert Volney*	*10,838 (PP)*
	Kennedy Swaratsingh	*7,778 (PNM)*
Tabaquite:	*Suruj Rambachan*	*14,310 (PP)*
	Farouk Mohammed	*5,350 (PNM)*
Tobago East:	*Vernella Alleyne-Toppin*	*7,649 (PP)*
	Gizel-Thomas Roberts	*5,623 (PNM)*
Tobago West:	*Dr Delmon Baker*	*7,693 (PP)*
	Terrence Williams	*6,811 (PNM)*
Toco/Sangre Grande:	*Rupert Griffith*	*7,941 (PP)*
	Eric Taylor	*7,285 (PNM)*
Tunapuna:	*Winston Dookeran*	*10,513 (PP)*
	Esther Le Gendre	*8,005 (PNM)*

Kamla's victory speech
May 24, 2010

"I am overwhelmed by your love!
I am humbled by your devotion!
I am honoured by your trust!

As Prime Minister-elect...As Prime Minister-elect of the Trinidad and Tobago...May I say how grateful I am by your overwhelming response to the People's Partnership. And may I thank God for the guidance that has brought us here to this victory.

Over the past month, I have asked for your hand, today you gave me your hand in trust; you gave me your love, support and confidence. I am so deeply humbled. The honour that you now accord me is without parallel. I accept it with deep gratitude and affection.

My brothers and sisters, your confidence today illuminates the theme of unity of all our peoples, to which we in the People's Partnership have devoted our lives. This is a victory of the people. You, the people, have won. The bells of freedom have rung resoundingly across our great nation. You have freely chosen the government you want to lead you. And the voice of the people is the voice of God.

The changing of the guard is an indicator that our democracy is still preserved and there can be nothing of greater importance for this nation. And tonight you have good cause to celebrate albeit in moderation. You have earned the right to feel good about what you have achieved.

But let this not be a night we say Kamla or the People's Partnership won, let it be said that the Trinidad and Tobago won. Let history record that each of you took part in a process that ensured the will of the people was carried out. Congratulations to the people of Trinidad and Tobago. And I wish to make special mention of Tobago. No longer will you have to feel like the ones left out. Tobagonians, welcome to your future equal participation in the affairs of our twin island state!

This victory only occurred because we listened to people from all walks of life. I pledge tonight that I will never stop paying attention to your needs. I will ensure that the leadership of the People's Partnership responds accordingly. No one will be left out. Tonight I offer my hand to all those who did not feel assured to give us their confidence today. I want to assure you that we will work for all of Trinidad and Tobago. We will work twice as hard to gain your faith and trust!

As a nation WE WILL ALL RISE!... The unbelievers said that they were mere words, a slogan and a flamboyant phase. Even when our opponents tried to downgrade our clarion call to unity, we built our collective strength and character around our belief that WE WILL RISE! Tonight I want to thank the chairman of the UNC Jack Warner...Jack Warner, thank you!

We were brave enough to face our challenges. To each of you, I offer a hand of genuine partnership in the important task of rebuilding our nation. Party loyalty to me after an election is of no more significance than the colour of your eyes or the texture of your hair or the colour of your skin. To the supporters of the People's Partnership I cannot begin to express how much your words of encouragement have inspired me.

This has been quite a journey for me, and one that has brought so many people by my side along the way. So it would be difficult to individually thank them all but it would be remiss of me if I failed to mention the dedication and support of my husband Gregory and my children.

It is never easy on a family when your wife and mother juggles her roles with her political life and so tonight I pay tribute to them for the way they have endured these years with love and selflessness... And to my niece, my special daughter, Lisa thank you my love for being there for me. Lisa endured and suffered so much during this difficult time, she bore the greatest trauma that can face us, that of a victim of criminals. Lisa I thank you and love you.

To Usha, Roopchand, Arlene, Vishnu, Karen, Silvy and Reesa all the ladies and gentlemen at Siparia constituency office and here at the Rienzi Complex...for the late nights and the long hours, for the dedication and the resolve, I thank you, and I love you all! May I also say a special thanks to the members, supporters and well wishers of my party the glorious United National Congress!

January 24 seems so long ago. It was 120 days ago that you gave me your sacred trust to lead our great party. Now I am so humbled to have delivered to you the government of the Trinidad and Tobago.

May I also thank all our UNC soldiers who laboured in the vineyards for the past decade during our most difficult days in opposition, all our members and officers who worked tirelessly to keep our party alive and keep our flag flying high and proud. I am so grateful for your work and sacrifice that has brought to this historic moment. I love you all and thank you from the bottom of my heart.

I express my gratitude as well, to the founder and former leader of the UNC the Hon. Basdeo Panday for his years of service and dedication to the cause of justice, equality and national unity. As Mr. Panday celebrates his 77 birthday (on May 25) from Rienzi Complex- Happy Birthday, Mr. Panday — we wish you a most pleasant and joyful day in the glory of the rising sun!...

But there can be no greater gratitude tonight than that which I express to all those who believed in themselves and this great nation of ours. Because of you we now stand on the cusp of a great moment in our history, one in which we begin the task of bringing people together to rebuild Trinidad and Tobago to make it safer, cleaner, more truly progressive than it has ever been before.

It will not be easy but the process is going to be as rewarding as it is challenging. And I begin that process from this very moment...

In fact, I can admit to you now that I had started working on what needed to be done before day one. Tonight, not tomorrow, tonight, I begin the task of selecting the most capable, competent, committed patriots to be a part of the leadership in the country's various ministries...And I will do so without fear or favour...I will do it for the common good of all the people of Trinidad and Tobago.

There will be continuity in all sectors of governance with a greater emphasis on consultation, accountability and retention of all critical policies that will be needed to ensure administrative and economic stability in transition.

There will not be the old politics of dismantling programmes and projects and plastering of new names just to stake a political claim, rather, there will be responsible, collaborative and proactive governance to provide the equitable representation and administration that every citizen, regardless of race or creed, deserves in this land.

Obviously, the process will require a level of consultation with the members of the People's Partnership and your representatives, and I am confident that we will share the same perspectives on what is required to get the job done effectively and immediately. I look ahead to the next few years with enthusiasm and great expectation. And I can assure you that I will lead a government filled with compassion and concern and with love above all.

The campaign promises must now become government policies. I can guarantee you a government that is accountable and transparent. You can hold me to the promise of the change, which you so positively voted for tonight.

As I heard the results coming in and saw the trend I knew the time had come. A new page had been turned in our nation's history and the responsibility to each of you is now on my shoulders. I will not let you down...I will not let you down.

I bring to my leadership not just political experience and government experience but I also carry into the office of the Prime Ministership the nurturing nature of a mother and grandmother and I will look after each of you all as my own.

And when someone asked me what was the first thing I would do as prime minister I instinctively replied "To visit a few Children's Homes and Schools." And having said that, it is what I intend to do...And I guess I said that because this is where the change must all begin...I want to say special thanks to the Congress of the People and our brother, Winston Dookeran...there will be no UNC, there will be no COP, there will be no PNM...we are one nation, we are one people and together we will rise...

In closing I wish at this juncture to pay special tribute to the Hon. Patrick Manning, Political Leader of the Peoples National Movement (PNM) who has been a most worthy and formidable opponent..

Whatever are our differences in ideology and policy Mr. Manning has given over 30 years of his life to public service. While we may not agree on approaches and programmes, we reserve and defend the right to disagree...

Tonight, however, I quite understand that for all of you that it begins with a nationwide celebration. But please, let us not lose a single of you tonight through recklessness and carelessness.

Be responsible. Don't drink and drive. Call the Arrive Alive team. May God bless you. May God bless our nation."

Manning graceful in defeat

Patrick Manning accepted his defeat gracefully in Monday's general election in Trinidad and Tobago and hinted that after 40 years in politics it is time to quit. In a brief address to disappointed supporters at the headquarters of the People's National Movement (PNM) in Port of Spain, the prime minister accepted full responsibility for the result.

He said he would meet with his party to discuss what needs to be done. He dropped a strong hint that he might retire, saying that whatever he does will be in the best interest of the party. He thanked supporters, especially young people. And he said he hopes that the incoming government would keep its promises.

"Yes we can"; T&T takes a quantum leap forward

Today, I offer my congratulations to the leadership of the People's Partnership Coalition and the citizens of Trinidad and Tobago for proving that democracy is alive and well in my country and that there is hope that they will fix the problems that face everyone.

I congratulate Kamla Persad-Bissessar and her team for a dignified campaign of hope and unity and salute Jack Warner for his patriotism in challenging the status quo in the United National Congress (UNC) and for his dedication and commitment, which has taken us beyond tribalism and divisiveness.

The journey is just beginning.

In April I wrote that it is worth it to fight for unity. I stated in that column, "Trinidad and Tobago is in the midst of a great revolution. The test is whether this People's Partnership will prevail and if it wins, whether it will do what it proclaims. If it does, then I can say with joy in my heart, "My country has agreed to grow up!"

Today, I am joyous for the resounding victory and acknowledge that we have indeed matured. We have grown up, but we must guard against complacency lest we begin sliding back down after inviting the nation to have faith and rise.

I put my faith in our Prime Minister-elect, Kamla, to keep her pledge to the nation to be a leader for everyone and to involve the people in decisions about their lives and their future. There are big hurdles to overcome. When you offer hope, you create expectations. Trinidad and Tobago is now looking to Kamla and her team to continue the process of healing and to deliver on the 120-day promise. We know that nation building is not a political campaign and we accept that the new government cannot do everything at once.

However, they must show that they are committed to create the just society they promised, and that they will begin the process of eradicating poverty, ending corruption and launching a frontal attack on crime. And I need not remind them that our seniors are expecting that $3,000 a month pension and our children are looking forward to the laptop computers for their book bags.

Failure to deliver amounts to a betrayal no matter how justifiable the reason because throughout the campaign, Kamla promised: "We will find the money." The government must also make good on its pledge to scrap the hated property tax and find a way to reform the tax administration and revenue collection system without creating the Trinidad and Tobago Revenue Authority (TTRA). They created great expectations and they must deliver.

The people have hired a new team based on the credentials it produced. The election campaign was the interview and having hired the applicant, they have now put the team on a 120-day probation. The people know they have the power to fire those who fail to deliver on their pledges.

Today, Patrick Manning is unemployed because he failed to remember that. After 9 years in office he had forgotten that the people had put him in office to serve them, not his friends and political allies. Manning broke a sacred trust with the people and no matter how much he pleaded with them, they exercised their democratic right to show him the door and boot him out of office.

The new kids on the block must be aware of that. Their entry into government will not make all our problems go away. But they must make a genuine start. Crime remains the country's number one problem. The partnership promised to attack it at the root. That's why it must immediately begin a poverty eradication programme, provide the protective services with the tools and the leadership they need to do the job and establish a governing system capable of solving the problem.

Patronage must end. And all the square pegs in round holes must be removed to get the wheels of government functioning effectively. That is not victimisation; it is progress.

In her victory speech Kamla said, "You have earned the right to feel good about what you have achieved" and she promised "a hand of genuine partnership in the important task of rebuilding our nation." She told supporters, "Party loyalty to me after an election is of no more significance than the colour of your eyes or the texture of your hair or the colour of your skin." We applaud her for that and we take her at her word!

That is the new society and the new system of governance that the people are expecting. And they will be patient and supportive only if she keeps that pledge and never breaks that sacred trust. And no matter what happens, the new administration must continue to defend democracy and freedom, including the right to freedom of association, of speech and the freedom of the media. For without a free media, democracy would be deformed. Had it not been for our right of free association and free expression and of media freedom, we would not be celebrating a people's victory today.

When historians write about May 24, 2010, they will note that it was the day the nation of Trinidad and Tobago took charge of its destiny and proclaimed with a single voice, "We are one people!"

Congratulations Trinidad and Tobago. You have given me hope that I can return home and know that all of us constitute a nation "forged from the love of liberty" where each of us will be equal and never again will be judged by the colour of our skins but by the content of our character.

That is the only way a nation progresses.

Congratulations Kamla, Winston, Errol, Makandal and Ashworth — and Jack Warner. And God speed ahead in the mammoth task ahead.

(May 25, 2010)

Section 6
The challenge of leadership

Heavy rains that immediately followed the election seemed like a divine test to see how the new administration would confront the challenges. Kamla responded as a true compassionate and caring leader and pushed aside inauagural celebrations to meet with officials of the disaster preparedness agency and later visited people in flood stricken areas. She rose to the challenge and set the tone for an administration dedicated to service.

The test begins for Kamla's experiment in participatory democracy

Kamla Persad-Bissessar takes the oath of office Wednesday afternoon (May 26, 2010), to become Trinidad and Tobago's first female prime minister following a landslide victory for her People's Partnership (PP) in Monday's general election.

That in itself is an historic event, but equally important is the coalition of interests that she represents.

The People's Partnership is a five-member coalition, hastily put together when Prime Minister Patrick Manning sprung an election on the country, hoping to catch the opposition sleeping.

Kamla had just won an election on January 24 to become the leader of her party — the United National Congress (UNC) — and had promised to unite all the opposition and defeat the governing PNM. On Monday night she did it.

But the government she will lead is not a UNC government, although the UNC by itself has a majority of seats in the 41-seat House of Representatives. It is a coalition that represents the liberal democratic views of the UNC, the more conservative policies of the Congress of the People (COP), labour, the poor and dispossessed and the regional agenda in the Tobago Organisation of the People (TOP).

It feels like an unworkable political accommodation, waiting for conflict to cause an implosion like the one that shattered the National Alliance for Reconstruction (NAR) in 1986 and led to the formation of the UNC. That was Prime Minister Patrick Manning's argument against a coalition during the election campaign for Monday's election.

What is interesting, is that the people accepted the coalition and rejected Manning and his PNM. The results show that the coalition won more than 430,000 votes representing nearly 60 percent of the popular vote and that the PNM support dropped by more than 14,000 votes over the last election in 2007.

What makes this different from other experiments, is that the coalition came together through intense private negotiation among the five partners and having forged an alliance the leader went to the people to seek their endorsement. In effect, Kamla kept her pledge to create a government of the people long before she had a majority and the people gave her what she requested. And now having got the mandate, she has promised that she will continue to govern with the people's consent and through consultation with them.

In 1986 when a similar arrangement propelled the NAR into office, the partners with conflicting ideologies became a unitary party with a common name, symbol and manifesto. It was almost stillborn because it was conceived through political expediency.

In 1995, the coalition that formed the government was produced after the election, so the people were not involved and had to accept a deal for which they had not agreed in advance. That too came apart although it lasted a little longer that the NAR experiment.

Now for the first time in Trinidad and Tobago politics, the people had a clear choice between the governing party and a coalition representing a wide cross section of interests from the elite to the poor and dispossessed. And the people chose the coalition.

The thought crossed my mind that this might be a crude form of "proactive proportional representation", in that it gives a voice in parliament to groups that would otherwise be silent in the legislature.

In its most common form PR allocates seats on the basis of popular support, which means that based on the votes cast on Monday the composition of the House of Representatives would have been different. However, the experiment in unity without creating a unitary party is interesting because it brings all voices together in a single chorus instead of a cacophony of competing agendas.

How Kamla constructs her cabinet will send the first important signal of how she intends to govern and will indicate who are the real beneficiaries of this new style of parliamentary democracy.

What she did was that rather than represent all the views proportionally through some complex formula, she brought together the political leaders of all those opposed to the status quo and negotiated a compromise that they could all agree to — a basis of unity. By doing things that way she was able to go to the voters ahead of time with a full disclosure about the collective strategy of the team and seek endorsement or rejection with all cards on the table.

It is a remarkable achievement that she was able to bring everyone together to negotiate a compromise position, while maintaining the independence of each party. That is potentially better than PR for a country such as ours. Thus, the voters have ostensibly endorsed a coalition of opposition interests based on the negotiated platform of all the parties. Whether the system turns out to be more stable or effective than a PR system remains to be seen.

When the euphoria of the election is over and the time comes to getting to the very difficult task of governing, ruptures may begin to form along ideological lines. The role of the prime minister in this parliament will be twofold: she must perform all the normal duties of a leader of a party and leader of government, but must also play a leading role in protecting the integrity of her coalition interests which makes it closer to the traditional PR system.

There is optimism for this coalition because unlike those cobbled together after indecisive elections on almost knee-jerk basis of unity the individual groups in this team worked out the details — and hopefully their differences — well in advance and the coalition was able to market itself as the better choice for Trinidad and Tobago. And the people agreed. Caution, courage, tenacity, and long-term strategy will be Kamla's most loyal friends in this parliament. She needs to beware of those who seek to flatter and she must foster a disciplined form of constructive criticism within her cabinet and caucus to maintain the basis of unity. That's the difficult challenge she faces. The task begins today.

(May 26, 2010)

PM Kamla's inaugural address

"My fellow citizens, it gives me great pleasure to address you for the very first time as Prime Minister of the Republic of Trinidad and Tobago.

This has been quite a journey for me. It is the summary of a life in public office that spans some 25 years but one, which most people will long remember for its past five months.

As you all know, I was elected on January 24th of this year as political leader of the UNC, and on February 24th became Leader of the Opposition and now I humbly received the honour to have been elected Prime Minister on May 24th 2010.

But that is as far as I will indulge myself in personalising the sequence of events, of far greater importance is enormous responsibility I now bear along with the leadership of the People's Partnership and our administration to address the urgent social issues at hand and move the nation forward.

Change has indeed come.

The time has arrived to open a new chapter in our nation's history. It's time for all of us to stand together side by side. Trinidad alongside Tobago. Members and supporters of all political persuasions, citizens all, arm in arm. Today we start the work of transforming the hope and promise of change into the reality of change. And while we leave the euphoria and the emotion of the election behind us, what we do not stray from is the unity the election has forged.

This morning we leave the labels behind and we move forward as one nation — all committed to the same goal — a safer, more prosperous and just Trinidad and Tobago where we all have opportunity and equality.

No more labels. No more prefixes of Afro and Indo nor North and South nor East West corridors. The election is over. It was a means towards an end. Now as citizens of Trinidad and Tobago we are all beneficiaries of the mandate given by the people. This is a victory for all citizens. Our love of country must now move to the forefront. And we must recommit ourselves to our nation and to ourselves.

We're not checking party cards or keeping notes on supporters' lists. The task of rebuilding Trinidad and Tobago will require the participation of everyone and you are all invited to sit at the nation's table. Our country has had enough of top down government. We're going to reverse that order of things.

Throughout the campaign, we were clear about our plans. And so today, we begin the process of making them government policy. My fellow citizens, the task ahead of us is challenging and we need all our nation's talent, all our nation's wisdom, all our nation's people on board with us. It's time to build a future that we can all share, hold pride in and pass on to our children with confidence. We have been given an immense opportunity for developing Trinidad and Tobago in ways many might not have thought possible.

The abundant talent of our people in so many spheres is world-renowned and we are blessed with rich natural resources. There is no reason why our nation cannot reach heights of development never seen before.

This development must not be measured in the grandeur of tall structures as an architectural manifestation of how far we have come but by the level of human development of our people, by the extent to which the needs of people have been satisfied, by the way things just work well, by the degree of safety and security that our people and the nation enjoy, by the enabling environment created for business to flourish and a renaissance of the arts and culture to emerge, by the mutual respect we hold for each other, by the level of education provided to our young ones and the quality of care given to our little children and by the success we achieve in addressing the very pressing social concerns such as poverty alleviation, domestic violence and child abuse.

These are just some of the ways in which our development must be measured. What happens from this day forward is in our hands. It is up to us. And so the challenge before us — is to stay as one people. We must never allow the seeds of separation to regain hold on our soil. This afternoon, the new chapter we turn is a fresh start for all of us.

Over the next few days I will be making the appointments of members of my cabinet following consultations with the leadership of the People's Partnership. I promise you it will be comprised of the most competent, committed and qualified individuals. On composition of the cabinet my administration will bring Tobago into the core administration of government. And I formally announce this afternoon that there will be an establishment of a Ministry of Tobago Development as we look to bring our sister isle on as equal partners in the development of our twin island state.

Our administration will be addressing social and economic restructuring in the medium term as we look to fast-tracking the changes so urgently required. We will be targeting ministries to give an account on specific deliverables within a timeframe, as an example, food production. This will be a performance driven formula that measures results and holds those in authority accountable to meeting their goals and objectives.

Under the Office of the Prime Minister, special emphasis will be placed on restoring the dignity and effectiveness of parliament. In this context, the Red House will remain the seat of the parliament.

Parliamentary oversight on key issues has gone into abeyance and in an effort to ensure parliament is not just a rubber stamp we will be making immediate steps to institute parliamentary reform under the Office of the Prime Minister.

The People's Partnership government I lead will be moving towards the delivery of an early budget after candid assessments are conducted on the state of the nation's finances and economy... and in this regard I shall be depending on my brother, Winston Dookeran. The budget provisions will be developed to give effect to the priorities of the new direction of our new government.

At the conclusion of this afternoon's ceremony, one of my first acts as Prime Minister will be to meet with the Head of the Office of the Disaster Preparedness and Management along with the Permanent Secretary in the Office of the Prime Minister, Sandra Marchack, to discuss the current flooding in various parts of the island and the impending increased level of flooding. Arising out of those discussions, a release will be issued on the decisions arrived at and the course of action to be taken.

This situation underlines the need of our new administration to fast track all assessment and begin the process of implementing both short term and long term solutions in so many areas including those such as drainage and irrigation. A tour of some of the affected areas was already conducted by members of the incoming administration this morning and a report is being compiled on the needs of the affected areas.

In light of the urgency of this situation and my need to address it I will now crave your indulgence to leave hastily and do apologise for having to forego the usual formalities that accompany occasions such as this.

On behalf of the government of the People's Partnership, may I thank you all for being here and to express once more my deepest gratitude to the people of Trinidad and Tobago for their overwhelming support.

May God bless you all and may God bless our nation.

Manning's resignation

The general election of May 2010 did not result in victory for the People's National Movement.

As political leader, I accept full responsibility for this result. I am of the view that the party should in these circumstances now proceed to elect a new political leader in the shortest possible time and in accordance with the party's constitution.

To facilitate this process, I hereby resign from the office of political leader.

May I also indicate that if it is the party's wish I am prepared to stay on as political leader until a new political leader is elected at which time it would be my pleasure to gracefully demit office.

I was first elected political leader on February 8, 1987 and it has really been a pleasure to serve the party these past 23 years.

I wish to thank the party's membership for the opportunity to serve at this level and for such a long time.

I wish also to assure you and through you our party's membership that I will give full support to the new political leader and would at no time operate in any manner the effect of which would be to bring the party into disrepute.

Yours in PNM,
Patrick Manning.
(May 28, 2010)

Kamla appoints first cabinet

Prime Minister Kamla Persad-Bissessar on Friday (May 28, 2010), told members of her first cabinet that she expects each of them "to dedicate all of your energies towards ensuring that the people's needs are being addressed." And she said each member must work on behalf of all the people, with the understanding that the "people are the government." She also banned the use of any party symbol while a minister is on official business.

In a brief address at the swearing-in of the cabinet, she said, "All of us are held accountable to the people. Ours is a monumental task but it is one which is equally rewarding because there can be no greater call than that of national service.

"We must accept no mediocrity. Neither must we contribute to it in any way. There must be no room for arrogance. We must be faithful to a leadership style that is firm but humble, passionate and impatient for great achievements but ever conscious of the correct procedures.

She added, "We have to be ever mindful that the nation is looking at us expectantly. No one out there expects excuses; they want results. No one expects us to create miracles, but simply to work hard enough as though we know could produce them.

"Lead by example. Follow by learning to listen. All of this is as much my mantra as it is your own. As of now, each of us is on trial. We begin to be tested as of this very moment.

"We carry a huge responsibility to get this nation back on track. So we must discover how to turn obstacles into opportunities, discover new ways of solving old problems. Inspire others by our enthusiasm and positive outlook. As members of the cabinet of the People's Partnership we are stewards of the nation's future.

"What a legacy we can leave behind. What an incredible privilege and honour given to us to serve in this way. What a phenomenal opportunity to make such a contribution to country.

"My caution is never to become aloof, never lose sight of the true purpose of the position you hold. Stay grounded. Keep connected to the people. Earn their respect by the way you serve them.

"As Chief Servant Makandal Daaga would say, the people are the government. We are servants of the people. We work for the people. Diligently and entirely, and always in their interest.

"The talent and commitment of this group assembled here this afternoon cannot be denied. Sure, many of you are new to this but that means you bring fresh ideas and new perspectives.

"Government cannot be about doing the same things and expecting different results. The days will be long and the nights sleepless but the rewards will come from knowing that we are improving the lives of others and creating the kind of nation of which we can all be proud.

"One of the hallmarks of our government must be that we serve every citizen with the same dedication regardless of their political affiliation. And we must never display any kind of party symbol during the conduct of our work as the government of Trinidad and Tobago in or out of Parliament.

"Transparency and accountability must be evident in all government matters. We must be exemplars of the society, returning sound, traditional values of ethics and morals back into government. Honesty must be one of the given qualifications of anyone who hopes to serve the people. Harness the best of our nation's human resources to give reality to the change so many voted for.

"Disregard which party any qualified individual comes from or what ethnic group or religion or anything else that defines them in any way other than their competency and genuine commitment to serve the people.

"The people are the government. Please take these words and frame them on every desk of each of your Ministries and recommit to them every single day of each month you are privileged to be in service to the nation.

"Thank you for coming forward in the way each of you has to contribute to the large task of rebuilding our great nation. I pledge to you all that I will be a leader who in turn listens and that my decisions will only be arrived at after collaboration and always in the interest of what best serves Trinidad and Tobago.

"There is no room for personal egos, no time for personal agendas, and no opportunity for self-glorification. This is not about us; it is about the people. And they have the power to dismiss us anytime."

"Congratulations to each of you. The entire nation now awaits your performance. And your job expectations actually began on Monday night so we have some catching up to do already so let me not delay you any further. God bless and guide us all as we embark upon this inspired journey of national service. And may God bless our nation."

(May 28, 2010)

Jack the giant killer topples Bas and Patrick and puts Kamla in charge

When Basdeo Panday and Jack Warner fell out in 2008, few would have thought that Jack would achieve the monumental task of removing Panday as leader of the United National Congress (UNC), helping install Kamla Persad-Bissessar as UNC leader and then soundly defeating Patrick Manning in a general election.

But in fewer than six months the Chaguanas MP — with the help of the people — did what most considered impossible.

How did it all come to pass? How did this simple, black man take on the leader of a predominantly Indian party and win? And how is it that this "*neemakharam*" was able to work against the founder of the UNC in the party's heartland, a constituency that has a 97 percent Indian population?

The answer is simple: Jack Warner had a clear vision of where he wanted the party to be and through effective communication and unsurpassed representation, he was able to achieve his goal of shaking the UNC out of its slumber, ending the PNM rule in Trinidad and Tobago and installing a government of the people.

When he started his "crusade" through the Movement for Change, few thought that he would get far. In fact the UNC leader at the time dismissed the FIFA Vice President, saying like all the others who dared challenge him, Jack would end up in the political graveyard.

But Jack had no intention of becoming another Panday casualty, even if it meant climbing a political greasy pole. He pressed on with demands to democratise the party of which he was an elected deputy leader and enlisted the support of several key UNC members including MPs Ramesh L. Maharaj and Winston "Gypsy" Peters.

The Movement for Change demonstrated professionalism in its organisation and it had a clear game plan, calling for internal elections that were long overdue and for change. It pleaded with the people to demand change, saying without it the party would not be able to change the government.

Panday resisted. But as the lobby for change grew more intense, Jack and his dedicated supporters and advisers created a Manifesto for Change and launched a nationwide campaign to demand action to fix the UNC's internal problems and get it ready to face the PNM in an election, which was not due until 2012.

He never once thought of forming a new party, because he insisted that the party Panday created in 1989 was the correct vehicle to get to government. He also felt the country was too small for a multiple-party system.

Panday's allies included the woman who won Jack's support for the leadership of the party and became prime minister following the May 24, 2010 general election. At the time Kamla Persad-Bissessar fought alongside "the chief" to keep Warner and his "pretenders" at bay. But like Jack, she knew that Panday was past his prime and that the party needed a new leadership in order to create the unity needed to defeat the PNM.

The real crack began at a UNC congress when one man stood up and told Panday to step aside and hand over the leadership of the party to Kamla. "It's not that I love you less," the delegate told Panday, "but I love the party more."

The die was cast and Panday eventually agreed to hold the internal election, hoping that party members would maintain the tradition of not opposing him. And when Kamla surprised him and many in the bosom of the party, she immediately won Jack's endorsement over his friend and ally, Ramesh L. Maharaj.

That earned him the title of "jumping Jack" from those who didn't understand his political pragmatism and his strength. That strategic repositioning was the turning point that would lead to the fall of two political giants within five months of each other, ending an era of "maximum leadership' in Trinidad and Tobago.

Jack pulled his troops together, disbanded the Movement for Change, which he said had achieved its aim, and mounted a strong campaign. Though he supported Kamla he kept his campaign separate from hers.

He stood alone as the candidate for chairman of the UNC, fighting Vasant Bharath, the St Augustine MP and close associate of Panday.

Kamla faced Ramesh and Panday, but Ramesh soon became an irritant linked to Panday and suffered the most humiliating defeat of his career. Panday's campaign was based on mudslinging without offering party members a clear reason why they should keep him as their leader.

Kamla on the other hand was focused and incisive, showing that while Panday had been an excellent prime minister he was unable to take the party back to government because he had lost his political currency. She offered a new vision of unity as a first step to defeating the PNM and the people gave her the mandate to lead.

On January 24, 2010 Panday suffered the worst defeat of his career, losing 10 to 1 against Kamla with only one member of his slate — Roodal Moonilal — winning election to the 18-member national executive. Jack won a landslide against Bharath. It took a month for the UNC caucus to come along, but once they installed Kamla as opposition leader she went after Manning with a determination to make the prime minister accountable for his misdeeds.

On the eve of an opposition no confidence motion, Manning pulled the plug on the parliament and a few days later announced the May 24 general election, which he lost. It was a Jack Warner hat trick: Panday and Manning down, with Kamla firmly installed as prime minister, heading a coalition that comprised all the groups opposed to the Manning government.

But none of this sequence of events would have been possible without Jack's patriotism, refusal to be wooed by the PNM, his effective communication and determination to back a leader. His focus was always on the big picture and he insisted on doing what was necessary to get his party into government.

With Kamlamania — which he silently helped create — still very apparent, the country had to make a choice between a woman who was a people's leader of a rainbow coalition and a government that has lost its way and collapsed under the weight of its leader's autocratic rule and allegations of the worst corruption ever seen in the country.

Those outsiders who were opposed to Jack or did not know him were quick to label him as a "political investor" and a "political opportunist." To Panday loyalists he was a traitor. But those who were in his inner circle — and his constituents — knew only a dedicated professional, a patriot who worked 20-hour days, seven days a week to create the change that made Trinidad and Tobago take a quantum leap to freedom from PNM rule.

When the historians write about the "yellow revolution," they would have to admit that Jack was indeed the nation's giant killer without whose help Trinidad and Tobago would not have been able to free itself from the bondage imposed by Patrick Manning and the PNM.

Jack's reward was to win nearly 19,000 votes, the highest ever for an MP in Trinidad and Tobago. And he did it without a campaign.

Today, this simple black man is the people's hero and everyone embraces him not for the colour of his skin or the texture of his hair but for the content of his character and the great love and affection that he shows to all.

(May 31, 2010)

Kamla moved swiftly to keep her promise to call local elections and while the Kamlamani of May 24 was still alive, she named July 26 as the date for the long awaited vote. It caught the People's National Movement by surprise.

No room for complacency

The euphoria that began with Kamla Persad-Bissessar's election as political leader of the United National Congress (UNC) in January has not yet subsided. That is the wave that she rode to Whitehall and she and the People's Partnership are hoping to carry the success into next month's local government elections.

But the opponent that the coalition trounced on May 24 has changed. Patrick Manning has disappeared as leader of the People's National Movement (PNM) and Keith Rowley is now firmly in charge, hoping to present a new PNM to the people and translate that into victory on July 26.

There is clear evidence that the opposition leader is cleaning house. The departure of Conrad Enill and Martin Joseph demonstrates that Rowley is purging the Manning elements and is being careful to preserve the integrity of the party. That had been his position in the election campaign. The "court martial" about which he spoke was swift and now that the PNM ship is in dry dock he has to move quickly to get her ready to sail — much quicker than he expected.

The PNM says it will be ready. And don't doubt it. The party is a well-established institution and Enill signaled that the impediment to its success has been removed so the party will regain what it lost — the support of thousands of supporters.

And that is why the People's Partnership should pay careful attention to what is happening, both in its own backyard and in the opposition camp.

Perhaps the most critical thing for the partnership in the next few days, leading up to nomination day on July 5, is to keep its house in order and ensure that its partners are happy with whatever arrangements are made for the local election.

There are loud rumblings from the Congress of the People (COP) about its "share" and some members are quite vocal about being pushed aside. That is the challenge for both the COP leader and Kamla — to keep the coalition together and to present another united front to the electorate if it hopes to win.

I speak of the need for vigilance as well because of the nature of our first past the post electoral system. If you look at the figures for the May 24 general election you will see a runaway victory for the coalition — 432,020 votes and 29 seats as opposed to the PNM with 12 seats and 285,354 votes, a loss of just over 14,000 over the votes in 2007 when the PNM won 26 seats. In spite of the swing to the People's Partnership the PNM kept its traditional support but the loss of those votes cost the party 14 seats.

The support for the partnership was most pronounced in traditional areas, where lopsided results gave the party the very high popular vote. In Chaguanas West, for example, Jack Warner polled more than 18,000 votes with his PNM opponent getting just over 1,300 votes. Jack could have had just got 1,400 votes and he would have won just the same. And that is what the partnership needs to watch carefully.

In theory, if the PNM had retained the support of the 14,459 people who refused to vote for the party in 2010 and had kept the support in the constituencies that it lost, the PNM could have won a majority, even with the coalition polling more than 400,000 votes. And if that sounds unbelievable, consider these figures, which show the number of votes that the PNM needed to win in each of nine traditional "PNM" constituencies:

- Toco/Sangre Grande — 266
- Arima — 572
- Tobago West — 883

- Lopinot/BonAir West — 1,058
- LaHorquetta/Talparo — 1,080
- D'Abadie/O'Meara — 1,121
- San Fernando West — 1,430
- Tobago East — 2,027
- Tunapuna — 2,509

That's a total of just 10,949. Had those voters remained loyal to the PNM, the party might have won a majority despite all Manning's misdeeds and the united front presented by the People's Partnership. In fact that was the gamble Manning took. And it is the picture the People's Partnership needs to keep in focus as it enters another election campaign.

Although Rowley is just taking over the leadership, the machinery for an election had been in place for a while and the prodigals are returning home, battle ready and determined to regain some of the power the party lost less than one month ago. Winning an election takes more than a fancy message and huge crowds; it takes effective planning and organisation.

On May 24 there was a swing away from the PNM, but it was not as significant as the result might suggest. It was the classic case of the government losing the election, giving victory to the opposition almost by default.

Much has changed since May 24. And each party will have to work hard to win votes. That is why there is no room for complacency on either side.

And may the best candidates win!

(June 22, 2010)

Does the PNM deserve forgiveness?

On Monday (July 26, 2010) citizens of Trinidad will vote in local government elections for the first time since 2003. Tobago does not vote in these elections. For four consecutive years former Patrick Manning used his parliamentary majority — which included current PNM leader Keith Rowley — to deny people the right to choose their local representatives. And at the same time he frustrated local authorities — especially those that were not PNM-controlled — by granting them financial crumbs to handle the mammoth task of serving their respective regions.

The Manning administration kept putting off the vote in order to hold consultations and put in place reforms to make the local government system better suited to the needs of the people. In effect they took away people's rights to vote while fiddling with the never-ending details of a reform package.

And now that Prime Minister Kamla Persad-Bissessar has done what she promised. The PNM is telling people they must deny the governing People's Partnership the right to represent them at the local level.

At Woodford Square on Saturday the opposition party declared, "The PNM is alive and well. We are troubled but not distressed and we cannot be destroyed." But the reality was a poor turnout for a rally that was meant to be a showpiece of the resurrected PNM under Rowley. Party vice chairman John Donaldson boasted that the fact that PNM was able to find "134 credible, intelligent people-oriented candidates in ten days, is a sign that we have already triumphed." And campaign chair John Rahael said people don't show up for local elections, which is why there were so few supporters in Port of Spain. Perhaps he should have looked at what was happening at Skinner Park before speaking. One commentator explained the poor turnout another way, saying now that the PNM has lost its ability to bully URP and CEPEP workers so it can no longer attract a crowd.

While some party jefes were boasting of the greatness of the PNM, Deputy political leader, Nafeesa Mohammed was using another approach, asking voters to forgive the party for all wrongs and give the PNM a second chance. If I am right, what the lady was saying is that the PNM actually did "wrongs."

That of course, is in conflict with her leader who has been boasting that the PNM has nothing "to apologise for", when he himself had denounced the Manning regime as the most corrupt ever.

The PNM cannot expect people to forgive the party for what happened when it continues to say it didn't do anything wrong. And the leader, not a deputy, must be the one to admit it. Rowley must go further. He must admit the abuse and waste, the corruption and the overall failures of his party, of which he was an active member, and then try to get a fresh start and ask for forgiveness.

The PNM doesn't deserve forgiveness for raping and plundering the treasury for its own benefit and the benefit of its friends and supporters; it must pay the price by answering before the courts of the land. Then, purged of its corruption, it would have a feeble case to present to the public. Until then, the people have only one choice on Monday.

And that is to elect candidates of the People's Partnership — a coalition that they elected to government two months ago on a platform of accountability, transparency and governance on behalf of the people.

In two months the Partnership under Kamla Persad-Bissessar has demonstrated that it intends to govern on behalf of the people and with zero tolerance for corruption. If anybody deserves a chance to get the people's vote on Monday it is the People's Partnership.

PP wins LGE; no one will divide us again - Kamla

Fireworks lit up the midnight sky over the Rienzi Complex Monday (July 26), as thousands celebrated with the leaders of the People's Partnership the landslide victory in Monday's local government election.

In a speech to supporters, Prime Minister Kamla Persad-Bissessar thanked everyone for the victory and pledged that she would not allow anyone "to divide us again." She said the people's victory is now complete with control of both the central and local government and added that "we are now best placed to begin the process of transformation and change".

On behalf of all the leaders of the People's Partnership the prime minister thanked everyone and expressed her heartfelt gratitude. "And I take this opportunity to recommit the People's Partnership to serve the people, serve the people, serve the people!" She pledged to keep "the faith that you have bestowed in us."

She said the result of the election is testimony of the commitment of supporters and "your country is eternally grateful...this is your victory and we will never let your down."

Persad-Bissessar also had a message for PNM supporters and their leader, Dr. Keith Rowley. To PNM members, she said as citizens they are entitled to all the benefits of the state. "This is a victory not just for the party I represent or the government I lead; this is a victory for the people... and everyone must benefit from it," she said. And she called on Rowley to put politics aside and work to build and transform the nation. "I offer an open hand of cooperation to work with us in making Trinidad and Tobago a better place for all our citizens," she said. "The change that is about to take place in Trinidad and Tobago will call for all our resources, it will require the support of every citizen and it will bring out the best in each of us," Persad-Bissessar said.

She spoke of the transformation of the society, to produce the highest level of creativity to foster a stronger "brotherhood and sisterhood, create a more caring and compassionate society, rekindle old, strong traditional values, inspire greater tolerance and acceptance and open a whole new world of promise for Trinidad and Tobago to finally become the nation we were always destined to be."

The prime minister also had a message for the newly elected members of local councils, telling them their work has only just begun. "I expect that each of the winning local government candidates will tonight begin preparing for the first day's work in the communities they represent," she said. And she warned that they would face an ongoing performance assessment. She urged everyone to celebrate, but do it in moderation. And she promised that "my love will always be there for you."

PNM must confess its sins in order to move on

If the rumours are true and Patrick Manning is really planning a political comeback by unseating Keith Rowley and taking over as the official Leader of the Opposition, he could easily do it. After all Manning handpicked the MPs now sitting in opposition, with the exception of Keith Rowley, so they might be tempted to revolt if the rewards are attractive enough.

Colm Imbert has already shown where he stands when it comes to Rowley, having come out swinging against the new PNM leader and blaming him for the PNM's defeat in last week's local government elections (LGE). And Amery Browne is also not a Rowley fan.

So if Manning wants to call in his chips he could easily have enough MPs on his side to deal a severe political blow to Rowley, who has already been wounded by the LGE "cutarse".

From the opposition leader's office, Manning could plot Rowley's political demise, starting with restoring the old guard in the executive or adding some cosmetic changes to demonstrate that he has a sanitised team. He could also get a "Manning" senate, meaning people like Penny Beckles would have to go.

Once in charge, he can commandeer the various party groups to call for a leadership review and since the party elects its leader through a delegate system unlike the UNC's one-member-one-vote, he could suddenly be PNM leader again. It is possible in theory. However, the real question is whether the PNM is that dumb to reinstate a maximum leader who has led them from the promised land to the political wilderness?

The results of the two elections that the PNM lost in as many months show something that may not be apparent to many — a political tit-for-tat in the two PNM camps. Rowley and his people undermined Manning to help cause the defeat of the PNM in the May 24 general election; the Manning loyalists returned the favour and boycotted Rowley for the LGE.

In fact, some of Manning's "disciples" who currently sit in parliament, refused to be get involved in the campaign as Rowley fought to win at least some credibility. If this political drama plays out according to the rumours it would be a gift to the People's Partnership because once again the two arch-rivals would be at each other's throat in parliament as they were before the general election.

And you never know what secrets might get exposed as each tries to outdo the other and in the process opens the PNM's pandora's box.

Rowley has so far failed to show strong leadership. Instead of taking charge and acknowledging that the party made mistakes, Rowley boasted that there is nothing for which the PNM should apologise. That *faux pas* totally embarrassed supporters who had hoped that their new leader would actually show leadership and make a break with the regime that he himself had called the most corrupt ever.

The problem is that Rowley remains in denial and expects that those who have always been "PNM til ah dead", will return to refloat the sinking ship, just because the captain and some of the crew have been replaced.

What happened on July 26 demonstrated that times have changed and people have confidence in themselves and in the People's Partnership, which has discarded race for a more sincere type of politics based on commitment and dedication to the people.

Those who blindly supported the PNM in the hope of getting protection from discrimination now understand that they have nothing to fear from Kamla Persad-Bissessar and the new political leadership. They are comforted because Kamla has extended her arms to all citizens, regardless of ethnicity, religion, class or political affiliation to join her in this new political revolution to rebuild a nation that had become divided and disfigured by Manning's failed policies and contempt for the people.

If the PNM hopes to prevent what appears to be an imminent implosion, it must first accept that it cannot be business as usual and begin by acknowledging that it made big mistakes and that it intends to fix the problems and rebuild the party. That could stop Manning in his tracks and give Rowley some breathing room. And if he expects to ever lead the PNM back to government, Rowley must learn from the example of the People's Partnership and build a party based on the PNM's original charter — a movement of the people, for the people, by the people.

The People's Partnership has already done that with its commitment to "serve the people, serve the people, serve the people." And so long as it remains on focus, stays on course and maintains its partnership with the people, the PNM would have to remain in the wilderness for a very long time.

Opposition infighting is bad news for T&T and PNM

The good news from the opposition People's National Movement (PNM) last week, was that it has ordered a "dispassionate, arm's length" view of the party following two successive election defeats. However, the bad news is that the divisions continue to get worse between the Keith Rowley and Patrick Manning camps, which could only get in the way or any meaningful change that might reinvigorate the party.

A strong and effective opposition is a vital component of Trinidad and Tobago's governance model, which is based on the Westminster system of parliamentary democracy.

The crushing defeat of the PNM in the May 24, 2010 general election, by the People's Partnership (PP), left the party gasping for air. And as if that was not enough, within days, the PNM drove Manning out of office and installed Rowley as opposition leader, subsequently acclaiming him leader of the party.

The new captain was unable to get the ship back on an even keel, in time to face the PP in a second election in as many months and Rowley sustained his first decisive defeat at the hands of Kamla, Jack et al. That July 26 loss put the PNM in a tailspin and exposed the very deep wounds that Rowley is now trying to heal. Or is he trying to cut off what he considers cancerous parts of the party?

His parliamentary colleagues, Colm Imbert and Amery Browne — both representing Diego Martin constituencies — left him alone for local government elections (LGE). And once the votes were counted and Rowley was bloodied and bruised, Imbert came out swinging, blaming the leader for the loss.

And that's where trouble lies.

Imbert, who had contemplated running for the leadership but pulled back for "peace in the party," does not accept Rowley. Neither does Browne and many of the Manning loyalists.

And Rowley has been courting certain people, who have been close to people like Imbert in the past, in a move seen by many as the political death knell for the former cabinet minister. There were even rumours, which Manning quickly put down, that the former leader was planning a comeback to remove Rowley and take back the job of opposition leader.

This kind of political drama is unusual for the party that Eric Williams built. But the *"wajang"* who Manning banished and then had to embrace for the general election, is showing some qualities that make some of his parliamentary colleagues very uncomfortable.

Like Manning, Rowley is showing that he has "maximum leader" tendencies and like Eric Williams, he is sending a message that who "doh like it" would have to go. So what the PNM's General Council is about to do is likely to cause a lot of in house damage before the PNM fixes its problems.

Its plan is to have a 15-member team conduct an analysis of the PNM's current situation and make recommendations. Rowley wants to include non-members. "The important thing is it is a good mix of skills. And most importantly it does not include people who have been so close to the wood that they can't see the trees," the PNM leader told reporters.

However, while that is taking place PNM insiders say Rowley is going after Imbert, putting the former Works Minister under intense scrutiny for his absence from the LGE campaign and the made disparaging remarks about Rowley's leadership. And Rowley is going after Browne as well. This seems to contradict the plan for any arm's length analysis of the party.

That's the same problem that caused the UNC's implosion following its defeat by the PNM in 2007. And had it not been for the strategic moves by Jack Warner and his Movement for Change no meaningful change would have taken place and the PNM might have remained in office for many more years. And that's what the PNM risks today. The bad news is that it has no Jack and instead of Rowley getting the PNM's act together and having its MPs work closely together to confront the new government, it is fighting its own.

And while it does this, it leaves room for the Kamla government to get complacent and even make critical missteps in the absence of a strong, united opposition to maintain the checks and balances that are so vital for effective governance.

Fortunately for Trinidad and Tobago, there is a strong commitment from the People's Partnership to good governance, accountability and transparency, so we might see quantum leaps ahead.

The first major test in the bad-news budget that is coming soon. That would be an opportunity for the government to either demonstrate to the nation it has what it takes to govern in tough times or take its first slide in popularity.

(August 8, 2010)

Section 7
New issues and major challenges

With two elections out of the way and the opposition People's National Movement trying to catch its breath and reorganise itself Trinidad and Tobago had to start returning to normal. But as Kamla and the PP would soon find out normal meant constant assault from forces opposed to the new administration. And in came in many forms.

This section begins with an issue that would haunt the government at all times — a dedicated few from the PNM working hard to discredit the new government.

Kamla's yellow dress was always green

The National Lotteries Control Board (NLCB) has tried to explain its full page ad congratulating Port of Spain Mayor Louis Lee Sing.

Acting Prime Minister Winston Dookeran, expressed concern about the ad in which Lee Sing, who was chairman of the NLCB during the Manning administration, is seen wearing a black PNM balisier tie.

NLCB Director Phyllis Borde offered an explanation for the ad, stating that there is nothing wrong in promoting someone when the person is doing something good. "We have always operated in a manner to give recognition to persons worthy of it," she explained. Borde said she will be writing Dookeran to explain "the way things are done at the NLCB." Isn't she getting things a little upside down? I always thought the owners/shareholders — in this case the state — tell the "board" how things are done.

Why Lee Sing alone? Is she suggesting that Marlene Courdray, the new mayor of San Fernando is not worthy of the office she holds? And what about the other mayors and heads of corporations? What is so special about Lee Sing and his balisier ties, that makes him alone worthy of recognition by a state organisation that saw it fit to spend thousands of taxpayers dollars on ads in the daily press?

Borde has an explanation for that too. "The NLCB does not have to congratulate everyone, and we make no apologies for congratulating Lee Sing since he has done a lot for the organisation during the time he served on our board," she said.

I beg to disagree. What he did for the board was his duty as chairman. He deserves no special treatment. But there is also something more important.

One of the issues raised was Lee Sing's balisier tie, the official symbol of the PNM. It has always been PNM policy for its top members to wear the tie on official business.

So it is strange that Borde did not know that and even stranger that her organisation put out an ad and did not see the picture of Lee Sing and the tie. "I was at the Mayor's swearing-in ceremony and we used a photo from that," she said. Well that in itself should raise a flag that Lee Sing was wearing the tie. I would suggest that she knew and is now trying to use spin to cover her tracks. Consider her other statement.

"We have done it in the past for several persons, including Prime Minister Kamla Persad-Bissessar wearing her beautiful yellow outfit shortly after her swearing-in ceremony, it's just what we do," Borde said.

Yellow is the colour that Persad-Bissessar used during the election campaign — a party symbol. So the insinuation is that if Kamla and her yellow dress are OK then Lee Sing and his tie should be acceptable too.

Well perhaps. Except for one significant detail.

Kamla was NOT wearing a "beautiful yellow outfit" during or shortly after her swearing-in. She was wearing a lime green dress. She wore it when she took her oath of office; she wore it when she left immediately afterwards for a meeting with disaster preparedness officials and she wore it later in the evening at a reception at the Crowne Plaza hotel.

The prime minister has been very careful about party symbols and has cautioned every member of her cabinet that party symbols must be absent whenever they are on official business. And she has been very careful not to wear any political symbol on official business.

So the suggestion that Kamla was wearing a "beautiful yellow dress" appears to me to be an attempt to justify the use of the other party's symbol. But worse, it's not true! It's a lie. The lady was wearing green.

The government determines policy for the NLCB and it is the government that should be telling the board "the way things are done at the NLCB." And as a citizen I would like to hear my government tell the NCLB board that it was out of line with the ad and further, that it must stop the abuse of taxpayers funds to promote its friends.

(August 22, 2010)

Police must not be allowed to hold a nation to ransom

Police are supposed to protect and serve. So when I hear police officers threatening not to help carry out a government's anti-crime plan I become angry, especially when this is happening in a country where someone is murdered every 12 hours.

I am speaking about Trinidad and Tobago and am reacting to the news that police officers are planning to boycott the government's crime plans, because they are angry at the new People's Partnership government's delay in concluding talks for better pay. Media reports quote one of their representatives as saying his association "may not be able to control its membership who...may engage in formal action which will be very detrimental to the proper administration and efficient functioning of any anti-crime plan."

I find that irresponsible, to say the least. No one should be allowed to hold a government to ransom and put an already frightened citizenry at greater risk. While I agree that police officers should be paid a decent salary and their working conditions improved, I also insist that police are essential service workers who, by virtue of their jobs, are on duty 24/7.

I recall hearing about those obligations from a police officer: "We are dedicated public servants who are sworn to protect public safety at any time and in any place...we are police officers, and we do what is right because it is right!"

No matter what the circumstances, what comes first is a duty and obligation to protect public safety. And you cannot do that by refusing to do your assigned duties or boycotting a government's anti-crime plan.

If the CEO of a company refuses to carry out the instructions of the board of directors, that person is fired. Let's bite the bullet and tell our police in Trinidad and Tobago that the same rule applies to them as well. Truth be told, we can do without a whole lot of them who are crooked and an impediment to upholding law and order.

The board of directors is the government and the shareholders of the company are the citizens of Trinidad and Tobago who pay the salaries of police officers. To quote my colleague in England, John Lindsay, "This is despicable."

There is no evidence that the new government is not paying attention to the needs of the police. All through the election campaign the People's Partnership promised to make sure the police have the tools they need to do their jobs. The Minister of National Security, the Prime Minister and the Finance Minister are aware of the needs as the government prepares its first national budget, which it will deliver in two weeks.

In this context, there is no need for this manner of blackmail from men and women who are duty bound to protect the country. It is unacceptable for our law officers to behave like factory workers. If they go ahead with their threats, the government should act decisively.

We need police officers in Trinidad and Tobago who are dedicated to serving the people, to protect life and limb and create a society where we can escape from our self-imposed jails and freely walk the streets again without fear of being robbed, raped or murdered. Any officer who refuses to accept that responsibility should find another job.

(August 25, 2010)

Can Rowley justify his own mutiny?

Keith Rowley appears to have found himself in a political straight jacket. The new PNM leader told supporters earlier this week the current government seems to be "more PNM than PNM" since it is keeping many PNM programmes. He made the comment as he tried to explain his party's rationale for voting for the budget.

One of his caucus colleagues was careful to explain, that there is a difference between voting for government policy and the appropriations bill.

Colm Imbert stated on an Internet chat site that MPs vote for the "appropriations" not the budget speech, which he said is a statement of government policy. That means, according to Imbert, when Rowley and the PNM registered their "Ayes" for the budget they did not agree to such things as the scrapping of the smelter or the CL plan. So his point is that it's OK to support the budget but at the same time slam the government.

Rowley didn't follow that line of logic.

Instead the opposition leader admitted that the PNM "ushered in" the People's Partnership, which he suggested is really a different incarnation of the PNM. But he had a warning, a reason why the new government is not fit to be in office. "Those who got it don't know what to do. They have no plan. They didn't expect to be in government...We ushered the People's Partnership into government half way into the term," he said.

Rowley admitted that the PNM "invited" change and that the voters' reaction in the May 24 general election was to the way the PNM leadership at the time managed the country, not that the policies were flawed. Rowley said the PNM elected not to play "stupid politics" and hurt the party's credibility so it voted for the budget, which contained PNM plans.

So what really is Rowley's point?

What we have experienced in Trinidad and Tobago since the electoral overthrow of Manning and the PNM, is a shift to good governance and a clear direction to improve the lives of the people. And contrary to Rowley's argument, the People's Partnership does have a plan — a good one — that it clearly outlined in its manifesto. That document was not something scrambled together for political expediency. And yes, it embraced some of the PNM's plans, which had the potential to work well under a government of the people.

The government assistance for tuition expenses (GATE) programme, for example, is being expanded and improved. And as a point of interest, GATE was really an improvement on the UNC "dollar-for-dollar" policy introduced under Kamla Persad-Bissessar's stewardship as education minister. What the People's Partnership government is doing is called continuity It's what's expected of a responsible administration.

Sadly, in the process it has inherited a lot of baggage from the Manning era, some of which will cost the taxpayer much more than anyone envisaged. The CL fiasco, the Offshore Patrol Boats (OPV) and the La Brea smelter project are examples of bad and costly decisions that the new government must now address.

The real problem for Rowley is that he campaigned against the PNM and his former leader and wanted nothing more than a PNM defeat. The People's Partnership won two elections based on its programmes and the failure of the PNM. That is the reality that Rowley cannot face. He is still in shock and hoping that he can convince his divided party that his mutiny was justified.

He is using the argument that, to make an omelet one has to first break the egg. The truth is the egg was a rotten one and the people discarded it along with the whole chicken coop. That's a matter the PNM must now address instead of trying to take credit for what the People's Partnership is doing.

And Rowley would do well to try to emulate the new kids on the block and redevelop his party as one that respects and represents the people, not only its parochial interests.

The people voted for change and so far, although there is obvious discontent in some quarters, they are happy with their decision because they are seeing a strong light at the end of the tunnel signaling true hope for a better Trinidad and Tobago.

And Kamla Persad-Bissessar and her colleagues know very well that if they become arrogant like the PNM and ignore the people, those who put them in office will fire them with the same zeal with which they elected them.

The people are still in charge of Trinidad and Tobago. And now, more than ever, they know it and understand their true power.

(September 29, 2010)

Is the PSA uprising really about money?

A comment made by Watson Duke, on Tuesday, made me wonder what is really behind the carnival atmosphere that surrounded the "Blackout Tuesday" protests by public sector workers.

"We told her (Chief Personnel Officer Stephanie Lewis) in no uncertain terms that she is working for a secret agency that is trying to overthrow the government. There are many different acronyms out there, there is CIA, PNM, many other acronyms," Duke told members of the Public Services Association (PSA).

While CIA might be far fetched and a stretch, it is no surprise that the PSA chief mentioned the opposition People's National Movement (PNM). After all, it is in the PNM's interest to foment this kind of labour unrest.

And what makes the story even more interesting is the presence among the PSA marchers of Dr. Amery Browne, the PNM MP for Diego Martin Central. Browne, who was part of the Manning government that created the problem that is now before the new People's Partnership government, said he was there to show solidarity with his constituents, who are civil servants. That is hypocrisy!

David Adullah who wears two hats these days — government senator and labour leader — was careful to point out that the problem at hand was a PNM problem, not one that the People's Partnership created. "We have to recognise the reality of the fact that many of the ills we now experience are due to the sins of those who were there before. We must never forget that," he said when he addressed the PSA workers.

And another trade union was quick to point out the same. Joseph Remy, president of the Communication Workers Union (CWU) noted that,"If they (the PNM administration) did what they should have done when they were in power, then we wouldn't be here."

Yet, if you pay attention to the way the PNM is spinning this, you would think that they were the ones who defended the PSA and the devils are the people in the new government. Duke knows the real story, which is why his comment is so interesting. Duke and the PSA were up in arms earlier this year against the Manning PNM administration over the PNM's attempt to scrap the country's two revenue agencies and fire thousands of workers. That was the PNM. And the people who fought the PNM on that were the same people who are in government today.

Duke's charge that the CPO is undermining the government, is one that Prime Minister Kamla Persad-Bissessar should not ignore. Perhaps the language is strong and perhaps the CPO is only acting on the instructions of the cabinet or the line minister.

However, it is a fact that there are people today in key positions, who are dedicated members of the old regime, who will do whatever they can to undermine and destabilise the present government. That is a fact.

Kamla's resolve to put away party symbols and treat everyone equally is admirable and I fully support her and her political colleagues on that. But the government must look carefully at who is doing what these days to determine whether Duke is right or not.

It goes beyond the CPO. In every ministry and even in Trinidad and Tobago's foreign missions, there are people who were loyal to the PNM and the Manning regime who continue to show that loyalty. Some of these people are clear obstructionists whose mission is to work against the government. The new ministers know it and some of them have made key changes. I am not advocating that the government should kick out PNM loyalists. On the contrary I want to see everyone involved in the business of making the government work. We voted for that! We changed things so we could have a more transparent and fully accountable government.

And the new administration has a responsibility to itself and every citizen, to ensure that it delivers on that key promise that has become the Kamla mantra: "Serve the people, serve the people, serve the people!"

That is why vigilance becomes important. If anyone in a key position — PNM or not — becomes obstructionist or refuses to do her/his job that person has to be removed. That is the only way this government can achieve its goals.

So while Duke's accusation might not be entirely true, the Kamla government is getting a black eye on the PSA issue, which is not of its own doing. The signal that Duke is sending is a very important one. Get your act together!

The CPO is holding firm on her one percent offer, which most people consider inadequate and insulting. According to Abdulah it should never be put on the table. But it IS on the table and the CPO appears to be firm in her position that it will not change. The government has backed her up, stating in a media release that to pay what the PSA wants would push the 2011 deficit to $12 billion and add to the recurrent expenditure.

I have no doubt that the figures are correct and the burden on the taxpayer would be immense. But by taking such a firm stand against the PSA and getting the PSA up in arms the PNM is in the classic position of having its cake and eating it too. The PNM under Manning deprived the PSA of the increases while it squandered billions on mega projects and useless initiatives like a $2 million flag and billion-dollar summits. It abdicated its responsibility and there are some people who say it probably helped engineer its fall to escape the wrath of the people. Rowley certainly wanted the government to fall so he could pick up the pieces and build his own little fiefdom.

And now that the people are screaming for their just due, they are standing on the sidelines and adding fuel to the fire, hoping the PSA issue will burn the new government.

Now is the time for a reality check. The People's Partnership needs to start paying very careful attention to what's really going on.

There is more to come, much more. And the PNM will continue to point fingers at the new government for all the ills for which it was responsible, including the CL fiasco, UDeCOTT and many others. The PSA issue is just the fever that alerts the body politic that there is an infection that needs powerful medicine to cure the illness.

(October 27, 2010)

Are we there yet?

If you have ever taken a road trip with children, you would have experienced the anxiety during the journey. "Are we there yet?" is the common refrain. And that seems to be what is happening with people watching the new Kamla People's Partnership government in Trinidad and Tobago.

It's only been five months and a few days, yet if you listen to people you would think that the government has been there for an eternity and nothing has happened.

In fact this government has achieved more in this short period than any government in Trinidad and Tobago. And it has been working with just the financial crumbs left by Patrick Manning and the PNM after their orgy of spending and waste. Still every time there is a negative report, the emails start flying around, the phone calls are fast and furious: "O Gawd, we in trouble! The government go mash up!"

Since May 24 I have been inundated with such calls and emails from party faithful, who all seem to feel that the sky is falling in. The end was near when Kamla asked for a review of the airport contracts; the government was "mashing up" when politicians in COP were trying to score points during an internal election; it was all over when the PSA called for mass protests; all hell is breaking loose because of the CL *bacchanal*. Look around folks. The sky is not falling in. Yes, some media reports would like you to believe that. The PNM's misinformation and political propaganda is aimed to making you believe it. And people's own selfish needs are adding fuel to all the rumours flying around. Don't get sucked in with Chicken Lickin' and fall prey to Foxy Loxy. I have been telling everyone who would listen that the PP government is not in trouble despite the propaganda that says so. Things are happening; the government is at work.

It took God a full seven days to create our world. Don't expect Kamla and her team to undo all the wrongs and fix every problem in less than six months! We gave them five years, so we need to have some patience. Haven't we experienced enough government mistakes in Trinidad and Tobago in recent memory?

The real anxiety from among supporters and many opportunists who have emerged like woodlice from the political woodwork, is Kamla's delay in completing the appointment of boards and making diplomatic appointments. There is every reason for the prime minister to be cautious and to check and double check everything.

In the old days, a party card was the essential credential to get on a state board. It didn't matter if you had the competence to serve or whether you understood what the company did. And some of the people demanding board appointments today still fall in that category.

What Kamla is doing right is making sure of a few things:

- No person is going to serve on more than one board
- Everyone appointed to a board would have the right credentials
- Everyone will have to go through a background check
- Party connection is not a passport to favours

You will likely say, if you look at some of the appointments already made, she has broken some of those rules. However, I would argue to make such a determination you have to understand all the relevant issues and know all the players. In such circumstances I would give the lady the benefit of the doubt.

There is grumbling as well about foreign postings. Obviously, she has determined that running things at home takes precedence over the overseas missions and foreign policy. She and her foreign minister appear to be in full control, so waiting a little while longer to find the right persons to serve cannot be a mistake.

One of our greatest faults is that each of us seems to be an expert in everything. We know how to run a political party; we know how to run a government; we know how to run state boards and everyone can be a diplomat.

I am sorry folks, it doesn't work that way. I know that our recent past has not provided good reason for trusting politicians and it will take some time to make the adjustment.

Kamla promised change. Change takes time. We are not there yet! The journey is just beginning. Have patience. And take time to enjoy it and to be part of the change.

(October 30, 2010)

Is Rowley a drowning man clutching at straws?

Keith Rowley is spending a few days in the United States hanging out with party faithfuls and getting standing ovations from the friendly, enthusiastic People's National Movement (PNM) crowds. It makes a pretty photo-op for a politician and would be something to celebrate under different circumstances and in different times.Not now.

The truth is, Rowley is taking all the basket and consoling himself that at least some PNM members love him, even if they live in a different country. What is interesting about this is that the party that Rowley leads cannot even get enough support at home to hold its annual convention, which it has had to postpone. One top member of the PNM told the local media recently that the party is having great difficulty getting delegates together for a convention.

A good leader would have asked himself *why?* And instead of running off to New York to take basket from a small group of supporters, he would have tried to fix the problems that he himself created when he decided to campaign against his leader and his party in the May 24 general election that toppled the Manning government. Once the deed was done Rowley gathered his troops and muscled his way into the leadership after hounding Patrick Manning out and making sure no one dared to challenge him for the post.

Manning has refused to disappear and the rumours from Balisier House are true, a counter coup might be in the works. However, instead of building support for his party and making a genuine attempt to rebuild and broaden its appeal, as he claims he is doing, Rowley is literally running away from reality and allowing himself be to flattered into thinking that he is a great leader and that PNM is a national institution that will rise again "and prevail."

He is doing it by trying to present the new People's Partnership government as the evil one, responsible for all the things that he and Manning created — the failure to pay contractors, the Clico *bacchanal*, the PSA unrest, the smelter in La Brea among others.

The PNM pulled that propaganda in 1987, but it is not working this time. It's primarily because Rowley and the PNM have no moral ground on which to stand. Having been a part of everything that the PNM represented he cannot now pretend to stand apart from the party. It doesn't work that way. And there is enough support within the Manning faction of the party to make Rowley uncomfortable at least if not to throw him out. And that explains why he is in New York.

If Manning or his hand-picked disciple makes a comeback to unseat Rowley, it would be because of Rowley's own incompetence as a leader. And such a development could well be the death of the party that Eric Williams built with people like Kamaluddin "Charch" Mohammed and others who had a much wider nationalistic vision than Rowley or anyone in the present PNM establishment.

The other primary factor that is hurting the PNM is this: While it lacks leadership and vision, its members are seeing those qualities in the new government and flocking to the People's Partnership (PP) where they are finding that they are being treated equally and with respect by a government that puts people first.

Manning and the PNM had historically operated on the basis of patronage, which ended up hurting the party and the leadership. Rowley, for all the boast of inclusivity, has embarked on the same kind of partisan and divisive politics that toppled the PNM from office on three occasions since independence.

The PP has come into office with a promise of clean, representative government based on accountability and transparency. The prime minister's mantra is "serve the people, serve the people, serve the people!" She is trying to do that in spite of the attempts by her detractors to show otherwise. One critical factor that makes the PP government stand out from all the other in Trinidad and Tobago is that it is not discarding people who happen to be former supporters of the PNM.

That strategy is confounding Rowley and working to undermine the very foundation of the PNM. It might be upsetting some PP supporters as well. However, it is a risk worth taking, especially since the members that make up the partnership have the same vision, which is true to the national anthem — "here ev'ry creed and race find an equal place." It is a kind of politics that is new to the country and it is working.

So if Rowley really wants to do something for the country, he should get serious about being a constructive opposition leader and work hard within his party to rebuild it by introducing policies similar to the PP, which was able to attract hordes of PNM voters in the last general and local elections.

Running off to New York and getting standing ovations might be good for the ego and present an impressive picture for the media. The real test for Rowley, is whether he can get the same from a PNM crowd back home. And the evidence suggests he can't. So the best advice for the PNM leader today is to follow the rules of good management: lead, follow or get out of the way.

(November 8, 2010)

PM exposes secret spy network; President, media on list of victims

Prime Minister Kamla Persad-Bissessar on Friday (November 12, 2010), provided parliament with full details of a covert spy operation that was authorised by the previous Manning PNM administration, to spy on prominent law-abiding citizens, including President George Maxwell Richards.

She said her administration cannot condone such behaviour, which presents "a clear and present danger to our democracy." She said it was a tragedy that the executive arm of the state sanctioned the illegal activity without reference to the elected representatives of the people and the parliament.

She said the "extremely dangerous precedent...shows that the country was being run by executive decree instead of parliamentary approval."

Persad-Bissessar said several agencies were engaged on the illegal activity and they reported directly to the minister of national security and the prime minister at the time, who was head of the country's National Security Council.

"In some cases this power was misused to spy on political opponents and perceived political enemies. In other cases no clear justification exists on the grounds for interception remain dubious and questionable."

The prime minister lamented the fact that while "our children were being kidnapped and the Anti-Kidnapping Squad (AKS) seemed powerless and unable to trace the several telephone calls demanding a ransom, the Security Intelligence Agency (SIA) was busy listening to our conversations — conversations of prominent members of society who had no connection with criminal activity."

The spying was widespread and involved people in various professions:

- members of the judiciary
- trade unionists
- editors and journalists
- media houses
- radio talk-show hosts
- comedians
- persons in the entertainment industry
- former opposition MPs
- government ministers
- sports personalities
- businessmen and -women
- newspaper columnists
- advertising executives
- county councilors
- lawyers and in some cases, the children of such persons

"Words cannot express the deep sense of personal outrage and hurt I feel about this matter," the prime minister said.

"Such an unwarranted and unjustified invasion of citizen's privacy is a cause for alarm. Why on earth would a government wish to engage in such unproductive illegal activity when the country was under siege as a result of criminal activity?"

She provided a list of victims of the illegal activity, which she said was code named "Operation News," which she said started in March 2005 and has been ongoing since then.

Politicians:
- The UNC's head office
- Constituency offices of UNC MPs
- Kamla Persad-Bissessar
- Anand Ramlogan
- Suruj Rambachan
- Gerald Yetming
- Wade Mark
- Manohar Ramsaran
- Roodal Moonilal
- Roy Augustus
- Winston Peters
- Robin Montano
- Jack Warner
- Fuad Khan
- Carolyn Seepersad Bachan
- Winston Dookeran
- Gary Griffith
- Anil Roberts
- Ashworth Jack
- Keith Rowley

Members of the judiciary who were targeted included:
- Chief Justice Sat Sharma, his wife Kalawati Sharma and his son Shiv Sharma
- Justice Herbert Volney
- Justice Rajendra Narine
- Madam Justice Carol Gobin

Persad-Bissessar said the media were also under attack, with the SIA eavesdropping on journalists. "Freedom of the press is enshrined in our constitution and the widespread wire tapping of journalists and the media houses undermines this important pillar in our democracy," she said.

She gave the names of some of the media personnel who were targets:
- Dale Enoch
- Sasha Mohammed
- Shelly Dass
- Francis Joseph
- Ian Alleyene
- Inshan Ishmael
- Ken Ali
- Devant Maharaj
- Peter O'Connor

- Camini Marajh

The trade union movement was also under attack in the illicit operation. Among the victims were:

- Errol Mcleod
- Clyde Weatherhead
- Rudy Indarsingh
- David Abdulah
- Robert Guiseppi
- Lyle Townsend

Other prominent persons included:
- former (AG) Commissioner of Police James Philbert
- former CEO of the San-Fernando city corporation Marlene Coudray
- comedian Rachael Price
- former Security Chief Mr. Richard Kelshall
- President George Maxwell Richards
- Sat Maharaj
- Ato Boldon
- Emile Elias
- former Chief of Defence John Sandy
- Gary Aboud

Manning did not even spare members of his own PNM. "The dictator was not content to spy on opposition MP's and the aforementioned list of persons. Former government ministers were also the subject of wire tapping," Persad-Bissessar said. The targets included:

- Colm Imbert
- Pennelope Beckles-Robinson
- Donna Cox
- Faris Al Rawi
- Keith Rowley

The prime minister said the illegal activity went beyond eavesdropping on personal telephone calls. The spy agency was also intercepting emails.

"One list provided by the Commissioner of Police contains the name of every single government minister in the People's Partnership. Sadly, Mr. Speaker the names of our children are also included on this list," she said.

"I regret the further intrusion into the private lives by virtue of this disclosure but I felt it necessary to do so to demonstrate by reference to hard evidence the depth and extent of the dictatorial operations of the former administrations."

"Under the former government, Big Brother seems to have taken a very keen interest in ordinary citizen's private lives and affairs. "I want to reassure you that I do not intend to move from Big Brother to Big Sister," she said.

(November 13, 2010)

Manning should be censured for making mischief

Patrick Manning seems to have a special gift for spreading misinformation. The latest episode is his allegation that Prime Minister Kamla Persad-Bissessar is building a "palace" for $150 million, which he claimed was bigger than the one that he built for himself at a cost of more than $175 million taxpayers' dollars.

My first reaction was that it was impossible for that building in south Trinidad to cost anywhere close to that. But like other citizens hearing it from a former prime minister who should be responsible, it was something to think about. It didn't take long for me to figure out what was really going and to understand Manning's motives.

Now that Kamla has produced the evidence to show that Manning lied, I would wager that Manning's intention all along was to mislead the parliament and inject doubt among citizens about where the lady found so much money to build her palace. It was part of his plan of misinformation that started the week before when he suggested that "dirty" money was used in the People's Partnership campaign for the May 24 general election. And in a statement Sunday he suggested that "drug money" might have been used in the construction of the home.

Kamla quite rightly put Manning in his place on that matter and has threatened legal action unless Manning makes a retraction and apology. Now he has repeated the malicious statements, making it personal.

The government is planning to deal with this issue on Wednesday (November 24), based on the Standing Orders of the House, which prohibit an MP from knowingly misleading parliament. But that doesn't seem to bother Manning, who is accustomed to making outlandish statements. Kamla has produced the evidence to show that the cost was around $3 million with another half a million needed to complete the structure so the matter should be closed. But Manning's insistence on pursing it with innuendos and no facts shows that his intention was to create mischief.

The former prime minister boldly proclaimed that he was stating "facts" based on evidence he had gathered. Yet he has not shown how he arrived at his figure. I would suggest that he cannot because he made up the "facts" the same way he made up the "facts" to try to smear Keith Rowley. For Manning, telling lies is ok so long as it suits his political agenda.

Does anyone remember his allegations in parliament against Rowley? He spoke of a missing $10 million and asked Rowley to account for it when he knew that no money was missing. And although government officials produced the documentation to prove everything was OK, Manning repeated his misinformation. And now he is going down that same road again, this time with the prime minister as his target.

Such irresponsible behaviour is unbecoming of a man who sits in the nation's parliament, especially when that man served as prime minister. There are several similar incidents, but I am sure you get the point.

Manning has demonstrated a level of irresponsibility that is even embarrassing his own party. His statement on Sunday (21 Nov. 2010) demanding full disclosure from Persad-Bissessar after she had in fact shown that everything is above board demonstrates his intention to maintain his mischief.

People usually see others as a reflection of themselves. Perhaps this is why Manning finds it difficult to accept that Persad-Bissessar could be honest.

(November 22, 2010)

What is Manning contemplating?

What is happening in the PNM?

A newspaper report Sunday, claims that there is a move within the opposition party to dump its leader, Keith Rowley, who contributed to the fall of his predecessor, Patrick Manning. The drama that is unfolding has an unusual twist and one of its principal players appears to be Manning, the man who described Rowley as a *"wajang"* after he kicked him out of the cabinet for challenging Manning's cozy relationship with the former head of UDeCOTT, Calder Hart.

Manning, the report suggests, is planning a political resurrection and is apparently working closely with the former PNM chairman, Franklin Khan, who had to resign his cabinet and party posts after he was charged with corruption. The charges were later withdrawn when the state determined than Khan's accuser was not a credible witness.

People who know Manning well, like political scientist Dr. Selwyn Ryan, are saying that the country should not underestimate the former PM. "Mr. Manning cannot be trusted at face value. He is using a strategy to recover centre stage with the assistance of the media," Ryan told the Sunday Guardian. "He was waiting for the right moment to return to the spotlight...He definitely has a strategy up his sleeves."

Manning remained silent for six months in parliament until recently when he surfaced with headline-grabbing accusations about the house in Phillipine that Prime Minister Kamla Persad-Bissessar and her husband have been building for the past eight years.

His distraction came after Persad-Bissessar exposed Manning and fingered him in an illegal wiretapping racket in which a special agency — the Strategic Intelligence Agency (SIA) — was eavesdropping on the private phone calls of citizens, including the head of state, the judiciary, top politicians and journalists.

The government has since passed legislation to use wiretapping legally if absolutely necessary and if sanctioned by the proper authorities. No more illegal snooping on law-abiding citizens.

But when faced with the prospect of defending his position, Manning chose to deflect attention and make slanderous statements about something totally irrelevant — Kamla's palace, as he called it.

Manning has also suggested that the attorney general is making up stories to implicate him in the illegal activities conducted by the SIA. Anand Ramlogan told parliament the former head of the SIA told him that Manning gave instructions to spy on people and went as far as suggesting the PNM was likely behind the spike in serious crimes. Manning responded with his own accusations. While denying any knowledge of the spying, he suggested that Ramlogan was telling a big lie. "I wish to ask the Attorney General to stop letting his fertile imagination run wild," he said in a media release. "It is most unbecoming for one who holds such high office and very unsettling for the national community who expect calm, rationality and sobriety from those who impact so directly on the security and stability of our nation," Manning added.

The innuendos in the rest of his statement are important. He suggested that Ramlogan's motive was to "grab headlines" since there is "very intense competition among many in the Cabinet now anxiously aspiring to succeed the Prime Minister."

That is deliberate '*khoochur*'. Manning is trying to create divisions within the People's Partnership by suggesting that Ramlogan is trying to upstage his cabinet colleague, Roodal Moonilal, the man named by the prime minister as her successor. Instead of trying to deal with relevant national issues and matters of national security Manning is making a juvenile attempt to create his own agenda while trying to plant a fox in the government's hen house.

His hope is that he could add salt to whatever minor wounds there might be in the partnership while advancing himself as a leader. He had been suffering from political *tabanca* for six months; now he appears ready to make his comeback.

Privately he has been plotting his revenge against Rowley through his silence and it seems that he is ready to make his play. I disagree with suggestions by some political pundits that Manning deliberately threw away the election because of the mess he had made. Manning invested too much to give it away. He had hoped for a double whammy in calling the snap election — to catch the opposition unprepared and also to dispose of Rowley forever.

He miscalculated both. And now after six months in the political wilderness during which he plotted his next moves, he has put the political shame behind him and is making a play to become a national leader once more. His problem, of course, is that he is so scarred by scandal and allegations of corruption that he cannot seriously expect anyone in the party to reinstate him.

However, he knows Rowley has made serious tactical missteps. The new leader has been trying to put his own stamp on the party, while making big blunders along the way. Manning's lips were sealed while all this was happening. And now that he sees Rowley politically wounded he is getting ready for the kill.

He already has some of his troops within the small parliamentary caucus. If he could infiltrate the party organs and the 41 constituency groups, Rowley could face the worse shock of the political career.

Whether Manning can engineer Rowley's fall will depend on how desperate the party is to pull itself out of the gutter in which it finds itself now with droves of supporters running off to become part of the People's Partnership. The attraction for those who are embracing the government is that the Prime Minister and her political allies have made it clear that this government is a people first administration that does not consider party affiliation as a prime factor in governing.

It means many PNMites who had feared victimisation from the new government remain comfortable in their jobs as they should. The obvious political millstones are being replaced, but those who hold office based on merit have remained there. The message is that PNM people have nothing to offer so they are deserting the once mighty party of Dr. Eric Williams and there is a big question mark today about whether the party will rise again and "prevail."

Manning and his allies are making the point that if it is to get out of the political quicksand it must find a new leader since Rowley has failed to invigorate the party. If the rumours turn out to be true we can expect to hear much more from the member of parliament for San Fernando East. And Trinidad and Tobago might soon see the wily and cunning Manning as a renewed fixture in the political landscape.

(December 5, 2010)

It's time for Rowley to stop the pappyshow

Keith Rowley — the *"wajang"* and "raging bull" that Patrick Manning fired — has had his revenge and now wants to be Prime Minister of Trinidad and Tobago. But the way he has been behaving lately suggests that he is working very hard at ensuring that it never happens.

For a long time now he has been trying to sway public opinion in his direction with some success. That is part of the political game and his right in a free and democratic society, so nobody should fault the PNM leader for that. However, there is a big difference between political campaigning and misinformation. And what Rowley did this week with his declaration about the property tax borders on mischief.

He summoned the media to raise the alarm that he had learned that the government was bringing back the property tax and making it more oppressive than the one it fought against — the hated tax that the Manning administration tried to inflict on citizens. The "Axe the Tax" lobby was so strong it shook Manning's confidence and might have helped him decide to call an election two and a half years ahead of schedule.

Rowley told reporters the government would try to "sneak" the tax in during the Carnival festivities on "unsuspecting citizens." And he conveniently left out the point that the valuation upon which the homes would be taxed would be based on older rates.

Prakash Ramadhar, the Legal Affairs minister who was previously the principal flag bearer for the "Axe the Tax" movement, had to clarify the matter. The Manning PNM was basing its tax on new inflated property values while the present government is using old values, he explained. In that context a lower percentage in the PNM tax was still higher because of simple maths. Three percent of $10 is much higher than 7.5 percent of one dollar. Simple. Not for Rowley. He didn't go there. That would not give him the required headline and face time on TV.

His mission was to create mischief based on misinformation. If he has seen the bill as he claimed he has then he would have known that he was not telling the whole truth. He was engaging in what Basdeo Panday famously called "lies, innuendos and half-truths.".

As if that wasn't enough, later in the week he demonstrated a lack of leadership when he decided to kill the "hanging" bill while saying his party is fully committed to executing convicted killers. When Attorney General Anand Ramlogan introduced the bill the opposition objected, saying that it was wishy-washy and unlikely to cause anyone to hang. That was and continues to be a point of debate depending on a person's point of view. But it has become irrelevant because the government "bent over backwards," according to Ramlogan, to amend the bill in line with what the opposition was demanding.

In effect it changed the agenda and caused the government to dance according to music of the PNM band in order to get the crucial opposition support needed to pass the bill. But that was not good enough for Rowley. Rowley wanted more than his ounce of flesh. He got all he wanted but he is still not happy, so on Monday (February 28, 2011) he is going to vote against the bill and kill it. It doesn't matter that a majority of citizens want to hang killers.

That defies logic especially since the PNM is saying all over the place that it supports hanging. Political expediency, it seems, is more important for Rowley than the welfare of the people. Just Friday (February 18, 2011), Penny Beckles was expressing optimism that the opposition would join the government to do what is best for the country. It looks like she didn't speak to her boss because while she might think the opposition wants to do what's best Rowley has a different agenda.

Rowley's behaviour is downright irresponsible. As leader of the opposition people expect him to be an alternative national leader. But he has to get serious about his job and end the weekly pappyshow.

He seems to have missed the whole point about the role of the opposition. The opposition is an integral part of the governing system and is expected to act responsibly to be the chief watchdog for citizens, keeping checks and balances on the government. The opposition's role is not to be obstructionist. Its role is not to knock down every single thing the government does, challenge every appointment and denounce every government move.

That's not how you win political points and it's not way you conduct the business of parliament. And it certainly is not the way for a leader to behave. Democracy demands a strong and reasonable opposition. It is time for Rowley to get serious about doing his job. He owes it to himself, his party and the people of Trinidad and Tobago.

(February 26, 2011)

PNM kills hanging bill

As expected, the constitutional amendment bill to reintroduce the death penalty for murder was defeated in the House of Representatives on Monday February 28, 2001.

Despite changes to the bill to meet the demands of the opposition the 11 members of the People's National Movement (PNM) present for the sitting voted "no." Point Fortin MP Paula Gopee-Scoon was not present when the vote was taken. All 29 members on the government side supported the legislation. House leader Roodal Moonilal was expecting the defeat and had said the PNM would have to answer to the people for its stand on the very important crime fighting initiative.

"We have made fundamental amendments to our initial version of the Bill—Constitutional Amendment (Capital Offences Bill 2011). We have made these fundamental changes to satisfy the demands of the opposition so that the final version is effectively the PNM's bill," Moonilal said over the weekend.

In wrapping up the debate, Attorney General Anand Ramlogan slammed the opposition for its position noting that according to a study done by Oxford University last November an overwhelming 91 percent of people surveyed said they favoured hanging as the punishment for murder. He made the point as he referred to the presentation of the opposition chief whip who said in her contribution to the debate that 85 percent of the population are in favour of hanging and that the PNM agrees with it in principle. However, Marlene McDonald told legislators that the bill was flawed because it would not cause anyone to hang. She also demanded that it be scrapped and redone because there was no consultation with the people.

Ramlogan took issue with the matter of consultation and read out a long list of measures the former Manning PNM administration took without any consultation with the people. However, he noted that he found one instance of a consultation over a one month period that cost the taxpayer more than $4 million. The AG pointed out that one of the recommendations of that consultation was that hanging should be restored as the penalty for murder.

Ramlogan said no matter how you look at it the people of Trinidad and Tobago are in favour of hanging convicted killers — even supporters of the PNM. During the committee stage Prime Minister Kamla Persad-Bissessar asked for a suspension of the sitting for a meeting between the Prime Minister and Opposition Leader Keith Rowley. However, Rowley refused, saying that an earlier request for such a meeting was turned down. During the various committee stages the opposition made no objections to any of the changes. However, when the final vote was taken all 11 members present voted no.

One story that created great uneasiness in 2011 was a decision by the Housing Development Corporation (HDC) to destroy productive farm lands in D'Abadie and Endeavour to make way for housing. The HDC stood by its decision, calling it government policy but the question that arose was which government.

It caused a farmers uprising and Food Production Minister Vasant Bharath found himself standing with farmers against his ministerial colleague Roodal Moonilal who had responsibility for the HDC. In the end Prime Minister Kamla Persad-Bissessar, who was away in Brazil at the time, intervened and settled the problem.

Let's grow food and build houses

When Vasant Bharat stood up against bulldozers in Spring Village in 2008 he was representing the cause of farmers in his St Augustine constituency and his actions were consistent with the policies of his party — the United National Congress (UNC).

The People's National Movement (PNM) was in power and the Housing Development Corporation (HDC) was under the control of Emily Gaynor Dick-Fode, who responded to the farmers' protest and ordered HDC boss Noel Garcia to halt the project.

When Bharath stood up with farmers Friday (April 29) he was doing what he did in 2008 as an opposition MP. When he told them, "You have a just cause", he was demonstrating consistency as an individual committed to the farming community as a politician representing a party — the UNC — that has always stood up in defence of agriculture and agricultural workers.

However, his action put him in an apparent conflict with his cabinet colleague, Housing Minister Roodal Moonilal, who expressed regret at the bulldozing of farmers' crops and offered compensation and relocation for those affected by the actions of the HDC on Easter Monday.

And it puts Prime Minister Kamla Persad-Bissessar on the spot. Would she penalise Bharath for standing up for government policy? Would she do the same to Moonilal for also following government policy? Moonilal made it clear on Thursday (April 28) following the regular cabinet meeting that there never was a question of housing versus agriculture. But he insisted that the lands at D'Abadie were earmarked for housing and that he would continue with plans to build houses there.

That is where there appears to be a clear policy conflict. While the present government is committed to both housing and agriculture it has identified itself as a humane and caring administration that operates on the basis of consultation with the people.

When Persad-Bissessar intervened from Brazil to stop the bulldozing she said while she appreciated and understood the urgent need for housing, the government must give equal consideration to farmers. She asked both ministers to find a solution and expressed confidence that the matter could be resolved in the interest and satisfaction of all concerned. It appeared so on Thursday but the events of Friday demonstrate that the optimism was premature. Farmers are now demanding Moonilal's dismissal. And Bharath's decision to stand with the farmers might be seen as evidence that he shares their views with respect to his cabinet colleague.

Of course Bharath wants no such thing. He made that very clear on Friday — that his presence with his "extended family" was not to criticise his colleague but to show solidarity and consistency, reminding everyone that when the HDC bulldozers showed up in Spring Village in May 2008 he was there to stop them.

Moonilal and Bharath both want to carry on with their agenda and deliver on the housing and agriculture promises of their government. In the process, his housing ministry may have erred in the lack of consultation. But Moonilal's insistence on building houses on land earmarked by the previous government for a residential development had offended many people, including supporters of the UNC in its heartland.

The question is whether there are no more suitable lands for housing in the vicinity of the farms that have been bulldozed. Bharath has been encouraging people to stay on the land and to grow food. Just a couple of weeks ago he told farmers occupying state lands they are welcome to stay while the state regularises their tenure, providing they cultivate the land

In the case of the D'Abadie and Endeavour lands there is clear evidence that the lands have been used for agriculture for many years. Bharath and his government have been saying they will ensure that arable land is not used for housing. That is a reasonable position given that Trinidad and Tobago has thousands of acres of land that can be used for housing.

So why didn't the HDC look for other suitable lands for housing? Why insist on one particular location, especially one that is producing food for the nation? That really is what has ticked off the farmers who are suggesting that Moonilal is acting contrary to his own government's policies. The task for the prime minister now is to decide on whether any of her ministers erred and to investigate what went wrong. But she must act swiftly to resolve this unnecessary impasse that could escalate into a political nightmare. The solution could be as easy as finding an alternative location for the housing project. After all, no one needs fertile land for that and there is without a doubt more available land in that constituency.

But there is a bigger and more sensitive issue to be resolved. That is, why did the bulldozers wreck so many acres of crops, necessitating state compensation when the HDC could have waited for the farmers to harvest their crops or look elsewhere to build houses. The HDC's view is that crops are cyclical, that the farmers were served notices and should have expected the arrival of bulldozers.

While that may be true, the whole episode demonstrates a kind of arrogance that is inconsistent with government policy and the character of its leader who has always put people first and has always acted with compassion and humility in dealing with people. The challenge that faces Kamla on her return home is to deal decisively with this matter. In opposition the UNC put people first; in government the UNC and the People's Partnership put people first.

There's room enough for food production and thousands of new homes. So let's build homes and let us grow food and feed our nation.

(April 30, 2011)

Kamla Persad-Bissessar promised transparency and accountability in her administration and when necessary she took decisive action against members of her own team. One of the first people to face Kamla's discipline was Mary King, the Planning Minister in the first cabinet.

Kamla fires Mary King

Prime Minister Kamla Persad-Bissessar on Tuesday revoked the appointment of Mary King as Minister of planning, economic, social restructuring and gender affairs, as well as a government senator.

The prime minister made the disclosure to reporters just after noon on Tuesday following a meeting she held with President Max Richards. The meeting took place at Knowsley, Port of Spain. The prime minister said she was deeply saddened by the action she had had to take. However, she said it was something that had to be done in the interest of all. She said it was the right thing to do. She promised that she would name a planning minister on Wednesday to replace King.

In a related development, the Congress of the People (COP), which is King's party, issued a media release stating that it met with King Tuesday morning to hear her views on the matter. It said COP is "of the firm opinion that the intervention of the Integrity Commission to launch a full investigation into the alleged wrongdoing on Dr. King's part is necessary." It added, "The COP remains faithful to our founding values and is committed to the concepts of natural justice, equality, fairness and integrity in public office."

(May 11, 2011)

PM's Facebook entry:

"Today I have received an advice from the Honourable Attorney General. Upon the basis of his opinion, I have decided to advise His Excellency the President of my intention to revoke the appointment of Mary King as Senator and Minister. It is a sombre decision, but one that upholds the principles of good governance and integrity in public office, to which my Administration remains fully committed."

Opposition Leader Keith Rowley found himself in deep trouble when he accused Attorney General Anand Ramlogan of meeting with staff at the T&T mission in New York and enquiring about the ethnic composition of the staff. Ramlogan immediately refuted that and even produced his passport to show that he was never in New York since assuming office. However, Rowley insisted that he did visit with staff and that his story was true.

However, Jyoti checked the facts and confirmed that Rowley was not telling the truth. The opposition leader had to eventually apologise.

Did Rowley really visit NY mission on Nov. 5?

Did Keith Rowley and Marlene Mc Donald go to the Trinidad and Tobago mission in New York on November 5, 2010 as they have claimed? Last week Trinidad and Tobago's ambassador to the UN and head of the mission wrote the permanent secretary in the foreign affairs ministry advising that checks revealed that Rowley did not visit the mission in November.

In his letter Rodney Charles said he consulted staff and reviewed the mission's records and has concluded that no such visit was ever paid "by either the Honourable Attorney General or the Opposition Leader in November 2010, or at any other time thereafter. Additionally, the Charge d' Affairs at the Mission at the said time, Ms Cheryl Ann Millard, has advised that no such meetings were held... In fact, at a staff meeting held on April 27, 2011, staff emphatically stated that they would wish not to be associated with the allegations being made," Charles wrote.

The next day Rowley accused Charles of distorting the facts and insisted that he visited the mission on November 5, 2010 and that he had a witness to prove. The PNM leader added that he cannot understand "how Mr. Charles would be in a position to say and to prove that nobody spoke to me or what they said, they didn't say to me. It is just preposterous."

Rowley's witness is his parliamentary whip, Marlene Mc Donald. She insisted she was aware of the comments made by staff of the UN mission in New York about a visit there by Ramlogan. "I was part and parcel of all the comments made at that mission with respect to the ethnic composition of the staff at the mission...No one could say we were not there," Mc Donald insisted.

Jyoti checked the records and we found that November 5th, 2010 was the national Divali holiday in Trinidad and Tobago and the mission in New York was closed on that day. No staff were present so Rowley and Mc Donald could not have officially visited on that day.

November 5, 2010 was a Friday and the mission was also closed on the weekend. The facts would suggest that either Rowley lied or he got his dates mixed up. The opposition leader has suggested that he would apologise "at the appropriate time."

Rowley has been inconsistent in his story all along. On Monday (May 16, 2011) he told reporters he has been conducting "very detailed investigations on the matter and at this moment I can tell that there is some confusion with the facts...At the appropriate time, the correct information and any relevant apologies would be forthcoming."

(May 19, 2011)

Workers must start asking their unions some questions

Trade Unions in Trinidad and Tobago have declared "war" on the government without telling their members the true cost of the demands or how their battles will help the average worker get a better quality of life.

The People's Partnership government inherited a near bankrupt treasury, which was the result of years of reckless spending by the previous government. Interestingly that government had no love for the working class yet none of the unions now clamouring for huge wage increases is talking about that.

What is clear is that the unions are behaving in a most selfish manner without regard to implications of their actions for the medium and long term in the country. The short-term result of their planned national strike will be to deprive the very people they claim to represent of basic services.

When the lights go out and the taps run dry everybody suffers. Yet that is exactly what the unions are threatening to do and they are asking for support for this action from the very people who will suffer most. It is time that the unions tell their members the demands for more money cannot be met without causing irreparable damage to the national economy that is just starting to emerge from near collapse.

The reality, no matter how you look at it, is that Trinidad and Tobago cannot meet the demands of the unions and contrary to what the unions are saying, you cannot borrow to finance recurrent expenditure and to pay wages; that is a formula for economic disaster.

Watson Duke and the Public Services Association understood that and backed down on their demands. If the other trade unions honestly pay attention to what is happening in the country and in the world they would do the same. The question is whether they care about the national economy and their membership or whether their political agenda to try to destabilise the government is more important. If you look at what is happening in the global economy, there is cause for worry.

The United States has just lost its AAA rating for its treasury bonds for the first time in 70 years. What that means is that it can no longer sustain the low interest rates that helped keep the economy afloat. Financial analysts say that it's the first sign that U.S. government will soon have higher borrowing costs, which means taxpayers will have to put out tens of billions of dollars a year to sustain the economy.

The ripple effect is that interest rates for consumers and companies seeking mortgages, credit cards and business loans will also go up. The real worry for the US is that investors will pull their money out of the system because they know that it is bad economics to believe you can spend yourself out of debt or tax yourself into prosperity. This is just plain common sense. And we all know that what happens in the US affects the global economy. It happened in 2008 and we have still not recovered.

So if workers in Trinidad and Tobago are smart they would start paying attention to what is really happening and tell their union leaders to explain a few things to them:

- They need to ask them to explain how they can have secure jobs when reckless strikes cripple the economy
- They need to ask them to explain how shutting off water and

turning off the lights will feed and clothe their children or provide better health care or other services
- They need to ask them to explain how they intend to get a better deal for them by trying to bite the very hands that feed them

Now is the time to ask these questions.

(July 7, 2011)

Trinidad and Tobago faced a security crisis in 2011 that included a plot to assassinate the Prime Minister and at least two of her senior cabinet ministers. Crime escalated and had been getting out of control. In one weekend seven people were brutally murdered. The government reacted with a state of emergency.

The presidential proclamation:

"Whereas it is enacted by Section 8.1 of the Constitution, that the President may, from time to time, make a proclamation that a State of Public Emergency exists, and B; that Section 8.2 of our Constitution, that the proclamation made by the President shall not be effective unless it contains a declaration that the President is satisfied that action has been taken, or is immediately threatened by any person of such a nature, and on so extensive a scale, as to be likely to endanger the public safety or deprive the community of supplies or services essential to life.

"And now therefore, I, George Maxwell Richards, President in pursuance of the powers conferred upon me that I am satisfied that action has been taken, or is immediately threatened by persons or bodies of persons of such a nature, and on so extensive a scale, as to be likely to endanger the public safety or to deprive the community or any substantial portion of the community, of supplies or services essential to life and a State of Public Emergency exists in Trinidad and Tobago."

Don't be fooled by Rowley's crocodile tears

Let us not be fooled by Keith Rowley's sudden concern for the killing of innocent people by murderers who have no regard for the law and know that they can kill and get away with it. The opposition leader is suddenly interested in meeting with the government to discuss crime and to cooperate to make legislative changes to facilitate the war on crime. He said Saturday fighting crime is not a political issue.

Where was that national spirit in February, Dr. Rowley, when you and your MPs voted down the bill to hang killers? All that was needed was the same "concern" and a little cooperation. Instead you and your MPs behaved like a gang and defeated the legislation that would have hanged those who kill and just walk away.

Even when Prime Minister Kamla Persad-Bissessar tried to reach out to you to make changes you behaved like a hooligan in the parliament and snapped at her, saying you would not talk with her.

Attorney General Anand Ramlogan quite rightly accused you and the PNM of taking a serious debate on hanging and transformed it into a "political gayelle," in which MPs were trying to outdo each other because their internal election campaign was coming. So much for crime and politics!

The prime minister continued to reach out to the opposition even when the bill was in the final committee stage; she even offered to suspend the sitting to try to find a compromise.

I am sorry, Dr. Rowley, you were not interested in talking or finding any means to deal with the criminal problem then and you are just playing politics today when you say you care. The prime minister had no choice but to accept defeat on the hanging bill but lamented that "at the end of the day it would be innocent people of this land who would suffer".

Ramlogan said in parliament on that fateful day that for "every murdered person and every murderer that escapes the hangman's noose, the PNM must be held responsible." He said he had tried the "diplomatic, friendly route" to give the PNM support, but the party failed to rise to the occasion because its political concern was not to "make the People's Partnership look good." He described the PNM's attitude as "political hooliganism of the worse kind" and accused the PNM of political obstructionism by "holding an entire country to ransom and standing in the way of a vision."

Today, Rowley's political deception and hypocrisy stand out clearly with his crocodile tears. We have said before that the government has a responsibility to fight crime with all the weapons it can muster. We know that it has been making a valiant effort and that crime has come down, despite the horrendous events of last week.

Rowley should be ashamed to even raise his voice on this matter to try to score cheap political points and try to pretend that he and his party care. Let us not forget that it is their former leader who said crime was not a problem, entertained gang leaders at the state's expense and also gave them lucrative government contracts.

The PNM never cared about ending crime and they don't care now. And that includes Keith Rowley and the whole PNM clan!

(August 21, 2011)

Rowley should learn to lead or just get out of the way

Keith Rowley continues to demonstrate that he lacks the competence to lead his party and the country. His latest declaration that the People's National Movement (PNM) is not prepared to associate itself with government's "incompetence, wrongdoing and ulterior motives" in declaring a state of emergency shows that his interest lies in gaining political points rather than dealing with the safety and security of citizens.

And it's also contradictory.

Last week he was all over the government for not dealing with crime and was offering to meet with the prime minister to find ways to deal with the problem. He said he was willing to discuss whatever legislative measures are needed and offered to cooperate with the government.

That was the same Rowley who refused to work with the same government and the same prime minister in February this year to find a compromise on the bill to hang murderers. He and his MPs killed the bill, which required a special majority to pass. Then last week, suddenly Rowley began shedding crocodile tears for the 11 victims of killers who died within a 48-hour period. And now that the government has acted, he is withdrawing his enthusiasm.

The problem is that Rowley continues to see everything in Trinidad and Tobago from his personal political bias without regard for the national good. Now he is dismissing the state of emergency as part of a plot to detain people "in certain parts of the country." It's a racist comment.

He told reporters Wednesday once detained, the government would invoke the Anti-Gang and Bail Amendment Bill to hold them without charge for as long as possible, hoping to get past December, and reduce the number of homicides between 2010 and 2011 for political reasons. "That was always the objective," he said.

Well hold it for a minute and analyse what Rowley is saying.

First he is saying the government is rounding up certain people according to where they live. Then, he says, they are holding them until December to show the number of murders is down. It seems to me that Rowley is admitting but not saying, that those people who are being "rounded up and detained" are responsible for the murders — or at least some of the murders — in the country. How else could he conclude that by locking them up the murder rate would drop?

And what is the message this wannabe national leader is sending to gang leaders and gang members? That he is on their side. I hope I am wrong, so I leave that for you to figure out.

The State of Emergency has become necessary because Rowley's former leader and the government of which he was a part refused to deal with crime. Under the Kamla government, the security forces had started to deal with crime and those who were hurt started to fight back with a vengeance. So the government acted. And it acted with the right formula.

This is the first time in Trinidad and Tobago that a government has had to declare a state of emergency specifically to deal with crime because those who ran the country until May 2010 looked the other way when criminals did as they pleased. The Manning administration refused to deal with the problem and chose instead to entertain gang leaders at taxpayers' expense and then hand them lucrative contracts.

It was Rowley's former boss who boasted that he knew Mr. Big who was the crime boss, yet Manning did nothing about it. It was the same "leader" who said crime was not a problem when hundreds were dying every year while he was prime minister.

Rowley's government had no plan to deal with crime. Under the PNM there were 2,868 reported murders between 2002 and 2009, with a record high of 550 in 2008. And all that the PNM was prepared to do was launch irrelevant public relations campaigns and waste money on blimps and expensive international consultants. If Rowley wants to lead he must demonstrate competence and rationality, not to mention caring for all citizens instead of only those who support him and the PNM. Those days are gone forever.

Kamla has shown that she cares about Trinidad and Tobago and the safety and security of all its citizens. The nation supports her move and it is time for Rowley to start learning to lead in a constructive manner. Otherwise he should just shut up and get out of the way.

(August 25, 2011)

One of the issues that Keith Rowley raised during the State of Emergency was that the government took the measure to attack people of one ethnicity. It was an emotional statement that he did not back up with any evidence but it created some doubt about the state's motives.

National Security Minister John Sandy shot back at Rowley with the evidence to prove that Rowley was wrong.

Afro Trinis commit majority of crimes in T&T: Sandy

National Security Minister John Sandy told Parliament Friday (September 2, 2011) Afro-Trinidadians commit most of the crime in Trinidad and Tobago and much of it is directed against other Afro-Trinidadians. He also noted that this group comprises the majority of the prison population in the country.

Sandy was speaking at the time in the debate to extend the State of Emergency, specifically on the president's reasons for agreeing to declare the emergency.

Sandy said of 72 percent of the 2,307 people murdered since 2006 were of African decent. That's a total of 1,668. He made the point to defend the government against opposition charges of racial profiling the crackdown on crime. Sandy broke down the statistics by year:

- 2006 — 390 murdered, 228 Afro-Trinidadians
- 2007 — 391 murdered, 308 Afro-Trinidadians
- 2008 — 547 murdered, 427 Afro-Trinidadians
- 2009 — 506 murdered, 383 Afro-Trinidadians
- 2010 — 473 murdered, 320 Afro-Trinidadians

"We must recognise that it is people looking like me who are being murdered, mothers like my mother, God rest her soul, who are out there weeping more than any other race," Sandy told the House of Representatives. "When we see the accused being led away, being led to court, in most instances, it is people who look like me with their heads bent, hiding from the cameras. We must stop that. This is why I am appealing to my brothers and sisters to stop that," Sandy said.

Sandy said in 2006 there were 2,678 people in prison of which 57 percent or 1,532 were Afro-Trinidadians. He said it has continued that way.

- 2007 — 2,726 prisoners, 1,464 Afro-Trinidadians
- 2008 — 3,012 prisoners, 1,610 Afro-Trinidadians
- 2009 — 1,886 prisoners, 1,776 Afro-Trinidadians
- 2010 — 2,412 prisoners, 1,300 Afro-Trinidadians
- 2011 — 1,734 prisoners, 890 Afro-Trinidadians

Sandy said too many young people are dying, leaving children without fathers. He noted that in San Juan one murdered gang leader left 15 children behind.

The minister strongly defended the emergency. "I remain confident that the decision was the correct one," he said. He added that if the government had not acted to prevent what was about to happen "1990 would have been a Christmas party compared to what would have happened....loss of life, the brutality and mayhem would have made 1990 a garden party."

Sandy said he remains confident that "this Government took the right decision in declaring a State of Emergency as I am convinced that we prevented a crisis of unprecedented proportions."

He added, "Two weeks later, the criminals are hiding from law enforcement officers," noting that people can now sleep at nights without fear. In addition, he said there is a resurgence of family life among the population. "That, Mr Speaker, is our objective, to take back our cities, streets, communities and our beloved nation from the criminals. Hard talk is not our strategy, hard action is," he said.

(September 3, 2011)

Don't give a moose a muffin

Keith Rowley and the PNM have no moral authority to speak about crime or how to deal with the problem that has become a cancer in Trinidad and Tobago.

They allowed crime to grow and did nothing about it except dump millions into useless public relations exercises and expensive "toys" pretending they were fighting back. Under their watch crime continued to grow while they looked the other way.

Prime Minister Patrick Manning chose to deal with crime by anointing crime bosses as "community leaders" and making deals with them to keep the peace when he should be locking them up and breaking up the gangs. He gave them lucrative government contracts as peace offerings. One top PNM official once said it would be political suicide for the PNM to demobilise gangs.

Is it any wonder then that the PNM is so opposed to the State of Emergency, which is aimed at dealing forcefully with crime?

Perhaps what is most worrisome in the declarations from the opposition PNM is the warning of what is to come in the aftermath of the State of Emergency. Colm Imbert and others from his party are saying the criminals would return with a vengeance and things would get worse.

My interpretation of that is that they want the government to behave like the PNM and let the criminals have their way. Let them continue to rob and kill people, and terrorise the nation instead of dealing with them for fear that things would be worse if you try to attack the criminals. They are saying we must be afraid of the criminals and let them have their way or things would get worse.

These people — the PNM and Manning — ran the county since Christmas Eve 2001 to their defeat on May 24, 2010. Every year they spent millions on crime; they knew how many gangs were operating and how many members they had; their leader knew Mr. Big. Yet crime grew every year and the number of murders and serious crime continued to grow. And now there is clarity about why it happened.

The PNM wanted it to be that way because many of those gang leaders and gang members were part of the PNM's voting block. And they didn't want to upset crime bosses for fear that they might be angry and go on the warpath.

The PNM crime strategy was to give criminals and gang leaders handouts to try to keep them in check. It didn't work and it can never work because if you give an inch to a bully he will demand a yard. It reminds me of a story I used to read for my kids about a moose entering the kitchen, causing fear and threatening to wreck the place. So they gave the moose a muffin and hoped he would be satisfied and go away. He didn't. Having learned his "strength" he demanded a glass of milk — and got it. He was now in control with those in the house cowering from fear.

This is how the PNM dealt with crime. Today it is telling the Kamla government to do the same. And it is acting most irresponsibly by injecting fear in the nation by telling them that since the People's Partnership refused to give the moose a muffin and a glass of milk, the animal would wreck the place.

Well, it ain't going to be so. Because the people who run the kitchen now are not afraid of the moose and they are going to deal with him. The People's Partnership is determined to deal with crime. They promised it and they are doing it.

(September 4, 2011)

PM Kamla says PNM didn't deal with crime

Prime Minister Kamla Persad-Bissessar on Sunday (September 4, 2011) used official statistics to show that the former PNM administration failed to effectively deal with crime and that under the watch of

Patrick Manning crime increased to unprecedented levels with murders reaching a high of more than 500 in 2008. She noted that with respect to murders, the average per year under the Panday UNC administration was 112; under the Manning PNM there were 3,082 murders — an average of 357 per year.

"There was a 218% increase in murders on average per year during the PNM's administration from 2002 to 2009 as compared to the UNC's regime from 1995 to 2001," she said noting that there were 126,978 serious crimes in the period 2003 to 2009. She said the reason why crime continued to get worse was because the PNM encouraged it. "Do you all remember the PNM leader meeting with the Head of the Jamaat during the 18-18 tie when his party was appointed the government?" she asked.

"Do you remember when he promised to give back to the Muslimeen the land at Mucurapo? And after there was a public outcry he relented?

"Do you remember how the Muslimeen campaigned for the PNM and mounted platforms urging support for that party and threatening those who didn't?

"Do you remember the images of Abu Bakr celebrating at Balisier House on election night? Do you remember that?" she asked MPs during debate on the extension of the State of Emergency.

"Do you remember that billions of dollars, not millions, hear me clearly, *billions* of dollars went into CEPEP and URP and into the hands of these gang leaders with their ghost gangs and funded their nefarious activities? What do you think happened with all the alleged contracts that these gang leaders received through the PNM? How can any government sit and talk about co-existing with criminals?"

She said the former prime minister "in the full glare of the public and the media" met with gang leaders at a hotel in the city to guarantee that they stayed in power. "It was so bold faced that when one of those gang leaders died, the PNM political leader and then prime minister is on public record as having said the country had lost a national hero," Persad-Bissessar said.

"The anointed "hero" was a gang leader whose criminal record was as long as from here to San Fernando East, someone who had publicly campaigned up and down the East West corridor for the PNM," she added. She said the People's Partnership government does not "negotiate and wine and dine with the gang leaders at hotels like the last administration did." She emphasised that, "The moment the PNM government of the day took the decision to negotiate with criminal elements in exchange for political support, it set off a dangerous course of events from which the country is still reeling today. The moment you sit and talk with an enemy such as that you have surrendered power; you have ceded constitutional power and legal authority to the gang leaders. How can any government sit and talk about co-existing with criminals?"

Persad-Bissessar said her government went after the "stock in trade" of gangs by swooping down on their supply of drugs. And she said the State of Emergency averted a planned retaliation from the gangs that represented a clear and present danger to national security and innocent law-abiding citizens of the country.

"The declaration of war by the State on criminals who terrorise our citizens was something they did not expect. After all, they had become accustomed to being treated as community leaders," Persad-Bissessar said.

She said while she was not at liberty to disclose the sensitive details of national security, it is a matter of public record the security services have, in recent times, made a number of important drug seizures that disrupted the "smooth flow of business" in the supply chain and jolted and weakened the entire network.

She gave examples of drug seizures:

- Marijuana — 1229 kilos seized for 2011 valued at $18.5million.
- Marijuana for the same time period in 2010 — 3295 kilos estimated at $49.5million
- Cocaine for 2011 — 8477kilos valued at $296.7million.
- Cocaine for the same period in 2010, 6750 kilos valued at $236.3million

"We responded decisively to preserve public safety and the results to date have vindicated our decision...Today the nation is safer because of that decision. The government has demonstrated that it will not allow the nation to be held to ransom by marauding groups of thugs bent on creating mayhem and havoc in our society," she said.

"Let us be clear about one thing. The state of emergency has worked. And it has worked not only because there has been substantial reduction in killings but also because serious crime is almost zero and road carnage halted...

"It has worked not only because we have arrested over one thousand criminal elements with hundreds on outstanding warrants.

"It has worked not only because caches of weapons and ammunition have been confiscated; but it has also worked because from the moment we took the tough decision to impose a state of emergency a crisis had been averted. And that is how I measure its success."

The prime minister concluded her contribution by thanking the protective services for their "yeoman service to protect and serve the people of Trinidad and Tobago." She also thanked community organisations, "the real community leaders," the business groups, the business owners and employers for their patience and understanding and for their support.

"I also want to thank the members of the national media, print, electronic, television and online for going well beyond the call of duty and even themselves experiencing some inconvenience to ensure that they keep the public well informed," she said.

"And of course, I thank every single man, woman and child who has made the sacrifice in different ways in order to ensure that the government and our nation can win this war on crime.

"The war on crime will continue! And for the sake of our citizens and in memory of those who did not live to see the day when the tide would finally be turned on criminals, we have no intention of losing this war.

"Today I stand before you because in our 15 month history in government, we have made our most difficult choice and most trying decision yet. This was neither an easy decision nor one taken lightly. But our nation needs action, decisive action, now. The nation needs political courage!

"There is a great evil stalking our land. Where others have shirked their responsibility, we have accepted it.

"That evil must be confronted with full force of our state and the full resolve of our people. Our nation has endured more than it could bear. Too many precious lives have been snatched away.

"The righteous blood of our brothers, sisters, sons and daughters has been spilled at the hands of the lawless, greedy, selfish, deviant and cruel. Today's actions may be painful but necessary. We must sacrifice now or we shall pay a huge price later.

"The state of emergency is bringing back respect for the rule of law and a balance to the scales of justice. Give your children a better future. Give them a sense of hope. Give them a fair chance. Don't let them suffer because of your silence. Allow them to live their dreams. Let them live longer. So that sons and daughters can bury their mothers. Instead of mothers burying their children. We are the children of history but the parents of the future. Let us join hands to create a brighter future for the sake of our children. It's now or never. NAIL THEM UP!"

(September 5, 2011)

Patrick Manning apologised to the nation Friday October 28, stating that he was not perfect. "I am sorry," the former prime minister said in a prepared statement that he read at a news conference in San Fernando. "I think it is time for me to apologise for those who feel or who would have felt disenfranchised by any action I would have taken over the years as prime minister or in any other capacity. I wish to humbly apologise to all of them and to say to the people of Trinidad and Tobago, I am sorry."

However, Manning did not go into details about his shortcomings and imperfections, saying: "I am not a psychologist." He declared, "It is not for me to decide what those imperfections are. I am careful not to go into any details. Whatever imperfections people perceive I apologise for that. Let's move on...I am not perfect. No human being is perfect, ladies and gentlemen.

He said it took four months to recover from the humiliating defeat at the polls and added that the time has come to intervene in the affairs of the nation. And he seemed to take a swipe at Keith Rowley. "I am not going to act like a mongrel, that is to say, a pothound. It is not my intention to run after every car that passes, not at all. What I propose to do is to intervene judiciously from time to time as I consider appropriate."

If you think Manning is quitting politics, watch for Santa Claus

Patrick Manning and his supporters really think people are fools. His Friday (October 28) "confession" exercise was meant to launch a comeback to his political career, despite his declared intention to retire at the end of the present term as the MP for San Fernando East.

If Manning had any real intention of leaving the political stage he would have done so immediately after his humiliating defeat on 24 May 2010 and his subsequent expulsion by his party to make way for the coronation of Keith Rowley.

If you read between his lines you would also see the hypocrisy. While he is saying he supports his leader, he is also suggesting that by attending meetings of important party institutions he might overshadow Rowley —

a sign that his arrogance has not waned. And then his comment about not being a pot hound barking at every car is a clear reference to the Rottweiler who now occupies the PNM kennel, chasing cars at every turn just to let his bark be heard. Manning on the other hand is presenting himself as the dignified dog of high breeding who would bark when it is appropriate and do so with forceful effect.

So far his barking has been no better than the pot hound chasing cars. The first pronouncement landed him is hot waters and got him expelled from parliament. And he was full of arrogance and defiance when he shouted in parliament during the budget debate, to which he made no contribution

No matter what he says Manning has no love for Keith Rowley today and never will. Their rivalry began many years ago when he fixed things to become PNM leader and cast Rowley aside. You may recall Manning's laments in the House of Representatives about how he had to endure Rowley's rage for years. He called him a "*wajang*" and a "raging bull".

The Rowley PNM has also kept its distance from Manning refusing to support him in parliament and letting him walk alone on his lonely march to San Fernando. It is noteworthy that a few PNM bigshots chose to walk some part of the way just in the off chance that Manning returns to be top dog.

The other part of Manning's confession is also to be taken with more than a grain of salt. "I am sorry," he told citizens through the media. He added that people expected him to be perfect and since he is only human, he inevitably failed them. You don't have to be God to govern fairly.

Manning had all the right conditions to be a good national leader but he squandered it with his corruption, nepotism, arrogance and partisan politics. And he chose to stand behind all the misfits and square pegs he put in round holes, including his friends like Calder Hart and spiritual adviser, Rev. Juliana Pena. Even when he was caught with his hand in the cookie jar he was still demonstrating his tendency to be a dictator.

He stood with Calder Hart and insisted that the man did nothing wrong. He denied any involvement of the infamous church at Guanapo when he was clearly directing the project. He personally guided the scholarship slush fund, making sure only certain people knew of it and got awards.

And he was not tolerant of any criticism. When two radio announcers knocked his fiscal policies he showed up at the radio station to intimidate the men and demand that the management of the station deal with them.

And when those of us in the media told him he was out of line his response was that he would do it again "if the spirit moves me."

If to err is human, then Manning should be magnanimous enough to forgive the PP government for some of its missteps. After all Kamla et al are also human. But Manning isn't really sorry about anything except that he miscalculated the outcome of the 2010 general election. If he had the slightest idea that he would be in the position he occupies today he would have stood his ground instead of calling an election. Today his *tabanaca* must have reached the peak seeing Kamla shaking hands with the Queen in Australia.

He promised some years ago that he would leave politics and become a preacher. His once close ally Louis Lee Sing advised him recently to do just that. If I were a betting man I would wager that Pastor Manning is not going to take the pulpit any time soon. And if Manning is really quitting politics, then I would expect Santa Claus to come down the chimney delivering gifts on Christmas Eve. Manning knows about that because he got his best ever gift one Christmas Eve from a man named Robinson.

National Security Minister John Sandy told reporters on 28 Nov. that plotters had planned to assassinate Prime Minister Kamla Persad-Bissessar and three senior cabinet ministers: Anand Ramlogan, Dr. Roodal Moonilal, and Chandresh Sharma on November 24.

He confirmed that Police Commissioner Dwayne Gibbs told him about the plot on November 18. "This plot to undermine the security and stability of the Republic of Trinidad and Tobago was to be executed on the 24th of November. Twenty fourth being a significant date in the political successes of the prime minister," Sandy stated.

"As a consequence, the prime minister was immediately alerted and briefed on the said afternoon, 18th of November, by senior members of law enforcement. Further gathering of intelligence over the five days following the initial report led to the arrest and detention of 13 individuals."

Sandy confirmed that he received legal advice to issue Detention Orders against four of them: a gang leader from Central Trinidad, a serving police sergeant, a businessman, and a former soldier. He said more such orders would soon be issued. The minister added: "By the end of the state of emergency we should have enough information against the suspects. If not they will have to be released. Investigations are still continuing."

Sandy stated the Prime Minister did the right thing by speaking about the plot since all kinds of rumours about a planned coup were already in circulation. He also confirmed that the CIA and MI6 are working alongside local law enforcement in investigating the plot.

The SOE worked. Now let's keep criminals on the run

The debate over whether the state of emergency worked or failed will rage over the next few days and weeks with some polarised positions.

My view is that it worked because it brought all crime down significantly and for the first time in years citizens felt safe in their homes and their communities.

The opposition and its supporters insisted from day one that the measure was not necessary and would not work. With nothing more than political expediency to guide their position it is likely that they will continue to hold that view.

Others will likely have constructive explanations and data to show that it was not the resounding success that it might have been. However, the bottom line is this: crime was out of hand, the nation was under siege by criminals and the government had to act. And all through the emergency the authorities acted responsibly.

During the Patrick Manning administration from 2001 to 2010 crime — especially homicides — rose dramatically each year, crossing the 500 mark in 2009 and peaking at 550 in 2008. Yet Manning and his National Security Minister Martin Joseph failed to acknowledge that something drastic had to be done to deal with the problem.

One of Manning's solutions was to bring together gang leaders, whom he called "community leaders," to discuss a truce. And he rewarded them with lucrative contracts. The result was even more gang warfare with many of the "community leaders" getting killed in the crossfire. Manning even ignored the advice of a committee led by Ken Gordon that recommended that a state of emergency be used in order to arrest the crime situation. He did not think it was necessary and considered the gang-on-gang killings to be collateral damage. He even suggested that the brutal murder of a young child was part of the gang warfare.

In fact, PNM insiders have reported that Manning did not want to go after gangs because many of the members were PNM supporters. The People's Partnership coalition led by Prime Minister Kamla Persad-Bissessar campaigned on an anti-crime platform and won a landslide; within the first few months in office the crime rate began falling.

However, regular policing was not enough and Persad-Bissessar acted on the best advice of the country's security and intelligence officials.

In declaring the emergency, the government's position appeared to be this: it is better to err on the side of caution. Just look at the figures. The state of emergency allowed the government to make available 5,000 soldiers and the intelligence of the Defence Force to join the battle against crime. Further, with powers of search and arrest, and the relaxation of the need to get warrants, the task of making a tough assault on the gangsters and criminals was made easier.

Whatever the critics might say there are some clear facts that point to a measure of success in the fight against crime. First and foremost, citizens felt safe for the first time in a decade. All major crime was down from petty thefts to kidnappings, rapes and murders. If you take murders alone you can conclude that the state of emergency was a success. There were 43 murders in 99 days. For the same 99 days in 2009 criminals killed 121 people and in 2010 the homicide numbers for the same period was 119.

The police statistics for the year from the beginning of 2011 to November 30 showed the number of murders at 306. For the same period the year before (the PP government took office on May 26) was 450. That's a drop of 144 or 32 percent. In addition, thousands were arrested and the security personnel had criminals at bay. Police and soldiers seized and destroyed illicit drugs valued at about $1.5 billion, took more than 200 illegal guns off the streets and seized thousands of rounds of ammunition.

These things were in the hands of people who were and continue to be a threat to the safety and security of the nation. The fact that the Director of Public Prosecutions (DPP) failed to prosecute hundreds of people does not diminish that reality.

The test today and in the months and weeks ahead is to maintain a strong police presence to continue to send the signal that it cannot be business as usual for those who want to break the law. The PP government has already introduced other measures to deal with social issues that contribute to crime.

The security forces have to be ever vigilant. The nation is grateful for their work during the state of emergency.

It is clear that things have changed for the better. There is much work ahead and the government and protective services have demonstrated that they are up to the task. There is hope, despite what the naysayers will preach today and in the days ahead.

(December 4, 2011)

Don't put on your campaign jerseys yet

Frankie Khan announced over the weekend that he is putting the opposition People's National Movement (PNM) on an election footing and went so far as telling reporters that the party will launch its general election campaign on January 10, 2012.

I am not sure what general election Frankie is planning for because the only one I know about is the one that is constitutionally due in 2015. And the prime minister has made it quite clear to everyone that she is not calling any election ahead of time.

So what is the PNM really doing?

If you read between the lines of this PNM soap opera you would understand that what is really happening is that the party that Keith Rowley heads is trying to play catch up with its former leader and MP for San Fernando East, Patrick Manning. All of a sudden Manning has regained his power of speech and has been holding weekly news conferences to do what Rowley should be doing.

In other words, Manning is behaving as if he is still the leader of the PNM although he professes support for his "esteemed" leader, the same one whom he described as a "wajang" and a "raging bull" and more recently a "pot hound" chasing every passing car. And the former prime minister, having licked his wounds from the sound cut arse he got at the hands of Kamla and the People's Partnership, is now calling for fresh elections.

Last week his boldness was most pronounced when he suggested that if the PP government could not do the job they should get out of the way and let others (read Manning and company) do it. Eighteen months ago more than 430,000 voters hired Kamla and her partners to run the country and they fired Manning and his PNM. Why does Manning think that anyone wants him back in power?

So here's the real story.

Manning is only the frontline poster boy for the real PNM players who are the hand in the glove guiding this drama. They know that the "pot hound" cannot lead the party back into government. So they have been playing a wild card to see if Manning has any remaining political traction.

And that is why Frankie and company up at Balisier House are talking about a general election campaign. They know they cannot force an election the way Kamla pushed Manning to pull the plug years ahead of schedule.

Sure the PP government has made mistakes and some big missteps. But the country is not yet ready to give up on the government. And nobody, especially PNM members and supporters, want another election because they know they will lose again. What the Rowley PNM is doing is trying to get some real support for Rowley. And they need to do it fast. That is the real issue.

The so-called election campaign that the party is planning is really to play down Manning and his supporters and see if they could get the party to rally around Rowley. That is a tall order, given Rowley's lack lustre performance so far.

And the real PNM power brokers — the ones with the money and influence who are playing their hand with Manning for now — will watch and see what happens next. They know Rowley is not the one and they are making a big gamble trying for a Manning comeback.

They know in all honesty that they have to not only try to rebuild the party but they also have to find a leader. None in the present crop is suitable, which presents the real dilemma for the back room power brokers.

That presents a real opportunity for Kamla and her team to do a post mortem on where they are today and figure out the best plan for where they must be in the next two years. Prakash Ramadhar is seeking to build his own political stock and is sounding off about a variety of issues that provide reporters with good copy. The truth is he too is under intense pressure from a faction in the Congress of the People (COP), which says it wants to stand on its own. But Prakash and the MPs from COP are not ready to walk away from government, no matter what they say.

So Kamla is right when she says the coalition is strong, even if for now it is so for political expediency. Which of the MPs on the government side really wants to sit in opposition? Nobody is moving because the reality is that if COP wants to walk, the UNC can stand alone. Kamla will still have a majority.

So to all those who are wondering what is really going on, here's the best advice: leave the campaign jerseys alone. There's no election coming for a long time!

(December 12, 2011)

Manning was not the only one trying for a comeback. Former UNC leader Basdeo Panday decided that it was time to "take back" the party and the former PM mounted a campaign to support a group of young people called Generation Next.

What's Panday trying to prove?

Recent political developments in Trinidad and Tobago could lead you to conclude that as the governing coalition approaches its mid-term, "has-been" leaders are seeking a resurrection, hoping to appeal to tribal instincts and catch the present leadership napping.

First, there is the spectacle of Patrick Manning, an elected MP and former prime minister, leaving the parliament in favour of his personal audiences with reporters through news conferences, to provide "solutions" to the nation's problems. He even had the audacity to demand fresh elections. This is the same Patrick Manning who called an election in 2010, nearly three years ahead of schedule and suffered a humiliating defeat due to the unprecedented corruption under his watch and his failure as a leader. Yet somehow he believes he has the moral authority to call the government to account.

And last week another former prime minister, Basdeo Panday, who also suffered a stunning defeat by Kamla Persad-Bissessar, called reporters to tell them of his plan to "take back" the United National Congress

(UNC) in internal election in March 2012. And he justified it by saying his plan is to take back the party that was "stolen" in 2010.

First, the UNC must not allow Mr. Panday to talk about a "stolen election." He has never provided the evidence to substantiate this claim. The red herring that he used to try to make a case after his defeat was that thousands of membership cards were hidden and not delivered to party members. Even Kelvin Ramnath, one of his supporters from the pre-UNC days and a member of the election team at Rienzi, acknowledged that was a non-issue since party ID cards were not required to vote.

For the first time in his political life someone challenged Mr. Panday for the leadership of the party and she beat him. The members of the party chose Kamla Persad-Bissessar 10 to 1 over him, because they felt that she was the best person to rebuild the party, unite the opposition and then beat the PNM in a general election. The developments of 2010 proved that the members were right on all counts.

Panday lost the leadership election in 2010 because people realised that he had lost his political currency and therefore no longer had the ability to lead or win an election. The UNC membership opted for an opportunity to get back to government and they said unequivocally that they did not want Mr. Panday because he could not deliver that.

Second, if he really feels he has a right to "take back" the UNC, Mr. Panday must come up with substantive reasons for doing so. He has failed to do that the same way he failed to provide any credible reason for his re-election as leader in January 2010. What he is doing is appealing to certain disgruntled UNC members who are unhappy with the coalition arrangements, hoping they might help to lead the charge and influence the youth to rally against the present leadership.

The sub-text of Mr. Panday's pronouncements is an emotional appeal to the UNC membership, telling them the current leadership has left them in the cold, having used them conveniently to achieve power.

Part of that emotional appeal will also be his claim that "outsiders" have taken control of "his" party and left its true supporters and workers empty-handed. It all comes down to political spite and revenge. Mr. Panday is determined to get even and push Kamla out from her position of power.

What is perhaps most interesting about his latest move is that he has dispensed with the old guard that deserted him when he lost the leadership of the party in 2010 to Kamla. Now he is looking for a new constituency and is targeting the youth. "I shall be speaking to you every day from now on, giving you advice on how we shall overcome," Panday has promised in his Facebook page.

Those who might be eager to latch on to Mr. Panday's campaign should acquaint themselves with the reality rather than blindly follow. Mr. Panday seems to be taking a page out of the PNM playbook to try to seize control of the UNC and find a backdoor to government, using the Nazi propaganda style of repeating lies and misinformation so often that they become fact.

The UNC needs to ask questions. The general membership and the youth, — especially the generation NEXT to whom Mr. Panday is appealing — should ask what Mr. Panday is really offering. His motives are extremely suspicious, to say the least. He seems to have retired the old line that those who hold office today did not stand in the rain and mud when the party was born. The reason is because those who did — people like Roodal Moonilal and Kelvin Ramnath — have moved on. Who were more loyal than them?

Others who had "worshipped" at Mr. Panday's feet have also moved on. People like Vasant Bharath, Tim Gopeesingh, Fazal Karim, Chandresh Sharma to name a few — have seen the futility of living in the past without a vision of the future. Today's youth, hopefully, are educated enough to ask questions. And the fundamental question that they must ask the former UNC leader is what can he do for the UNC that the present leadership cannot.

They must ask him why the UNC — a party that the people control, not the leader — rejected him in 2010. Ask him for solutions. They need to also ask him why his "apostles" have all left and the real reason why he is trying to woo the youth. And Generation Next — today's youth — must ask themselves why they need the prop of a failed 78-year-old leader to fight their cause. If they really have cause to fight the current leadership, why do they lack confidence to do it themselves?

In 2010 Trinidad and Tobago demonstrated that it had grown up politically when it dispensed with both Mr. Panday and Mr. Manning and accepted a coalition of interests to take them forward into the 21 century. Now is the time to move forward. And Patrick Manning and Basdeo Panday are not the leaders to take Trinidad and Tobago in that direction.

(December 19, 2011)

Section 8
Testing time for PP as T&T turns 50

The year 2012 started with a state visit to India by Prime Minister Kamla Persad-Bissessar. It should have been a normal affair except for the hoopla around one incident that Opposition Leader Keith Rowley and some citizens blew out of proportion.

This opening commentary addresses the storm in a teacup created by the Prime Minister's respectful gesture of bowing to her elders, in this case, the President of India when she was presented with the Chief Guest honour at the annual Pravasi event.

Opposition Leader Keith Rowley said Persad-Bissessar should not have bowed before a foreign leader. He said the act was "indicative of subservience". Persad-Bissessar told reporters: "I make no excuses or apologies for showing respect to my elders."

Rowley should not be offended by Kamla's act of humility and respect

Keith Rowley is deeply offended by something that happened in India, during the visit to that country by Prime Minister Kamla Persad-Bissessar.

The prime minister was on a state visit and she was also celebrated as the Chief Guest at the annual *Pravasi Bharatiya* Divas event in Jaipur, Rajasthan. The event on January 9th was a celebration of Indians living abroad and people of Indian origin. Persad-Bissessar was invited to attend and receive the honour because of her status as the first woman of the Indian Diaspora to become the prime minister of a country.

The person who made the presentation to the prime minister was India's president, Pratiba Devisingh Patil. In keeping with her personal style and Hindu tradition, Persad-Bissessar attempted to touch the feet of the president, whom she recognised as her elder; the president stopped her in the act and hugged her instead. It is something that Kamla has done here at home, showing respect for her elders and even performing *aarti* for them; she did it as recently as last year's Indian Arrival Day celebrations, when she paid tribute to pioneers.

The opposition leader and leader of the People's National Movement is upset because he sees the act as "the ultimate subservient of superiority and inferiority being demonstrated." He told supporters at a political meeting: "I am a citizen of Trinidad and Tobago and I take umbrage at my prime minister going to anybody's country and kissing any office holder's foot." He added, "Nobody sent the prime minister abroad to represent her religion or her race."

The question that Rowley raises is whether as the head of government the prime minister was bowing before the head of state of another country. That seems to me to be taking the issue too far. I certainly did not see it that way and most people who come from the Hindu tradition, like me, would see it only as a mark of respect that is common in Hindu and Indian society. Kamla does this all the time at home, paying respect to her elders and her priests. So in that context, she was only following her tradition.

I don't think Rowley is being fair when he goes the distance he is going on this matter. Throughout the visit the prime minister acted according to the normal diplomatic tradition, following all the accepted protocols.

The event in Jaipur was for all intent and purposes a private one ... and from all reports, a very emotional one. The Indian media reports said people wept openly when Kamla received the award. For that one moment she was representing herself, her ethnicity and her connection with India, the land she referred more than once to the "grandmother" of Trinidad and Tobago citizens of Indian origin.

The opposition leader also displays a level of cultural ignorance when he asked if President Obama, whose father was a Kenyan, would be expected to "bend down and kiss the foot of somebody in Kenya because his grandfather came from Kenya." (By the way, Obama bowed to Japanese royalty as a mark of respect when he visited Tokyo in 2009.)

Kamla was following a tradition that is thousands of years old. It is a tradition brought to Trinidad when the first Indian arrived in the British colony of Trinidad in 1845, a tradition that the Indian community kept alive and handed down to their children, who passed it on to future generations.

We agree with Rowley that we are "a proud nation." And we urge the PNM leader to see this issue in its right context and perspective.

I disagree that Kamla's gesture was an act of subservience. And I state categorically, as someone who has known her and worked closely with her for more than a decade, that Kamla is fiercely nationalistic, as she should be. That is why she made the point in her speeches in India that India is not our mother.

Kamla understands her obligations to the nation and acted commendably during her state visit. But she is also a cultured Hindu woman who follows a tradition that offers lessons in respect, humility and charity.

I respect her for it, and so should all us.

Ira Mathur, who is a prolific writer and commentator, also wrote about that issue in one of her columns, which I have reproduced unedited. Ira kindly consented to this and I thank her for sharing her work in this publication.

Ira Mathur
We need more humility

"The image of the Prime Minister bowing to the feet of the President of India was both ridiculous and revealing. The gesture has a specific genealogy: anyone subjected to Bollywood torture—forced to watch the movies— knows what it signifies: an ostentatious display of peasant virtue which is neither humble nor innocent. Anyone not schooled in this sign system would misunderstand this."—

Raymond Ramcharitar, columnist at the Trinidad Guardian

"If you go there in your personal capacity you can do that but when you represent all the people of Trinidad and Tobago, do not go and kiss anybody's foot on my behalf. Its the ultimate subservience..superiority, inferiority being demonstrated."

Opposition Leader Dr Keith Rowley

I hold both these men in high esteem, but I absolutely disagree with both Dr. Rowley and Mr. Ramcharitar in their assessment of the 30-second gesture of the Prime Minister Kamla Persad-Bissessar bending down to touch the feet of the Indian President Pratibha Patil when she was being awarded the Pravasi Bhariya Samman award.

It was absolutely correct. To do otherwise would have been rude. In fact, the gesture endeared this country to all of India.

And no, I am not a Kamla boot-licker, don't belong to any political party, no, I do not want a 'wok' in the PP Government, and no, it's not because I was born in India. But let's go back before we go forward.

Years back, like many students studying abroad, I was very politically active as a student in Canada and the UK. The world was much more black and white then. There were right and left wing ideologies, there was the cold war, and there was labour, the conservatives and the liberals. There were parties who believed that the state needed to provide a huge safety net for the vulnerable and there was Margaret Thatcher.

There were marches against nuclear weapons and against apartheid. There were the communists, socialists, and capitalists. At least you knew who was who. And what you could expect. And who, by voting for a party, you yourself represented.

Back home, the political debate was not about how we could free ourselves of our colonial wounds, how all our people could realise their full potential through development and education. The ideology of development was absent in the corridors of power.

It's as if we were suffering from post traumatic stress and locked ourselves into the safety of the politics of protest and race. Your vote was never free. It was tied to the race you happened to be born into. As a journalist you become a kind of a confessional and people everywhere said they felt they belonged to the downtrodden race including the French Creoles (who feel invisible.)

Our brightest stars, the late economists Lloyd Best, Frank Rampersad, William Demas, with UWI, LSE, Oxford and Cambridge degrees, and a deep sense of what it meant to be West Indian, could have led us into development but we were too busy protesting. Massa day was done. Indian would rise one day. Oddly, on the ground, there was peace.

Abroad, the Indian, African and European collectively owned the roti, the steel pan and the magnificent seven flew the same flag at the Oval. Wined with the same gestures for Carnival. Still, no development of fundamental values.

The conversation on every political platform, from every political party, stayed the same, how corrupt they were, and how we needed to get them out. Whoever came into power was going to have to deal with the IMF or the boom, or the slump, and just changed the name of the dependency programme they were going to put in place.

There are four generations of people in this country who have worked in previous incarnations of Cepep and Colour Me Orange. There was no development. Go back.

In 2002, when Winston Dookeran, then governor of the Central Bank, got economist Prof Jeffrey D Sachs to speak at the bank's lecture series he had already been pronounced by The New York Times "the most important economist in the world.".

"What is globalisation? Simply this," said Sachs. "The way countries and people are interlinked. HIV/Aids is a far more tragic effect of globalisation than September 11. Three million people die of HIV/Aids every year; 9,000 people die every day from it; 25 million are dead; it has affected over 65 million people. It has left Africa isolated, drowning in the cycle of disease and poverty. One-sixth of the world, led by the US, is doing well with globalisation. Everyone else is being left behind.

"The premise that globalisation creates equal opportunity is false because some countries haven't even had a chance to join the world economy.

"Geography, climate and history have already decided which countries have a head start. For example, countries in which slavery was practised, where there has been a wanton devastation of natural resources, are absent in the globalisation process. Brain drain, disease, social instability, geographical isolation, have left a fifth of the crippled world out of the race."

What of Trinidad? He warned us then that despite our oil and gas, our per capita income (US$8,000) is roughly half that of Barbados (US$15,000) which invests far more in health and education. Development will come not by hanging on to oil prices, but by investing in our people. He thought it "dismal" that 30 percent of our secondary students dropped out, that only 10 percent make it to university, compared to US's 85 percent, Europe's 50 percent.

I looked around the auditorium then at Crowne Plaza and scarcely anyone was listening. The next day's news carried more scandal, and with our impotent rage went after another scapegoat which allowed us to bury our heads in the sands while pretending we were dealing with serious stuff. As a people we continue to give our power away to politicians and public figures.

What Sachs didn't say was that slavery and indentureship destroyed our most important resource. By stripping a people of dignity, separating families, coercing them to change religions, forcing them to neglect their native languages, forget their villages and cities by geographically cutting them off from their ancient histories and oral traditions we were virtually shorn of our humanity.

As it is, the neglect of education (400,000 among us are functionally illiterate) has left us without a voice. Powerless, dependent on hand outs, bereft of the soul of ancient civilisations, or oral traditions that could comfort us, make us self reliant, humanise us, we turned blank, harsh and empty giving us among the highest murder rates on the planet in a non-warring country.

That's why a country like Spain could have up to five million unemployed but is practically murder free because the people still have intact families, a solid sense of their identity, and a broad education where shame is not working as a cleaner, (especially when one is qualified as an engineer) but depending on someone's handout.

Back to the gesture. We need more. We need more humility. We need more respect for elders. We need to see joy in service. We need to be able to say please, thank you, sorry, after you, keep our word; keep time, without feeling small. It could be a boost to our entire tourism and service industries. Service should make us feel tall, not small.

She was not "kissing" someone's "foot." She was bending down, as perhaps millions of Indians were doing all over India, and some in Trinidad (my son, on leaving for university bent down to touch his grandfather's feet and was blessed) not to put herself and her country down, but to show that we have respect and ask for blessings from the most highly revered, non political woman in India today, the President, Pratibha Patil.

The PM was at the time being awarded with the Pravasi award for her achievements in the Indian Diaspora as a "great grand daughter" of India. The tradition is that no one touches anyone's feet. The younger person shows respect for the wisdom, love and sacrifice of the older person. The elder immediately holds the bowing younger by the shoulders, and hugs them in a gesture of blessing. There are many similar African and Asian greetings. Indians also put their hands on their hearts when being complemented or thanks. Humility is humanity.

That there is not just grace in humility in that gesture, but economics that allowed the world's largest democracy to break out of poverty through its ancient values of hard work, humility and sacrifice to become one of the most powerful in the world, then we will understand the true meaning of that gesture.

The real poverty we are battling now, is the poverty of the spirit which stands ready to destroy us. We have to regain our humanity from somewhere. Why not here with a prime minister's gesture?

(February 2012 — With permission)

The People's Partnership that defeated the Patrick Manning PNM administration in 2010, was under extreme stress during 2012, leading to the withdrawal of one member, the Movement for Social Justice (MSJ). The problem arose initially because the group, which was originally led by Errol McLeod, felt that it was not getting fair representation within the PP government.

That led to the resignation of McLeod from the MSJ and the anointing of David Abdulah as the group's leader. Abdulah was both a government senator and the general secretary of the anti-government Oilfield Workers' Trade Union (OWTU) led by Ancel Roget, who had vowed to do all within his power to cause the fall of the government.

It took political skill and a genuine need for compromise on the part of the prime minister to keep the coalition together, especially since she had to also deal with rumblings and threats from the Congress of the People (COP) over the defection of one of COP's members, Marlene Coudray, to the United National Congress (UNC). Coudray, who was the mayor of San Fernando, then ran and won the post of Deputy Political leader of the UNC, which caused COP to demand Coudray's dismissal.

The following commentaries deal with those issues and the OWTU's mission to destabilise the government.

McLeod's departure from MSJ won't damage coalition

Don't press the panic button! The sky is not falling down and the People's Partnership is not about to crash because Errol McLeod is no longer heading the Movement for Social Justice (MSJ), one of the five groups that comprise the governing coalition.

What has happened was inevitable, since McLeod's colleagues declared war on the government and threatened to bring down the government over their demands for a better deal for workers.

David Abdulah, who now heads the MSJ, will probably make an attempt to formally keep the MSJ in the partnership. He was one of the leaders of the Axe the Tax movement with the current Congress of the People (COP) Leader Prakash Ramadhar and helped bring the MSJ into the partnership.

The labour minister has given himself some flexibility, since as leader of a belligerent labour body, he found himself in a straight jacket having to carry out his ministerial functions and also fulfill his leadership role in the MSJ. It was obvious he could not do both, given the nature of the issues involved. So he did the wise thing. By keeping his job in the cabinet the MSJ maintains a voice there and can help influence policy.

With respect to his constituency, nothing changes. The coalition is not a unitary party and that is what makes it workable in spite of the developments on Sunday (January 22, 2012). The five groups that signed on to work together have their individual identities and philosophies, which allow for dissent without the risk of coming apart as the NAR did following the historic 1986 general election.

The People's Partnership experiment will continue to work simply because unlike most coalitions that come together after a general election, this was a political group that worked out its agenda ahead of the election and presented a common platform for governance, which the electorate endorsed.

While the UNC received a majority of 21 seats on its own in 2010, to Kamla's credit, she kept the coalition together and gave its individual members a generous helping of the political pie. What is important now is how the next act in this political drama plays out.

It is obvious that the key people in the MSJ want to get out of the partnership. But they cannot have their cake and eat it at the same time. For now they are content with leaving McLeod where he is. However, they will have to draw the line and McLeod would have to either stay in cabinet as an independent (or join the UNC) or leave.

Leaving would rob the MSJ or any influence it might have in governance and Abdulah would lose his comfortable senate job. He cannot lead a movement that is bent on overthrowing the government while sitting in parliament as a representative of the government.

The question that commentators will be tossing around in the next few days is whether the MSJ can morph into a strong labour party and expect to have any significant impact in the next general election.

That's unlikely given the history of such movements in Trinidad and Tobago. When Basdeo Panday created a labour party, the United Labour Front (ULF), in 1976 it had a much stronger following than the MSJ has today. And all the labour heavyweights were included, among them the OWTU's George Weekes.

However, the ULF split along ethnic lines. Panday's sugar workers and Raffique Shah's cane farmers migrated from the DLP giving the ULF the "opposition" traditional constituencies that remain today safely in UNC hands. The rest of labour remained loyal to the PNM.

The political landscape has changed but the nature of labour has not. Businesses and many of the primary definers in society would always be wary of a labour party in Trinidad and Tobago because of the kind of leadership such a party would have. Without their endorsement, no party will win government.

So for now, the partnership stands and the MSJ as a political institution presents no great threat to the governing coalition, especially the UNC. McLeod occupies what is traditionally a safe UNC seat so if he really wants to stand with his labour colleagues Kamla could show him the door. The other political question that will become part of the national conversation is, whether COP will remain in the group.

There are two significant reasons why it will: if it leaves, it won't be able to influence policy and secondly, the UNC can govern with its 21 seats. COP has six and TOP has two of the 29 seats. And COP's leader is sitting in what is probably one of the safest UNC seats in the country. COP's establishment outside of parliament might want out but those inside, including the political leader and the president of the senate, would see value in trying to effect change from inside.

COP's dilemma is that it wants to present itself as the conscience of the society and those clamouring for a divorce feel that the present government is already tainted. If that is so, COP must take responsibility for some of it and cannot expect to walk away unscathed.

Its difficulty in resolving this issue is whether it can be a strong independent movement outside of the partnership. COP was born out of the UNC and many of its members were UNC, including the former and present leaders. COP's strength in 2007 was because of the disenchantment with Basdeo Panday. Kamla's leadership changed that and weakened COP since many who had left returned home to the UNC, including the present Attorney General, Anand Ramlogan, and Transport Minister Devant Maharaj.

COP would have to rebuild without the traditional UNC constituency and that is going to be an uphill struggle. COP's boast that it caused the electoral victory in 2010 is without merit, but that discussion is for another time.

Trinidad and Tobago's experience with multi-party politics, has shown that it doesn't work. The risk for COP then would be, that it would face demise if it were to leave. No matter what we think and what we say, there have been two parties that have mattered since 1956 — the Afrocentric

PNM and the various incarnations of the original People's Democratic Party (PDP) that drew its support from the Indian community.

For COP (or the MSJ) to be a threat to the UNC, it would have to demolish the party the way Panday did with the DLP in 1976. That is unlikely, given the strength of the UNC today with a new popular leader in Kamla Persad-Bissessar and her strong supporting team. No election is imminent and Kamla has three years to maintain control and strengthen her hand. Anyone who wants to stay in the game would be wise to remain on Kamla's side.

(January 19, 2012)

Rowley must start leading instead of just being a rabble rouser

"rural /roŏrəl/ adjective — in, relating to, or characteristic of the countryside rather than the town: remote rural areas."

Keith Rowley continues to amaze me. For a politician who has been around as long as Rowley you would expect that he would put his experience in government and opposition to good use and come up with creative, winning plans to get his party back in government some day.

However, it seems every time the opposition leader makes an "important pronouncement" he either confuses the issue further or makes no sense.

His latest idea of dismantling the Ministry of the People and Social Development, which Prime Minister Kamla Persad-Bissessar created on assuming office, is a good example of going in the wrong direction.

Rowley promised supporters this week that if the People's National Movement (PNM) forms the next government of Trinidad and Tobago, he would establish a Ministry of Rural Development. The opposition leader told a rural gathering of PNM supporters this week that "logistically" rural communities are always left behind.

"In order to ensure that rural communities are not left behind as we progress as a nation there will be in the cabinet of Trinidad and Tobago a Minister of Rural Development whose responsibility will be to co-ordinate what the nation has to offer to ensure that rural communities get their fair share and they get it in a timely manner," he told the gathering. "We will have no Ministry of the People," he declared.

Well first of all, under the present government, the cabinet makes sure that it coordinates what the nation has and it makes sure that through all its ministries and agencies that rural communities get their fair share and they get it in a timely manner. In addition there is The Rural Development Company of Trinidad and Tobago that Rowley's former boss, Patrick Manning, created in 2005 as a Special Purpose State Enterprise Company mandated by the Ministry of Local Government to improve living conditions in rural communities.

Tell us something that we don't know, Dr. Rowley. And also ask yourself first why rural communities are "logistically" left behind, as you claim. That is PNM logic and PNM policy.

Times have changed since the PNM left office. The philosophical thrust of the current People's Partnership government is to focus on rural neglect and other areas of underdevelopment. In fact Kamla and her team have been making every effort to reach into rural Trinidad and Tobago to deliver services with the same urgency as in the towns and cities. It's called national development.

Development is taking place at a pace that Rowley and the PNM cannot comprehend. And all of it is happening within or below cost. The Kamla government is exploring new areas and going where no government has ever gone before.

For the PNM, rural Trinidad and Tobago has always been the place to go to *mamaguy* people for votes every five years and then disappear until the next election. And that's exactly what Rowley was doing.

If I understand Rowley right, he is suggesting that the poor, dispossessed and destitute only live in rural areas, so he would create a Rural Development Ministry just to look after their needs. Every ministry in the government is responsible for the welfare of the entire nation — for schools, utilities, roads, amenities.

But in the PNM playbook, rural equals non-traditional PNM constituencies so rural always equaled "neglect". This government — that is the Kamla led government — has dismantled that idea and its whole development thrust includes the rural communities. No one is left behind!

I have heard the PNM complain that the government is only developing UNC and COP areas, which adds credence to the point I am making. A new road with proper box drains in Papourie Road, Barrackpore became an issue of "biased development" for the PNM. When PM 1 went there, it was the first time a prime minister of T&T had gone so far south. Not even Basdeo Panday. The truth is that the PNM had shamefully neglected all the rural areas, which is why Rowley can say unashamedly "logistically rural communities are always left behind."

Works and infrastructure, local government, public utilities, finance, trade and investment, national security, education, tertiary education, agriculture, people ministry, gender and youth affairs and the others are all focusing on development across the country, regardless of rural or urban classification; for the current government of Trinidad and Tobago development means a holistic approach to nation building.

It has discarded the PNM style of building white elephants to show off to the world, in favour of educating itself on the needs of the people and then developing programmes and projects to help where help is most needed. You see, for Kamla, hunger and poverty are not reserved for rural communities. Which community in Trinidad and Tobago has been more neglected (by the PNM) than Laventille and its environs? And they certainly don't fit the definition of rural.

The structure of government, even under the PNM, was designed for developing the whole country. However, under Patrick Manning and Keith Rowley development meant doing favours for friends and supporters.

Patrick Manning created whole communities of unemployed, when in one spiteful, political decision he closed an industry that had sustained the nation and kept a community of nearly a quarter million alive and vibrant. And to compound the spite, he refused to give the former sugar workers their entitlements and allowed the billion-dollar assets of the company to be plundered.

He had hoped to destroy the base of the opposition but underestimated the resilience of the people. And Rowley is making the same mistake, based on his personal bias and the discriminatory behaviour of his party.

Unless the PNM remakes itself as a truly national party, that recognises and accepts the diversity of Trinidad and Tobago and develops a genuine development plan for the entire nation regardless of where people live, it will remain in the political wilderness for the next 40 years. The party is a relic of rum and roti politics of the past and Rowley is not making it any better.

It is time for Rowley to start leading instead of being just a rabble rouser. *(Rabble-rouser — noun : a person who speaks with the intention of inflaming the emotions of a crowd of people, typically for political reasons.)*

(January 23, 2012

On January 24, 2012, Kamla Persad-Bissessar celebrated her second anniversary as leader of the United National Congress at a party rally. She used the opportunity to reiterate her vision for the party and the country. The speech was also a call to action for those who would be running for election to the party's national executive.

Kamla's vision:

"Our party is bigger than any individual; you demonstrated two years ago that you understood that and you made the correct judgment in changing your leadership. Two months from today you will face the same challenge — to choose wisely so that our party will remain strong, united and in government ... to continue to serve you.

Ask questions and demand answers.

And remember always, that we in the UNC have a clear vision of what our country must be ... it must be that proverbial village that nurtures and raises every child...

It is a vision that extends beyond the home and into the community... It is a vision where we give more than we receive.

The greatest charity is to be each other's keeper, to stand together to help one another. My vision is one that sees our people celebrating that which brings us together, not what sets us apart ... a vision of a new society that we fashion with discipline and where we open our doors to one another and welcome the best human values.

It is a vision of a new society with respect for each other and the preservation of human dignity...

It is a vision of a country where the poorest have the same opportunity as the most affluent, where we treat the differently abled with respect, where we care for the elderly with dignity for their contribution through their toil be it in field and factory or anywhere else ...

It is the vision of a society where every family has a home, where no one goes hungry, where the entire community raises every child as its own, where every woman and every child and every elderly person is respected, where everyone who wants a job can acquire one, where people are rewarded and acknowledged in accordance with their respective contributions...

My vision for our nation is one where our government is guided by the highest moral values and ethics, where government is accountable to the people ... It is a vision where the media must be free to report and probe as a fourth estate of governance, to be the guardians of democracy to generate debate and discussion on matters of national interest on which citizens can act...

It is a vision of continuing service to you the people ...

As a mother and grandmother I know the value of love and compassion ... and as I leave you tonight, I pledge to embrace everyone in unity, so that we will live as one family, under God, enjoying and sharing the bounty of our land.

We must never again engage in divisiveness ...we must always celebrate our diversity and our rich heritage. Let us live together, dream dreams together and build a nation of equals where each of us would be free and free from fear.

This is my vision for you in the UNC and our country. And I promise you I will not fail you.

And so I ask you once more to put God in front and let us walk behind ... and let us live the way the Almighty meant it to be — one family, dedicated to our mother Trinidad and Tobago."

So what's wrong with a welfare state?

Some critics of Prime Minister Kamla Persad-Bissessar are slamming her for "creating a welfare state" with her announcement of water, electricity and transportation subsidies for pensioners and other qualified citizens.

Before we create the impression that "welfare state" is a bad word or something retrograde, let's understand the system. By definition it is:

"a social system that allows the state to assumes primary responsibility for the welfare of its citizens, in such matters as health care, education, employment, and social security." In that context Trinidad and Tobago has always been a welfare state and there is nothing fundamentally wrong with it. Canada is also a welfare state. What is wrong is when we have a citizenry that becomes so dependent on the state that people refuse to be productive.

Trinidad and Tobago has not gone the route of Canada in developing a full welfare state, although in areas such as education it has surpassed Canada. Successive governments going back to Eric Williams have been making efforts to improve the welfare of citizens.

Kamla and the People's Partnership are moving the process ahead and doing it quicker than their predecessor administrations because of their approach to fiscal management. In other words they are finding ways to make their dollars work harder for more people.

So giving free electricity and water to certain people might ostensibly put an additional financial burden on the state and its taxpayers. But that is not necessarily so. Kamla operates on the premise that managing the state must be done with the same care and accountability as running a home. You look after everybody and spread the resources to ensure that no one is left out.

By the very definition above, Trinidad and Tobago is a well-developed welfare state, looking after the healthcare, education, employment and social security of its people. I would argue that it needs to develop the system even further to provide state-managed employment insurance, state pensions and a financial support system for people who need the help. It must go beyond what NIS now offers. And it needs to fine-tune some of what it does to make it more effective.

In health for example, Trinidad and Tobago offers free services, but only at the hospitals and health centres. It means a mother with a sick child might have to wait hours to see a doctor at a public institution or pay a hefty fee at a private clinic to see a doctor. Compare that with Canada where the state regulates the fees that doctors charge and pays doctors directly for service provided to anyone.

If you need a doctor you go the clinic and he or she bills the government for it. Doctors are taxed at source and that generates revenue to help pay for the system. In Trinidad and Tobago you have to pay for every visit and I would wager that there are very few doctors who are honest about their revenues in paying taxes.

Further, Canada has a single tiered system, which means that the state pays for doctors' visits, hospital care, and a host of other health services. It is illegal to have a private hospital unless that hospital operates within the rules of the Canada Health Act and the state pays the bills.

In Trinidad and Tobago many doctors undermine the health care system because they encourage patients to use private facilities — and pay thousands — when the public system is just as good. I have had angioplasty in Toronto without paying one penny; my brother in Trinidad paid TT$100,000 for the same service. In principle it should be free in T&T too, but the two-tiered system allows the double standards and exploitation where doctors malign the public system for their own benefit.

Every system in the world can be exploited by some. However, with proper planning and management the welfare state is affordable and creates a better society in which people are treated fairly and equitably.

It works well within a capitalist system too, so the private sector and the corporations need not fear the term "welfare state." In fact, such a system provides welcome support to everyone, even the rich and famous.

There's no need for anyone to apologise for creating support systems for those who need them. That's what Kamla promised and that's what she is doing. God speed to her and her team!

(January 30, 2012)

Doctors must honour their oath and put patients first

Health Minister Dr. Fuad Khan acted swiftly last week and changed the rules for all ambulances operating in Trinidad and Tobago.

The move was a reaction to the refusal of personnel in an ambulance from the South West Regional Health Authority (SWRHA), to offer assistance to a woman who asked them to help her get her dying child to the San Fernando General Hospital. Citing company rules, they said they were unable to assist. The SWRHA confirmed that they were following the rules.

Stacy Simon's 21-month-old baby boy, Akile Simon, died in his mother's arms moments after she was denied help by the technicians in the ambulance. On learning of the matter last Sunday (29 Jan.) Khan expressed "disgust with the lack of compassion" and he pledged to take "a harsh decision with respect to the ambulance service." He did.

On Wednesday Feb. 1, the minister said he would change the policy to make sure that nothing prevents paramedics from stopping to help people in need so that no one in such a situation will ever again be refused medical care, regardless of the circumstances. "An ambulance means that you have everything in there to take care of a person in need...So once you put the word ambulance on your vehicle, it has to have the basic equipment and qualified personnel. If you don't have that then they will have to call it something else," he said. Simon told reporters, "I am happy that the minister has stepped in to correct a wrong."

Now the minister has launched an investigation into another aspect of the same story, which did not get the kind of media attention as the actions of the ambulance technicians.

According to media reports Simon took her child to the Gulf View Medical Centre in San Fernando, where she was treated shabbily and in a most unprofessional manner by a doctor there.

The Express report said the doctor, who asked not to be identified, said the baby showed no signs of life so he advised Simon "to seek medical attention at the Accident and Emergency Department of the San Fernando General Hospital (SFGH)." He admitted that he knew that the child was clinically dead. "There were no signs of any activity. The pupils were dilated," the paper quoted the unnamed doctor as saying, adding that he advised the mother to take the child to the hospital although he knew the infant was dead. And according to the mother, the doctor didn't even tell her that her child was dead.

It seems from the report that the doctor was more concerned about other issues. "The patient was brought in without any warning. I was seeing another patient. No appointment. Just rushed in," he told the Express. "Yes, I told her take him to the emergency of the San Fernando Hospital...where you need to do post-mortem, an autopsy. And that could not be handled in private settings."

Dr. Khan is justified in investigating the actions of the doctor, whose callous treatment of a woman and a dying child took second place to his personal concerns. His selfish attitude is contrary to what citizens should expect from doctors whether they operate in the private or public service.

It seems that the doctor was annoyed that the woman showed up without an appointment and less concerned about the patient, a dying child. He knew that the baby was dead, did not bother to tell the woman so and instead passed on his responsibility as a physician to the hospital while offering no assistance to the distraught woman.

When one doctor behaves likes this he taints the entire medical professional. Those who show such disdain for human life and suffering should be removed. I know that there are good doctors in the system. I have five nephews and nieces working in the public system and they are all very dedicated, as they should be. My brother was the country's Chief Medical Officer until his retirement and service to patients took precedence to everything else. Dr. Khan himself has demonstrated in his professional life that his patients come first.

I urge the minister to act with the same urgency that caused him to change the ambulance rules and deal with this matter so that citizens could feel confident that those who practice medicine in Trinidad and Tobago are true to the The Hippocratic Oath, which commits them to caring for patients.

Their oath states: *"I will remember that I do not treat a fever chart, a cancerous growth, but a sick human being...I will remember that I remain a member of society with special obligations to all my fellow human beings, those sound of mind and body as well as the infirm."*

That's what every doctor pledges to do. That is what every citizen expects of a doctor, be he or she in the public service or working in a private clinic or office.

The practice of medicine is not a business in which its practitioners treat humans as commodities; it is a profession in which the care of every patient is sacred and must come first. Those who fail to do this do not deserve to be doctors. And in a just and fair society, they should be removed with dispatch.

(February 5, 2012)

Kamla still strong but protests will continue

It is no surprise that we are seeing an acceleration of anti-government activities in Trinidad and Tobago these days. It is normal that some people would feel that their expectations have not been met with the haste they expected and that they would want to vent their frustrations in any number of ways. That's expected especially when a new government is approaching its mid-term.

However, the intensity of some of the protests suggests that there is more to them that just people feeling let down. The charge that there is some organised plot to embarrass MPs and the prime minister, in particular, might be valid.

I say that because, the opposition People's National Movement (PNM) stated clearly last December it is launching what it called a general election campaign. Party Chairman Franklin Khan made the announcement at the PNM's General Council Meeting held at Balisier House, stating that the campaign to "engage" the population would begin on January 10, 2012.

"The PNM is putting its troops out on election footing given the fact that after 18 months the government of the day has no developmental plan for T&T," Khan told reporters in December. So there is a campaign! And it's not going to stop.

We live in a democracy and must respect people's rights to protest.

The People's Partnership came into office on a wave of national support that spilled over from the intense leadership campaign that saw Kamla take over the United National Congress (UNC) from its founding leader, Basdeo Panday.

The Kamlamania was bound to subside, although I would argue that Kamla still enjoys popular support across the board, in spite of the missteps. It is primarily because she is a genuine people's politician who has always worked hard among the people. When she put her inauguration celebration on hold and changed her dancing shoes for wellington boots and ventured into flooded areas within hours of becoming prime minister, Kamla was acting out of genuine concern for the people.

Sure it created a great photo-op of a leader in action, but she followed up with compensation for people and immediately tried to deal with the people's problems. And that has been her style all along. Whenever a problem reared its head she stepped in and found a solution. And it is her dedication to unity and compromise that has kept her coalition together in spite of rumblings from labour and some elements of the membership of her coalition partners.

So when people accused her of refusing to meet with demonstrators in her own backyard last week, it raised the question of whether the demonstration was genuine or one orchestrated to cause embarrassment.

Tossing burning tyres at vantage points across a stretch of roadway running several miles, certainly didn't appear to be a normal spontaneous move to raise concerns about potholes and poor drainage. The question is why didn't these people do what others in the Siparia constituency have done when they had an issue — take it to the MPs office.

Kamla has always been one of the most popular MPs long before she became PM because of her excellent representation and an efficient machinery at her constituency office. She keeps in touch and responds.

People have a right to demonstrate and fuss when they feel that they are not getting what they expect. However, causing inconvenience and putting on a show for the media doesn't solve problems.

It is clear that the opposition would have a vested interest in creating disturbances, while at the same time it is also clear that all the people's expectations are not met. The PNM as an opposition will exploit every opportunity it can find to hurt the government. It's Rowley's style.

Kamla and the People's Partnership must find their own methods to clearly tell the people what they have been doing, what they intend to do so that people will understand that it takes time to rebuild a nation that the very PNM almost destroyed through its greed, corruption and failure to govern on behalf of all the people.

(February 6, 2012)

(Postscript: The demonstrators admitted later that they did not address the issue as they should by taking their complaints to the MPs office and some of them apologised for their actions)

When Patrick Manning suffered a stroke in January 2012 people feared the worst. However, although the former PM survived, he became an absentee MP because of his illness. Would ill health cause the longest-serving MP in T&T to hang up his gloves?

Battle for San Fernando East

It appears inevitable that there would soon be a battle for San Fernando East, the constituency that Patrick Manning inherited from Gerard Montano in 1971. Manning was the chosen successor after Prime Minister Dr. Eric Williams decided, following the 1970 Black Power uprising, that white men had no place anymore in his People's National Movement.

Manning's entry into politics was effortless; 1971 was the year of the no vote campaign by the combined opposition and the man who would later become prime minister, entered parliament without a vote being cast in his name.

Now a stroke and other health issues have hastened Manning's departure from active politics. While parliament has granted him leave for 90 days while he recuperates from the stroke that knocked him down on January 23, his party has raised the matter of whether he would be able to continue. They are already talking about a by-election and tossing around names as possible candidates.

Manning had already stated publicly, that he would not seek re-election at the next general election, so it is logical to expect that under the present circumstances he will either resign his seat or parliament may have to declare it vacant. Either way, it would open a very interesting fight.

The open warfare between the current leader of the PNM, Keith Rowley, and Manning was highlighted after Manning fell ill. While Rowley and the party tried to play it down, inside sources in the PNM reported that Manning's wife, Hazel, refused to let Rowley see her husband and slammed the door on him.

That opening act set the stage for a battle for turf if and when Manning demits office in San Fernando East. It is clear that he remains influential and commands popular support, so the PNM would be wise to let the constituency choose the next MP. But the current leader is not winning points these days for his political wisdom. San Fernando East is already talking about nominating Hazel, although it's doubtful if she would want to run.

For one thing, she would want to spend time with her husband and nurse him back to good health. For another, she has always been shy of the electorate. She served in cabinet following the 2001, 2002 and 2007 elections without ever being elected although she could have been nominated in any of a number of safe PNM seats. Both she and her husband preferred nepotism to electoral democracy.

The question for the PNM is, whether it would allow San Fernando East to make the decision, or whether Rowley would insist on his nominee for the seat. Rowley would likely go for the latter in order to assert his leadership, which would then draw clear battle lines between those loyal to the former PM and supporters of the present leader. Such a development would erode some support within the constituency and provide an opportunity for a candidate of the People's Partnership to make a play, and possibly win, the seat.

That is a real possibility, given the demographics and the voting pattern over the past few elections. There were 22,967 registered voters in 2010, the same number as 2007; the number in 2011 was 23,106. The highest vote that Manning ever received in his constituency was in 2002 when he won with 10,772. His opponent from the United National Congress (UNC), Carol Cuffie-Dowlat received 5,557 votes.

By 2010, the same opposition candidate appearing for the Congress of the People (COP) in the People's Partnership, increased her vote to 6,109 while Manning's support was at 9,736, a loss of about one thousand votes from his best performance, with some of it going to his opponent. The interesting thing about these figures is that the opposition was encroaching on Manning's support with 3,627 votes separating them.

The figures mean that there are about 8,000 'free' or floating votes in the constituency. That invisible vote could make the difference and change the political tide in San Fernando East, if the partnership could pick up at least 3,000 floating votes.

If Rowley decides to let the constituency have its way, it might be more difficult for the partnership candidate to win. On the other hand, if he insists on having his own candidate and the UNC or COP candidate is a strong person with no negative political baggage the PNM vote could decline, as it did in some key constituencies in 2010, and help the partnership.

Some PNM bloggers are already saying that Penny Beckles should replace Manning. That would be a horrible strategy for the PNM because of two key factors: she is from Arima and doesn't know or understand San Fernando East, and she is the woman Manning rejected twice in the 2007 election. If she runs in Manning's turf, many Manning loyalists might stay away or register a vote for her opponent.

It's early in the game still. Manning could make a miraculous recovery and return to parliament, in which case it would be business as usual. However, the prognosis is not good and those who have always wanted to see Manning's back would be eager to help ease him out the door.

That means San Fernando East could see an epic battle between PNM for supremacy and the real electoral fight to determine who will be the next representative in parliament. It would be a splendid opportunity for the partnership to demonstrate that it could enter enemy territory and walk out victorious. It would be a tall order indeed. However, anything is possible in politics. Look at all that has happened in two years!

(February 7, 2012)

Choose a side Abdulah; you can't have it both ways

David Abdulah is a government senator and leader of the Movement for Social Justice (MSJ), one of the five members of the governing coalition. He has stated often enough that the MSJ supports the partnership. Yet, Abdulah is at the same time wearing a different hat as an executive member of the Oilfield Workers Trade Union (OWTU) and is at the forefront of the union's impending strike against the state-owned Petrotrin.

A strike at the company is a no-win situation for both sides and could cause irrecoverable damage to the company and the national economy. And Abdulah knows it.

Abdulah would argue that workers have a right to use the one weapon that they have — the ability to withhold their labour — when they feel they have not got a fair deal. And indeed workers have that right. But shutting down Petrotrin at this time is nothing short of driving a stake into the company's heart.

The question that arises in this matter is whether Abdulah and the OWTU leadership are looking at the big picture and being honest with the membership. Or are they using misinformation and fiery rhetoric to create mass hysteria among the workers and cause them to act as a mob.

Based on media reports, it seems that the company is offering more than a fair deal to the workers, although OWTU President General Ancel Roget is harping only on the fact that Petrotrin is holding fast to its five percent wage offer. Both Roget and Abdulah know very well that the deal is more than that.

In fact, Roget and his union went into these negotiations asking for a 75 percent increase, which everyone knows is ridiculous given the state of the global economy. He is insisting that he has changed that position but is not saying what he is prepared to accept. In the meantime the union is setting up camp, ready to deprive workers of a livelihood and create chaos in the country. Already motorists are in panic mode and the strike has not even started.

I cannot help but conclude that the motivation for their action is highly political. Comments by Roget leave no doubt about this, since he has stated that his intention is to inflict harm and that Prime Minister Kamla Persad-Bissessar would pay the ultimate political price for not bending to give the union what it wants. And Abdulah — who should know better as a government insider — should be helping to solve this problem rather than adding fuel to the flame.

This is the same kind of misinformation by the labour movement that caused Watson Duke to become a pariah and a target of scorn by other union leaders and some of his own members in the Public Services Association (PSA). Duke signed on to a deal that was best for his members and the same happened at the port. But ask those like Roget about it and they will tell you, without presenting verifiable evidence, that it was a betrayal.

Take a look at what Petrotrin is offering and you would realise that the OWTU is misleading the Petrotrin workers. An ad by the company points to the fact that when the package is taken together Petrotrin workers are getting real increases of between 24 and 39 percent. Where else can a labourer earn $11,895.47 a month in Trinidad and Tobago?

If I were a Petrotrin worker I would demand full disclosure from my union about the negotiations and ask why the union is asking me to go on strike. This is a political move and Abdulah must make a clear choice about the side on which he sits; he can't have his cake and eat it too.

If the MSJ wants to belong to the governing coalition, it must act responsibly. The truth is the prime minister has been most generous on this matter. She could easily show Abdulah the door and let the MSJ depart without it doing any harm to her government. Roget wants to destroy the government and he is using workers at Petrotrin to help him.

The workers are the pawns in this game and while I expect certain people to behave this way out of political expediency, I cannot accept that Abdulah should be allowed to be a part of this destructive movement while enjoying the perks of being in the inner circle of the governing political establishment.

(February 16, 2012)

Roget's "war" more important than a settlement at Petrotrin

Ancel Roget's personal declaration of "war" is a deliberate attempt to try to embarrass the government of Trinidad and Tobago in the eyes of the international community while trying at the same time to inflict serious economic damage to the state Petroleum Company, Petrotrin.

And while the president general of the Oilfield Workers Trade Union (OWTU) is accusing the company and the government of strong arm tactics to "intimidate" workers, he is the one who has been using inflammatory language in what is clearly political posturing to advance his personal agenda.

This is not just an industrial matter and the more you look at it, the more you realise that Roget is driven by his politics, not the love and welfare of the workers. A strike is not going to benefit the workers and it will certainly weaken the company's ability to pay any more than it can today.

Roget had been talking about "shutting down" the country long before we got to the impasse, which he now blames on the government, and more precisely the prime minister. In fact he accused the government, as did Keith Rowley, of declaring a state of emergency to restrict the labour movement. He has accused Prime Minister Kamla Persad-Bissessar of riding the backs of workers, "to win the 2010 general elections," which is a fallacy. He has pledged to bring down the government and declared that at the next election "we would get them out."

The "we" is the trade union movement, which is affiliated with the Movement for Social Justice (MSJ) led by OWTU's David Abdulah. And the "them" includes, for now at least, the MSJ. Roget's political statement might suit his own purpose but it won't put food on the table for the people he is about to deprive of an income. Of course that doesn't worry him because he continues to have his income and perks, paid by the striking Petrotrin workers who won't have any.

Roget knows that the eyes of the world would be on Trinidad and Tobago this weekend and into next week. He knows that Carnival attracts international media attention. And that's his motivation for the dramatic plan to shut down of the oil company.

He wants to make a public statement through commuter chaos. It's not that gas will run out, but he is making sure that he creates enough doubt to cause panic. In fact he is hoping that there will be chaos. Pay attention to his words. The government will "fall flat on its face" he told reporters, adding that it will happen because "fuel supplies to the public will be greatly affected once strike begins." And recall what he said last week: "This is war! A strike is meant to hurt...Prepare to play mas long after Ash Wednesday."

This is a man with a political agenda that does not include the stability of the company he is targeting or the country. He is not advancing the cause of the workers but doing everything he can to hurt the government and the country, since the energy sector is the lifeblood of the economy.

Worst of all, Roget is using this strike to slash the wrists of the company and bleed it to death. His reckless actions could tarnish the image of the company on the global scene and lower Trinidad and Tobago's standing, perhaps even lead to a hit on the country's economic and financial credibility.

And the very workers who are shouting insults to the company and the government today, could be deprived of jobs because of the irresponsible action of Roget and the other union leaders who are dragging the workers into a strike that would benefit no one. With the global economy still in a slump, a loss of production in the energy sector would cause serious damage that would take years to repair.

That's ok with Roget. That is what his "war" is all about. And he's not worried about the workers who will end up losing their jobs when his little war is over. Such "collateral damage" is inevitable, he would argue. He will continue to speak his fiery, combative language and spread misinformation and urge workers to make sacrifices in order to keep the struggle alive and win the war.

Roget is walking down a dangerous path that will hurt families across the country for a long time to come. His former colleague, Labour Minister Errol McLeod, is still trying to find a way to prevent this strike, but it is clear that Roget wants the walkout more than he wants a settlement.

(February 17, 2012)

Rowley's gamble could inflict critical political injury on him and his party

Keith Rowley and his allies have always had a vision of him leading the People's National Movement (PNM) and the government of Trinidad and Tobago. However, Patrick Manning ensured that he kept Rowley in check, although in his "remake" of the PNM he handed Rowley one of the three positions of deputy political leader.

Rowley openly challenged Manning, more than once, but remained in the inner circle until he touched Manning's achilles heel — Calder Hart and UDeCOTT — demanding accountability.

That *"wajang"* behaviour got him fired and sent to the back bench from where he plotted his revenge, while Manning continued to attack him both outside and inside the parliament. When Manning, facing the political Kamlamania tidal wave, called an election more than two years ahead of time, Rowley saw his opportunity. He fought to get nominated as a candidate but silently plotted to try to make the PNM lose, even talking about a "court martial" for the captain of the ship when the election was over.

The tide had changed and the People's Partnership swept the PNM out of office with only 12 PNM members surviving, including Rowley and Manning.

Rowley went for the jugular, demanding Manning's immediate resignation and literally chasing Manning out of the party's headquarters. He subsequently squeezed out all opposition and "won" the leadership unchallenged. However, he was always uncomfortable with the crown that he placed on his head, knowing that his party was clearly divided.

For a while, Manning watched silently, then he made his play, offering the nation an apology for his mistakes. "I am not perfect. No human being is perfect, ladies and gentlemen," Manning told reporters at a news conference. "I was not perfect in the governance and I am sure that along the way it is not possible for any leader to conduct the affairs of any country and for such a long time without by the decisions he makes, initiates, or for which he holds responsibility, to not adversely affect some people" he declared.

Manning's move was clearly an attempt to undermine Rowley's leadership. It was also a clear indication that certain power brokers within the party were testing the waters to see if Manning had retained any political currency.

Rowley had been stumbling and was clearly not the man to take the party back to government. And Manning had lost his political lustre forever. Still there were those who wanted Manning back.

Now with Manning out of the way because of a serious stroke, Rowley is flexing his political muscle with a motion of no confidence in the prime minister. This is a serious matter and Rowley knows that by sheer numbers alone he will lose. Still, he is climbing a political greasy pole hoping to secure his leadership by appearing to be on the attack against a government that the PNM claims has failed. He might even be hoping for a miracle like the one that propelled the People's Partnership into office. It is a dangerous gamble.

What can Rowley say to inflict damage when there is clear evidence that the People's Partnership government has done more for development in 20 months than Manning, Rowley and the PNM did in the eight years since the 2001 presidential coup that handed Manning the leadership of government?

Rowley has lost credibility even in the eyes of many members of his own party. And his only hope of redeeming himself from this is to reveal something that is so powerful that it takes precedence over everything else.

He cannot hope to raise the same issues that he has presented over and over again and expect to influence public opinion. So the real danger for Rowley and the PNM is the boomerang effect, where this will fly right back at them with the PP government blowing its trumpet about all that it has achieved in 20 months.

He is sitting on a wall and like Humpty Dumpty he could lose it all. In effect if he fails to inflict heavy political damage on the prime minister as he hopes then he has a moral responsibility to accept his failure and resign. That might give the PNM a real opportunity to rebuild itself as a strong national party that can offer the PP a real challenge when the next election comes in 2015.

(February 27, 2012)

(Postscript. As expected, the PNM did no damage to the PP and did not reveal anything new. Rowley claimed that he achieved what he set out to do but not all PNM members agreed.)

Now is the time for the PNM to get rid of its albatross

Where does Keith Rowley go from here?

It is clear that his move last week was to assert himself, coming so soon after his arch rival Patrick Manning was felled by a stroke and effectively removed — for now at least — from the political stage.

Rowley had used a cloak and dagger approach to get the People's National Movement (PNM) leadership and Manning — like Basdeo Panday — could never let go. So he remained a thorn in Rowley's side and never forgave his former deputy leader for helping bring down his government and taking over the leadership.

Manning and Rowley walked together and even hugged for the cameras. The member for San Fernando East even pledged allegiance to the new leader of the PNM and said he would leave politics. But deep inside there was no forgiveness. It was mutual.

Rowley ignored Manning in his democracy march from the Red House to San Fernando, and did not support him in his motion seeking to change the rules regarding the Privileges Committee of parliament. It was a tragic display from the once mighty PNM. Rowley and four others abstained; the MP who seconded Manning's motion — Alicia Hospedales — was absent when the legislature voted.

What was clear was that Rowley's revenge was a continuing process and he would not be satisfied until Manning was out of the way. So Manning chose to report to the nation, starting with an apology for mistakes he made. And he promised to keep watch on what was going on in his "defence" of the nation, stating that he would not be a pot hound "chasing every passing car." What humiliation for Rowley! Demoted from rottweiler to pot hound.

Inside the PNM, Rowley was never stable. His major cause célèbre was the removal of the Balisier tie that had been a mandatory wear for MPs on official business both in and out of parliament since the days of Eric Williams. When Manning suffered a stroke and Rowley, in all hypocrisy, went to visit, Hazel slammed the door in his face, dramatising the hurt she felt for the injustice meted out to her husband by Rowley and his supporters. So once Manning was out of the way Rowley decided to take charge. It was a bad move.

Rowley and his team had nothing of merit to offer, no "mark to buss." Instead, they afforded the People's Partnership a splendid opportunity to blow its trumpet and remind the national population of the reason why the PNM is out of office. It also provided PP politicians the best chance they would ever have to go after Rowley. And they did.

Moonilal exposed a plot for a palace coup (which as expected was denied). Jack told Rowley there are two things he would never see — God's face and the PM's chair. Kamla denounced Rowley as a man who betrayed his own political family. And she promised to take on "anyone of you, anyplace, anytime." But she made it clear that unlike her predecessor, she is in no hurry for an election.

The end result of nearly 28 hours of debate — as the Hansard will show — is that there was indeed a lot of "sound and fury" signifying nothing, except, the end of Rowley's career. Some big wigs in the PNM — including Port of Spain Mayor Louis Lee Sing — had cautioned Rowley about his motion, especially with it coming in the weeks before the UNC's internal election. And many of them have not been amused by the embarrassment in the parliament.

Whether the PNM will admit it or not, Rowley will now face an inquisition even from some of those who shouted "absolutely yes" in favour of his motion in parliament Saturday (March 3). Rowley fought for more than a decade to reach where he is, even scheming and undermining his leader. So he will not walk away or roll over and die. However, those inside the party who understand the nature of politics will have to tell him the truth — that he is, today, the albatross around the neck of the PNM. And he will have to go.

And for the sake of democracy, let's hope that when the PNM finds a new leader it will be a person who will offer much more than just small change!

(March 5, 2012)

Lee Sing is new Rowley target

It looks like Louis Lee Sing is in trouble for warning his political leader that the no confidence debate would backfire on him. Now Keith Rowley, with political egg on his face, is trying to shoot the messenger for expressing the views of many within the party and warning of the consequences of an ill-advised motion of no confidence that, as predicted, backfired on Rowley and made the People's National Movement (PNM) look bad.

And Rowley is attempting the same cloak and dagger kind of assassination that he used to take down Patrick Manning. He is getting PNM members to stage a coup and take away Lee Sing's job as mayor of Port of Spain. Of course he is distancing himself from what is happening, saying only that he would let the party decide if it wants to bring disciplinary charges against Lee Sing. However, he has made it clear that Lee Sing's intervention was not welcome. "No general likes to know that...the first time the enemy fires his salvo, you turn tail and start firing on your own troops. No general likes that," Rowley told reporters on Monday, March 5.

It is clear that Rowley is not going to tolerate dissent within the PNM, never mind that he talks about democracy. For years he fought like a worm in a guava to get Manning out of the way until he went too far and challenged Calder Hart. Manning kicked him out and the quiet fight became an epic public conflict.

Rowley eventually had his revenge when he openly campaigned against his leader in the 2010 general election while telling the PNM faithful not to desert the PNM ship. Once the election was over, he and his loyalists ejected Manning from the leadership and from the PNM headquarters. He then made sure all challengers were moved out of the way so he could inherit the party, something he desperately craved. In the nearly two years since the dramatic turn of events, Rowley has disappointed his party and those outside who had become fed up of Manning and had hoped that Rowley would add value to the party and rebuild it as the dominant institution it once was.

He did neither. He lacks the ability to control and lead his small parliamentary caucus. And instead of being a responsible opposition leader, he is getting a reputation as a rabble-rouser, often raising issues without proper research. His racist accusations against Attorney General Anand Ramlogan stand out as one of the more glaring episodes of a Rowley misstep. It was a blatant lie.

Rowley has also failed to take the PNM forward into the 21st century, keeping it right where it was back in 1956 — a single ethnically based political organisation that keeps the society polarised. At the same time he continues to find fault with the highly successful experiment in democracy that has propelled Kamla and her partnership into office as a truly representative organisation of the people.

Now that Lee Sing is seeing beyond tomorrow and suggesting that the party become more democratic and responsible, he has become a target. That says a lot about Rowley and his leadership.

I have known Lee Sing for more than 30 years and I can say one thing about him that those who know him will corroborate — he is dedicated to his party and puts party ahead of individuals. That is why when Manning had run his course, he had no difficulty with bidding his friend farewell.

The party's movers and shakers are not pleased with Rowley and neither are they happy with the conflicts and confrontations that have been hurting the party long before the 2010 election. After two years, they know that Rowley is not going to take them back to government. And that has Rowley on the defensive, attacking every shadow that crosses his path.

Rowley is an angry man. Anger is a dangerous thing; it creates fear and instability and erodes freedom because it causes people to clam up and not speak out. It is a fatal attribute of a weak leader whose selfish tantrums cause damage instead of solving problems. Rowley's dilemma is how to take charge while standing in a political mine field that he helped create.

Sooner, rather than later, the PNM would have to decide if it wants to keep Rowley and remain where it is or move into the 21st century with a leader who is willing to build a truly national party and get back to government.

(March 6, 2012)

Leave Kamla alone

The latest People's National Movement (PNM) "expose" about Prime Minister Kamla Persad-Bissessar borders on the ridiculous and reminded me of the words of Plato, the Greek author and philosopher: "Wise men talk because they have something to say; fools, because they have to say something."

It seems that the PNM believes it must keep talking and exposing imaginary scandals and keep making all kinds of allegations at its weekly news conferences, even if, like the proverbial fool, there is nothing to say.

What are the latest "allegations," as Marlene McDonald, put it?

- Three nephews of the prime minister, who live abroad, might have stayed at her official residence, used facilities reserved for the PM in her official capacity and may have had a meal or two "at taxpayers' expense"
- Her sister might have stayed at the official residence
- Why has she used a national security helicopter to travel within the country?
- Why does Kamla hold meetings at her private residence?

In keeping with her policy of transparency, Kamla has explained all these things as she has done with other frivolous issues raised by the PNM opposition over the past two years. There has been no abuse. And surely, a PM deserves some flexibility in conducting her daily affairs.

Perhaps someone should remind the PNM of the role of the opposition in our parliamentary system. The opposition's main role is to question the government of the day and hold them accountable to the public. However, it must do so in a responsible and constructive way. And as an alternative government, it must do more than challenge the policies of the government; it must produce different policies where appropriate.

An active opposition would debate legislation vigorously in the House of Representatives and, during the Select Committee process, ensure legislation receives careful consideration. And where there is a truly responsible opposition, it will sometimes agree with government if the solution proposed by the government has wide support and is soundly based.

Does that sound like the PNM opposition? You be the judge.

What we have got from the PNM in the past two years, is a lot of sound and fury with no constructive ideas. The target is always Kamla — what she is wearing, how much her shoes cost, what time she goes to bed, who are her friends. And their whole motivation is to try to get something to stick on Kamla the way Patrick Manning's "Hart" was exposed.

There is a reason for that. The PNM sincerely believes that if you tell lies often enough and keep a constant attack on the leader, you will eventually cause the fall of the leader and then "all fall down." Manning boasted in parliament that he used that strategy to bring down the Robinson NAR government and Keith Rowley was part of that scheme.

They did it with the Panday government and brought down that government with help from some of Panday's top ministers. Now they are hoping to do the same with Kamla. The trouble is that people are seeing through Rowley and his team and even "PNM till ah ded" supporters are starting to "*stueps*" with the way the opposition is conducting its affairs.

A case in point was the no confidence motion that Rowley brought to parliament that wasted everybody's time and gave the government the best opportunity yet to boast of its achievements since taking office.

If you go through the news archives over the past 21 months, since Rowley muscled his way into becoming leader of the PNM, you will find very few instances where the opposition has performed as it should.

On the hanging legislation it kept saying that it supports the execution of convicted killers, yet it voted down the bill. Rowley walked away from the Joint Select Committee on procurement for no good reason while saying he wants to see strong legislation to encourage transparency. And in their weekly rants, they seem to forget that they have a past that is less than glorious.

What about Manning's lies about the PM's house? And what about Rowley's lies about Anand Ramlogan going to New York and complaining about the ethnicity of staff at the Trinidad and Tobago consulate there? And his most recent lie about a former SIA director having a government contract?

The Nazis based their propaganda on fabricating "truths" and speaking and presenting them so often they became "facts." The PNM understands that well. And it is working hard to use that strategy to try to destabilise the present government.

There is one problem with it. They are forgetting that the people of Trinidad and Tobago now know how to listen, judge and make decisions. They have grown up; they can no longer be seduced by the PNM the way Eric Williams did it for 30 years.

Can the PNM honestly say that Patrick Manning's sons or relatives never dropped in for a cup of tea? And what about the millions the former PM squandered on entertainment expenses while spending many millions more flying all over the place in a private jet leased from his friend's company.

Kamla is running a good government and managing quite well in crossing all the hurdles she faces. The PNM would be do well to understand that there is a strong, united government in place and the only way it would defeat Kamla and her team is for it to get serious and start behaving responsibly.

The people know what they want and they know they have the power to elect leaders who lead. That's why they put Kamla there. And Rowley and company would remain where they are in perpetuity unless they become a truly national party and start acting in the national interest and as a government in waiting.

Here's my message to the PNM: Leave Kamla alone! She has a country to run ... and she has to fix the mess you created.

(March 22, 2012)

It didn't take long for the Congress of the People (COP) to start picking a fight with its coalition partners, especially Kamla and the UNC. It was triggered by Marlene Coudray's defection to the UNC. However, Kamla refused to be blackmailed or coaxed into shoving COP out of the door.

It's time that COP gets over its political tabanca

Prakash Ramadhar and the Congress of the People (COP) must show leadership and political maturity and stop behaving like kids in a schoolyard brawl.

When the leaders of the five groups came together to form a coalition to fight the 2010 general election, one of the fundamental areas of agreement was that each of the parties would maintain its identity and its philosophy.

They agreed that the common denominator was their collective desire to rid the country of the People's National Movement (PNM) under Patrick Manning and introduce a new system of government. Ramadhar's predecessor Winston Dookeran was the leader who signed the declaration. And he has always remained committed to the partnership. Last year, while he was still leader of the party, Dookeran told the membership, "We will make it work. Despite criticisms, COP will do its utmost for the People's Partnership coalition government to be sustained in power." Dookeran called the coalition of interests a new era of politics, which he said has now become a new mode of governance. "Trinidad and Tobago is now in that alliance, and COP will continue to uphold its historic responsibility," he said.

One of the fundamental areas of agreement in the Fyzabad Declaration was to establish mechanisms for the achievement of consensus and the partners agreed that, "they will abide by the spirit and letter of the Constitution and law of Trinidad and Tobago" and to propose legislative changes as are necessary to give effect to the will of the people. That spirit and letter of the constitution gives an individual the right to freedom of expression and the freedom to join a political party of his/her choice, which is what Marlene Coudray did. She exercised her constitutional right and as UNC Deputy Political leader Roodal Moonilal said last week, she does not have to apologise to anyone for that.

The COP is making a big fuss and suggesting that Coudray's move to the UNC is damaging to the coalition and Ramadhar even told reporters Tuesday that he considers it a power grab by the UNC to take charge of the San Fernando City Corporation. He also wants Coudray fired and replaced by a COP mayor. The truth is COP never wanted her as mayor and is now shedding crocodile tears, suggesting that the UNC stole "its mayor."

What Ramadhar has failed to address is whether COP had been fair to its member and why it treated her with contempt.

She was denied an opportunity to run for the San Fernando West seat in 2010, which according to all projections ahead of the vote, would have been a safe seat for COP. The party handed it to Carolyn Seepersad-Bachan, who won the seat as expected. COP compounded the slight to Coudray by refusing to nominate her for the mayoral post after the coalition won the

2010 Local Government Election. It was the UNC that stepped in and made her mayor.

In making accusations about UNC's intentions COP has conveniently sidestepped these issues and seem to be focused only on suggesting that the UNC is wrong and out of place when COP must take responsibility for Coudray's loss of confidence in the party to which she once belonged.

Ramadhar needs to also remember that he himself tried to "steal" Kamla in 2007 and later, inviting her to "come home to COP." And why hasn't he and COP made a fuss about some of the high profile people in the UNC who were members of COP — people like Attorney General Anand Ramlogan and Transport Minister Devant Maharaj who fought seats as COP candidates in the 2007 general election and then returned to the UNC when Kamla became leader. And has he forgotten that he too came from the UNC?

The fact that Coudray won a seat on the UNC's national executive is a statement of confidence in the UNC as an all inclusive party, while COP's rantings are lowering its standing within the national community.

One of the things that has always made this coalition an example of political maturity, is its ability to function as a single unit while each component part maintains its identity. Unlike the NAR's "one love" experiment, the PP is not a homogeneous party; it is a cross section of interests, representing the diversity of Trinidad and Tobago.

Each party must respect the other, but at the same time COP and its partners must also respect the right of individual members to make choices. And if those choices mean walking away from COP to the warm embrace of another party, then COP must accept that as the individual's democratic and constitutional right. At the same time it must ask itself *why*?

If there are genuine issues tearing the coalition apart, by all means the leaders must meet, discuss them, arrive at a consensus and move on. However, the Coudray affair is a manufactured crisis; COP must get over the political *tabanca* on this and focus on what are the real issues facing the partnership and the government.

(March 28, 2012)

COP's gamble could be costly and lead to its own demise

If the Congress of the People (COP) has genuine concerns with the way the People's Partnership is functioning, then it has every right to sit with its partners and work out the details in the interest of the government of which it is a part, and the people of Trinidad and Tobago.

However, I cannot agree that the Marlene Coudray matter is important enough — or even valid — as a reason for COP leader Prakash Ramadhar and his executive to want to mash up the partnership. Unless the COP leadership changes it attitude, they could soon face the reality that the party doesn't have the support or credibility to make any significant progress on the national political front.

In coalition politics, minority partners generally have control since the survival of a government depends on their critical votes. However, in Trinidad and Tobago today, that is not the case. Even if COP were to walk out with its six MPs Kamla and the UNC would still have a majority of 21 and the real losers will be COP and the people of Trinidad and Tobago. The partnership would be weaker and COP would no longer have any influence on national policy. But Kamla's government won't fall.

Kamla has always reached out to the members of the partnership, listening to their concerns and responding to their needs. COP, for example, has benefited much more from the partnership arrangement than if the proportional representation formula were used as a yardstick to determine allocation of political resources.

The president of the senate is COP. At the cabinet level, COP controls the ministries of finance, planning, sports, public administration and legal affairs. And many of its members hold important board positions, including chairmanships of state companies.

COP must seriously ask itself this question: which of the six COP MPs really wants to walk away from cabinet, knowing that such action would leave the UNC fully in charge of government? Prakash is going about this the wrong way. And his demand is undemocratic.

It is wrong to tell the PM to fire a mayor; she does not have that right. The council elects a mayor, so the democratic thing to do is to let the council consider the arguments and decide for itself whether it has confidence in the mayor. To do otherwise contradicts the political philosophy of COP and the other members of the partnership.

The truth is, this political tantrum is making COP weaker. And if it insists on creating a mountain out of this molehill, its support will slide further.

Let us not forget that COP began as a splinter group of the UNC that morphed into an independent party. Once the "offending" part of the UNC was excised from the body the majority of the disenchanted UNC followers returned home to the UNC, among them high profile people like Anand Ramlogan and Devant Maharaj, both of whom are senior members of the cabinet.

COP was a hybrid of disillusioned UNC members and activists, former members of the National Alliance for Reconstruction (NAR) and certain middle and upper class citizens who rejected the People's National Movement (PNM), but were too aloof and arrogant to associate with the "common folks" who comprised the UNC rank and file. To put it bluntly, they didn't want to be associated with "cane field" Indians.

The moment Kamla removed Basdeo Panday as leader of the UNC, COP's fortunes diminished; the UNC became stronger with the warm embrace of a leader who was ready to unite the opposition and prepare to govern. That determination to find compromise led to the historic Fyzabad Declaration and the dawn of a new era of participatory democracy in Trinidad and Tobago politics.

Kamla and her colleagues in the four other political movements that formed the People's Partnership were determined to find common ground on which to unite and determine policy to take Trinidad and Tobago forward.

Theirs was a coalition of interests that was different from anything Trinidad and Tobago had ever seen. In the sharing of the seats for the general election, Prakash got St Augustine, one of the safest UNC constituencies in the country, the one that eluded Winston Dookeran in 2007 when he led COP against the UNC.

Dookeran saw the political light that Kamla rekindled and became the first to join hands with the UNC in an historic alliance that changed the politics of Trinidad and Tobago forever. Today, with the return of the prodigals, the UNC is stronger than it has ever been and it has shed the ghost of racism that had haunted it for a long time.

Both Kamla and chairman Jack Warner are determined to lead a party that represents Trinidad and Tobago's diversity and to continue to support the coalition of interest that saw the political demise of Panday and Manning. COP now has a choice to stay within the partnership and keep its identity while being able to influence policy or it can walk away with its MPs and cause its death by suicide.

I would wager that Prakash would find it difficult — if not impossible — to take his MPs out of government even if he takes COP out of the coalition. How Prakash concludes this matter will determine whether he is a leader or just another rabble-rousing politician.

(April 1, 2012)

Partnership will stand - with or without COP

Kamla Persad-Bissessar has used her political instincts and personal charisma to first of all create the People's Partnership, and over the past two years, she has made use of her skills to keep the partnership together. On Monday (April 2) she returns to the negotiating table to try to find a solution to the Coudray affair that has threatened to fracture of the coalition.

Last week, the leader of the Congress of the People (COP), Prakash Ramadhar, was furious and even suggested that if the matter was not resolved to his satisfaction he would walk away. It reminded me of Ralph Maharaj in 2001, right after the UNC had won a clear majority despite the PNM's campaign that focused on alleged UNC corruption. Ralph painted himself in a corner when he told TV6 reporter Rosemary Sant that unless the UNC dealt with the issue of alleged corruption to his satisfaction he would consider leaving.

Basdeo Panday, who was prime minister at the time, reacted angrily at a public meeting a few days later. "Who want to walk could walk," he said at a UNC meeting at the SWWTU hall on Wrightson Road, Port of Spain. The rest is history. Maraj together with Ramesh L. Maharaj and Trevor

Sudama left the party and tried to stage a coup by cutting a deal with then opposition leader Patrick Manning to oust Panday.

That led to fresh elections in December 2001, the 18-18 tie and the presidential coup that saw President Robinson appoint Manning prime minister, justifying his actions on the basis of selecting a leader who would bring "morality and spirituality" to government.

Don't expect any such drama in this administration.

In fact, what is most likely is that Prakash and COP will have to climb down and eat humble pie.

Following Sunday's (April 1) COP emergency meeting, Prakash was already presenting an exit strategy when he backtracked on his threat and announced that while he stood firm on the Coudray matter he would continue to support the partnership and the government. It was a different story a few days earlier when he threatened to walk away from the coalition.

He really has little choice because he is not standing on firm ground. Having declared his hand without proper consultation and consideration of the facts, the COP leader now finds himself in a rather awkward position.

At least one high profile COP MP is distancing himself from COP's position and from the leader. Anil Roberts made it very clear in an interview with the Guardian media that he won't walk with Prakash if that is the option his leader chooses. And he has chastised Prakash for making unreasonable and unlawful demands of the prime minister by telling her to fire the mayor of San Fernando.

Prakash first suggested that the Fyzabad Declaration establishing the partnership stated that, COP would nominate mayors for Arima and San Fernando. When it turned out that the declaration only dealt with the general election and outlined broad principles of agreement, Prakash then remembered that it was a "gentleman's agreement" that provided a guarantee to COP, that it would have a mayor in both jurisdictions.

What is clear is that the ground is shifting from beneath the feet of the COP leader. While he has the support of his executive and many of COP's members the critical facts and logic in his arguments don't stand up.

It is absolutely clear from all the evidence in the public domain that COP did not support Marlene Coudray to be mayor of San Fernando. It was the UNC that nominated her although COP supported her in the election in the council. COP wanted another candidate who was unacceptable to the UNC. So since August 2010 the UNC had control and COP knew that

Marlene was not a COP mayor. It is dishonest, to say the least, for COP to wait two years before raising the matter as an issue of concern.

The only reason why COP is so angry is because Marlene's defection and subsequent election to a post of deputy leader in the UNC has embarrassed the party. COP's arrogance is what caused it to react in the manner it did. Its argument therefore that the UNC reneged on a "gentleman's agreement" should have been raised in 2010 because if it is a valid argument today it was even more valid in 2010.

Kamla is right to stand firm. Marlene's tenure as mayor is not her business. The council must decide if it wants to keep Marlene as mayor or not and Prakash knows that. So when he meets with the rest of the PP leaders on Monday, he should be prepared to accept that he is out of line.

Whatever happens, Prakash has already put himself and COP between a rock and a hard place. No matter how it ends, COP will be injured. As for the partnership, it will endure and the government will remain standing. That's what makes this experiment in coalition politics so interesting.

Kamla made sure she embraced everyone as they were, unlike the NAR coalition that dissolved the political parties and formed a single party that imploded because there was no room for dissent, discussion and compromise.

Trinidad and Tobago, as Basdeo Panday once noted, is too small for partisan politics. Kamla understands that better than all the political leaders in Trinidad and Tobago today. She sincerely believes that Trinidad and Tobago's diversity must be represented in its government because that is the only way that a government can understand the needs of the people and respond appropriately.

COP, the MSJ and the other coalition members are only individual parts of the whole. By all means, they must represent and fight for their respective constituencies but in the final analysis, they must recognise that they collectively represent all the people and that is why the people put them in office.

(April 2, 2010)

Trust Kamla to keep partnership together

I continue to be confused about the position of Congress of the People (COP) leader Prakash Ramadhar on the Coudray affair and his party's lukewarm relationship with the rest of the members of the governing coalition.

This is what Ramadhar told the media Thursday (April 12), at the end of the an inconclusive fourth partnership meeting on the matter: "Where the future of our country and our partnership may be jeopardised, I ask how could anyone in honour hold on to the office they did not gain by work? I can tell you what my position would be if there was harm to my country, I would be the first to stand down and allow things to go forward."

That's a clear message to Coudray that she is, in his view, the problem and that she just has to walk and the problem is over.

Ramadhar's contention is that Coudray's position was not earned in the same way that an MP earns his/her seat and that a mayor is a political appointee, not a true people's representative. In that context, he said, all it takes to remove a mayor is the political will. And he appeared to be pointing fingers at Prime Minister Kamla Persad-Bissessar, suggesting that she is dragging her feet on resolving the impasse.

Ramadhar is standing in political quicksand and instead of trying to get a helping hand out of the mess he is sinking deeper while blaming everyone but himself.

Kamla is doing what she does best: avoiding a hasty decision and allowing the stakeholders to argue over the matter so that at the end of it all, the partnership will arrive at what's best for the coalition and the country.

She reiterated on Wednesday (April 11), the guiding principle among leaders would be "that we all put the greater good as foremost in our minds in making our decisions." And she assured the media that she intends to hold the Partnership together.

However, in politics a day is a long time. So as an observer on the outside and a citizen who cares deeply about what happens to Trinidad and Tobago I trust that the leaders — including Ramadhar — would act responsibly and quell this storm in a teapot and move on with the people's business of creating the just society that Kamla and the partnership promised.

But coming back to Ramadhar. How can he now blame Coudray for putting the country and the partnership in jeopardy? In the first instance, COP treated the lady with contempt by refusing to let her run for the San Fernando West seat in the 2010 general election when it knew that she could win. She came close in 2007 when it was a three-party contest.

Secondly, COP is also avoiding discussion on the fact that, while it did not propose Coudray to be mayor, she has been — with the blessing of the UNC — the mayor for two years. Yet no one in COP complained about Coudray or the running of the San Fernando City Corporation, until she showed up last month at Rienzi Complex in the company of UNC jefes, Roodal Moonilal and Suruj Rambachan to file her nomination papers, to run as a candidate for one of the posts of deputy leader of the party.

Suddenly, the UNC was "poaching" and when she won a high profile post in the March 24 UNC election COP's embarrassment reached its peak with the chorus from the leadership that she must be fired

Ramadhar is the one who is putting the partnership at risk with his poor leadership in the handling of this matter. And by extension, he is causing harm to the country. So if we take him at his word — "I would be the first to stand down and allow things to go forward" — he should resign.

If Ramadhar and his chairman, Joseph Toney, had approached this matter professionally from the beginning there never would have been an issue. But in typical COP style they preferred to wear their morality and integrity on their sleeves and make a public display.

The Coudray affair only became an irritant because the lady decided that she had enough of COP and wanted a political change. That is her democratic and constitutional right. COP has always pledged to fight for and uphold citizens' rights, yet with political egg on its face, it chose to use emotive language like "poaching" and "disrespect" to malign the UNC.

Kamla could have said to Ramadhar, "take your MPs and go" and still have enough strength to govern. However, she knows that would have been unethical and immoral since the electorate voted for a partnership, a coalition that collectively pledged to rid the country of the PNM plague and make Trinidad and Tobago better.

She pledged in 2010, to unite her party and the opposition to create the broadest coalition of interests in the country; she achieved that and won the endorsement of the electorate.

In the past two years there have been disagreements and quarrels, as is expected in a family with such a cross section of interests. However, in the end the leaders always kept the big picture in view and arrived at consensus on what was best for the coalition, the government and the country.

Kamla did not have to include everybody and perhaps she would have still won the 2010 general election. That was never her intention. She ran for the UNC leadership on the slogans: "We deserve Better" and "United We Win" and since then has been doing all within her power to keep this group together for the good of the nation.

If COP sincerely believes that the Coudray matter — which in my opinion is quite low on the scale of national priorities — is the issue for which it must leave, then the other leaders should wish them well and let them go. The government will survive and perhaps some COP members might choose to stay. You may recall when ANR Robinson tossed out the "ULF elements" from the National Alliance for Reconstruction (NAR) government, some ULF MPs — including Winston Dookeran — refused to leave with Panday.

Has COP surveyed its membership on this? Does the party and its floor members sincerely believe that COP can walk away and become a powerful alternative? Has COP asked its sitting MPs how they feel?

When COP took birth as a protest movement, under the leadership of former UNC leader Winston Dookeran, the political mood in Trinidad and Tobago created the ideal opportunity for fresh political thinking and what Dookeran called "new politics". Things have changed dramatically since then. Basdeo Panday and Patrick Manning have both disappeared from the political radar and Kamla is fully in charge.

Some of the UNC insiders are saying she can do it alone and perhaps she can. But that was never her intention or style; she believes in unity and is a coalition builder. The lady I know as the Prime Minister of Trinidad and Tobago will continue to do all within her power to continue to offer a warm embrace to everyone because she knows that the days of partisan politics are gone forever and political success depends on a leader's ability to represent and serve all the people, all the time.

(April 13, 2012)

COP's rumblings were shaking the confidence of some supporters of the government and when the Movement for Social Justice (MSJ) started making unreasonable demands, Kamla found herself in the difficult situation of managing the government and a restless coalition fed by certain members of the MSJ whose agenda was in conflict with the government's. The new MSJ leader was wearing two hats and it was not long before he had to make a choice.

Labour's best deal ever is to remain a part of the People's Partnership

Prime Minister Kamla Persad-Bissessar has declared the COP tantrum involving Marlene Coudray is over, although some COP members may not necessarily agree. But the grumbling within the People's Partnership is not going away immediately.

Kamla is still facing what is perhaps a more contentious issue. And it's coming from the Movement for Social Justice (MSJ), which is a far more belligerent group that the Congress of the People.

The MSJ has sent the Prime Minister a list of 10 demands that it wants her to address before the government celebrates its second anniversary on May 24. The 10 issues as outlined by the MSJ are:

- Settlement of negotiations in a fair and equitable manner consistent with the free collective bargaining process
- Fair share of state resources to communities and the equitable distribution of jobs
- Reduced rights of land tenure and massive increase of lease rates to farmers without consultation
- Governance: process of constitution reform and local government reform, addressing state sector governance, cutting all forms of discrimination, political victimisation, corruption, nepotism and patronage

- Getting rid of the odious system of contract labour in the public service and state sectors
- Privatisation, especially of Petrotrin (Trinmar's acreage) and First Citizens
- Advancing the agenda of labour law reform
- The protection of the livelihoods of fisherfolk
- Implementing the cultural sector agenda, as committed to in the manifesto
- Establishing a policy position so as to stop the use of force by the police service to frustrate, intimidate and stop the legitimate and peaceful activities of civil society, including peaceful protest action by workers and the rights of the media

The government has dealt with, and is dealing with, some of these issues; others cannot be resolved with the haste that the MSJ expects and Kamla may not have jurisdiction to deal with some of them. The MSJ knows that, so what really is its point?

David Abdulah finds himself in a rather awkward position. The MSJ leader is walking in big shoes inherited from Errol McLeod, the man who committed the MSJ to the partnership. And like McLeod, he must choose between his dual role of government senator and general secretary of the Oilfield Workers Trade Union (OWTU).

The OWTU has already drawn a line in the sand. President General Ancel Roget is on record as saying he wants to bring down the government and has pledged to do what's necessary to achieve that whenever the next election comes along. That leaves Abdulah little wiggle room to negotiate in good faith.

The question for Abdulah is, whether he really wants to lead a labour party from outside the partnership that would not be able to win an election or whether he would find areas of compromise so that labour could still have a seat at the cabinet table and influence national policy. He cannot have it both ways, especially with Roget and some other MSJ members continuing to remain opposed to meaningful dialogue.

And the real question is this: Does the OWTU really want to resolve the issues raised by the MSJ or does it want only to bring down the government by using the MSJ as an excuse to achieve its agenda?

The OWTU alone is not the MSJ, although Roget seems to have taken it upon himself to be the voice of the party. Unlike his labour colleague

Vincent Cabrera who has talked openly about forming a labour party Roget's obsession is with bringing down the government.

The MSJ can benefit the most from being a part of the governing structure and influencing state policy on more than labour issues. However, to do it, it must be prepared to work with its coalition partners in a spirit of compromise and consensus. In reality, there is no MSJ MP in government. McLeod fought the 2010 election as a candidate of the UNC and therefore his leader is Kamla. She could easily tell Abdulah if the MSJ is unhappy and does not wish to work with the partnership it could leave.

She won't. That is not her style. And it is in conflict with her principles and her commitment to the people of Trinidad and Tobago. That's why she did not push aside COP. The partnership that she put together is the first political grouping in Trinidad and Tobago that truly represents all sectors and classes in the country. And no one should expect everything to be perfect. Kamla has said herself that one of the virtues of the partnership is that its leaders know how to argue and disagree.

Each group has its own political philosophy and operates independently. No one was asked to unite into a single party. However, there was enough common ground to bring them together for a single purpose. That remains the most important issue today and when Abdulah sits down with his colleagues to discuss the MSJ's demands, he must do so with the understanding that Kamla must act both as the leader of the partnership and the prime minister of the country. She must separate her dual responsibilities and where there is a conflict the needs of the country must take precedence over those of her political allies.

Kamla is committed to creating a new society with respect for one another and the preservation of human dignity, where the poorest have the same opportunity as the most affluent, where every family has a home, where no one goes hungry, where the entire community raises every child as its own, where every woman and every child and every elderly person is respected, where everyone who wants a job can acquire one, where people are rewarded and acknowledged in accordance with their respective contributions.

Hers is a vision of continuing service to the people. And that is not in conflict with labour or what the MSJ desires for those who support it. She remains committed to end divisiveness and to celebrate Trinidad and Tobago's diversity and rich heritage so that everyone can live together, dream dreams together and build a nation of equals.

Labour must understand that the electorate is today much wiser and more in tune with issues than it was 36 years ago when Trinidad and Tobago launched its first true labour party — the United Labour Front (ULF), led by the trio of Basdeo Panday, George Weekes and Raffique Shah. That was a powerful movement that had mass support. But the support evaporated when voters had to make a choice between their labour representatives and the people they wanted in government.

The dysfunctional labour body of today is nothing close to the 1976 mass movement that failed to win popular electoral support. And Abdulah and Roget must understand that they face political annihilation if they try to turn the tables on the government. Workers today need the same "bread, peace and justice" for which they fought in 1976 and they are still not prepared to hand their government to belligerent trade unionists who refuse to understand the difference between rhetoric and good governance.

(April 20, 2012)

Labour united in 1976 but failed to win power

In 1966, a new political party made a bold attempt to achieve a breakthrough in Trinidad and Tobago's polarised ethnic politics. It failed.

The country was still divided between supporters of the People's National Movement (PNM) and the Democratic Labour party (DLP), the two major parties in the country.

The Workers and Farmers Party (WFP), believed that the country had enough of racial politics and entered the political area on the premise that it could change that and convince people to vote for principles that were above the narrow ethnic divide. Among the people in that movement were Basdeo Panday, a young lawyer, and George Weekes, the respected leader of the powerful Oilfield Workers Trade Union (OWTU).

The experiment failed miserably. The electorate rejected the idea and the party. All its candidates lost their deposits, including Panday and Weekes. They regrouped later after Panday had taken control of the sugar union, hoping to realise the same dream of a party of ideas, involving anyone who shared the vision regardless of race, religion or social standing.

Panday spoke about it in an interview with People magazine, which is quoted in the book, *Crisis*, edited by Owen Baptiste (Inprint 1976):

"By the end of September 1974, I had won the struggle for guaranteed work and I felt I had the loyalty of the workers. I went to George Weekes... and I told him that the time had come to continue the job we stated in 1966. We had to unite the workers in such a way as to get rid of the racial antagonisms that prevailed. We proposed a rally in December 1974 but because of some internal problems in the OWTU we postponed it to February 18".

The venue was Skinner Park. Twenty-five thousand people — workers and non-workers — attended the launch of the United Labour Front (ULF) and heard speeches from Panday, Weekes and Raffique Shah, who was the leader of the country's cane farmers. Journalist Raoul Pantin called it "the biggest labour rally ever held" and described the ULF as a serious force to be reckoned with.

In the Sunday Express of February 23, 1975 he wrote: "Here was a clear demonstration of joint action by the two biggest sectors of the labour force. And the fact that one section was rural and Indian and the other was urban and black only heightened the occasion. So whatever the government or anybody else might think the fact is that on Tuesday the workers in oil and sugar showed they could stand united around a common cause."

The motive of the new labour body was clear. Shah had told the crowd, "We must now consolidate and institutionalise the power which we now have to get control of the state." That never happened. In fact it was journalist Jeff Hackett who touched on what was perhaps the most significant issue of the day. Writing in the Express, Hackett wondered if Panday had become "the fair, fearless prince who would lead his people out of the wilderness."

He suggested that Panday might be the natural successor to the "broken Democratic Labour Party (DLP) dream" and become the new "Baba" in the sugar belt, a reference to Bhadase Maraj who had been a champion of the Indian working class and also a political arch rival of Dr. Eric Williams and the governing PNM.

While the rally stunned the nation, the events that followed failed to materialise into political power. Labour had united the races under a common banner of "bread, peace and justice" but the people refused to be seduced by the slogan, "let those who labour hold the reins." And ethnicity proved to be a more powerful motivator than labour unity.

In the general election of 1976, the PNM was returned to power. And Hackett's speculation turned out to be right. Panday had indeed become the new messiah on the plains of Caroni. The man who had hoped to end racial politics, soon discovered that despite his efforts he had not succeeded in creating a winning labour party; all he had done was to replace the DLP as another Indian party.

The ULF failed to attract any significant support among voters in the non-traditional DLP areas where people saw Panday as the leader of the party. For example, Panday's non-Indian candidates Errol McLeod (Oropouche) and Paul Harrison (Caroni East) won easily in traditional DLP (Indian) constituencies, demonstrating allegiance to a leader. Other ULF candidates like David Abdulah (Tunapuna) and John Abrahams (Pointe-a-Pierre), both respected OWTU members, were defeated by the PNM because oil workers did not see Weekes as the ULF leader.

Labour might have fared better in a more focused campaign, but Williams and the PNM were on a high and won a clear majority of 24 seats; the ULF won 10 and for the first time the PNM lost the two Tobago seats, which went to ANR Robinson and Dr. Winston Murray of the Democratic Action Congress (DAC).

Today, labour is again agitating for recognition. It claims that it represents the largest constituency in Trinidad and Tobago. There is no doubt that the majority of the electorate are "workers." The question is whether these voters are prepared to risk their future and the country's future by electing trade unionists to government. It's not that there is anything fundamentally wrong with electing a trade union leader. After all Panday led one of the better governments in Trinidad and Tobago.

However, his United National Congress (UNC) was not a labour party. And once in government Panday realised that he had work closely with the "parasitic oligarchy" that he had denounced in his years fighting for the cause of workers. The reality is that effective governance requires more than desk thumping trade union negotiators. Yes, labour parties have governed in many countries including Great Britain. However, they were much more than a group of trade union activists.

If labour is serious about getting organised into a political movement that expects to win power, it must first rebrand itself as a responsible organisation that can see beyond the short sighted needs of the worker alone. To run a country requires a commitment to everyone, not just one group or tribe.

While labour was in upheaval and COP was flexing its political muscle, Rowley was getting into a political fight with one of the more vocal and high profile members of his part. Louis Lee Sing had rebuffed Rowley for exposing the PNM to ridicule in his failed no confidence motion against the Kamla government and Rowley was not amused.

Is Lee Sing getting ready to lead the PNM?

What is Louis Lee Sing's next move?

The mayor of Port of Spain told reporters on Monday (April 23), he is not interested in seeking a second term and that he wishes that the position were one that was open for election rather than appointment.

Is he saying that his relationship with his political boss, People's National Movement (PNM) leader Keith Rowley, is so strained that he won't get the nod for a second term? Or is he saying that he would be willing to challenge the PNM status quo and run in a local election for the post of mayor if that were an option? Or perhaps he is setting his sights on bigger, more important national politics.

Whatever the truth, you can be sure of one thing — Lee Sing is a political junkie who is no quitter. And he probably has had enough of cutting track for goutie to run. Louis is an effective communicator, understands how to make media work for him and is a smart strategist. He is a loyal and dedicated member of the PNM and has been so for the more than 30 years that I have known him personally and professionally. And he calls it as he sees it, even if you don't agree with his points of view or politics.

You might recall, that while the mayor's daughter-in-law joined Manning on his walk to San Fernando, Lee Sing called Manning's "democracy march" foolishness and added that those "who continue to follow Mr. Manning like Karen Tesheira, Mustapha Abdul-Hamid [and] Gary Hunt" should know better and recognise that "the population is tired with that kind of thing."

Louis made it clear that from where he stood the responsibility for the sad state of the country today rested "in the laps of Patrick Mervyn Augustus Manning." He said Manning should just go home, open his church and preach the gospel.

And he got himself in political hot waters with Manning's successor as well when he told Rowley and the party jefes that the recent no-confidence motion in the prime minister was not only ill-timed, but also afforded the government an opportunity to shore up its support. He went so far as suggesting that PNM members felt that the motion amounted to "collusion" between Rowley and the prime minister.

The mayor slammed the administration of the party, noting that recent events "suggest to me the leadership of our party has elected to pursue an archaic and less than democratic approach to party governance."

Rowley was not amused and suggested that the Mayor's "untimely" intervention was not welcome. "No general likes to know that when you go into battle...the first time the enemy fires his salvo, you turn tail and start firing on your own troops. No general likes that," Rowley said when asked about Lee Sing's stand.

So with both factions of the PNM gunning for him, where does Louis stand? That's the most interesting political question today.

He is probably standing at the right place, at the right time and could very well be eyeing Rowley's job. And don't be surprised if many of the big shots and behind the scenes movers and shakers in the party are thinking the same thing.

It is common knowledge that they are not happy with Rowley. They also know that Manning has run his course and it is time for the MP for San Fernando East to be sent to the political glue factory.

After two years, they know that Rowley is not going to take the PNM back to government; Rowley's lack lustre performances have been getting worse every time he tries to take on the government.

I wrote in a previous column that Rowley is an angry man. Anger is a dangerous thing; it creates fear and instability and erodes freedom because it causes people to clam up and not speak out. It is a fatal attribute of a weak leader whose selfish tantrums cause damage without solving problems. Rowley's dilemma is how to take charge while standing in a political mine field that he helped create.

Sooner, rather than later, the PNM would have to decide if it wants to keep Rowley and remain where it is or move into the 21st century with a leader who is willing to build a truly national party and get back to government. Perhaps this is the first signal that Louis could be the chosen dedicated PNMite who is willing to embrace change and lobby to take the party forward by breaking the mould that Eric Williams used to fashion the party more than 50 years ago.

The challenge for Louis, if his focus in the PNM leadership, would be to adopt a new style of politics devoid of ethnic loyalties and tribalism. In other words, he would have to be willing to create his own version of the people's partnership in which everybody is represented and all can believe that she or he is equal. And that includes the Indians who are already watching with suspicion because the mayor has taken the "Indian" out of their "Indian Arrival Day."

Trinidad and Tobago has moved well beyond the hegemonic party style that has always characterised the PNM. Both Williams and Manning preferred to "win alone and lose alone" in preference for collaborative coalition politics.

We have progressed from the time when Williams wrote his People's Charter, which still looks good on paper but has failed in practice. The PNM is no longer "great" and it can only "prevail" if it does some introspection, admit that it has lost its way and resolve to become a forward looking, national movement of the people, for the people. That would be a good move because it would create a stronger opposition to keep checks and balances on the government. And for the People's Partnership, it would also be a warning that there is no room for complacency.

(April 25, 2012)

COP needs to be careful it does not shoot itself

Some members of the Congress of the People (COP) never wanted to be a part of the coalition of interests that came together and won the 2010 general election. And now, having got a weak leader in Prakash Ramadhar, they are exploiting the Coudray matter and publicly demanding concessions from the People's Partnership. They are also objecting to legislation to make the switch from the Privy Council to the Caribbean Court of Justice [CCJ]. The Privy Council has always been T&T's final court of appeal so this change would mean that the CCJ would take on that role.

But don't despair. The sky is not falling. The government that more than 432,000 citizens put in office is not about to fall, even if Prakash walks away from the coalition and leaves cabinet.

Let's be honest about a few things. Despite COP's arrogance and boast that *it* won the 2010 election, the reality is that if it had opposed the United National Congress (UNC) led by Kamla Persad-Bissessar it would likely have not won the six seats it now has. In fact, that is what Patrick Manning was counting on. When he called the election prematurely the leader of the People's National Movement (PNM) was hoping to capitalise on a fragmented opposition, expecting that they would split the anti-PNM vote and let him win again.

Kamla, Winston Dookeran and the other leaders — Errol McLeod, Ashworth Jack and Makandal Daaga — demonstrated a sense of patriotism and nationalism that Manning never expected; they came together for the good of the nation and the people embraced them. Each unit in that coalition of interest pledged to remain true to its principles while working together to develop common policies for governing Trinidad and Tobago. And that's why the people accepted the partnership as a single political unit and voted overwhelmingly for them.

For the first time in Trinidad and Tobago, there was a political organisation that represented everyone — from the poor and dispossessed to the privileged and affluent and everybody in between. Unlike the NAR that imploded shortly after the historic 1986 general election victory, the People's Partnership represented an entirely new and different political thinking. It was not a single party, but a coalition of interests.

The partnership agreed to represent its various constituencies and engage in dialogue and consensus, a genuine part of the new politics that COP boasted about as one of its great strengths. Now COP is a dissident group within that coalition. Its language is not in keeping with the rationale for establishing the partnership and it also contradicts the agreement of the leaders of the partnership, including COP's leader.

Here's what COP chairman, Joseph Toney told reporters: "Until this matter is resolved, that is the matter of the mayorship of San Fernando, the national council instructed the national executive and the political leader that they wanted to go on record that the COP reserves the right to revisit our relationship with all the units that form the People's Partnership." And here is Ramadhar's contribution: "We will not accept any alternative compensation for the breach of the agreement by the UNC." He added that his party "would not be bought."

On the call for a referendum on the CCJ he said, "We would exercise our independent discretion...If we do not believe it [legislation] is in the interest of the people of T&T, for now and for the future, we will take the decision to either vote against legislation or to abstain from voting."

What emerged out of Sunday's (April 29) national congress of the COP on the Coudray matter, is that the party made it clear that it has no confidence in its leader and would not abide by his decision. And they made him contradict himself — again. In addition it demonstrated that despite of its commitment to new politics and democracy it prefers to resort to political blackmail and bullying to try to get its ounce of flesh.

In the first case, let's be clear about the Coudray matter. That is a red herring that would never had been an issue if Coudray had not won a seat on the UNC's national executive. COP created the problem when it refused to nominate Coudray as its candidate in the 2010 election after she came second in the 2007 election and could have easily won San Fernando West. COP compounded it when it refused to nominate her to be mayor of San Fernando in 2010. It was the UNC that supported her and the UNC used its majority in the corporation to guarantee that she became mayor. COP grudgingly voted for her. So if there was an issue with COP not having its mayor in San Fernando the issue is two years old, so why raise it in 2012 only when Coudray suddenly emerged as a high profile member of the UNC?

If COP operates from a position of accountability and transparency here are some questions that it must answer for its membership and the electorate:

- Whose position is the party articulating when it makes these statements?
- Did COP consult its membership or at least the people of the six constituencies it represents?
- Why is the leader flip flopping on important issues?
- Are the COP MPs going to accept this
- Are other COP members like the planning minister and the president of the senate going to go along with this?

The reality is that if you analyse what COP is saying today you would see that nothing has really changed except for the rhetoric and political posturing. COP was supposed to be independent and retain its identify and its principles. That is what it says it will do from now on.

But wait. That raises other interesting questions. Is that an admission that it was dancing to the beat of another band all along and suddenly it has discovered its error? Was it not being true to itself and its principles over the past two years?

Prakash has found himself between a rock and a hard place in this political dilemma. He has shown that he is a weak leader who is unable to make a decision and stand by it. And COP has sent a message to the public that after all it is just another political party seeking to gain power for itself even if that means trampling on its partners. It seems that it is content to mash up the partnership if it doesn't get what it wants just like the kid who runs home with his marbles when he loses at the game.

Kamla has put Prakash in his place and made it clear that the Coudray matter is closed. And on the other matter of a referendum on the CCJ that the party raised Sunday, she has also stated emphatically that she does not agree with COP.

The next chapter in this drama is yet to be written. COP would be wise to do some self-analysis and take a look in the mirror. It might believe it has the strength to fight the partnership and walk away but in the end the people will be the ones to pass a final judgment.

And as Kamla has said repeatedly, the people are the government. COP needs to always be conscious of that. The people know they have the power and they will use it when the time comes.

(April 30, 2012)

Prime Minister Kamla Persad-Bissessar used all her political skills to firmly end the bickering that was threatening the survival of the People's Partnership. In a day of tense negotiation and frank discussions, she settled the matter. At one point the media even ran a breaking story that Kamla had fired Prakash. Jyoti acted more responsibly and through its contacts inside the cabinet room, it learned that all was well and that no one was fired. And that is what Kamla reported to the nation when the talks were over.

All's well that ends well, but stormy seas lie ahead

It's not over. But for now the crisis has past and the storm has abated. However, no one should get complacent because stormy seas still lie ahead as the People's Partnership ship of state sails on.

When Prime Minister Kamla Persad-Bissessar summoned her cabinet for an emergency meeting Wednesday (May 2), she knew that it would be tough one. At the end, she emerged as a stronger leader, demonstrating once again that she is a person dedicated to the principles of consensus and unity. And her coalition remained in tact, much stronger than when the troops gathered for their discussion.

"Why else do we get involved in politics?" she asked as she reported to the media. She explained that unlike her predecessors she had no need to crack a whip or get anybody in line. What was needed, she explained, was discussion and consensus, which is exactly what happened.

Kamla made it clear that, "No minister has been fired. No minister will be fired. No minister has resigned. And no minister has indicated any desire to resign." There was a lot of discussion among all ministers and each of them accepted that the government must be guided by the principle of collective cabinet responsibility. "My government is very strong...the cabinet is very strong and I have not picked up one dissonant voice that seems to be saying, 'I do not want to belong to this partnership or I want this partnership to break up." she said.

Those who had a specific agenda and the Trinidad and Tobago *bachannal* society, were quick to feed the rumour mill with misinformation and report as fact that Kamla had fired Congress of the People leader Prakash Ramadhar from her cabinet. The Express newspaper, which doesn't often update stories online, carried a breaking news story that Prakash was fired. The Guardian media's reporter at the scene said she had reliable information that Kamla had done the deed. And at COP's operations centre the troops had gathered with COP chairman Joseph Toney. He told the Express later, "I want to especially thank all the national executive members and others who came out to the Operation Centre in solidarity to plan a way forward if the rumour was indeed true." And he said "We await a report from our political leader."

Inside the room with his colleagues at the Diplomatic Centre, Prakash took a beating for the public pronouncements he had been making, culminating in what amounted to a rebuke of the prime minister. His own MPs were unhappy and pointed out that he could not continue along such a destructive path. In the end he agreed and all the members of the cabinet pledged full support for the partnership and the government.

However, Prakash still has to face the vocal COP officials and members who will be calling for his head on a platter because they didn't get their pound of flesh. They had pushed their leader to the brink and the irresponsible posturing almost caused a fracturing of the partnership on the eve of the coalition's second anniversary.

They will not give up easily. How Prakash treats the issue now will determine whether he saves face nationally and whether he has a future as a political leader. He had already painted himself in a corner. Wednesday's cabinet meeting saved him from disgrace and all credit must go to Kamla for demonstrating that leadership is not about autocracy but about compromise and understanding.

She could have fallen for the COP bait and either fired Prakash or put him in a doghouse. She chose neither because she knows that the reason she worked so hard to build a coalition in the first place was to give a voice to everyone. So while she and her government could have survived without Prakash and COP she understood that such a situation was ethically wrong and contrary to the principles that brought the partnership into being. The people voted for a coalition of interests that pledged to govern with professionalism, transparency and ethics; she was not about to break that bond with the people.

The next step is for Prakash to stand up to COP and let them know that he is the leader and that he and his ministerial colleagues will make this coalition work. If they are unhappy with that, then he would have one of two clear choices: remain committed to the government and the coalition or hand over the leadership of COP.

For COP, the latter would be a political death sentence since the strength of the party lies with its parliamentary caucus. No matter what its leaders outside of cabinet might think, the party will not be able to stand alone and win an election if it walks away from the coalition today.

It's a message that the Movement for Social Justice must also heed as it prepares for battle with its partnership members.

For now all is well. It's going to continue to be stormy seas as the government enters its third year. There will continue to be stress and tensions. However, if each component part of the partnership is determined to hold on to the principles enunciated in the Fyzabad Declaration and fight to make Trinidad and Tobago a better place, the partnership will survive to 2015 and beyond.

With Kamla as the leader, chances are good for that to happen. She has demonstrated that she is committed to Trinidad and Tobago and to service to the people. And that is the commitment that will hold this coalition together.

(May 3, 2012)

Resolving the COP problem was one step in the right direction but Kamla still had to deal with another member of the family — one that felt it had a greater entitlement than the others. In the end, the inevitable happened.

Time for Abdulah to make up his mind about the PP

There is a clear distinction between a member of the People's Partnership and a member of a party within the partnership. But it seems to me that that is not clear to the Oilfield Workers Trade Union (OWTU), which has been behaving as if it is the Movement for Social Justice (MSJ).

The MSJ is one of the five members of the People's Partnership coalition that is the governing political group in Trinidad and Tobago. Its former leader, the man who committed the MSJ to the partnership, used to be the head of the OWTU. So that alone could cause some of us to believe that when the OWTU speaks the MSJ speaks and if the OWTU is angry with the government all fall down for the partnership. But that is not so.

The fact of the matter is that, the OWTU is just one of the groups that make up the MSJ and while it is most vocal in its anti-government stand it remains just a member of the MSJ and that must not be confused with who or what is the MSJ.

For a long time now, the OWTU has been leading the charge against the government of prime minister Kamla Persad-Bissessar with its President General Ancel Roget saying at every opportunity he gets that his mission is to bring down the government.

If you listen carefully to Roget, he sounds so much like the opposition People's National Movement (PNM) that you are likely to ask what is his official PNM title, and wonder where is his red shirt and a balisier tie? (Never mind Rowley doesn't like the tie anymore but the real 'PNM till ah ded' types love their tie). So when Roget and the OWTU issue an ultimatum to the People's Partnership they are damn well boldface and out of place.

Roget and company are ready to leave, but leave what?. They are saying on May 24 if they don't get what they want they are leaving. Don't take it from me. Here is what they are saying:

"At the stroke of midnight May 24th 2012 they [the government?] will not have the involvement of the OWTU in any dimension whatsoever. Our vehicle is ready to reverse, reverse like you never reverse before out of that nonsense and that charade they call the People's Partnership."

The OWTU is a little mixed up here. When Errol McLeod signed on to the partnership he didn't do it as a former OWTU boss; he did it as the leader of an activist group called the Movement for Social Justice, which was not even a political party. So when the time came for him to put his name on a ballot paper he put it next to the rising sun of the United National Congress (UNC).

MSJ the party came afterwards. And when Errol realised that his friends in the OWTU were behaving like bullies and thugs, trying to blackmail him and the government, he walked away and decided to focus on his real job as the minister of labour. So if you do the reality check, Roget and his OWTU boys are trying to bring down the government pretending that they are the MSJ.

So it is time for David Abdulah, the new MSJ leader, to show some leadership and tell Roget and the OWTU that they are members of the MSJ, just like the other labour groups and they do not speak for the MSJ.

But is David ready to do that?

He has a little bit of an identity problem. Sure he is a government senator, has stood on the platform with Kamla and the other leaders of the partnership and pledged the MSJ's commitment and support. But when he goes home to the OWTU (he is the union's general secretary) everybody begins to shout him down and tell him they want to get out of the partnership.

And David has some heavy baggage as well. He has always been the kind of guy to stand up and fight. After all, that's why he gets the big bucks as a top dog in the OWTU. So when the OWTU decided to shut down Petrotrin he was right there waving the flag, ready to go to a battle that would have wreaked havoc on the national economy and hurt the government of which he and the MSJ are a part.

When Wayne Kublalsingh and his friends in Debe decided to block some bulldozers and stop work on the highway to Point Fortin he was there too. So David has a little problem, which can become a really big one.

A doctor will tell you, David might be afflicted with a condition called dissociative identity disorder (DID), or multiple personality disorder, which manifests itself as the presence of "two or more distinct identities or personality states that recurrently take control of behaviour."

So sometimes he is a rabid trade unionist joining the OWTU chorus to denounce the government; then he is a fighter for the little guy; and then he is a government senator standing firm with the government that he will fight the next day as the leader of the MSJ (Or is it that he too thinks the OWTU is the MSJ?)

The MSJ gave the government until May 24 to settle 10 issues or else it will walk away. That ultimatum has really come from Roget and the OWTU, which is why they feel that when they walk away on May 24 it is the MSJ that is walking away. And that is why David has to cure his DID really fast. The smartest thing he could do now is to understand that his 10 demands are unreasonable and he and the other members of the partnership should sit down and make sense of the whole thing.

Even a head honcho labour consultant like Robert Giuseppe knows that David and Roget and the rest of MSJ are making a mistake in threatening the partnership. What does Giuseppe think? "I think that is a nonsensical way of looking for changes. You can't give a deadline on issues that are broad and so expansive. You can give a deadline in terms of at least saying let's sit down by that date and arrange a sort of accommodation where we can continue to develop as a real coalition."

He's right. But perhaps the rabble rousers never wanted a resolution, just an excuse to try, like some of the COP members, to harm Kamla and the partnership and perhaps cause the government to fall.

What they didn't count on, was the strength of a lady who has always known what she wanted and still does. Kamla has been nice so far but she can also be brutal and surgical in dealing with cancers that threaten to hurt the body politic.

So if the OWTU wants to leave that is its business; it has nothing to do with the partnership. The union is a member of the MSJ, which up to now remains a member of the partnership. David and the MSJ might decide they want to leave. That would be a bad move for them but they are big boys so nobody has to hold their hands to tell them what is right or wrong.

(May 3, 2012)

PP remains strong because it welcomes dissent

I have been reading a lot from commentators and persons who write on online blogs and chat groups about what is right and what isn't about the People's Partnership (PP) in Trinidad and Tobago. And one of the things that strikes me, is that the majority of comments seem to focus on the belief that the partnership is in trouble because of dissenting views.

What is wrong about this perception is that the flexibility of holding dissenting views and expressing them among partnership members is exactly what makes this coalition strong and what will likely make it endure.

Many people are making the mistake of comparing this political arrangement with the National Alliance for Reconstruction (NAR) that resulted in the first ever defeat of the People's National Movement (PNM) in a general election. It isn't the same. The fundamental difference between the two is that NAR was a single party with a single constitution and all its members were expected to accept that. Although the parties that comprised NAR were individual entities with their own political philosophies, each decided to dissolve into a single unit, giving up that independence.

Therefore, while TAPIA continued to exist, the political arm became a part of NAR. It was the same with ANR Robinson's Democratic Action Congress (DAC) and Basdeo Panday's United Labour Front (UFL), which as the official opposition in the 1976 and 1981 parliaments, had the greatest degree of legitimacy among the political groups. Some commentators disagree with that, noting that in the 1981 general election it was the predecessor to NAR, the Organisation for National Reconstruction (ONR), that had the highest percentage and numbers of votes among the opposition parties.

ONR won 91,704 (22.2 percent of the popular vote), but failed to win a seat primarily because of the defects in the first-past-the post system. ONR, DAC, TAPIA and the ULF merged into one party and contested the election and won because of its combined strength and also because the

Chambers PNM had collapsed under the weight of allegations of corruption, highlighted by the infamous declaration by cabinet minister Desmond Cartey: "*all ah we tief*".

The magnitude of the NAR victory was a loss for the minority elements in the party and when differences arose between Robinson and Panday, it was easy for Robinson to tell Panday he could leave if he didn't approve of the way the government was conducting its affairs. Panday obliged and created CLUB 88 (the Caucus of Love, Unity and Brotherhood), which later became the United National Congress (UNC), both under the chairmanship of Dr. Rampersad Parasram.

Robinson had enough MPs to maintain a very strong parliamentary majority, but his autocratic management of the cabinet caused internal problems. This was compounded by the poor state of the economy and unpopular measures that had to be taken, which led to the uprising of 1990.

There are fundamental differences between NAR and the PP that many journalists, commentators and analysts have failed to acknowledge or consider in passing judgment on the state of the PP.

1. NAR was a single party; the PP is a coalition of five groups representing a coalition of interests involving the full spectrum of Trinidad and Tobago society
2. NAR operated with strict party rules; the PP accepts that each member of the group has its own identity and is expected to continue to develop according to its priorities while continuing to function as a single unit in matters of governance
3. NAR tolerated no dissent; the PP welcomes dissent and discussion so that through constructive dialogue it could arrive at consensus on what is best for Trinidad and Tobago
4. This coalition of interest is a radical departure from the style of government that Trinidad and Tobago had known since 1956.

It differs from the marriage of convenience between Panday and Robinson, that led to the 1995 UNC administration because it determined *before* the election, that it would be a coalition and established rules that would govern the partnership. The electorate knew that in supporting the PP it was endorsing a common set of ideas to govern the country but at the same time was accepting that each of the parties was independent.

In 1995 the NAR, the UNC and the People's National Movement (PNM) of Patrick Manning ran their separate campaigns, attacking one another's platforms and policies. Then UNC united with NAR for the sake of forming a government, in spite of the glaring differences in their respective approach to governing.

In 1995 people voted for single political parties, yet they had to settle for a coalition due to political expediency. Had Manning and the PNM not committed to standing alone, the coalition might have been very different from the one that governed between 1995 and 2001.

In the PP case the Fyzabad Declaration made it clear that Kamla would lead the group, that each was an independent unit and that collectively they agreed on a common set of principles to govern.

That flexibility remains today, but few commentators, journalists and analysts see and accept the fundamental differences. They have been so indoctrinated by the single party syndrome that they fail to see that dissent is an integral part of this coalition.

Kamla has made that clear on several occasions. "We know how to argue and we know how to agree," is how she has explained "quarrels" in the coalition.

It is normal and expected, therefore, that each group will have its individual priorities that it would present to the parliamentary caucus, to cabinet and in meetings among the key political stakeholders.

This is why the Congress of the People (COP) stated its grievances and why the Movement for Social Justice (MSJ) has its own set of concerns that it wants Kamla and the PP to address before the end of the month.

The whole thing threatened to go off the rails when the members chose to go public to express concerns before meeting with the leadership, to vent frustrations and try to find consensus. From the time the election results were announced on May 24, 2010 it was clear that Kamla's UNC had a clear majority. That didn't change her approach. She and the UNC had made a pledge to the people to unite the opposition and build a new Trinidad and Tobago. They have vowed never to renege on that.

The PP is a work in progress that will continue to face obstacles, but Kamla remains determined to keep the partnership and the coalition together. Unlike Robinson in 1987, she has refused to flex her political muscle. Compromise and consensus remain the watchwords that she hopes would insulate the coalition.

The experiment in coalition politics has worked because of the innovation by the People's Partnership. In a society that is as diverse as Trinidad and Tobago, it is the best political system.

For now, the PP remains comfortable because its main opposition, the PNM, is stuck in the past and has refused to accept this new politics of participatory democracy. That could change. And if it does, the partnership would have to become even more vigilant because it would open other possibilities for the political groups outside of the PNM and the UNC.

(May 8, 2012)

Labour advancing political agenda at the expense of workers

There is no pretence anymore.

Ancel Roget and some of his colleagues in the labour movement have only one interest today and it has nothing to do with the workers they represent; they are intent on creating unrest with the hope that they will destabilise the People's Partnership (PP) government and cause it to fall.

The fact that the unions represent a substantial part of the membership of the Movement for Social Justice (MSJ), also raises the question about whether David Abdulah, as both leader of the MSJ and an executive member of the Oilfield Workers' Trade Union (OWTU), can morally be a part of this anti-government movement and still remain a government senator and an insider in the governing coalition.

Roget's latest move against the government, is to throw his support with what he perceives to be a popular pressure movement — the Highway re-route group led by Wayne Kublalsingh. Roget and his friends declared that they have now engaged in an "epic battle" against the development of a section of the highway to Point Fortin. And if you needed the smoking gun as evidence that this is much more than a community trying to protect their interests, you have to listen to how Kublalsingh describes the new alliance. "This new political formation will defeat this political elite," he told reporters.

The "political formation" will neither bring down the government nor solve any problems. What it will do is place additional hurdles in the way of development and at the same time push Abdulah between a rock and a hard place. And the stress is already showing.

As the leader of the MSJ, Abdulah represents more than the OWTU and the more vocal labour bodies that are screaming for the government's blood. The MSJ comprises unions other than the OWTU and he cannot allow one group to bully the others into submission. And the most important question today is this: How can he honestly and ethically work within the OWTU, knowing that Roget's aim is to use the union as his base to undermine the government? How can he do that and still lead a party that is a member of the governing coalition?

Roget, as president general of the OWTU, has already made it clear that his union is leaving the MSJ before the end of May, even before giving the PP an opportunity to resolve the issues the MSJ has put on the table. This means that Abdulah, as an executive member of the OWTU, would have endorsed that unless Roget has made a unilateral and dictatorial decision on behalf of the union.

The MSJ has found itself in a political straight jacket because as a member of the coalition it has a responsibility to stand up with the partnership and should be attending next week's celebration to mark the second anniversary of the election victory. But some of Abdulah's labour colleagues — mainly the OWTU — are pushing him in another direction. This dissident element in the MSJ doesn't want to be a part of the coalition and is suggesting that Abdulah must not attend that rally.

The MSJ leader cannot continue to sit on the fence and try to please both sides. He must make a choice and he must do it in the next few days. If he continues to keep the MSJ in the political coalition he must state so and then stand publicly with his colleagues in Chaguanas next Thursday.

That would likely mean that he would have to hand over the leadership of the MSJ while continuing to be a government senator and an executive member of the OWTU, which would be quite annoying for Roget. On the other had he could chose to follow the line clearly outlined by Roget and his battle-ready union friends to create a new political protest movement aimed at undermining the government, walk away from the government and cause labour to lose its voice and influence within cabinet.

The choices are clear. Now the ball is really in Abdulah's court and how he plays it will determine where labour truly stands. And more importantly, it will determine Abdulah's political future.

(May 18, 2012)

Abdulah must show leadership and resign as a government senator

The worst kept secret in Trinidad and Tobago is secret no more. David Abdulah stated on Monday (May 21, 2012), that the Movement for Social Justice (MSJ) would not attend the second anniversary rally of the People's Partnership on Thursday.

In a lengthy statement, the leader of the MSJ outlined his reasons for the decision, noting that in the opinion of the MSJ has changed very little since the election of 2010.

"The MSJ is concerned about reports that the state sector governance culture has not changed after 2010.

"All that has happened is that faces have changed: nepotism, discrimination, patronage and corruption are still the order of the day in too many enterprises. The "winner take all" culture of the PNM is very much alive in the view that it is "we time now" and party loyalties count for more than merit in appointments," he said.

In his flowery rhetoric, he did not provide evidence to support his charges, choosing instead emotive language to justify his decision and demanding a government committed to "social justice, equity, peace and sustainable livelihoods for all."

Abdulah, as expected, blamed the People's National Movement (PNM) for the culture that the MSJ has denounced and stated that the society "cannot go through another process of dashed hopes and the failure of good governance unless there is hope that we can finally get it right with a political leadership that demonstrates that strength lies not only in votes or the mobilisation for rallies, but in articulating a clear vision which citizens help to shape and own."

He said that includes generating the confidence in citizens, "that principles are being upheld, the right policies are being implemented, and that good governance is being practiced." He said that is the context in which the party has decided not to attend the rally.

I do not wish to comment on the merits of the arguments presented by Abdulah and the MSJ for its decision not to attend the rally. That will come at another time.

However, what I find most curious about the MSJ's position is that Abdulah is today highly critical of everything the government has done in two years yet just a couple of months ago he was waving the coalition flag, standing shoulder to shoulder with members of the People's Partnership, rallying the troops to support Prime Minister Kamla Persad-Bissessar in the opposition no confidence motion. Yet his statement is clear that nothing has changed since 2010.

Today he is denouncing the very government that he was praising just two months ago. The question that is most pertinent today is at which time was he being a hypocrite — during the campaign in support of the PM against the PNM motion or today? Surely he could not have believed in March that everything was just fine and suddenly today determined everything was wrong since 2010. That defies logic and it is something that he would have to explain to the people.

Also, I note that Abdulah is asking members of the MSJ who have been appointed to state boards, to resign "with the exception of the tripartite (labour, business, government) boards." I wonder, however, why he is not showing leadership in this regard and why he is not resigning his position as a government senator. How can he, in all honestly, decry the government and the partnership today in such strong language and continue to sit in parliament to represent the same government?

There is another equally important issue. Abdulah is the general secretary of the Oilfield Workers' Trade Union (OWTU), which has stated publicly on several platforms that it intends to bring down the government. By association, Abdulah is part of the movement to topple the government.

It is therefore most unethical and hypocritical, for him to be a part of a movement to undermine the government and continue to pretend to represent the views of the government by occupying a seat as a senator.

I refuse to believe that it is because he is reluctant to give up his senator's monthly salary of $16,000 and the perks that come with the office. Surely, someone who is clamouring for governance based on "policies that are based on social justice, equity, peace and sustainable livelihoods for all," would want to demonstrate that he can walk the talk. I expect that when the prime minister returns home Abdulah would greet her with his resignation from the senate. If he doesn't he would leave her no choice but to fire him.

(May 22, 2012)

(Postscript: Abdulah chose to resign from the senate and take the MSJ out of the coalition)

The People's Partnership celebrated its second anniversary in government with a rally in Chaguanas on May 24, 2012. It was a celebration for everyone in the spirit of unity that characterized the government and parties that make up the coalition. One surprise feature of the event was a tribute to Kamla by a pro-PNM entertainer. That offended a lot of people, which is to be expected. However, I was deeply bothered by the reaction of a prominent national figure. And that prompted me to write this commentary.

Music that celebrates humanity cannot be imprisoned within the narrow walls of racism

I have read the lyrics of the song by Jamaican-American artiste Tarrus Riley over and over again and I have watched the music video trying to understand what it is about the song and the music that makes it so exclusive to women of African descent that it becomes "insulting" for an artist to sing it in tribute to a woman of a different ethnicity.

Pro-PNM calypsonian Sugar Aloes, made a surprise appearance on the stage of the People's Partnership on Thursday night (May 24) and sang "She's a queen" in tribute to Kamla Persad-Bissessar, who is the prime minister of Trinidad and Tobago and political leader of the United National Congress (UNC).

The use of the song in this context — of serenading Kamla — is nothing new. It has been done before and no one made an issue of it. However, now that a man who has opposed the UNC in his music and always supported the People's National Movement (PNM) has performed it for Kamla, it has become offensive and "insulting" to black women, at least in the eyes of one prominent and high profile woman.

Pearl Eintou Springer, a vice chairperson of the Emancipation Support Committee, told the Express newspaper the song should never have been sung for Kamla. "We have this one song "She's Royal" for black women that I use all the time when I work with young black people. Suddenly, it is taken out of the context and taken into a political situation."

Riley's tribute was likely originally intended for women of African descent. However, the lyrics do not give it any exclusivity and could be just as appropriate for any woman anywhere. It is unfortunate that Ms. Springer has chosen to use a wide racist brush on this occasion and by so doing she has tainted her own cause in the struggle to emancipate women.

Music that celebrates humanity cannot be imprisoned within the narrow walls of racism.

Helen Reddy's iconic song, "I am woman" is by a white woman in tribute to women everywhere. Should one consider it insulting as well when it is performed for a non-white woman? Kamla has used "I am woman" as well as Bob Marley's music — "No Woman no Cry" and "Everything's gonna be alright" — in her political campaigns as well as in apolitical events because of the significance of the music and the lyrics. There is nothing offensive about that.

Why is it suddenly offensive for the use of Riley's music, which falls in the same category as Marley's and Reddy's work? Is it because a "PNM till ah ded" artiste decided to sing a tribute to the woman who defeated the PNM?

In 2010, I was convinced that we had past that stage of racism and partisanship when we embraced the People's Partnership, a coalition that represented and still does, everybody in our country, regardless of ethnicity, social standing or religious beliefs. I might have been wrong; we still have a great distance to travel.

Those of us who still wear ethnicity on our sleeves to justify our actions and rationalise our decisions, need to change those views and see us all as one, because that is what we are.

People of African origin have suffered the greatest indignity that the human race has ever inflicted on itself. But we have to move forward as Martin Luther King did when he delivered his historic "I have a dream" speech. Recall his words, spoken on August 28, 1963: "I have a dream that my four children will one day live in a nation where they will not be judged by the color of their skin but by the content of their character..."

Those were the words Basdeo Panday used in 1989 when he implored our citizens to rise and embrace his new movement — the UNC — and join his crusade to end discrimination and prejudice in Trinidad and Tobago.

Kamla and the People's Partnership are dedicated to those same ideals, to create a just society in which all of us are equal. Each of us needs to banish our fears and join hands to help. Our society has been divided for too long by people who have been so conditioned by prejudice that they find it hard to let go.

Let us live in a state "where the mind is without fear, where the world has not been broken up into fragments by narrow domestic walls...". Let us follow the dream of Rabindranath Tagore and live together in harmony and celebrate our diversity to let our country "awake."

We are one country, blessed with a rich heritage of different cultures and a plurality of views. And now is the time to free ourselves of the chains of the past and make the hope expressed in our national anthem a reality: "Here every creed and race find an equal place."

After 50 years, let us stand strong and rise with pride and sing the lyrics of everyone who celebrates humanity and freedom. Only then can we sincerely believe that "everything's gonna be alright!"

(May 26, 2012)

Time for labour to remove the mask

It's Labour Day again, a national holiday that celebrates a turning point in labour relations in Trinidad and Tobago. It commemorates the start of a strike in 1937 to protest inhumane working conditions, low wages, racism and exploitation. The work stoppage that began in the oilfields in southern Trinidad spread rapidly into the sugar belt to become the first major attempt at uniting oil and sugar workers.

The labour riots of 1937 resulted in turmoil and the colonial administration, labelled the populist trade union leader Tubal Uriah 'Buzz' Butler a threat to national safety.

It was his friend and labour comrade, Adrian Cola Rienzi (Krishna Deonarine), who shielded Butler and kept him in hiding until the colonial government betrayed Butler with a promise of safe passage, to testify at a commission of enquiry into the events of June 1937. Once he came out of hiding they arrested and jailed him.

June 19, 1937 is also a dark day in our history because it is the anniversary of the brutal murder of a policeman named Charlie King who was sent to Fyzabad to arrest Butler. In a speech to supporters Butler asked whether they would allow the policeman to arrest him. They responded by turning into a murderous mob that attacked and killed the police officer.

That historic place, Charlie King Junction, where labour gathers every year to celebrate, stands as a reminder of both the triumphs and successes of the labour movement over the decades since 1937 as well as the dangers of a mob mentality that turns men into beasts.

Today, labour is in upheaval again not because of working conditions and the state of labour relations, but because some leaders and union executives have a specific anti-government agenda driven by parochial interests and political ambition.

The bitterness is so intense and so personal that OWTU's president general Ancel Roget, has told labour leaders who do not share his views that they are not welcome to join the celebrations in Fyzabad, while at the same time declaring that Labour Day is about unity, democracy and social justice. The contradiction defies logic.

Just two days ago David Abdulah, under pressure from Roget and others, announced the withdrawal of the MSJ from the governing coalition. He also said he is quitting as a government senator. Abdulah told reporters on Sunday (June 17, 2012) he had to leave because "For them (the government) it is not about changing the system of governance but rather changing faces because it is "we time now." We do not see this approach to politics and governance being altered in the near future."

Yet Abdulah, just weeks ago, was singing the praises of the same government and the same leaders he is now condemning.

In his born again labour incarnation, he has squandered the best opportunity labour has ever had of sitting at the seat of power and participating in the governance. The mask he now wears has robbed labour of something precious and made Abdulah a puppet of men like Roget.

However, the government does not share the bitterness. Prime Minister Kamla Persad-Bissessar has reaffirmed her administration's pro-labour policy and pledged to continue to create better conditions for all.

Abdulah is masking his true intentions behind his rhetoric, saying he wants to have good government "that takes into consideration and seeks the well-being of every citizen regardless of race, religion, age, gender, party affiliation or geographical residence...[that] will lead to the greater happiness of all; the reduction in the feelings of dispossession, disenfranchisement, hopelessness, cynicism, exclusion and even anger that are all too prevalent throughout the society."

If Roget and company had not blinded him, he would have noticed that he was already a part of such a government and that there was no need to look beyond where he was. Roget and the OWTU leadership dragged him over and demanded that he leave the government because they never wanted to seek the interest of workers and the dispossessed. Never mind what Abdulah will tell you, they cared only about their partisan interests and their political agenda, which includes efforts to destabilise and bring down the government.

They have refused to ask the tens of thousands of workers of the country what they want. For them, democracy is defined by a few men in blue shirts who plot to put hurdles in the way of progress and to hurt the very workers they claim to represent. That is why they wanted to shut the state energy company, Petrotrin, and cause irrecoverable economic damage to coincide with the opposition motion of no confidence in the prime minister. The coincidence is stunning.

On May 24, 2010 something remarkable happened in Trinidad and Tobago. The people endorsed a partnership that was honest enough to say in advance "we will not agree on everything, but we will serve you." That coalition of interest that took office was the first government that represented *all* the people from the poor and dispossessed to the privileged elite. And the woman who led that movement has reaffirmed that her government will protect the "rights, enhance the benefits and improve the comfort of workers."

At the same time she has made it clear that her agenda goes beyond narrow, partisan interests. "We must, however, govern fairly and responsibly in the interest of the entire nation," she said. "This means that as we govern, the greater good must never be sacrificed for political expediency or partisanship."

It is a message that every citizens needs to heed.

In the past two years Kamla has demonstrated that leadership is not about confrontation and bullying but about dialogue, compromise and consensus. The People's Partnership remains strong because the woman who leads it understands that the people are the government and she is in office only to serve them.

It is time that labour remove the mask and follow the same path. If it does, that would be a quantum leap forward for workers and for Trinidad and Tobago.

(June 19, 2012)

Labour still has the best representation in the PP government

"If you are not with us you are the enemy".

That is the mantra of people like Ancel Roget, president general of the Oilfield Workers' Trade Union (OWTU), who has made himself the spokesperson for the labour movement in Trinidad and Tobago and for the Movement for Social Justice (MSJ).

It was his bullying that caused David Abdulah, who is general secretary of the OWTU, to walk away from the governing People's Partnership. In his haste to toe the Roget line, Abdulah forgot what he himself had been saying for the past two years — that the government had done a remarkable job of improving conditions for workers.

Not all trade unions support the Roget and the OWTU agenda, which is to destabilise the government and try to engineer the collapse of the present administration. And that is an annoyance for Roget, who suggested on the Labour Day platform Tuesday that those who don't share his views are traitors to the working class. He called on supporters to "call out" their fellow comrades who are "selling out." He said, "You have to name them and point them out."

His definition of "selling out", seems to mean anyone who has refused to defy the state and those who have seen wisdom in settling outstanding industrial agreements — 36 of them — that had been pending under the former Manning People's National Movement (PNM). He himself settled some of them! What is perhaps most interesting is that Roget and company didn't have a problem with the delays when Manning and his administration ignored labour.

So when Watson Duke and his executive reached agreement with the government for what Duke considered an excellent package, Roget decided that Duke "sold out". Now TTUTA has said it doesn't want to be part of any political movement, so Roget's next target would be TTUTA's Roustan Job.

Roget claims to represent a democratic movement, but so far, he has failed to get the general membership of labour unions to stand publicly behind him in his declared intention to overthrow the government, not even his colleague in the SWWTU, Michael Annisette, who might also be a "sell-out" for accepting a good contract for port workers.

We have past the stage in Trinidad and Tobago of rabble rousing, desk thumping militants, who behave like schoolyard bullies and hope that they can have their way whenever they shout. Workers in Trinidad and Tobago want stability, not chaos. They need to know that every new day brings hope for a better life for them and their families. They know that bullying and threats cannot deliver those things.

When the government moved the minimum wage to $12.50 an hour, from the $9 an hour where the PNM had kept it since 2005, it was because of a deep concern for workers while also taking into consideration that for workers to survive businesses must also prosper. That is the difference between a caring government that seeks the national interest as opposed to trade unionists with a narrow, selfish interest.

Now is the time to call out people like Roget. When he told workers to go on strike, did he cut his fat income and compensation package as head of the OWTU? His bread was nicely buttered. Did his sidekick, David Abdulah, stop taking his salary as a government senator and as an executive member of the OWTU?

Workers had none of that. Is Roget committed enough, like Jack Warner, to take a salary of $1 dollar a month and hand the rest to a charitable foundation to provide help for the workers?

Workers need to ask these questions.

They need to ask Roget, how they would be better off when the unions destabilise the economy and cause businesses to close shop and leave. That is where Roget could take the country with what is clearly a destructive agenda while pretending to stand up for the rights of workers.

If workers truly care about their future, they should start paying attention and stop listening to useless posturing by those who cannot deliver anything but instability and chaos. The labour movement still has the best representation in government through a leadership that cares and a minister of labour who spent his life in the service of workers. They don't need Roget to preach his hate and venom.

(June 20, 2012)

The People's Partnership government is engaged in a multi-billion dollar project to extend the Solomon Hochoy Highway from Golconda to Point Fortin. It's a project that was on the drawing board by the PNM administration and the new government decided to go ahead with it.

However, a group led by environmental activist Wayne Kublalsingh took issue with the project and tried to stop work on a section of the highway, claiming that building on that route would cause serious damage to the environment while dislocating families who had been there for generations.

The Highway Reroute Movement set up camps in the way of the construction equipment, halting work. By the time Jack Warner changed portfolios from works and infrastructure to national security, the highway project was way behind schedule because of the blockade. So he asked police to do something about it. When officers moved in and demolished the protest camp, the issue dominated the national conversation for weeks with critics alleging that the state was trampling on the rights of citizens.

Progress means some inconvenience

The overwhelming response to what happened Wednesday (June 27) at the Highway Re-Route Movement camp in Debe has been negative.

Long before anybody knew the facts, Jack Warner had become the demon, attacking "poor innocent folks."

I'm always bothered by such knee-jerk reaction. And having read reports from both sides of the story and knowing some of the background from writing about it, I think people are shutting their eyes to reality.

Jack claims that Wayne Kublalsingh slapped a law enforcement officer; Kublalsingh says that's not true. However, Kublalsingh has corroborated Jack's story that he was there to try to prevent the soldiers and police from demolishing the camp. Kublalsingh has also suggested that what happened Wednesday would solidify a political movement against the government. That has not got a lot of airplay.

Kublalsingh is getting support from known political players, especially the Movement for Social Justice (MSJ) and its most vocal member, the Oilfield Workers' Trade Union (OWTU). It is common knowledge that the OWTU has vowed to do all it can to bring down the government and Kublalsingh has boasted that the support of the union would strengthen his political muscle. These facts are mostly absent from most of the media reports and the online condemnation of the minister and the state.

If you pause and reflect on this movement and scratch the surface, you will find beneath a political movement that is determined to do whatever it can to cause the fall of the People's Partnership government. And it is using people as pawns in its game, many of whom sincerely believe the whole issue is about them.

Sure there are some people who would prefer not to move. After all they have lived in that stretch of land for generations and have built their lives around it. But there are others who are ready to move. And Kublalsingh and company are preventing them from doing so, in effect violating their rights.

Ramesh Lawrence Maharaj, who has now joined this protest political group, is the one person who should remember that sometimes you have to get out of the way for progress.

He and Hulsie Bhaggan fought in much the same manner to block the Guaymare section of the Uriah Butler Highway more than two decades ago, burning the constitution and holding protests over an extended period of time. In the end the state won and after years of unnecessary delay, the government built the highway, which everyone has welcomed.

When Jack was the works minister, he suspended work on the disputed Mon Desir/Debe section of the highway to Point Fortin, to allow technocrats to have another look to see if the route can be changed. He agreed to temporarily stop work entirely in that section. That was more than a reasonable compromise.

But what did Kublalsingh and his supporters do? They insisted that they would set up camp and try to bully the state into letting them have their way. That is not how you conduct a negotiation. Still the authorities didn't bother them. Then they pulled the Indian Arrival Day stunt in Debe, trying to embarrass the prime minister. That also failed. It is clear that they were not interested on a compromise; they would have it their way or no way. So when the issue came up this week both Jack in his new incarnation as national security minister and the new works minister, Emmanuel George, decided to do something about it. And they did!

The state must take decisions that appear harsh at times in the interest of the wider population. You might recall a squatters land grab at Cashew Gardens in central Trinidad. People were just moving in and putting up homes on state lands hoping that the government would just give in. It didn't work.

Roodal Moonilal read the riot act and moved in. The tough action was condemned but in the end the problem was solved. There is a right way and a wrong way to do things and all that the state was saying is that if you want land and housing do it the right way. And Moonilal as the housing minister is working with the Land Settlement Agency to help everyone who needs a home.

The digression is important because it addresses an inherent lawless attitude among our people who feel that all they need to do is burn tyres, block roads and set up camps — all illegal activities — and they would get their way. And those who have a strong anti-government agenda compound the problem when they take such action, hoping it would undermine the government and cause its eventual fall.

Whatever the merits of the Highway Re-Route Movement, the fact remains that the state has an obligation to conduct its affairs without hindrance. Having offered to study the proposals and having halted the project, a responsible group would have waited for the result before escalating their action. But that didn't happen. And there are reports that some people in the community have been threatened for failing to support the re-route agenda.

It's important to look at the whole picture. Did Jack and the law enforcement officers break the law? It doesn't appear so, but if they did then there is a way to handle that as well. Jack himself has said so. "If any laws have been breached, there are ways of having that resolved. My advice has been and continues to be that the lands belong to the government and the campers are occupiers and they are there illegally and therefore the best advice I can give is the one given to me by the Attorney General, which is that they are there illegally," he told reporters.

The People's Partnership government has made it clear that it wants to develop the country — the whole country, not just the urban areas. It means that to do this some people would have to make sacrifices and compromises. Those who live along the path of the new highway have been offered fair compensation and some of them are happy to accept it.

But Kublalsingh and his supporters are not interested in compromise and solutions. Theirs is a political movement determined to overthrow the present administration. And in that case the state has every right to protect its interest on behalf of all its citizens.

(June 28, 2012)

The facts show Jack did nothing wrong

As more information emerges about Wednesday's demolition of the Highway Re-Route camp on state lands in Debe, it is becoming clear that neither Jack Warner nor anyone involved broke the law or did anything wrong.

Yet, if you listen to the national conversation and the anti-government propaganda on this, you would think that Jack is some kind of ogre whose mission is to trample little people with no regard for their rights.

This is what happened. Soldiers tore down an illegal structure on state property and police were on standby to keep the peace. Dr. Wayne Kublalsingh admitted that he tried to block the soldiers from carrying out their assignment; police arrested him but did not lay any charges. Ministers Jack Warner and Colin Partap were present but did not direct anyone or get involved in what was happening. What exactly did the ministers do wrong? Consider the facts:

- The Highway Re-Route Movement, by its own admission is a political group (*"This new political formation will defeat the political elite": Kublalsingh*)
- The group is supported by organisations that have stated openly that they want to topple the government (*"We say there will be a political price to be paid...and it is coming soon." OWTU President General Ancel Roget*)
- The group and its supporters have been illegally occupying state lands (*"The reality is that the people have no right to be there in the first place..." AG Anand Ramlogan*)
- Some legal personnel have stated clearly that there was no breach of rules (*"A dispassionate examination of the facts*

would lead one to the conclusion that Mr Warner's effort...is legal and unobjectionable." Former Judge Larry Lalla)

- Their action has hindered development and resulted in losses to the state of millions of dollars (*"I will get all of the details and what it has cost so far and what it has potentially cost this Government every day that the work on the Highway cannot go on." Works Minister Emmanuel George*)

- The attorney general advised the relevant ministers that they have the right to take control of the land and continue their work (*"The advice I gave to Mr. Warner a long time ago is that this type of lawlessness should not be tolerated," AG Ramlogan*)

- The army was asked to remove the people and destroy the camp. During the operation the head of the army was directing the activities (*The military officers were directed by the Chief of Defense Staff, Kenrick Maharaj..." Jack Warner*)

- The minister asked the police to be present to maintain law and order (*..the police were sent by ACP Fitzroy Frederick... he is the person to whom I spoke." Jack Warner*)

- Neither Jack Warner nor his junior minister Colin Partap directed any officer or soldier (*"I was there observing; I did not say a word to anyone; I folded my arms." Jack Warner*)

- People verbally abused the minister and used racist remarks against him (*"I want on behalf of the constituency of Oropouche East to apologise to Mr. Jack Warner for that attack on him in that way on the soil of Oropouche East." Roodal Moonilal, MP*)

I did not make up these facts that have been reported in the national media in Trinidad and Tobago. They are in the public domain. If these are the facts, I ask the question again, what rules did anyone breach?

What happened is that the government acted as a government should. It moved in to end the kind of lawlessness that is too common in the country today. Warner made that point very clearly when he spoke with the media. "Everyone in this country wants to sponsor lawlessness," he said. "They believe lawlessness is something they must give some kind of fame to; I don't believe that...If people believe that the way to get by is to support and sponsor and promote lawlessness, I and my government don't," he added.

It's no longer business as usual. People do not have the right to burn tyres, block roads, grab lands and bully the government — in effect just break the law and then expect the authorities to look the other way and apologise. People are mixing up the right to hold dissenting views, to protest and to disagree with the state, with breaking the law.

Nobody has said Wayne Kublalsingh and his followers do not have the right to protest and to demand that they be heard. Moonilal made that clear: "This is a matter for the police and the National Security Services. Mr Kublalsingh and his group are free to continue protest activities within the law," he said.

What the authorities did is make it clear that Kublalsingh and his followers do not have the right to occupy state property and hinder development. Moonilal reiterated that point: "We must also respect the rule of law and the re-route people were clearly in breach of the law."

The AG has said anyone who believes the state acted outside of the law is free to go to the courts to seek redress. According to Ramlogan, "If they have a legal case then by all means I encourage them to take it to court. But you cannot blackmail this government and bully us and hold us to ransom because what you are doing is holding the people of Point Fortin, Debe, Mon Desir, all those persons to ransom. This matter will affect hundreds of thousands of lives."

The judiciary is not an arm of the executive so no government minister can influence what happens in the courts. If Jack was wrong or the protective services officers acted improperly let those who are aggrieved take legal action and the courts would make a judgment.

(July 1, 2012)

Why does Rowley want to waste Parliament's time again?

Doublespeak is a trademark of politicians in Trinidad and Tobago. Today, the opposition People's National Movement (PNM) and its leader, Dr. Keith Rowley, are making it a fine art.

Take the latest example of how the PNM and Rowley are behaving with respect to the demolition of the illegal Highway Re-Route camp in Debe last week. The PNM is furious and has made Jack Warner its target. In fact the moment Prime Minister Kamla Persad-Bissessar appointed Jack as minister of National Security, the PNM was "damn vex," probably because it was frightened that Jack might bring crime under control, something the PNM could not do with its blimps, SAUTT and all the million-dollar hit-and-miss crime fighting schemes dreamed up by Patrick Manning and Martin Joseph.

So now Rowley and his tribe want to hang Jack. But they should know that if you want to hang a Jack you must have the right cards — and they don't. They are calling the demolition of the camp a serious national crisis, so serious that the opposition leader wants Kamla to recall parliament immediately to deal with it.

His "deep concern" for this group lends credibility to the suggestion that this is part of the opposition's master plan to try to try to pull down the government. After all the movement has admitted that it is a political entity and its allies include anti-government unions like the Oilfield Workers' Trade Union, which has said it will do all it can to topple the government. And then there is Movement for Social Justice (MSJ), which used to be a part of the People's Partnership until Ancel Roget bullied David Abdulah to leave.

Wasn't Dr. Rowley the man who said the illegal occupation of State lands is anarchy and that the PNM would not tolerate a state of lawlessness or political disorder? That's when he was a minister in cabinet. So going after people who illegally occupied state lands was right then and is wrong now? No wonder nobody is taking Rowley and the PNM seriously these days.

The question that arises is this: Why are Rowley and company so vocal in their support for this group that has illegally occupied state lands, hindered national development and might have already cost the state millions of dollars by their actions? And to make their case in favour of Wayne Kublalsingh and his supporters they are deliberately circulating misinformation about what really happened in Debe last week Wednesday. The critics are saying Jack was directing the security operation when in fact he was just there as an observer.

Let's be fair. If you want to knock Jack and the government find just cause but this Re-Route thing is not the smoking gun. The state acted on legal advice from the attorney general to remove people who had been illegally occupying state lands. It used soldiers to do it and had police on site to keep the peace.

That's what happened. How this translates into a national crisis that warrants the recall of parliament and the calls for Jack's head truly beats me.

Rowley is a master of doublespeak. He should check his own record before bad mouthing people. He was throwing out people who illegally occupied state lands and offering no apology for doing so. So why is he shedding the crocodile tears for this group?

When he was dealing with illegal occupation of state lands as a cabinet minister Rowley stated that the PNM would not encourage "lawlessness and land-grabbing." Now that he is sitting on the other side, "lawlessness and land-grabbing" is not only acceptable but he and the PNM are making heroes and martyrs of the people who are breaking the law.

As far back as 2004 Rowley was going after people illegally occupying state lands. Commenting on a land grab at Cashew Gardens he said, "This is anarchy." He said then lawlessness was one of the greatest impediments to national development. But what is he doing today? He is encouraging lawlessness and cuddling with people who are hindering national development. He is following his former leader who used to cuddle gang bosses, whom he had christened community leaders.

It's strange how time and circumstance can alter how politicians view what is right and what is wrong!

(July 3, 2012)

A thought for Emancipation Day: Are we free yet?

Emancipation Day symbolises a continuing quest for freedom. In 1834 Britain released an entire race from servitude, but it was only a small, first step to freedom from economic and social bondage.

Nearly two centuries later, freedom continues to be an elusive dream for so many of us everywhere.

In a world that accepted and tolerated the legitimacy of apartheid, where ethnic cleansing and racism have ravaged entire societies, where hate devours reason, where the mind is still in chains, where economic interests are stronger than human dignity, freedom is yet to be won.

Emancipation Day is a time to recognise that we have made progress. But it is also a time to acknowledge that the journey is incomplete. It is about reflecting on the struggle of people everywhere, a struggle for equality, dignity and freedom, a struggle against the greatest indignity humanity ever inflicted on itself.

Trinidad and Tobago was created through the labour of slaves, and sustained through a new system of slavery in the years of indentureship. All our people are the product of our history of servitude. And Emancipation Day is about all of us. The journey to freedom is a long one. As we celebrate Emancipation Day, let us continue to travel the road to freedom as one people, one state, committed to equality and dignity for all.

(August 1, 2012)

As part of the celebration of Trinidad and Tobago's 50th year of independence, Prime Minitser Kamla Persad-Bissessar held a national day of prayer. We conclude this section with her message at that event on August 26, 2012.

PM Kamla verbatim
National Day of Prayer
August 26, 2012

"My fellow citizens of Trinidad and Tobago, today represents a glorious day in the life of our nation when citizens gather in recognition of our many blessings, to place God at the forefront of our every step.

It is always my belief that I have always held throughout my life, above all things, to place God in front and walk behind; and today's demonstration of belief in the supremacy of God over our lives, over our nation and over our future fills me with profound joy.

I am deeply delighted to welcome you all this evening, to join hands, to bond with each other by sharing our beliefs and our prayers, as we bow before God in worship and appreciation for our blessings.

As a strong and united nation, of people who are descended from many ancient cultures and traditions, it is a tribute to the human spirit, that we can gather today and with goodwill share our own diverse beliefs in prayer and thanksgiving. The past 50 years of independence has seen our nation reach glorious heights of achievement in so many spheres whether it be the arts, culture, sports, music and science. And today is an appropriate time to pause, reflect and give praise and thanks for the abundant blessings.

We have come a long way in 50 years.

Aside from our moments of patriotic pride and elation in our successes, there have been moments of great anxiety, loss and sadness. At times, by virtue of our human weakness, we may even have questioned our faith as we looked around us wondering how we would ever rebuild our lives, our communities and our nation.

It was always in these moments that we called upon the knowledge possessed by history, the fortitude of our ancestors and most of all, the supreme wisdom of God. And in all things, with God's mercy, we have triumphed.

Much of our celebration as a nation at 50 has been dedicated to honouring our past and how yesterday's action created today's greatness.

At times we remember the words of our past leaders and elders.

At times we seek comfort in the events of the past and attempt to emulate the courage that our parents and grandparents summoned.

At times we look back at the development guideposts from history, in order to understand those we wish to set for the arrival of a more enlightened tomorrow. There can be no purpose whatsoever to a world we create for ourselves that is not enriched by a value based society. One in which honesty and integrity count for more than ill-gotten gains. One in which fairplay counts for more than winning at all costs.

For our lives must be ultimately measured by the quality of our character rather than by the quantity of stuff acquired or the positions held.

As a society, let us measure how far we have come and where we need to be by how compassionate we are, how sharing we are, how tolerant we are, how understanding we are, how grateful we are.

For there can be no great nation without great people, no great accomplishment without great purpose and no greatness at all without great humility.

And we have a responsibility to pass on these values to our children, to sow the seeds of these values that will enrich their lives and ensure the development of our society over the next 50 years. As the saying goes: "If you plan for one year, plant rice. If you plan for ten years, plant trees. If you plan for 100 years, educate children."

I remember well, the story of a little girl from a rural district who walked barefoot to school, a little girl who went hungry many a night, a little girl who nevertheless never felt ashamed nor was never made to feel that poverty was a curse but a lesson in compassion and an inspiration to help.

I am that little girl who knows I must never forget those lessons life taught and the guidance my parents gave. The legacy we build must surpass what we inherited by the work of others before us.

It is here that I would like for us all to pray for former prime minister and President Arthur N.R. Robinson, former prime minister Patrick Manning, and Justice Wendell Kangalloo, each of whom remain unwell at this time. We pray for their strength and recovery. They have all served their nation well.

Brothers and sisters, this year we cross the threshold into a new dawn, with a future coming at us at a much greater pace than ever before. We must therefore prepare for it and ensure that the legacy we build will be one that is befitting of our appreciation of the past and of the future people of Trinidad and Tobago.

For us to achieve this, your help is needed.

As we join hands in our journey into tomorrow, let us pray together, work together, aspire together and achieve together as a nation. Let us build a society of purpose, unity and respect. Let us build a society that is free from crime and violence and secure in its freedom — a society which takes pride in its liberty, guards its freedom jealously and exercises that freedom responsibly for the good of our country.

Let us thank God for all he has given.

Let us pray for his guidance and for his healing hand to touch us all as we take our first steps towards achieving a century of achievement in Independence.

Let us walk together in faith and unity, in the spirit of freedom and with the assurance that God shall always remain in front of us, whatever the future may bring.

May God Bless you all, May God Bless Trinidad and Tobago."

Epilogue
We still have a long way to go

I came home to be on my native soil as our country celebrated 50 years of independence. But it was a sad occasion for me to witness the divisiveness and hatred that threatened to taint the celebrations to mark such an important milestone in our development.

The bickering over the programme of events and the decision by the party, whose leader took us to independence, demonstrated a level of pettiness that I thought had vanished a long time ago. What I saw was a reminder that for some politicians, partisan interests are more important that the national good.

And while we celebrated with cultural shows, flag waving and fireworks, I remained deeply saddened by the absence from it all by the People's National Movement (PNM), whose leader, the late Dr. Eric Williams, stood with the leader of the opposition, the late Dr. Rudranath Capildeo, 50 years ago to proclaim the birth of our nation, "forged from the love of liberty" and dedicated to the pledge that here "every creed and race" would find an equal place.

What was so wrong that the country's oldest national political party, the one that governed us for nearly 40 of our 50 years of independence, could not stand with the people to say, "Happy Birthday, Trinidad and Tobago"?

That level of divisiveness tells me that the PNM has lost its focus and is no longer a national party, but one dedicated to its tribe alone, loyal only to people who see things through its lens — and everybody else is an outsider.

That's a tragedy. We are one people regardless of which party we support, how we look and how we worship. We are, first and foremost, citizens of a free society, one family with a common destiny.

Over the years we have demonstrated that we can argue and disagree but in the end we accept the will of the majority; we have seen peaceful political change and we have put down rebellions that threatened our freedom and democracy. Why then must we — on an occasion worthy of celebration — become so divisive that we cannot even talk with one another?

Surely that is not the lesson we want to leave with our children, who will have the task of caring for this nation when we are gone. If we are one, let us stop the partisan nonsense and live like one. Poverty, hunger, homelessness affect us all the same. And they have no race, religion of political stamp.

Earlier this year, PNM Leader Keith Rowley told the nation in an Indian Arrival Day message: "While some unprincipled people have over the years found it in their own self-serving interest to create and promote racial divide, Trinidad and Tobago's history illustrates, for the most part, a level of racial togetherness of which we can be proud."

If Dr. Rowley sincerely believes that he should have put aside his political differences and celebrated with all of us 50 years of our independence in order to show leadership, which is what the country needs from those who aspire to govern.

While the PNM's motivating factor for its boycott of independence celebrations may not have been race, its pettiness and juvenile behaviour demonstrated that we still have a long way to go before we can call ourselves mature.

Prime Minister Kamla Persad-Bissessar acknowledged in a speech some time ago that accepting change can sometimes be difficult for those who must hand over power.

"It's difficult to convince those that have been seated at the dining table for such a long time that they must make room for us, that there must be an equal numbers of places for all to share, that no one is to be excluded because they are of a different colour or because of their religious beliefs, or because they have different lifestyles and preferences, nor because they happen to be a woman...

"Many resist change in the name of equality, preferring instead to preserve the status quo. But we simply will not allow that...invitations are hereby extended to all and sundry to sit at the table," she said.

The ugly political tribalism that disfigured Trinidad and Tobago in the past, must never be allowed to return and retard progress; we as a people must understand that there cannot and must never again be a "we and dem."

We are 50. Let us behave like the adult we should be!

And now - it is time to close the book.

Forty years is a long time.

Just think of how our world has changed since 1972, or more specifically February 16, 1972, the day I began my career in journalism and broadcasting at Trinidad and Tobago Television (ttt).

We wrote news copy on typewriters in those days — old manual ones. My children and many others from their generation have never seen such a machine. We didn't have cell phones and blackberries and computers. The PC was not even invented. Our news was shot on negative film; portable video cameras and videotape came along much later. Even the portable machines weighed 50 pounds! (Today we do broadcasts on an iPhone.)

Sure we had videotapes. A one-hour tape was on a huge metal spool, 12 inches in diameter and the recording machine took up half a room. And if you messed up a live to tape recording you just had to start all over again because editing videotape was not a viable option. Well, there was a way to edit but just a few of us knew how.

We didn't have the Internet and Skype. There was no 24-hour news service so the "world" was not as small and as close as it is today. We relied on the BBC and the Voice of America to tell us how the world was doing. In those days we didn't even have our own source of wire copy. However, we managed to tell stories and tell them well.

And people remember me for that, even though I left home a long time ago.

In the 40 years since I first entered Television House at 11a Maraval Road, Port of Spain as an employee I have seen and done a lot.

I've travelled to places I never expected to see and met people from all walks of life from simple ordinary folks trying to find a way to live, to presidents, prime ministers, kings and dictators. I've also met movie stars and international performers.

Among them all, I felt closest to ordinary people, telling their stories and calling officials to account. My advocacy journalism offended officials and those who had power, but it helped to give a voice to the voiceless.

My sources were sacred and remain known only to me to this day despite death threats and at least one attempt on my life.

In Canada, I had the honour of being a part of the team that inaugurated what was then the world's second 24-hour all news cable news service. However, unlike CNN, we were a distinctly Canadian service.

I edited the historic newscast that launched the service at 7 am on July 31, 1989 — and thousands more for CBC Newsworld. We produced a dozen a day for nearly 10 years; I lost count after the first few years. My job offered an opportunity to work with some of the finest journalists and other media professionals I've ever known and to be a part of one of the most trusted and respected news organisations on our planet — CBC, The Canadian Broadcasting Corporation.

I covered all manner of stories during my 40 years and produced and presented many award-winning documentaries. I interviewed influential people like Donald Woods and Oliver Tambo as well as regional and world leaders; I sat in the White House next to the Oval Office, walked with Michael Manley in the bloodiest election Jamaica ever experienced and reported on the uprising in Grenada that saw the murder of my friend, Prime Minister Maurice Bishop, and the subsequent American invasion.

At the Non-Aligned Summit in India in 1983 I was among journalists covering more than 100 world leaders, including international pariahs at the time like Yasser Arafat. Two countries at the NAM summit — Iran and Iraq — were at war, yet were at the same conference.

At Newsworld we were witness to the end of communism and the fall of the Berlin Wall; we were first to report on the invasion of Kuwait and the war that followed. And yes, we also had superb coverage of the 1990 failed Muslimeen coup in Trinidad and Tobago, thanks to my sources and excellent relationship with leaders and my colleagues in journalism back home.

We worked hard at providing Canadians with an honest picture of the country in a way only live television could. Canadians would no doubt remember Newsworld's (now Canadian News Network) pioneering coverage of the Oka crisis and the horrendous stories of the abuse at the Mount Cashel orphanage in Newfoundland, told with raw emotion by the victims themselves — uncensored.

I entered the world of journalism during the "golden days" when we had no agenda other than a commitment to truth and fairness, integrity and honesty. That's the world of journalism I knew; I still try to do it that way. The book you are about to close is mostly a collection of my raw and honest opinion, a diary of a private citizen observing from afar, developments in Trinidad and Tobago.

Now, after four decades, I feel it is time to retire, to spend time with my family, especially my precious grand daughter, Aurora.

There is an old Chinese saying: "When you reach the last page, close the book." Am I there yet? I am not sure I am ready. There is still so much work to do, so many stories to tell.

Appendix
Remembering ttt
A Personal View

The institution that gave birth to my journalism career closed in 2005 after more than 40 years. It was a tragic passing for all of us who were part of an institution that was, "the eyes of the nation" from the date of its first broadcast to coincide with our independence. I wrote this "epitaph" on the urging of Farouk Muhammad, the first native Programme Director at ttt, the man who hired me in 1972. It is one of several similar pieces from an online blog ttt pioneers.

How do you write an epitaph for ttt?

How do you find a few words to summarise an institution that is as old as our nation? Where do you begin? And where do you end? ttt has been a part of our lives for more than forty years. It has been our eyes and our ears.

Over the decades it has brought us closer together, taught us about ourselves, created an understanding of our diversity, unearthed some of our greatest talent, presented some of our best stories and kept us in touch with our world.

The institution that ceased to exist on January 14, 2005, was a poor shadow of the vibrant (and profitable) ttt I knew. But it was, after all, the only national broadcaster – the people's station, a reflection of our society, our people, the conscience of a nation.

Today the heart of ttt has stopped, but it had been on its deathbed for a long time, afflicted with a disease brought on by its own inability to accept change and move forward into the modern broadcasting era. It deteriorated soon after its unfortunate marriage with the other state broadcasting organisations and the reluctance – or impotence – of its owners and its managers and directors to provide the strong medication required to resuscitate it. But that's for another time.

Much has already been written about ttt's demise. And journalists, commentators, historians and politicians will have much to say in the weeks, months and years from now. Today I want to add my thoughts as we end an era in broadcasting in Trinidad and Tobago.

Now is not a time to mourn; it is rather a time to celebrate what ttt represented to all our people. I want to celebrate what it meant to me. I want to remember the ttt that was there when the Union Jack came down, the eyes of the nation that saw a country take birth and its Parliament constituted. The ttt I remember is the one that connected with the people, the organisation that reflected – or tried its best to reflect – the nature of our society, our unique social structures, our art and culture. It was also a news organisation that was at times bold and pioneering.

The generation that's witnessing the end of this broadcast era doesn't know the ttt I knew. Today's generation is polluted by American mass culture, by sensationalism and reality television and they demand more glitz than substance. That is their right, I guess. But I believe it is our responsibility, our duty, to educate them about their loss.

Today is a day to pay tribute to the pioneers who entered uncharted waters and created ttt. From the technicians and prop men to the on-air 'stars', from the office floor to the boardroom and that small dedicated group of pioneering television journalists, among which I count myself. We were witnesses to history at home, in the region and beyond.

ttt was also a dream maker. It opened doors for journalists, producers, artists and performers and allowed talent to grow and blossom. I lament the demise of an institution that gave me and so many of us an opportunity to go beyond hope and live dreams.

The nation will remember only a few names and fewer faces, but it must collectively say thanks to everyone, the army of dedicated men and women who built and nurtured ttt and made it ours.

I want to begin with a step back to a time when ttt was still a novelty, when a television set was a mystery. It was a time when its on-air personalities were national icons. I want to tell you a story about a teenager from the countryside, where "young men had dreams and old men waited to die"[1], where hope for a better life faded with the end of the day and took

---

[1] From Michael Manley's THE POLITICS OF CHANGE

birth again with the rising sun. ttt gave wings to that young man's dreams and took him beyond the village, allowing him to travel from the ghettos to the White House, to meet kings and paupers, presidents and despots, telling stories about people and their lives and the world in which we live.

I was that young man who dared to dream. And ttt allowed me to live those dreams, made me a storyteller. And I shared those stories with a nation that was willing to see and hear. I was proud to be a part of a national broadcasting organisation, to work alongside some of the finest media personnel I have known.

Today I write stories for Canadians, seeing the world through Canadian eyes. Over the years since I left ttt I have produced thousands of newscasts, covered scores of major national and international events, witnessed the rise and fall of dictators, the birth of nations – events that have changed our lives and charted a new course for this planet. Yet I still have dreams of returning home to tell our stories about all of us. Sadly, I won't be able to do it on ttt.

Back in 1963 while I was in high school, my father succumbed to my nagging and bought the family's first television set. It was an act that was to change my life forever. That night I watched television at home for the first time. It was the moment I had only imaged. Now I could put away my Reader's Digest and enter another world, one with sound and vision and the drama and passion of life.

We watched a documentary about penguins. And later, the news. When Peter Minshall said, "Good Evening" I saw myself. That's what I was going to do, no matter what it involved. In the next few days we watched cricket, listened to Mervyn Telfer tell us in every commercial break about "McQueen caps, worn by cricketers everywhere". We saw Lloyd Rohlehr interview some unimportant guest and Hazel Ward present the weather, briskly and carefully scratching graphics on a chalkboard as she went along. (Many years later Hazel told me the story of how Barry Gordon put her live on the air doing the weather report while she thought she was doing a rehearsal.)

In the days, weeks and months following that first encounter with this magic medium, our TV attracted the entire neighbourhood to watch all the staples of the sixties – I Love Lucy, Maverick, Bonanza, 77 Sunset Strip, Perry Mason, The Beverly Hillbillies, Happy Days. My father was particularly fond of Dan Matthews, the no-nonsense cop played by Broderick Crawford on Highway Patrol. Ma preferred Lucy and Granny of the Beverly Hillbillies.

ttt was still a foreign medium, waiting to move from infancy and grow up alongside the nation to become a chronicler of our society.

I didn't like the crowds and perhaps that's why I was attracted to news and current affairs shows, which the crowds didn't like. I was intrigued with Walter Cronkite's "You Are There", with his authoritative voice informing us that, "All things are as they were then, except You Are There". I was always there, even today. Cronkite's book, A Reporter's Life, and his own narration of it are two of my prized possessions.

Each week as I watched Cronkite, I imagined myself telling stories about people, their lives and their world. It was my first lesson in television journalism. And I never stopped learning.

Soon I was teaching myself, mimicking Cronkite, retelling the stories, writing scripts secretly to avoid the ridicule of others who could never understand my obsession with television. I was reciting every commercial seen on the tube even the one with a matronly white woman telling us about our own Angostura and inviting us to "try a little Angostura". And I was singing the Texaco jingle, "You Can Trust your car to the man who wears the star, THE BIG, BRIGHT, TEXACO STAR." It's amazing how things that happened 40 years ago remain etched in one's memory. In those early days television was as alien as the Christmas Cards with snow that I would send to my teachers and friends.

By the 1970s ttt had become an integral part of my life and the lives of our people. In ten years it had demonstrated its relevance and its necessity. Under the guidance and direction of Programme Director, Farouk Muhammad, it was producing its own shows, appealing to the people and creating opportunities for our nationals to enter this new world both in front of and behind the cameras.

Its programming included such shows as Issues and Ideas, Time to Talk, It's in the News, Teen Dance Party, Youth Talks Out, Heritage, Scouting for Talent, Mastana Bahar, Indian Variety, Twelve and Under, Mainly For Women, Play of the Month, Hibiscus Club, Community Dateline, Know Your Country, and many, many more.

Producers like Hazel Ward, Horace James, Oswald Maingot, Errol Harrylal, Shaffique Mohammed, Victor Daniel, Tony Lutchman and others were working with our talented pool of engineers and technicians to produce high quality national shows that reflected our country, our people and our culture. And they did it with minimal television facilities and equipment, but with commitment and a passion for excellence.

On the air we had equally talented home grown talent: Hazel Ward, Clyde Alleyne, Mervyn Telfer, Holly Betaudier, Horace James, Wilbert

Holder, Melina Scott, Sham Mohammed, Pat Matura, Allyson Hennesey, Brenda Da Silva and many others. And our news and current affairs personnel included Trevor MacDonald, Don Proudfooot, Lloyd Rohler, Jimmy Wong, Peter Minshall, Bobby Thomas, June Gonzalves, Yusuff Ali, Hans Hanoomansingh, Dale Kolasingh, Neil Giuseppi, Salisha Ali. I joined that impressive list much later as did Gideon Hanoomansingh and Dominic Kalipersad, and those who came afterwards.

All of us shared a common goal to produce television for Trinidad and Tobago that was relevant, timely and designed to create a better society, sharing our diversity and creating understanding and appreciation in our multi-ethnic, multi-religious society. It is what made ttt a great institution that cannot be replicated.

By 1972 I was teaching English, Literature and History at a high school in Couva. But I couldn't wean myself from the idea of telling stories on TV. Then my life changed. I responded to an ad for television technicians and was invited to Maraval Road for an interview with Farouk Muhammad.

When I walked into Farouk's office I didn't know what to expect; I was totally unprepared. Farouk didn't get up or even invite me to sit; I didn't have a chance to say "Good Morning."

I will never forget the next few moments: his first reaction and my response. "You look like a reporter," he said. "That's what I would like, but I don't think you're looking for a reporter", was my spontaneous response. He invited me to sit. And we talked, I about my dreams of telling stories on TV, he about plans for expanding local television production, focusing on more news and current affairs. It didn't seem like an interview; it felt like he had just found someone he had been looking for. And I thought I had arrived in the Promised Land. It was an important beginning.

My career didn't follow the script when I began my television career on February 16, 1972. I became a trainee technician and learned the basics of lighting, sound and other aspects of television production from Errol Harrylal, a martinet, a dedicated professional and one of the best television instructors I have known.

It was an intimidating experience, but a truly rewarding one. Victor Daniel gave me the first opportunity to write a television script; then in 1973 the real dream started taking shape when I was transferred to the newsroom. It was that corner on ttt's second floor that shaped my life, my career and my future, making me one of the professionals who contributed to making ttt what it was.

Yusuff Ali was the News Director and he gave me the first, perhaps most important lesson of my career. "This journalism business," he told me, "is really simple. You tell stories that people want to hear and you have to tell them well so they'll watch and listen."

Then he pulled up his chair to his typewriter and started writing a story to demonstrate what he meant. It began, "Hundreds of people waved placards in front of Whitehall this morning..." About a year later he gave me a lesson in broadcasting: don't read, talk. Farouk Muhammad explained it better, pointing out that television is an intimate medium that talks to one person at a time.

I learned a lot from all of them: Farouk, Yusuff, Ed Fung, Dale Kolasingh and Neil Giuseppi and many of the others who passed through ttt, people like Hazel Ward, Bobby Thomas, Don Proudfoot, June Gonzalves, Victor Daniel, Oswald Maingot, Horace James, Raffie Knowles. And from people who would call up to offer advice and also criticism.

The small short-wave radio on Yusuff's desk was my dearest companion. Every afternoon it allowed me to listen to the BBC and the Voice of America in Special English. It taught me how to write, how to read and how to speak.

Before long the team broke up. Yusuff, Ed and Dale left in quick succession leaving Neil and me – both in our late twenties – to run a newsroom with four trainees: Verne Burnett, Afzal Khan, Liz Aqui and Mary Mouttett. Angela Fox was there from time to time, helping as a casual writer.

Neil had a new vision for Panorama, which I shared, a vision that was driven by hard news and current affairs. Together we began a revolution in television journalism in Trinidad and Tobago that dispensed with soft, trivial matters, opting instead for hard news and stronger television journalism.

"We're just wasting time writing wire copy," was the way he summed it up. They were the magic words. It was as if a spell had been broken. The next day I was on the road with the newsroom's only sound camera, with a frustrated Gerry Vieira, my cameraman, wondering, "How yuh going to get all this on air today". We got it to air, all of it. And we did it again the next day, and the next.

We were finding stories about people and their lives, letting them tell their stories in their words; we were holding the bureaucrats and officials accountable. No one and nothing was immune or sacrosanct. I was everywhere, from the city to the villages. And Neil was in Port of Spain, working with studio equipment, also creating stories and putting together the show.

We had taken up a challenge and together we were determined to prove that youth and professionalism were indeed compatible. And we operated on the journalistic principle that our first obligation was to the people. And the people had a right to know what was going on in their world.

The country started noticing. Government ministers and bureaucrats stopped taking the people for granted because we were prepared to ask probing questions about the things people wanted to know.

Panorama was scooping the newspapers, Jai Parasram and Neil Giuseppi became household names and people were calling us from everywhere with leads, and positive comments about the value of ttt in their lives. One afternoon we received a one-line news release from Whitehall, which stated that "based on a report on Panorama" the government had ordered an inquiry into the PTSC. One year later the commission found exactly what I had reported about safety concerns with the corporation's buses.

There were dozens of similar stories that brought government response and solutions. Sometimes it brought the wrath of ministers; and often, the condemnation of ttt's ultra right wing chairman, James Alva Bain. ttt and our small news team had started to make the government and other primary definers in the society accountable, demonstrating that ttt was indeed a fifth estate in our democratic system.

Neil focused on indepth interviews about current affairs at home and abroad. I spent my time finding stories outside. We had changed the news paradigm from an urban based, diary-driven agenda to a people-based national one. We found the news where it was happening.

Early in my career a BBC producer told me that I should think of television as the ultimate coincidence, combining sound and vision to create an illusion of reality. Neil and I were going one step further: we were presenting reality, not an illusion. And Herb Nixon of the Canadian Broadcasting Corporation (CBC), where I now work as a journalist, told me to "let the story live."

Jeremy Taylor, the number one television critic of the time who rarely had pleasant things to say about ttt, found that he liked "the direction Panorama was taking under Neil Giuseppi" after it "unleashed a new secret weapon" called Jai Parasram. We were not out to get anybody; we were just telling stories that needed to be told. And people liked what they saw and heard.

We covered all the big stories. From regional summits to natural disasters, we found ourselves where it was happening. Nobody could tell stories the way we did because no one had sound and moving pictures. We were able to show the horror of Jonestown, the devastation of hurricanes, the wastelands created by an erupting volcano, the passion and the mayhem of Jamaican politics, the tragedy of Walter Rodney's untimely death, the battle for the Malvinas and so much more.

And at home the little, dispossessed people could now speak about their frustration, their problems and concerns and expect a response from the officials and bureaucrats who had always been inaccessible to them. That is what ttt was and that is what we have lost.

My several awards for Excellence in Journalism that sit in my library are a reminder of the glory days on ttt and the great loss we have suffered. But they are also a reminder too that I must continue telling stories.

And that's why I am telling this one.

Ed Fung's masterpiece documentary series, Our First Decade, remains one of ttt's finest current affairs works ever. It was produced at a time when we had few resources. His tour of China and the Far East with Dr Eric Williams remains one of examples of why ttt was part of the heartbeat and the soul of the nation.

Neil's outstanding coverage of Walter Rodney's death and the Guyanese elections, my eight-part series on Jamaica, my reports on the historic Non-Aligned summit in New Delhi and the OAS General Assembly and our annual News Reviews all contributed to making ttt more than a commercial broadcasting organisation. A private television station would not have gone so far to tell stories to make them relevant to Trinidad and Tobago audiences. They would have been content to pull down an Amero-centric report off CNN.

We did what we did because of professional pride, leadership, teamwork and a passion for excellence. We were the messengers serving the nation, with ttt as the medium.

We were also breaking new ground with special live coverage of major events including the historic nine-hour live telecast of Pope John Paul's one-day visit to Trinidad. And my own pioneering production in which we had the first live television picture out of Tobago: election coverage co-hosted by Dominic Kalipersad in Tobago and Jones P. Madeira in Port-of-Spain. What ttt lacked in finesse, it produced in relevant, national broadcasting. And that's what Trinidad and Tobago has lost.

The ttt that became a part of the National Broadcasting Network, seemed to lack the will and the enthusiasm to do the same in spite of modern, more efficient tools and additional staff.

Commercial media see value only when the bottom line stays in black; a national broadcaster serves a nation, building bridges, maintaining its culture, and preserving its heritage.

Today, the eyes of the nation are shut. And the doors at 11a Maraval Road are bolted. The broadcasting industry is one of the most competitive in today's world where globalism has changed all the rules. The ease at which the Internet and satellite television can transport us from deep space to the devastation of Asia by a tsunami makes it difficult to operate on a level playing field.

The marketplace in Trinidad and Tobago, with a proliferation of media, makes it imperative for any government to chart a new course for public broadcasting. In a nation such as ours, there will always be the need for a national broadcasting network, no matter what you call it.

Perhaps one of the greatest models is the Canadian Broadcasting Corporation, a respected public broadcaster that has been established by an act of parliament and is funded mainly by the treasury, with a board of directors keeping more than an arm's length from the government.

CBC recognises its social responsibility to the nation based on the premise that freedom of the press is central to the democracy and the defence of civil liberties. Its programming, as stated in its mandate, is "predominantly and distinctively Canadian, reflecting Canada and its regions to national audiences, actively contributing to flow and exchange of cultural expression, contributing to Canada's shared national consciousness and identity, reflecting its multicultural and multiracial nature while being responsive to the evolving demands of the public. Its journalism is consistent with freedom of expression, independence and the highest professional standards."

In a way it sounds like what the ttt I knew tried to do and did reasonably well, despite its myriad problems. The later version of this institution that became tied to other media seemed lethargic, almost suicidal. Perhaps its demise was inevitable.

We trust that out of the ashes a true, independent national broadcaster will emerge, one that celebrates our nation and its people, an institution in which journalists will operate with the highest professional standards of fairness and accuracy.

Democracy can only flourish when there is a free and independent media. Every government – especially in small, emerging nations – owes a responsibility to the people to ensure that they have access to media through public broadcasting. After all, the people own the state enterprises, not the government.

Whoever takes up the job of leading the new public broadcaster, must accept the responsibility to do it on behalf of the people, to represent the nation, to celebrate its diversity and highlight that which brings us together rather than sets us apart.

When the new public broadcaster is born, it must be all that and also ensure that it's free and independent voice is heard loud and clear as a fifth estate, ensuring that nothing is ever done to silence dissent and fair comment. Media, especially the people's media, must never prevent "today's minority from becoming tomorrow's majority".

Dr Lenny Saith promises a better product saying that, "...the wait would have been worth it". We want to take him at his word and wish him and the government of Trinidad and Tobago God speed in this project.

Jai Parasram – Toronto: January 2005